United States Policy in
Latin America

United States Policy in

Latin America

A Decade of Crisis

and Challenge

DISCARDED

Edited by John D. Martz

University of Nebraska Press
Lincoln and London

Library of Congress Cataloging-
in-Publication Data

United States policy in Latin America :
a decade of crisis and challenge / edited
by John D. Martz.
   p.   cm.
Includes bibliographical references
and index.
ISBN 0-8032-3162-8 (alk. paper). —
ISBN 0-8032-8189-7 (pbk. : alk. paper)
1. Latin America — Foreign relations —
United States.   2. United States —
Foreign relations — Latin America.
3. United States — Foreign relations —
1981–1989.   4. United States — Foreign
relations — 1989–1993.   5. United
States — Foreign relations — 1993–
6. Latin America — Foreign relations —
1980–
I. Martz, John D.
F1418.U718   1995
327.7308 — dc20
94-40410
CIP
SECOND PRINTING: 1997

To Federico G. Gil
Mentor, Colleague, and Friend

Contents

John D. Martz

Introduction

With the dawning of the 1990s, the global community unexpectedly found itself confronted by a significantly different configuration of forces. The collapse of the Soviet empire and the decomposition of Communist rule in Eastern Europe ushered in the post–Cold War era. Power relationships have been altered and are in the process of redefinition, while basic assumptions of international relations dating back over half a century must now be questioned; many must be discarded, to be replaced by the foundations of a new world order. While the process of rediscovery and renewal goes forward, it is clear that nations are currently experiencing a period of transition, out of which will come a reformulation of world politics for the early years of the twenty-first century.

At this moment some regions of the world seem more profoundly affected than others, but none are immune to the impact of recent events. Certainly this is true in the case of Latin America. Hemispheric relations raise many questions with which nations have been grappling for years, yet they are now placed within a different international setting. Moreover, new linkages are being formed, and although the influence of the United States remains profound, here too new patterns are gradually being formed. The roles and perceptions of the Latin American nations are in flux, while the United States seeks to place its hemispheric policies within a broader context. As a consequence, the Colossus of the North faces both global and regional realities that call for a rethinking of goals, objectives, and national interests. This identification of problems and the formulation of policies will require fresh and new insights, ones flowing in no small part from previous experience. In this time of transition, a blend of the old and the new is very much the order of the day.

Much has changed since the 1988 publication of *United States Policy in Latin America: A Quarter Century of Crisis and Challenge, 1961–1986*. That volume was intended as a contribution that goes beyond the headlines of the moment. As noted in my introduction, it was designed to provide more than the journalistic and quasi-academic collections that emphasize immediate problem areas and policy disputes. This is not to denigrate the merits of the latter genre. On at least two occasions I have collaborated to produce precisely such works: with Lars Schoultz, *Latin America, the United States, and the Inter-American System* (1980), and with E. Michael Erisman, *Colossus Challenged: The Struggle for Caribbean Influence* (1982). While such works meet a genuine need, they also emphasize current events to such a degree that their shelf life is brief. In contrast, *A Quarter Century of Crisis and Challenge* sought a distinctive identity that would render it less transitory. Happily, it was received by colleagues and critics as having achieved this goal.

Three identifiable perspectives were incorporated. The first part consisted of four chapters dealing in chronological order with U.S. administrations since 1960; these began with the Kennedy-Johnson years, continued through the Kissinger era and then the Carter administration, and closed with discussion of Ronald Reagan's first term. Emphasis was placed less on a recounting of major events than on analytic discussion of policy orientations and objectives, especially as influenced by the principal decision makers on Latin American policy for each administration. This in turn helped to raise questions that were addressed in the second part, where attention was focused on four specific instances of crisis management. One such event was selected from each of the four periods of government. The Dominican intervention was chosen for the Kennedy-Johnson years, and policy toward Marxist Chile was examined for the Kissinger period. The Carter administration was discussed in the context of the 1978 Panama Canal Treaties and the first Reagan term with regard to the Argentine-British war in the South Atlantic. Thus the reader was provided with examples of outright U.S. military intervention; economic and political pressures; peaceful resolution of a long-standing controversy by diplomatic means; and, lastly, the failure of negotiation to prevent recourse to armed force and war between two sovereign nations.

The third part presented the four concluding chapters, in which selected policy problem areas were discussed. Issues were raised that had been on the hemispheric agenda for years and that continue to preoccupy policy makers in the United States and Latin America. It was manifestly impossible to include all important problems, but at least some exemplary areas were examined in some detail. These included the debt crisis; the continuing upheaval in Central America and the Caribbean; the enduring hostilities between the United States and Cuba; and, finally, a consideration of democracy as perceived differently from Latin and North American perspectives. In the last of these, I concluded the volume by calling for renewed attention to and understanding of the meaning of democracy, its applicability to diverse societies, and the historical legacy of the Americas.

More recently, events and circumstances seemed sufficient to justify a second volume. Drawing upon the comments of a large number of reviewers in both the Western Hemisphere and Europe, along with my own sense of the prevailing literature, the question became one of organization and emphasis. Having concluded that the 1988 volume retained value in its own right, I rejected the possibility of a mere updating—one in which some chapters would be untouched while others would be rewritten to incorporate the most recent events. At the same time, the organizational foci of the first volume retained a relevance and validity that need not be abandoned. The result is a framework that incorporates some of the old while reaching out to areas not previously treated.

A Decade of Crisis and Challenge therefore returns to major themes of its predecessor in part 1. Policy making and crisis management constitute the dominant preoccupations, picking up where the earlier book left off. The first chapter deals with the entire Reagan period. This is followed logically by consideration of the Bush presidency, with the discussion carrying through the national elections of 1992. The two remaining chapters in part 1 then turn to specific cases of crisis management, one each for the Reagan and the Bush administrations. The first looks at the U.S. choice of military action in Grenada. In the second instance Panama resurfaces, this time revolving about the use of force to remove an unsavory dictator whose record included drug trafficking as well as mockery of a U.S. administration with which he had once collaborated.

In part 2, attention is directed toward bilateral relations between the United States and several of its neighbors. Some reviewers had criticized this omission from the first book, where such materials were largely limited to the problems in Central America and the Caribbean. Given the opportunity to introduce different materials that space had prohibited earlier, this led to the four chapters dealing successively with U.S. relations with Mexico, Brazil, Central America, and Cuba. One can always quibble about choices in such situations, and specialists whose countries are excluded may carp at the editorial judgments. In fact, my own long-standing research interest inclines me toward including Colombia and Venezuela, at the very least. But I will continue to write about them elsewhere. For a collection such as this one, the importance of Mexico and Brazil amply justifies their selection. Central America as a region continues to present a wide range of issues important to Washington, while also reflecting lessons for decision makers. Cuba's status has been altered by the global collapse of Communism, but it still holds a special place in North American eyes. Large numbers of U.S. citizens still retain an interest in Cuba, unlike most other American nations.

Finally, the chapters in part 3 return us to broad problem areas that bid well to endure into the next century. Two of these focus on policy areas that were excluded from the 1988 volume: the hemispheric drug war and the interrelated questions of immigration and human rights. In addition, the debt crisis and its implications for economic development extend the 1988 discussion. While chapters might also have dealt with environmental issues and other areas of concern, space is finite and choices unavoidable. Consequently, the two final contributions sketch broad internationalist and Americanist perspectives. The first considers hemispheric policy within the changing context of world affairs, while the second brings the volume to a close with a reconsideration of democracy, democratization, and its meaning for the formulation and implementation of U.S. foreign policy.

As was true with *A Quarter Century of Crisis and Challenge,* this volume is marked by certain themes that run through the individual analyses in recurrent fashion. Policy objectives are subject to the impact of broad ideological perspectives on world affairs, as well as on the regional circumstances in times of crisis. Patterns of decision making are strongly influenced by the personality and style of individual leaders—both the presidents and their advisers. North American public opinion is also a factor that affects policy decisions.

While some fundamental notions of the national interest have held constant, these are often interpreted and reinterpreted in order to meet the preferences of major policy makers. There is often a tugging and hauling over the ordering of priorities, as proved to be the case with the two recent Republican presidents. While their precepts were similar, differences in personality and leadership have influenced the character of their policies toward Latin America.

Robert A. Pastor seeks to penetrate the public mask and popular image of Ronald Reagan in the first chapter. In so doing he highlights some of the contradictions with which that president confounded friend and foe alike throughout his public career. Within the context of hemispheric policy, Reagan was almost obsessively preoccupied with Central America, while devoting precious little time or attention to the rest of the Americas. Pastor also draws contrasts between the first and second terms, especially related to the president's difficulties with Congress. Notwithstanding the long-standing Weltanschauung that placed all international problems within the context of the struggle with the so-called Evil Empire, Reagan could casually turn aside such considerations with a smiling shrug when it seemed politically useful.

In the case of George Bush, we find an internationally minded president of pragmatic inclinations who paid Latin America relatively little attention. Howard J. Wiarda, drawing upon his own experience as a close observer of the Washington scene, describes both the policies and the key personnel of the Bush team, from Secretary of State James Baker on down. Domestic political considerations were foremost in the thinking of the latter, as was evident in the approach to Central America, to Noriega in Panama, and to the problem of drugs. Hemispheric affairs were conducted with a minimum of fanfare, domestic and congressional opinion was minimized as much as possible, and the high profile of the Reagan years was diminished. The ideological content of the 1980s gave way to a perspective that, under George Bush, relegated policy toward Latin America to a much less visible position vis-à-vis other foreign issue areas. The contrasts between the Reagan and the Bush administrations were also evident in the handling of specific Grenadan and Panamanian interventions.

For Ronald Reagan, as Michael J. Kryzanek points out, the Grenada adventure was reified as a major foreign policy success. All stops were pulled out to present it to the public as a triumphant defense of national security. It was also hailed as an example of efficient crisis management based upon finely calibrated cost-benefit analyses. Yet the blunders of the military action were manifest, ranging from logistics and communications to breakdowns in intelligence. Washington policy makers presumably honed their skills for subsequent problems in Central America, while there was an intensified ideological resolve to continue the anti-Marxist crusade in the hemisphere. Even so, it is surprising, notwithstanding the simplistic optic of Cold War conflict that characterized true Reaganites, that the president himself in his memoirs later identified the Grenadan action as one of the most important taken during his eight-year incumbency. This was also one of the very few references to Latin America in the entire book.

The military action against Panama by the Bush administration was not only conducted on a much larger and more ambitious scale but also involved much more challenging problems for U.S. decision makers. It was striking in its wholly unilateral nature, as contrasted with the action against Grenada. Steve C. Ropp notes the government's parallel attention to economic, diplomatic, and military options. His analysis highlights the importance of domestic public opinion and electoral considerations in the minds of decision makers. The policy-making process again reflects the importance of individual leaders, based on personality and leadership style in addition to previous experience. This consequently redramatizes one of the thematic threads running throughout the book. In addition, Ropp sees the thinking of key decision makers as influenced by the lessons of earlier crises, most particularly that of Grenada.

In part 2 the analyses shift gears to examine the evolution of bilateral relationships, incorporating background material that has a bearing on current conditions and policies. George W. Grayson sorts out the complexities of Mexico's relationship with the United States, most particularly the recent movement toward the North American Free Trade Area. President Carlos Salinas de Gortari's reforms importantly included a redefined relationship with the United States, the cornerstone of which has been NAFTA. The impact of Salinas's personality and policy choices has been exceptional, even granting the tradition of strong presidential leadership in Mexico. From his time as planning and budget secretary under Miguel de la Madrid Hurtado, Salinas articulated a vision that moved toward fruition under his own administration at the turn of the 1980s and after. In the end, as Grayson concludes, the movement toward North American integration will profoundly influence bilateral relations as Washington and Mexico City approach the twenty-first century and a new framework for foreign policy.

In Brazil the United States has found itself dealing with a nation that has emerged as a newly industrialized country (NIC). Brazil had already achieved a degree of autonomy from the Colossus of the North. Largely overlooked by both the Reagan and Bush administrations, Brazil developed foreign policy interests and commitments that extended far beyond traditional links with Washington. Moreover, it progressively distanced itself from the United States, just as Mexico in contrast with building a more intimate cooperative relationship. Eul-Soo Pang concludes that prospects for the decade ahead do not bode well for bilateral ties. Here again, stark contrasts emerge between the Brazilian and the Mexican cases. In neither, however, was there as much domestic debate and partisan conflict in the United States as had been true of Central America and the Caribbean during the past decade.

Policy vis-à-vis Central America is carefully traced by John A. Booth, running from the Carter administration through the 1980s to the present. Changes instituted by the Bush administration reflected the new presidential style as well as perceptions of policy priorities on the part of the incoming team of decision makers. Management produced significant adjustments in U.S. policy toward the region, leading to a clear "cycling down" of security interests for Central America. In a different sense, the same is true of contemporary Cuba, as Enrique A. Baloyra suggests. Cuba watching has been powerfully affected by the collapse of international Communism, and security concerns have become less basic to the bilateral relationship with the United States. Cuban foreign policy toward other nations has also been altered, as Baloyra explains in sharpening an understanding of its regional position. His vivid blend of science and art goes far toward new and important insights at a time when the future course of events on the island is ever more problematic.

The contributions to part 3 carry us into policy areas that bid fair to remain relevant for years to come and that carry high priority for virtually all the nations of the Americas. Both bilateral cooperation and multilateral hemispheric action will be necessary for a gradual amelioration of these policy areas. A prime example is the problem of drugs, as William O. Walker III describes tellingly. When Colombian drug boss Pablo Escobar escaped from prison in July 1992, for example, it was far more than an embarrassment to Colombia and César Gaviria. It also complicated relations with the United States. Meanwhile, the drug networks running through portions of Venezuela, Ecuador, Peru, Brazil, and Bolivia remain active, as do related activities of the drug industry in Europe and the United States. The drug war rages on, decision makers debate policy options, and the devastating impact of *narcotraficantes* deepens, despite the December 1993 killing of Pablo Escobar.

At the same time, the ongoing debt crisis is scarcely less crucial to the Americas, if in a somewhat less direct fashion. Riordan Roett, a contributor to *A Quarter Century of Crisis and Challenge*, returns to the subject while linking it to socioeconomic development. He summarizes the debt crisis of the 1980s and proceeds to the Brady Plan, the Enterprise for the Americas, and other recent policies, leading in turn to a consideration of economic liberalization and what he views as the Januslike dichotomy of Latin America, a region now internationally creditworthy yet possessed of the overpowering social agenda inherited from the lost decade. With the unfolding of the 1990s, he sees the challenge as one of linking new flows of investment capital to social investment. Meanwhile, areas not covered in the earlier volume embrace U.S. policy toward immigration and human rights. Christopher Mitchell recounts attitudes and actions through the 1980s and closes his chapter by evaluating the work of both government and concerned interest groups in dealing with these problems. He concludes that difficult policy choices lie ahead and that past experience offers "only ambiguous guidance" for decision makers.

In the two final chapters, Joseph S. Tulchin and I undertake broader summations of policy interests and perspectives toward Latin America. In his inclusion of global preoccupations and of more fully internationalist perspectives, Tulchin underlines the growing importance of Latin American relations to the world at large. This constitutes a crucial development that is fundamental for the reshaping of links with Washington. The United States can no longer set its hemispheric policies on the back burner, nor can it deal with the Americas in paternalistic isolation from the rest of the international community. My own contribution turns our attention more directly to the Western Hemisphere, renewing previous assessments of democracy. The North American proclivity to export democracy—however poorly or ambiguously conceptualized—has remained at the center of U.S. preoccupations. I suggest that recent experience has provided little source for cheer, while at the same time reiterating the fundamental importance of understanding democracy and its values for decision makers and political leaders throughout the Americas.

In any such collection, consensus is at best difficult and, in any event, undesirable. As with *United States Policy in Latin America, 1961–1986*, the issues and policy problems are complex. There is no royal road to understanding nor to the resolution of controversy. Thematic variations are inevitable as our contributors—with both public and private experience in Latin American affairs—seek to illuminate the events of the past decade and project our thinking more lucidly toward the twenty-first century.

Part One

Policymaking and Crisis Management

Robert A. Pastor

The Reagan Administration: On Its Own Petard

For 'tis the sport to have the engineer
Hoist with his own petard.
    William Shakespeare, *Hamlet*

By 1980, Americans were frustrated with the world and impatient with their leaders, who seemed unwilling or unable to stop Soviet-Cuban advances, anti-American revolutions, and even increases in oil prices. The American people, according to two public opinion analysts, felt "bullied by OPEC, humiliated by the Ayatollah Khomeni, tricked by Castro, outtraded by Japan, and out-gunned by the Russians. By the time of the 1980 Presidential election, fearing that America was losing control over its foreign affairs, voters were more than ready to exorcise the ghost of Vietnam and replace it with a new posture of American assertiveness."[1]

Ronald Reagan tapped this frustration better than any other candidate in 1980. His campaign was a ringing declaration that the United States could and, if he were elected, would again take charge of its destiny and the world's. His vision of the world was uncluttered with complexity. All one needed to know was that the United States was engaged in a global struggle against Soviet Communism. "The inescapable truth," Reagan stated, "is that we are at war, and we are losing that war simply because we don't or won't realize we are in it . . . [and] there can only be one end. . . . War ends in victory or defeat."[2] During a war, leaders do not have to make difficult trade-offs between competing values because victory is the single goal. For Reagan, events were interpreted and became significant only through this organizing prism: terrorism was manipulated by a single source, the Soviet Union;[3] human rights was a fight against Communism;

economic development could succeed only if Marxists were removed and the state reduced.

In no region was Reagan's worldview applied with more clarity
and vigor than in what he called America's "backyard." Through two
terms, the Reagan administration's policy toward all of Latin America was focused disproportionately on three small countries in Central America: Nicaragua, El Salvador, and Panama. "Reagan has become an obsession for us," said Tomás Borge, minister of interior of
Sandinista Nicaragua, "and we've become an obsession for him."[4]
This interacting obsession had a curious mirror-image effect in
which the United States and Nicaragua utilized similar instruments
to confront the other.

At the same time, the large countries in South America resented
the lack of interest of the United States in their problems of debt and
democratization. The Reagan administration responded to their initiatives with cold shoulders or stiffarms. U.S. policy toward Latin
America was skewed not only in its zealousness and focus on Central America but also in the way that it enlisted military dictatorships in Argentina and Panama on its side, sometimes against democracies like Costa Rica. The results of this approach will be
assessed at the end of this chapter, which will tell the story of Reagan's journey from making war against Nicaragua to becoming a victim of his own strategy.

Background

During the presidential campaign, Reagan's positions on Latin America offered a stark contrast to those of his predecessor. He was the
leader of the opposition to the Panama Canal Treaties that were negotiated and signed by President Carter on 7 September 1977. Reagan insisted that the United States retain an exclusive right to operate and defend the canal, and he warned that if the new treaties were
approved, Panamanian general Omar Torrijos would tilt the nation
to the left and give the canal to Cuba and the Soviet Union. Even
William F. Buckley and John Wayne disputed Reagan's arguments,
but Reagan struck a responsive chord in the American people, and
he was able to use his stand on the Panama Canal Treaties to build
support for his nomination as Republican party candidate in 1980.

Panama was only the starting point for his differences on Latin

American policy with Carter. Reagan defended both Pinochet's Chilean government and the Argentine military regime in its war against "a well-equipped force of 15,000 terrorists." He also criticized Carter for antagonizing friendly military dictators with his policies on human rights, arms control, and nonproliferation.[5]

Jeane Kirkpatrick, whose criticism of Carter so endeared her to Reagan that he would appoint her ambassador to the United Nations, wrote that the Democratic president had "contributed . . . to the alienation of major nations, the growth of neutralism, the destabilization of friendly governments, the spread of Cuban influence, and the decline of U.S. power in the region."[6] She did not offer an alternative prescription, except by implication. In her censure of Carter's policy toward military regimes and her distinction between authoritarian and totalitarian governments, she implied that U.S. policy should be determined solely by a regime's friendliness. No matter how tenuous its legitimacy or how repressive its actions, a friendly regime should receive U.S. support because the alternative is uncertain or worse.

A group of five conservative academics who called themselves the Committee of Santa Fe issued a report, warning that the Caribbean was "becoming a Marxist-Leninist lake. Never before has the Republic been in such jeopardy from its exposed southern flank. Never before has American foreign policy abused, abandoned, and betrayed its allies to the south in Latin America." The committee recommended abandoning the human rights policy because it "has cost the United States friends and allies and lost us influence. . . . The reality of the situations confronted by Latin American governments that are under attack . . . must be understood not just as a threat to some alleged oligarchy, but as a threat to the security interests of the United States."[7] The 1980 Republican party platform adopted a similar stance. It deplored "the Marxist Sandinista takeover of Nicaragua" and demanded an end to aid to the regime. The principal message of the platform and of Reagan's campaign was that Soviet-Cuban power was advancing in the world and the United States must devote all its energies to rolling it back.[8]

"The morning of an Administration," Alexander Haig, Reagan's first secretary of state, noted in his memoirs of the first eighteen months of Reagan's administration, "is the best time to send signals." Haig wanted to send just two: "our signal to the Soviets had to be a plain warning that their time of unresisted adventuring in the Third World was over and that America's capacity to tolerate the mischief of Moscow's proxies, Cuba and Libya, had been exceeded. Our signal to other nations must be equally simple and believable: once again, a relationship with the United States brings dividends, not just risks."[9] The administration chose to send the Soviets the first signal by drawing a line in Central America; it sent the second signal by embracing military governments in South America.

On 23 February 1981 the State Department issued a White Paper that presented "definitive evidence of the clandestine military support given by the Soviet Union, Cuba, and their communist allies to Marxist-Leninist guerrillas" trying to overthrow the Salvadoran government. Alexander Haig condemned the "externally-managed and orchestrated interventionism" and promised "to deal with it at the source." The administration increased military aid and advisers to El Salvador. Haig also proposed a blockade and other military actions against Cuba in meetings of the National Security Council in early June 1981, again in November 1981, and finally in February 1982, but his proposal was rejected because Secretary of Defense Caspar Weinberger feared another Vietnam, and the military worried that the Soviet Union might respond forcefully in another part of the world. Others in the administration doubted that Congress or the public would accept such action without a Cuban provocation, and White House political staff did not want to divert the president and the public from domestic economic issues, especially a tax cut. Haig, by his own admission, was "virtually alone" in arguing for a blockade that Reagan himself had advocated during the campaign.[10]

Whatever the effect of the administration's signals on the Soviet Union, their initial impact on El Salvador was counterproductive. The struggle in that country was not, at that time, between the Marxist guerrillas and the government; the Marxists had been defeated soundly in their January 1981 offensive. The struggle was between the government and rightist elements, and the latter interpreted statements by the president and Haig as indicating support for them in their battle against Napoleon Duarte, the leader of the Christian Democrats and Salvador's junta.[11]

The administration's highest priority was to defeat the insurgency by modernizing Salvador's military. The head of the U.S. military team was instructed to negotiate an aid program directly with the military, thus undermining Duarte.[12] One month later, Salvadoran rightist leader Roberto D'Aubuisson told the press that, based on his meetings with "members of Reagan's group, the Reagan administration would not be bothered by a takeover" that eliminated the Christian Democrats from the government. Recognizing the seriousness of D'Aubuisson's threat, the State Department endorsed Duarte and warned against a coup. The White House, however, equivocated: "We just don't have a view on that."[13]

As the right wing became more repressive, the Salvadoran guerrillas (FMLN) gathered more support, but instead of changing its strategy, the Reagan administration blamed the Sandinista government. Carter had suspended aid to Nicaragua in January 1981 because of evidence that it was sending arms to the FMLN.[14] U.S. ambassador Lawrence Pezzullo used the possibility of renewing aid as leverage in negotiating with the Sandinistas, but despite an apparent halt in arms transfers, Reagan terminated the aid program on 1 April 1981.[15] Assistant Secretary of State Thomas Enders then discussed an agreement with the Sandinistas to reduce their military relations with the Soviet Union and Cuba and prevent any future arms transfers to the FMLN. The Sandinistas were not inclined then to negotiate their external relationships, and the Reagan administration was so dubious about negotiating with the Sandinistas in the first place that Enders had no support for probing Managua's position.

Having "tried" negotiations, the administration decided on a more confrontational approach. An NSC meeting on 16 November 1981 made the pivotal decision, formalized in Directive no. 17 signed the next day by President Reagan, to fund and direct a secret anti-Sandinista guerrilla force, the Contras. In briefing the intelligence committees in December 1981, CIA director William Casey described the proposal as a $19 million program to set up a five-hundred-man force aimed at the "Cuban infrastructure" in Nicaragua that was allegedly training and supplying arms to the FMLN. The House Intelligence Committee approved of interdicting arms from Nicaragua but was skeptical whether that was Reagan's objective.[16]

In March 1982, the Contras destroyed two bridges in Nicaragua. The Sandinistas condemned the United States and declared a state of emergency. Thus began a downward spiral in which the political space in Nicaragua was systematically reduced, the government became more militarized, and the United States found itself locked in indirect combat with a small nation.

Repairing Relationships for the Common Struggle

The Reagan administration's anti-communism and its decision to distance itself from its predecessor led it to embrace military governments in Latin America that the Carter administration had treated coolly because of human rights violations. As his first Latin visitor, Reagan invited Argentine general Roberto Viola in order to underscore the break with the past. Argentines had already absorbed the difference. Carlos Saul Menem, who would be elected president of Argentina in 1989, said: "I was in jail when Reagan won, and those who held me captive jumped for joy." On the eve of his visit, Viola's government arrested three Argentine human rights activists. Instead of criticizing Argentine repression, State Department spokesman William Dyess took aim at Carter's policy: "We want good relations with Argentina. Any abnormality in relations is due to a large extent to the public position this country took regarding human rights practices in the country." The meeting went well, beginning a period of cooperation that culminated with Argentine support for the Contras.[17]

On 1 March the administration also improved relations with Chile by restoring Export-Import Bank financing and inviting the government to participate in joint naval exercises. It stopped voting against loans in the international development banks to the military governments of Argentina, Chile, Uruguay, and Paraguay. Jeane Kirkpatrick visited Chile in August 1981 and said that the United States intended "to normalize completely its relations with Chile in order to work together in a pleasant way." She would not meet with several human rights activists, and they were arrested after her departure.[18]

Whereas the Carter administration had sought ways to be responsive to the Third World, the Reagan administration described the "so-called Third World . . . [as] a myth—and a dangerous one."[19] Reagan also reversed his predecessors' efforts to curb arms sales and nuclear proliferation. During its first two years, the Reagan administration sold more than twice as many arms (in dollars) as were sold during Carter's four years.[20] In 1982, overturning Carter's decision, Reagan authorized the export of 143 tons of heavy water and a computer system for Argentina's nuclear program without demanding safeguards. The administration claimed that the sale would permit it to influence Argentina to stop completion of an enrichment plant, but, as it turned out, the sale facilitated the completion of the plant one year later.[21]

Coping with Constraints

In his memoirs, President Reagan wrote that "one of the greatest frustrations during those eight years was my inability to communicate to the American people and to Congress the seriousness of the threat we faced in Central America."[22] It was not for want of trying. The "great communicator" gave more speeches on the region than on any other foreign policy issue. His purpose was to obtain aid for the Contras and the Salvadoran government and his language was unequivocal. Central America, Reagan argued, "is simply too close, and the strategic stakes are too high, for us to ignore the danger of governments seizing power there with ideological and military ties to the Soviet Union."[23] While warning Congress of the consequences of not supporting him, Reagan also tried to secure support by responding to some of the criticism of his program. To counter the impression that he viewed the region's problems solely in East-West military terms, Reagan proposed an innovative one-way free trade agreement called the Caribbean Basin Initiative (CBI); he toned down his criticism of Carter's human rights policy; and he established the National Endowment for Democracy to promote freedom. Many members of Congress supported these initiatives, but fewer accepted Reagan's policies toward Nicaragua and El Salvador.

In addition to Congress's attempts to change his policy, several Latin American governments also tried to contain his efforts in the region. In January 1983 foreign ministers from Venezuela, Colombia, Mexico, and Panama met on Contadora Island in Panama to explore alternatives for ending the East-West conflict in Central America. Reagan recognized the seriousness of both the congressional and the Contadora constraints, but he never ceased to try to overcome them.

While attention was focused on Central America, Reagan's first and only use of direct U.S. force in the region occurred on the small island of Grenada. In mid-October 1983, a faction of the Marxist regime killed Prime Minister Maurice Bishop and several of his colleagues. The English-speaking Caribbean, one of the few genuinely democratic regions in the developing world, was shocked by the violence, and six neighboring governments invited the United States to join them to remove the regime. Reagan decided to invade, although the bombing of the marine barracks in Lebanon two days before may have had as much influence on his decision as the safety of the medical students, who in any event were endangered more by the invasion than by the de facto regime.[24]

Although U.S. forces met little resistance on an island the size of Martha's Vineyard, Reagan viewed the invasion as a triumph and vindication of his campaign theme: "Our days of weakness are over. Our military forces are back on their feet and standing tall."[25] The invasion was condemned by most states in the OAS and the United Nations, but it was popular in Grenada and the Caribbean, and this influenced opinion in the United States.

In an attempt to obtain a bipartisan boost to increase aid to Central America, Reagan asked Henry Kissinger to chair a commission and issue a report in January 1984. Its analysis of the indigenous causes of the crisis differed from the administration's, as did its conclusion that local revolutions posed no threat to the United States.[26] The administration, however, deftly chose to agree with its other conclusion, that Soviet-Cuban involvement required a strong U.S. response. On 3 February, claiming bipartisan support, Reagan asked Congress to fund a five-year, $8 billion aid program to Central America.

In an election year and with a widening budget deficit, many members of Congress wanted to avoid the aid issue. But the president would not let up until the spring, when his effort was jeopardized by the disclosure of CIA involvement in the mining of Nicaragua's harbors.[27] A second reason Reagan could not persuade Congress was that few believed he was genuinely interested in negotiations. Reagan tried to allay that suspicion by sending Secretary of State George Shultz, who had replaced Haig in 1982, to Managua for talks in June. But evidence disclosed later during the Iran-Contra hearings confirmed that Congress's skepticism was justified. In a secret NSC meeting on 25 June 1984, Reagan said that the purpose of Shultz's trip was to deceive Congress, not to negotiate: "If we are just talking about negotiations with Nicaragua, that is too far-fetched to imagine that a Communist government like that would make any reasonable deal with us, but if it is to get Congress to support the anti-Sandinistas, then that can be helpful."[28]

With the economy improving, public opinion surveys suggested that the only issue standing in the way of Reagan's reelection was peace. He therefore stopped pressing for Contra aid, and Congress passed a bill with an amendment sponsored by Representative Edward Boland that barred funds for the Contras. Boland said the amendment "clearly ends U.S. support for the war in Nicaragua."[29] Reagan signed the law on 12 October 1984, but he also told his NSC adviser Robert McFarlane to "assure the contras of continuing administration support—to help them hold body and soul together—until the time when Congress would again agree to support them."[30] This was the mission assigned to NSC staff member Oliver North. The CIA withdrew its aid to the Contras, but Director Casey personally advised North on setting up a covert operation outside the government to provide funds and supplies to the Contras. North's operation began when the law said it should stop, and it continued until aid was approved in the fall of 1986 and his operation was disclosed.

None of this was known during the election campaign of 1984. Reagan was then talking peace and negotiations, defusing the argument made by Democratic presidential candidate Walter Mondale 'hat Reagan's reelection would mean a deeper war in Central Amer-ı. In the end, Central America played a small part in the voters' cal-lations, and President Reagan won by a landslide.

agan's National Liberation Strategy and North's Compass

.agan used his 1985 State of the Union message to dress up his ontra program into a doctrine on wars of national liberation: "We ıust not break faith with those who are risking their lives on every continent from Afghanistan to Nicaragua to defy Soviet-supported aggression and secure rights which have been ours from birth. . . . Support for freedom-fighters is self-defense." On 21 February Reagan candidly described his goal as seeing the Sandinista government "removed in the sense of its present structure," and he said he would not quit until the Sandinistas "say uncle."[31] After some representatives insisted that other steps like an embargo should be tried before overthrowing the government, Reagan obliged, decreeing an embargo on 1 May.

The next month, after President Daniel Ortega visited Moscow, the administration found the votes in Congress to approve $27 million in nonlethal humanitarian aid for the Contras. This was the first time that Congress openly debated and affirmed support for a movement whose aim was to overthrow a government with which the United States had diplomatic relations. U.S. actions provoked the Soviets to increase their aid to Nicaragua. By the end of 1985, the Nicaraguan army was using sophisticated military equipment to suppress the Contras, and Reagan decided to ratchet up the arms race. In the summer of 1986, Congress approved $100 million for the Contras—75 percent of it military aid.

Oliver North's operation to provide arms to the Contras using funds from the profits of arms sales to Iran was exposed in October 1986, the moment when congressionally approved military aid to the Contras began to flow. North and John Poindexter, the NSC adviser, were dismissed then, and one year later the congressional committees that investigated the affair issued their report. They found the president ultimately responsible, although not legally culpable. During the congressional hearings, Poindexter said that he hid the key decisions from Reagan, thus saving his presidency. (After Reagan left office, Poindexter changed his story at his trial, claiming that Reagan knew. Reagan testified but could recall little.[32])

Even during the investigations, Reagan never ceased trying to win support for the Contras. His main adversary was not the scandal but the Arias peace plan signed in August 1987 in Esquipulas by the five Central American presidents. The plan called for democratization through national reconciliation and an end to outside support for insurgencies. All five presidents asked Reagan to end aid to the Contras, but Reagan called the plan "fatally flawed" and reaffirmed his request for military aid as the only way to bring democracy to Nicaragua. In a chilling confrontation with Reagan at the White House, Arias told him: "We agree on the ends but we disagree on the means. You want democracy in Central America by imposing it with bullets. I want democracy by imposing it with votes."[33]

Reagan insisted that the Sandinistas would negotiate and hold free elections only if the United States gave military aid to the Contras. Congress disagreed. It rejected aid and was proven right when negotiations in March 1988 between the Sandinistas and the Contras yielded a cease-fire. Nicaraguans could not negotiate under the continuing pressure of Reagan's approach.

Another negative product of the administration's obsession with the Contras was the relationship it cultivated with Gen. Manuel Antonio Noriega, the commander of Panama's army. Noriega had long been a CIA "intelligence asset," but his value was enhanced in 1983 when he became head of the army. From then until at least 1986, Noriega helped the Contras and coordinated attacks against

the Sandinistas in exchange for at least $300,000 and an understand-
ing by the Reagan administration that it would overlook his corruption and control of Panama's politics.[34] This deal came unstuck in
June 1987 when a senior Panamanian military officer accused Noriega of killing a political leader, manipulating the election of 1984,
and skimming profits from a wide range of drug-related activities.
This revelation generated a powerful civic reaction in Panama.[35]
Noriega arrested the leaders of the opposition. The Reagan administration suspended aid and encouraged President Arturo Delvalle to
fire Noriega in February 1988, shortly after he had been indicted in
Miami and Tampa for drug trafficking. Instead, Noriega fired Delvalle. Washington then imposed economic sanctions and withheld
money for the canal. This strategy brought the Panamanian economy to its knees while Noriega reveled in his defiance of the United
States.

While the United States concentrated on Central America, the
rest of Latin America was undergoing a profound transformation.
Democracy, which had begun to replace military regimes in the late
1970s, continued its sweep. In 1985, competitive elections were held
in Brazil, Uruguay, Guatemala, and Grenada, and power was transferred peacefully from one civilian government to another in Bolivia
and in Peru, the first time in forty years for the latter. Two long-
standing Caribbean dictators also fell, raising hopes that democracy
might emerge from the ruins. Forbes Burnham, who had ruled Guyana for twenty years, died in 1985, and Jean-Claude Duvalier, whose
family controlled Haiti for almost thirty years, fled the country on 7
February 1986. The United States stopped aid to Duvalier in the closing moments of his regime, but Reagan denied that the United
States had forced Duvalier to leave.[36]

Many of the new democratic governments feared that Reagan's
Contra war could polarize their countries and divert the United
States from the debt crisis. Foreign ministers from four new democratic governments—Argentina, Brazil, Uruguay, and Peru—joined
the original Contadora countries in a meeting with Shultz on 10 February 1986 to request that the United States open talks with the Sandinistas and stop funding the Contras. Reagan ignored their request
and refused to meet them. The newly elected presidents in Central
America tried again. Guatemalan president Vinicio Cerezo invited
his Central American colleagues to a summit meeting in Esquipulas, Guatemala, on 25 May 1986 to discuss peace in the region and

the idea of a Central American parliament. The administration tried to block these efforts and displayed little interest in the debt crisis, although this was probably the most serious cause of fragility for democracies in the region. Enders dismissed the debt crisis in 1982 as "basically a question between borrowing governments and the markets themselves."[37] But by 1985, Latin America owed $368 billion, and it was impossible to ignore the crisis or view it as strictly a private matter. Annual debt service payments consumed nearly 44 percent of the region's foreign exchange. In just four years—1982 to 1985—Latin America transferred $106.7 billion of capital to the United States and other industrialized countries to service its debt, making it a larger exporter of capital to the United States in this short period than the United States was to Latin America during the entire decade of the Alliance for Progress.[38] Only when the region seemed about to set up a debtors' cartel in the fall of 1985 did Secretary of the Treasury James Baker offer a plan. He suggested that both private and development banks increase funding to the major debtor countries if they adopted market-oriented reforms. The Latin Americans welcomed the plan but said it was not enough. They wanted more loans and reduced interest rates. But in an important shift from previous calls for a new international economic order, most governments recognized that they needed to change their economic policies. Argentina instituted a severe austerity program in June 1985 and Brazil followed seven months later with a similar plan. The decline in oil prices at the time also compelled Mexico and Venezuela to accept market-oriented reforms and trade liberalization.

The other issue that engaged the United States and Latin America was the expanding trade in cocaine. The Drug Enforcement Administration estimated that the amount of cocaine imported into the country increased nearly twentyfold between 1981 and 1987. The administration preferred an enforcement strategy to cut off supplies and prosecute traffickers, whereas the Latin Americans insisted that the only effective approach was to reduce demand. Thus, drugs too became a cause for increased tension rather than collaboration in inter-American relations.

The Legacy of Ronald Reagan

On assuming the presidency in 1981, Ronald Reagan believed he had a mandate to confront and defeat Communists in Latin America and reassure "friendly" military governments that had been alienated by the Carter administration's policies. Reagan defended El Salvador, destabilized Nicaragua, invaded Grenada, and dismantled Carter's policies on human rights and arms control. In his second term, Reagan's approach broadened: he professed a commitment to human rights, democracy, and negotiations; he implemented a one-way free trade plan for the Caribbean Basin; his secretary of the treasury proposed a plan for the international development banks to address the debt issue. Yet the evolution in his policy should not obscure the tenacity with which he held to his initial and central objective: to change the Sandinista regime.

Latin America changed in the 1980s. The assertiveness of many Latin American governments appeared a permanent fixture in international relations in the late 1970s, but a decade later, assertiveness was replaced by national self-preoccupation. This change was less the result of external American efforts than of internal pressure derived from debt and democratic transition. Concerned about reelection and coping daily with financial crises, Latin America's leaders became more moderate and realistic.

The United States did not convince Latin America or impose its worldview on the region's leaders. Nor did the Reagan administration adapt to the region's concerns. Instead, Latin America and the United States each concentrated on its own priorities. This does not mean that Latin America had no influence. The CBI was Jamaican prime minister Edward Seaga's idea. Contadora diplomacy constrained the Reagan administration from undertaking more forceful actions in Central America, and even the Caribbean exercised a silent veto on Reagan's actions against Grenada until the regime self-destructed.

Reagan deliberately cultivated an image of detachment from the daily work of government, and in evaluating his presidency, one needs to distinguish between the man and his administration. Reagan's aloofness served him well when he faced the Iran-Contra questions, but beyond that case lingers the puzzle of someone who tried to affect a Churchillian style of leadership and yet also seemed unaware that members of his cabinet were almost at war with each other even as each pursued his own policy. In his memoirs, George Shultz, who had replaced Haig as secretary of state in 1982, expressed frustration that "the president did not impose discipline within his administration."[39] Instead of doing its job of coordinating policy, the NSC staff embarked on its own operation.

In his memoirs, Constantine Menges, who worked at the CIA and the NSC under Reagan, describes himself as the guardian of Reagan's Central American policy against the maneuvers of Shultz and other senior administration officials.[40] Menges could never explain why the president consistently allowed Shultz and others to hijack his policy. Like North, Menges was fired from the NSC yet continued to refer to himself as one of Reagan's few loyal followers. In Menges's memoirs as well as in those of Haig, Shultz, North, and even Frank McNeil, a State Department official who worked on Central America during the 1980s but opposed the Contra policy, Reagan's *name* is constantly invoked for contrary policies but Reagan's *person* is absent. Edmund Morris, the biographer who watched Reagan up close for the last three years of his presidency, confessed to being baffled by the man. Morris's only relief was in learning that "everybody else who had ever known him, including his wife, is equally bewildered."[41] Oliver North captured that quality when he wrote that Reagan was "almost always scripted" and that he "didn't always know what he knew."[42] Shultz put it bluntly in his memoirs: "President Reagan simply did not seem to grasp what was actually going on."[43]

One needs to understand how Reagan used language before one can decide whether there is more or less there than meets the eye. Trained as an actor but having an intuitive grasp of power, Reagan never permitted anyone to upstage him. Using his words to please his audience, he projected sincerity and yet did not really mean what he said, so his words were not as dangerous as his critics feared nor as true as his followers hoped. When Reagan said the national security of all the Americas was at stake in Central America, his critics feared he was going to war, and his supporters hoped he would. Both were wrong. All Reagan was doing was trying to scare Congress into supporting his program.

In the end, Reagan seemed more committed to certain policies than almost any other politician, and yet he was actually less committed. That explains why he ran so hard against the Panama Canal Treaties and then dropped the issue entirely when he became president. It explains why he was so committed to the Contras and then did not utter a word when his successor abandoned them in the bipartisan accord of 1989. And yet he was such a good actor that he retained a devoted following regardless of what he said.

To evaluate his administration's policy, one can start with his own objectives. How successful was Reagan in undermining Communism in the Caribbean Basin? There is no disputing his success in replacing a Marxist regime with a democratic government in Grenada. Reagan vividly recalls the invasion as "one of the highest of the high points of my eight years,"[44] a curious comment considering the size and significance of that island.

Beyond that, the record is either mixed or poor. If one judges the Contra strategy by whether U.S. interests and concerns in Nicaragua were better or worse off at the end than at the beginning of Reagan's term, the policy faltered: there were fewer moderate leaders and less tolerance for political dissent in Nicaragua; the Sandinistas were much more militarized and dependent on the Soviet Union and Cuba; the human toll was tragic for such a poor country; the war and the embargo severely weakened the economy and lowered the morale of the civic opposition, who felt that the United States only cared about the Contras. Even with this high cost, some might see the Contra policy vindicated by the defeat of the Sandinistas in the February 1990 election, except that Reagan himself said that the Sandinistas would never permit a free election unless Congress approved military aid to the Contras; Congress rejected both the aid and Reagan's argument, and Congress was proven right.[45]

The cost of the Contras in the United States was also high. No single incident stained Ronald Reagan and his presidency as much as the Iran-Contra affair. Several senior administration officials were convicted of criminal charges stemming from that scandal. The congressional investigation concluded: "Enough is clear to demonstrate beyond doubt that fundamental processes of governance were disregarded and the rule of law was subverted."[46] Reagan was faced with the sad choice of either acting unaware of this project or assuming responsibility and facing the prospect of impeachment. The smart strategy was to look stupid, and that's what Reagan did, but the American people didn't believe him. A *New York Times*/CBS News poll in early 1989 found that 52 percent of the American people thought that President Reagan was "lying when he said he did not know that the money from arms sales to Iran was going to help the contras."[47]

One could argue that U.S. policy helped make the Salvadoran military more professional, but its war against the Left moved no closer to success because Washington opposed land reform, stymied negotiations with the Left, and failed to exert sufficient pressure on the military to stop the death squads. In Panama, the administration found itself stuck in a hole that it had dug for itself, with no prospect of pulling Noriega out.

How does the administration fare using criteria weighted in favor of human rights? In every authoritarian Central American country except Nicaragua, the main struggle for democracy in the last decades has been against the Right. The Reagan administration refused to fight that war, fearful of dividing the non-Communist forces. Only in El Salvador in December 1983 did the administration deliver a message to the Right. Otherwise, the administration sometimes delivered *Congress's* message on human rights, which was better than none but no substitute for a policy.

The administration's efforts to improve U.S. relations with military regimes miscarried, ironically because many were replaced by democracies. Although Reagan changed direction in his second term and tried to take credit for the new democracies, most of the newly elected presidents in South America risked his displeasure by acknowledging the contribution of his predecessor.[48] The administration does deserve some credit for bringing democracy to Argentina, but by a convoluted route. The Argentine generals thought that if they helped the United States in Nicaragua, then Washington would help or at least acquiesce when Argentina seized its strategic prize, the Malvinas, in April 1982. But the United States first negotiated as a neutral and then supported the British, leaving the generals feeling betrayed.[49] Their disastrous defeat finally forced the military to give up power to civilians in a free election. For his part, Reagan admits in his memoirs that he tried to dissuade English prime minister Margaret Thatcher from an unconditional victory for fear that it would lead to a violent overthrow of the military dictatorship in Buenos Aires "by leftist guerrillas."[50] This was an utterly implausible scenario, and Thatcher was unmoved by Reagan's appeal.

In justifying its confrontation with Nicaragua, the administration discovered and then elaborated on a commitment to democracy. Most important, it informed the military throughout Latin America that U.S. support for them depended on their acceptance of civilian, democratically elected governments. Even though the administration disliked the radical approach of Peruvian president Alan Garcia, it was careful not to antagonize him or give a green light to the military to overthrow him. This was the first time that conservative Republicans had been willing to work with Social Democrats in Latin America in preference to stable, military regimes. Therefore, although the administration did not facilitate transitions toward democracy in the region, with the possible exception of Chile, and failed to use its influence to help consolidate the new regimes, it deserves credit for preventing the new democracies from being overthrown.

The Reagan administration's approach remained unilateral without apologies. It listened to its friends less and sought to divide regional efforts more than any other administration in the postwar period. The administration showed a blatant disregard for international law and organizations. Instead of bringing evidence of Nicaraguan subversion to the OAS, the Reagan administration released it as a White Paper. Instead of bringing Nicaragua to the World Court, the administration was dragged there by Nicaragua and then refused to accept the court's jurisdiction. By 1985, the administration stopped pretending to seek a multilateral approach to the region's problems, and the assistant secretary of state began defending unilateralism:

We can't abdicate our responsibility to protect our interests to a committee of Latin American countries. . . . the notion that if we have interests at stake we should ask Latin Americans what to do about it is wrong. . . . They want to know what we are going to do. They want to know if we have the guts to protect our interests, and if we don't, then they are going to walk away, and that is the way it should be.[51]

The Reagan administration is unlikely to be remembered for its foreign economic policies since it sidestepped the debt issue after helping Mexico reschedule its debts. It did initially improve relations with Mexico, but by the end of Reagan's term that relationship had been strained by differences on Central America. Its CBI was a positive program, but it did not compensate the region for the adverse effect of Washington's reduction of sugar quotas. Overall, during the Reagan years, the gross domestic product of Latin America and the Caribbean declined by 8.3 percent.

President Reagan's legacy in Latin America and the Caribbean is thus an ironic one. He accomplished least in the area where he tried the hardest—Central America—and most in the area where he did the least—democracy. He combatted Communism in the hemisphere, but he did so by polarizing the debate in the United States. He sought democracy in Central America but presided over a constitutional scandal that brought his presidency to the brink of disaster. He was proud and optimistic about democracy's progress in South America at a time when the region grew increasingly pessimistic about its social and economic prospects.

Perhaps the most intriguing irony of the Reagan administration was that its strategy toward Nicaragua gradually came to resemble the Communist strategy against which it was directed. Ronald Reagan, the arch anti-Communist, gave his name to a doctrine that was a replica of the Communists' support of national liberation movements. The administration's role in organizing, training, and supplying materiel for the Contras was the same role it accused Nicaragua of playing with Salvadoran guerrillas. Reagan's reliance on propaganda, covert actions, and deceit was modeled on Soviet activities. The obsession with overthrowing the Sandinistas led Reagan to ally with Manuel Noriega, a drug dealer, and threaten Oscar Arias, a Nobel Peace Prize winner.

To be sure, the United States had supported coups in Latin America before, but it had never publicly acknowledged its support for an army of insurgents dedicated to overthrowing a government with which it had diplomatic relations. It had never supported as large an insurgency for so long or incorporated that policy into presidential doctrine. In many ways, the administration forged a policy that reflected the revolutionary style of Cuba more than that of previous U.S. administrations.

To defeat the Communists, Reagan adopted their tactics while he jettisoned America's strength, its respect for the rule of law. At a moment of unprecedented opportunities for inter-American cooperation among democracies, the United States chose to pursue its war against Nicaragua alone. In the end, Reagan hoisted himself on the self-defeating tactics of his despised adversaries.

Notes

This chapter is adapted from chapter 4 of my book, *Whirlpool: U.S. Foreign Policy toward Latin America and the Caribbean* (Princeton, N.J.: Princeton University Press, 1992).

1. Daniel Yankovich and Larry Kaagan, "Assertive America," in *Foreign Affairs: America and the World, 1980* (New York: Council on Foreign Relations, 1981), p. 696.

2. Quoted by Ronnie Dugger, *On Reagan: The Man and His Presidency* (New York: McGraw-Hill, 1983), p. 351.

3. In an interview with the *Wall Street Journal* in 1980, Reagan stated this view without reservations: "The Soviet Union underlies all the unrest that is going on. If they weren't engaged in this game of dominoes, there wouldn't be any hotspots in the world" (cited in ibid., p. 353).

4. "Interview with Tomas Borge," *Playboy* (September 1983): 67.

5. See Dugger, *On Reagan*, pp. 382–83; and Ronald Reagan, "The Canal as Opportunity: A New Relationship with Latin America," *Orbis* (fall 1977): 551–61.

6. Jeane Kirkpatrick, "U.S. Security and Latin America," *Commentary* (January 1981): 29. Her other article was "Dictatorships and Double Standards," *Commentary* (November 1979).

7. Committee of Santa Fe, *A New Inter-American Policy for the Eighties* (Washington DC: Council for Inter-American Security, 1980), pp. 2, 20–21.

8. Republican National Convention, *Republican Platform* (Detroit, Mich.), 14 July 1980, pp. 68–69.

9. Alexander M. Haig Jr., *Caveat: Realism, Reagan and Foreign Policy* (New York: Macmillan, 1984), pp. 96–97.

10. The principal source for this summary of the debate within the administration was ibid., pp. 98–100, 117–40, but two other articles were helpful: Don Obendorfer, "Applying Pressure in Central America," *Washington Post*, 23 November 1983; and Leslie H. Gelb, "Haig Is Said to Press for Military Options for Salvadoran Action," *New York Times*, 5 November 1981. During the presidential campaign of 1980, Reagan said, "Suppose we put a blockade around that island [Cuba] and said [to the U.S.S.R.], 'Now buster, we'll lift it when you take your forces out of Afghanistan.'"

11. In an interview with *Time* on 5 January 1981 Reagan suggested postponing the land and banking reforms in El Salvador, and the Right in El Salvador rejoiced. An article by Viera Altamirano in Salvador's *El Diario de Hoy* the same day praised Reagan for rejecting "a policy of appeasement toward Communism" in favor of a confrontational approach.

12. Napoleon Duarte, interview by author, 26–27 July 1983, San José, Costa Rica.

13. Juan de Onis, "Haig Opposes a Coup by Salvador's Right," *New York Times*, 5 March 1981, p. A9.

14. Some of this evidence was released in the White Paper in February 1981, but the most credible and important proof was not released until September 1985. See U.S. Department of State, *Revolution beyond Our Borders*, September 1985, No. 132, pp. 7–10.

15. American ambassador Lawrence Pezzullo, interview by author, 30 July 1985, New York City.

16. For a chronology of the Reagan administration's covert decisions on Nicaragua, see U.S. Senate and House Select Committees on Secret Military Assistance to Iran and the Nicaraguan Opposition, *Iran-Contra Affair Report*, 17 November 1987 (hereafter Congress, *Iran-Contra Report*).

17. I am indebted to Mick Anderson's *Dossier Secreto* for bringing Menem's observation to my attention. The quote can be found in Alfredo Leveo and José Antonio Díaz, *El heredero de Perón* (Buenos Aires: Planeta, 1989), p. 17. Jackson Diehl, "State Department Official Sees Role for Argentina in Central America," *Washington Post*, 10 March 1982, p. A18, 12 March 1981, p. A16.

18. John Dinges, "Kirkpatrick Trip Upsets Opposition in Chile," *Washington Post*, 13 August 1981, p. A25; Raymond Bonner, "Chilean Exiles Appeal to Mrs. Kirkpatrick for Help," *New York Times*, 22 September 1981, p. A16.

19. This was Haig's characterization. See also Reagan's speech on developing countries, *New York Times*, 16 October 1981, p. A12.

20. Sam Dillon, "U.S. Arms Sales to Latin America Skyrocket," *Miami Herald*, 28 November 1982.

21. Milton R. Benjamin, "U.S. Is Allowing Argentina to Buy Critical A-System," *Washington Post*, 19 July 1982, pp. A1, A4; "Argentina's Blow to U.S. Nonproliferation Policy," letter by John Buell to *New York Times*, 29 November 1983, p. A30.

22. Ronald Reagan, *An American Life* (New York: Simon and Schuster, 1990), p. 471.

23. Department of State, President Reagan's Address to the National Association of Manufacturers, 10 March 1983.

24. For an analysis of the justifications for the invasion, see Robert Pastor, "The Invasion of Grenada: A Pre- and Post-Mortem," in Scott MacDonald, Harald Sandstrom, and Paul Goodwin, eds., *The Caribbean after Grenada: Revolution, Conflict, and Democracy* (New York: Praeger, 1988).

25. Juan Williams, "President Defends Using Force," *Washington Post*, 13 December 1983, p. 1.

26. *The Report of the President's National Bipartisan Commission on Central America* (New York: Macmillan, 1984).

27. "Senate, 84–12, Acts to Oppose Mining Nicaragua's Ports; Rebuke to Reagan," *New York Times*, 11 April 1984, p. 1. For a full account of what the CIA did, see David Rogers and David Ignatius, "How CIA-Aided Raids in Nicaragua in '84 Led Congress to End Funds," and "CIA Internal Report Details U.S. Role in Contra Raids in Nicaragua Last Year," *Wall Street Journal*, 6 March 1985.

28. Excerpts of the document were reprinted during the North trial in the *New York Times*, 14 April 1989, p. 9, and later declassified. In the meeting, McFarlane criticizes Nicaragua and other "Marxist-Leninist regimes" for using negotiations as "tactical exercises," but Reagan did the same thing (p. 10).

29. Congress, *Iran-Contra Report*, p. 41.

30. Ibid., p. 4.

31. Cited in Loretta Tofani, "'Contra' Cause Is Just, Reagan Says," *Washington Post*, 31 March 1985, p. A22.

32. Poindexter told Congress: "The buck stops here with me. I made the decision." At Poindexter's trial, his lawyer argued that "the President was the driving engine behind his [Poindexter's] actions" and his client was a victim of "a frame-up." David Johnston, "Poindexter Is Found Guilty of All Five Criminal Charges for Iran-Contra Cover-Up," *New York Times*, 8 April 1990, p. 1.

33. Cited in *FBIS*, 29 October 1987, pp. 6–7.

34. See David Lyons, "Noriega Was Spy, U.S. Concedes," *Miami Herald*, 31 May 1991. Also see a document submitted by the U.S. government to the U.S. District Court of the District of Columbia in *U.S. v. Oliver North* (No. 88-0080), esp. pp. 40–42.

35. For two balanced assessments of these events, see Margaret E. Scranton, *The Noriega Years* (Boulder, Colo.: Lynne Rienner, 1991), and John Dinges, *Our Man in Panama* (New York: Random House, 1990).

36. In a press conference on 11 February 1986, Reagan said that the United States provided an airplane for Duvalier, but when he was asked if he gave "him any strong advice to leave," the president responded: "No. And he never asked us for any." Reprinted in the *New York Times*, 12 February 1986, p. 10.

37. U.S. Department of State, Thomas Enders's Address to the Inter-American Press Association, 30 September 1982, Chicago.

38. The data are from Naciones Unides Comisión Economia para América Latina y El Caribe, "Notas sobre la economia y el desarrollo," December 1985, pp. 16–18.

39. George P. Shultz, *Turmoil and Triumph: My Years as Secretary of State* (New York: Charles Scribner's Sons, 1993), p. 964.

40. Constantine C. Menges, *Inside the National Security Council: The True Story of the Making and Unmaking of Reagan's Foreign Policy* (New York: Simon and Schuster, 1988).

41. "Official Biographer Puzzled by Reagan Persona," in the newsletter of the Miller Center of the University of Virginia (spring 1991): 3–4. Frank McNeil, *War and Peace in Central America* (New York: Charles Scribner's Sons, 1988).

42. Oliver North, *Under Fire* (New York: HarperCollins, 1991), pp. 11–14, 17.

43. Shultz, *Turmoil and Triumph*, p. 814.

44. Reagan, *An American Life*, p. 458.

45. Reagan expressed his "disappointment that the House voted to remove the pressure of the democratic resistance on the Sandinista regime,"

saying that the Sandinistas would never negotiate seriously and permit a free election without such pressure. *New York Times*, 25 February 1988, p. 8.

46. Congress, *Iran-Contra Report*, p. 11.

47. Thirty-three percent said he was telling the truth. The poll was taken from 12–15 January 1989. See p. 14 of the mimeo.

48. For example, Uruguayan president Julio Sanguinetti described "Carter's efforts" as "very important," particularly as compared to Reagan's policy. "We Fought in a Great Silence: Interview with Sanguinetti," *Newsweek*, 10 December 1984, p. 17.

49. General Galtieri described the "excellent" rapport established with Reagan and the "deception . . . bitterness . . . [and] betrayal" he felt when Reagan didn't support him. Oriana Fallaci interview, *Washington Post*, 13 June 1982, p. C5.

50. Reagan, *An American Life*, p. 360.

51. Elliot Abrams interview, "Big Sticks and Good Neighbors," *Detroit News*, 12 September 1985.

Howard J. Wiarda

From Reagan to Bush: Continuity and Change in U.S. Latin American Policy

George Bush did not have the same strong, firm, ideological beliefs about the world as did Ronald Reagan. Ronald Reagan did not have a powerful, Ph.D.-level, analytical mind; but he had a shrewd poker-player's touch as well as strong feelings, sentiments, and instincts—often quite noble and politically effective ones—that he applied to both domestic and foreign affairs.[1] Bush was more a pragmatist, a moderate, a centrist—some would say a chameleon, who seemed to change his color with every shift of the political winds. Reagan came out of the Right or Goldwater wing of the Republican party, whereas Bush emerged from the Nelson Rockefeller–Gerald Ford wing of the party. While Reagan had strong beliefs, his presidency also evoked strong emotions both for and against; in contrast, Bush, lacking strong ideological moorings, evoked no such strong reactions from either supporters or foes. Bush's pragmatism and moderation, after the more ideological presidencies of Jimmy Carter and Reagan, were positive factors in his 1988 election: the public clearly wanted a more centrist, moderate, problem-solving regime. At the same time, the pragmatism and moderation that helped Bush in the 1988 campaign later opened him up to the charge of lacking values, "vision," and direction.[2]

As president, Bush did not do a great deal positively or constructively for Latin America or pay it a great deal of consistent attention. At the same time, overall U.S. relations with Latin America at the end of his term were probably better than they had been in decades. Some of the changes for the better were due to Bush policies, but they mainly had to do with larger global events—such as the collapse of the Soviet Union and the end of the Cold War—over which the administration had only limited control. After the fevered attention and passionate debates about Latin American of the Carter and Reagan years, U.S. policy under Bush once again settled down and reverted to a posture of "benign neglect." But it is in precisely this context of a reversion to a level of indifference or neglect regarding Latin America that U.S. relations with the area have achieved perhaps their highest level in decades. It is toward the deciphering and explication of this apparent paradox that the present chapter is directed.

The 1988 Election Campaign

As the vice president under the heir apparent of Ronald Reagan, who served as president from 1981 to 1989, George Herbert Walker Bush did not need to form elaborate coteries of foreign affairs advisers and campaign staffers for his presidential campaign of 1988. Bush was expected, with some modifications, to follow the policies of Reagan; continuity rather than change was anticipated to be the hallmark of the Bush administration. In addition, Bush had the advantage of a foreign policy team already in place: it was called the U.S. government. Incumbency, even as a vice president, gives a candidate enormous advantages and means that he is able to draw upon the personnel, position papers, and expertise of the entire U.S. government.

Nevertheless, the Republican National Committee and the Bush campaign, headed early on by Ronald Kaufman, did establish in the spring of 1988 a series of foreign policy advisory panels, including one on Latin America. The Latin America panel was headed by William Perry, who had served for a time as presidential adviser on Latin America on the National Security Council (NSC) and was then a senior fellow with the Center for Strategic and International Studies (CSIS). Also on the panel were George Fauriol, director of the Americas Program at CSIS, and myself. The Bush advisory panels were centrist rather than Reaganite. Their purposes included drafting language on Latin America for the platform committee of the Republican convention coming up that summer, preparing speeches for the candidate, formulating "talking points" for the fall presidential candidates' debate, and elaborating more detailed policy recommendations for a future Bush administration.[3]

Such panels, however, serve several functions, not all of which involve serious policy formulation. William Perry and other panel members took their responsibilities seriously and prepared position papers dealing with Cuba, Mexico, Brazil, and overall Latin America policy that were well thought out, carefully crafted, and politically moderate—in keeping with the candidate's views. But these advisory panels, as in all election campaigns, also served as a place to assign individuals who donated generously to the party and who wanted a sense of participating in the campaign, who had previously served as ambassadors or government officials, or who simply wanted to be part of the Bush election effort. The quite diverse origins, motives, and constituencies of those who served on the advisory panels meant that the position papers drafted were political documents as well as integrated policy statements, designed to satisfy diverse groups and to keep everyone loyal to the campaign. Some of these papers and statements were used by campaign officials and the candidate; in other cases, new language was substituted at the Republican convention by, among others, Senator Robert Kasten of Wisconsin, who headed the platform committee. As a politician, Kasten had his own agenda, which was not always the same as that of the think tank scholars who served on the advisory panels.

The foreign policy differences in 1988 between Bush and Democratic candidate Michael Dukakis are familiar and need not be repeated in detail here. Bush favored continued research on and the eventual deployment of the Strategic Defense Initiative (SDI), whereas Dukakis denounced it as a "fantasy" but later indicated he would support limited research on the program. Dukakis opposed the Midgetman intercontinental ballistic missile, opposed plans to increase American naval forces by two aircraft carrier groups, and opposed building the Ground Wage Emergency Network (GWEN). Dukakis expressed reservations about the B-1 and Stealth bombers, but later gave them his OK. In contrast, Bush enthusiastically supported all these new weapon systems.[4] Dukakis wished to reduce drastically the Department of Defense budget; Bush wanted to keep it at then-current levels.

Specifically on Latin America, Dukakis opposed aid to the anti-Communist resistance in Nicaragua (the Contras) and denounced the Reagan administration's Central America policy as a "fiasco." Instead, he favored working through the Organization of American states (OAS), which most analysts at that time considered a moribund organization. Dukakis expressed strong support for the peace plan of Costa Rican president Oscar Arias, which called for an end to *all* military assistance in the area but was criticized by Reagan administration officials as ignoring U.S. interests and not providing sufficient guarantees for democratization in Nicaragua. Bush publicly supported the policies of the administration of which he was a part and particularly the multifaceted approach to Central America derived from the 1983–84 Kissinger Commission: economic and social assistance as well as military aid, diplomacy combined with pressure, public aid as well as foreign investment, support for democracy and human rights, as well as defense of U.S. strategic interests.[5] Bush favored the Arias peace plan so long as it was modified to take into account U.S. interests in Central America. On Latin America's international debt, Dukakis favored a multilateral approach and indicated that some share of the debt should be forgiven, while Bush preferred an incremental approach that avoided passing the burden of Latin America's unpaid debt onto U.S. taxpayers. Dukakis's statements also indicated that he shared many of the counterculture's views on American foreign policy: the CIA, the Defense Department, and maybe the U.S. government itself were "morally evil" forces that needed to be reined in.

A candidate is judged in political Washington not just on his own statements, however, but also on the quality of the team of foreign policy advisers who assist him during the campaign and will, presumably, accompany him to Washington and occupy high foreign policy positions if he is elected. In Dukakis's case, his chief foreign policy advisers were Madelyn Albright of Georgetown University and Albert Carnesale and Joseph Nye of Harvard University. On Latin America Dukakis received advice from former Carter administration assistant secretary of state for inter-American affairs Viron P. Vaky, former Carter administration NSC member Robert Pastor, former Carter administration Department of Treasury official Richard Feinberg, and Inter-American Dialogue executive secretary Abraham Lowenthal. All these persons are liberal, but none could be said to belong to the radical fringe of the Democratic party. Reports coming out of the campaign, however, indicated that while Dukakis gave these advisers a hearing, his own views announced privately to other aides were considerably to the left of his main advisers.[6]

To the extent the 1988 election was decided on foreign policy issues, Dukakis came to be widely seen by the electorate as being weak on defense and not very tough or well informed on U.S. foreign policy. In this regard he was similar to earlier Democratic candidates George McGovern and Jimmy Carter. All this was in contrast to Bush, whose basic policy of peace through strength was widely viewed as more realistic. In November Bush won a resounding victory with 53 percent of the popular vote and 426 electoral college votes.

The Presidential Transition

The time between the general election in November and the president's inauguration on 20 January is a critical one. In the expectations of political Washington, it is necessary for a new administration to "hit the ground running." That is, it must have all its personnel in place and its plans and programs ready to go so that on and immediately after inauguration day it can appear to be dramatic, innovative, and fully in charge. If it is not ready, a new administration is quickly branded by the press as inept, unprepared, and indecisive. The public seldom pays very much attention to the personnel and policy choices made in the two and a half months between election and inauguration day, but in fact these are often the most critical times of a new presidency. Several points should be made in this connection with regard to the Bush administration.

First, it should be said that the new president himself was highly experienced in foreign matters—the most experienced foreign policy president since Richard Nixon and Dwight Eisenhower. As vice president under Reagan, a former CIA director, former ambassador to China, former congressman, and businessman in the oil industry, Bush had a wealth of foreign affairs experience. Moreover, he enjoyed foreign policy issues and made it clear that he would be his own chief foreign affairs adviser.

Second, the president recruited a highly experienced and able foreign policy team at the highest level. James Baker, the president's campaign manager who had previously served as secretary of the treasury and as chief of staff of the Reagan White House, had his choice of Bush administration positions: he became secretary of state. For the NSC Bush chose Brent Scowcroft, who had also been NSC director under President Gerald Ford and who was known as an able but self-effacing adviser who would clearly allow Bush to run his own foreign policy. For the chairmanship of the Joint Chiefs of Staff Bush selected Gen. Colin Powell, a man who understood political as well as military affairs and who had also served as national security adviser under Reagan. At the CIA Bush had William Webster, a lawyer and former FBI director who had a clean image and who would defer to Bush and the foreign policy professionals. Bush nominated former senator John Tower to be secretary of defense, but that nomination was derailed in the Senate; later reports indicated that the White House was not displeased that the Tower nomination did not go through, because then former congressman and Ford White House chief of staff Richard Cheney could get the nomination.

Not only was this an experienced team at the highest levels, it was also a group that was used to working together. Alone among recent American administrations, the Bush administration largely avoided the personal rivalries, the "bureaucratic politics," and the turf battles that had characterized the Carter and Reagan presidencies.

Third, the new administration was very careful in selecting subcabinet (assistant secretary and NSC) officials. This is the level where most of the policy decisions are made and where most of the work is done in any administration; yet it is a level that often receives very little attention from the press or the public. In the case of the Bush administration, James Baker exercised oversight over all appointments at this level, but he relied heavily on a team of younger officials who had previously worked for him at Treasury or in the White House: Dennis Ross, Robert Zoellick, Margaret Tutwiler, and Robert Kimmitt. These officials, especially Ross, screened the appointments for Baker and therefore played a significant role in setting the tone for the administration's entire foreign policy. Their strategies and choices, accordingly, merit closer analysis.

First, these Baker protégés took care of themselves: Ross was named director of the Policy Planning Office at State, which now under Baker took on far greater importance as a way of bypassing the department's cumbersome bureaucracy; Kimmitt became undersecretary of state, the third-ranking position in the department; Tutwiler became assistant secretary for public affairs; and Zoellick was named State Department counselor. Second, Ross (and Baker) determined not to keep *any* of the Reagan administration foreign policy advisers, which meant policy would soon shift quite dramatically in many areas of the globe. For example, all those officials associated with Jean Kirkpatrick's foreign policy positions in the Reagan administration were now obliged to leave. Third, Ross (and Baker) determined to recruit only experienced foreign policy *practitioners* to foreign policy positions, not ideologues. This meant, among other things, that only one or two people from either the conservative American Enterprise Institute or the far-right Heritage Foundation (both of which had supplied approximately thirty of their scholars each to the Reagan administration) were appointed to a major position in the Bush administration. These criteria for recruitment also help us understand why Bush's foreign policy was almost universally acclaimed for its expertise and accomplishments in the processes of foreign policy making but criticized for its lack of vision. This was from top to bottom (Bush, Scowcroft, down through the NSC and the foreign policy-making departments) a *process administration* but one (in contrast to Carter or Reagan) that was not very good at formulating goals or purpose.

A key battleground was at the NSC. Under Reagan, the NSC, and particularly its three-person Latin America staff, had largely and rather consistently been comprised of conservative ideologues. First, the Bush team downgraded the Latin America staff to two positions instead of three; then it brought in foreign policy professionals from the State Department to staff the positions rather than Reagan-type true believers. The State Department people brought into the NSC were experienced officials in accord with the Ross-Baker-Scowcroft-Bush criteria, but they were often weak on Latin America or on conceptualizing Latin American development. The one sop to expertise and to conservatives was the appointment of Ambassador Ellis O. Briggs to the chief Latin America position at the NSC. Briggs was hardly an ideological conservative, but he recognized that the FMLN in El Salvador included Communists as well as independent Marxists and also that it was necessary to keep some sort of pressure (not necessarily the Contras) on the Sandinista government in Nicaragua. Briggs soon was enmeshed in policy disputes with other more "pragmatic" officials in the administration and was sent off as ambassador to Portugal. Thereafter, the NSC's Latin America contingent consisted *exclusively* of foreign service professionals with both the strengths and weaknesses already alluded to.

Perhaps the most interesting battle was over the position of assistant secretary of state for inter-American affairs, the State Department's chief Latin America position. Early on, several names had been put forward by diverse groups and interests, but among those who had served on Bush's campaign advisory team there was remarkable consensus on what qualifications were necessary: a person who spoke Spanish, knew Latin America (especially Mexico, since that was where interest was now centering), had previous government experience, knew the business world (because of the rising emphasis on trade issues), and was probably a lawyer. William Perry, who had chaired the Republican National Committee's Latin America advisory panel, even had a candidate in mind whom he brought to Washington and talked up among Congress and the press: William Helander, a shrewd and pleasant New York lawyer who was a middle-of-the-road conservative and had practical experience helping business entrepreneurs in Latin America.

But James Baker resented this effort by "outsiders" to try to tell him whom to appoint to the Latin America position and particularly resented Helander's being paraded around Washington as the nominee-designate without Baker's prior approval. In addition, Baker already had in mind a plan to diffuse the explosive and politically damaging Central America situation, and this called for a person very different from Helander. Baker hence chose Bernard Aronson to be assistant secretary. Aronson knew no Spanish and had never spent any time in Latin America, which rendered him unacceptable to professional Latin Americanists, but those were precisely the traits Baker was looking for. Baker wanted no one who had been "tainted" by Latin America or who was a party to the ideological battles over Central America in the 1980s. Aronson was, moreover, a liberal Democrat, a former Democratic party official, and a supporter of Walter Mondale (against Ronald Reagan) in 1984. Conservatives grumbled that if they had wanted a liberal Democrat in charge of Latin America policy, they would have voted for Michael Dukakis. But to no avail: Aronson was Baker's choice, Baker had prestige and backing in the press and Congress, he had Bush's backing, and the opposition to Aronson was hence brushed aside. The sop to the conservatives was that Aronson had once written part of a speech expressing support for U.S. aid to the Contras. There were no sops to Latin Americanists.

Changing Central America Policy

Secretary of State Baker was known to feel that under President Reagan, Central American policy had been handled poorly. Central America had proved to be terribly divisive, it had provoked considerable popular opposition to the president, and it had gotten strong elements in the religious denominations, the media, the Congress, and other groups hostile. Not only had Central America provoked a fractious domestic debate but the spillover from that nastiness had also damaged the president in his efforts to deal with other areas such as NATO or the Soviet Union. To the preeminently political Baker (then, as now, the president's chief campaign manager, regardless of the official position he held), Central America was thought to be a can of worms. If President Bush moved to the right on Central America, he got it from the religious, human rights, and liberal lobbies; if he moved left, he got it from the Reaganites and the conservatives.

Baker recognized, in addition, that there were no Central American votes out there, unlike the situation with regard to Israel, Greece, and Cuba, where domestic ethnic/nationality groups do make their voices strongly heard. To Baker, Central America was a lose-lose situation: there was nothing to be gained and much to be lost from continuing the Reagan strategy. It would be far better, Baker reasoned, to finesse Central America, get rid of it, solve the problem, and go on, thus enabling his president to concentrate on bigger and better things. That is why, after all, Bernard Aronson, totally lacking in Latin America experience or expertise, was appointed to the assistant secretary position. Aronson, it was assumed, would be able to work with and implement a deal with the congressional Democrats; in addition, and a definite advantage from Baker's perspective, Aronson was, unlike other prospective candidates for the assistant secretary's position, unencumbered by the legacy of the domestic ideological and political wars (there is no other word) over Central America policy in the 1980s.[7]

The negotiations for a deal with the congressional Democrats began as early as November 1988, within two weeks of Bush's election and only one week after Baker's nomination as secretary of state. In these early stages Baker himself conducted the negotiations and quickly arrived at a framework for an agreement; Aronson would be involved later, in the detail and implementation stages. Baker's quick attention to Central America, however, did not mean that he accorded the area high priority; rather, his goal was to dismiss Central America as soon as possible.[8]

In seeking to finesse the Central America problem Baker had several goals in mind. First, he wanted to remove an issue that had the potential to damage *his* president (Bush)—as it had earlier damaged Reagan—or to hurt his reelection possibilities. Second, he wanted

Bush and himself to be free to go on to other things deemed more important—a NATO summit in Europe and a meeting with Soviet president Mikhail Gorbachev in Malta—without being encumbered by the albatross of Central America, which had damaged U.S. relations with its allies and was a nonconstructive issue in U.S.-Soviet relations. Third, Baker wanted to establish a cooperative, working relationship with Congress so that, even in a situation of divided government with the White House held by one party and the Congress dominated by the other, his president could get his legislative agenda passed as compared with the deadlock in executive-congressional relations that had existed often under Reagan. In short, by settling the rancorous Central America disputes, Baker sought to buy political space for his president. Note that *every one* of these motivations has to do with U.S. domestic politics; none of them has to do with Central America per se.

The pact involved the following basics: the Congress agreed to continue to provide *nonlethal* humanitarian aid to the Contras fighting the Sandinista regime, through the scheduled February 1990 election in Nicaragua. This provision was intended to put pressure on Nicaragua to continue its democratization but without providing any new weapons or ammunition to the Contras. At the same time Congress made it clear that U.S. aid to the Contras *would* end: any new aid would, after 30 November 1989, have to be approved by no less than four committees of the Congress—a virtual impossibility. The nonlethal aid the Congress did vote was to be used chiefly to feed and clothe the Contras, to get them *voluntarily* to disarm and resettle inside Nicaragua, and in the process eventually (after the February 1990 reelection) to disband their military base camps in Honduras and Costa Rica and to close down the Contras' political offices in the United States. Meanwhile, Secretary Baker agreed to try to reach a political settlement of the Nicaraguan conflict by working through the Arias peace accords, but modifying them so that U.S. security concerns in Central America could also be met.[9]

The issue was very controversial all through 1989 and on into early 1990. Some conservatives accused the Bush administration of selling out the Contras and of putting too much faith in the democratic intentions of Nicaraguan president Daniel Ortega, whom it was assumed would either cancel the election once the Contras were defanged or rig them so his Sandinistas would win. Ellis Briggs at the NSC became unhappy when the Central American presidents' meeting in Tala, Honduras, determined to close down the Contra camps in December 1989, *before* the scheduled Nicaraguan election; he was also distressed to see the Contra leaders abandoned by the State Department. This conflict between the NSC and Aronson at State, who was following Baker's scenario to finesse Central America, led to Briggs's departure from the NSC and his reassignment as ambassador to Portugal.[10] Senator John McCain (R-AZ) and other conservatives continued the attack, criticizing the Democrats in Congress for agreeing with the Central American presidents on the mandatory (the earlier agreement said it was voluntary) closing of the camps before the February 1990 election, thus violating both the letter and the spirit of the earlier accord.[11]

Meanwhile, the administration had entered into negotiations with the Soviet Union to put pressure on the Sandinistas to run an honest election. In the spring and summer of 1989 Aronson met repeatedly with his Soviet counterpart, Baker brought the issue up with Soviet foreign minister Edvard Shevardnadze, and Bush mentioned it to Gorbachev at their summit. The Soviets hemmed and hawed on the issue for a time but did intercede with the Sandinistas to carry out a democratic election. At the time, observers speculated that there must have been a U.S. quid pro quo (cessation of U.S. aid to UNITA in Angola or to the *mujahadin* in Afghanistan, for example) or else why would the Soviets be willing to put pressure on their client? The answer is that even at that time the Soviet Union was in desperate economic and political shape (although few U.S. officials yet understood the full severity of the crisis); and when the possibility was raised (not a threat or a "deal") that U.S. trade credits and goodwill would be dependent on the Soviets' helping to secure honest democratic elections in Nicaragua, the Soviets agreed to talk to Ortega.[12]

The Soviets, like virtually everyone else, assumed the Sandinistas would win. Either they would win the election fairly on the basis of their popular support or they would rig things. With the presence of international advisers (insisted on by the United States and eventually agreed to by the Soviets), it would be hard to fix the elections once the ballots were counted; but it was widely assumed the Sandinistas in the months before the election would use their control of the media, the police, the army, the government, and their own ancillary groups (for women, students, peasants, etc.) to guarantee a favorable result. The United States had provided funds and other support to the opposition, but even the officials in charge of distributing the largess were pessimistic that it would produce results and convinced the Sandinistas would win. No one—not the CIA, President Bush, Secretary Baker, various pollsters—predicted the opposition victory.

The administration was so sure the Sandinistas would win, in fact, that in the weeks before the election it had worked out a deal with the Sandinistas. The essence of the deal was this: the Sandinistas would stop their attempts to destabilize neighboring countries, stop aiding the guerrillas in El Salvador, stop their attempts to spread revolution in Central America, work out a timetable to send most of their Cuban, Soviet, and Eastern European advisers home, and stop importing offensive military equipment from Eastern Europe or the Soviet Union that the United States saw as a security threat. Given the Soviets' economic and political problems and their desire to stop aiding Nicaragua anyway, this was a realistic strategy on the part of the Sandinistas. The United States, in turn, agreed to allow the economic embargo against Nicaragua to run out in April 1990 (when it was scheduled to expire anyway), to stop aiding the Contras (already largely accomplished through the administration's agreement with the Congress), and to enter into diplomatic discussions with the government of Nicaragua to settle remaining issues. The United States was so eager to extract itself from Central America that it intended to carry out this agenda regardless of who won the February 1990 election. The administration's rationalization was that, regardless of the outcome, it could say that it stood for democracy in Central America and was willing to work with any elected government no matter its stripe.[13]

But the electoral result turned out even better than that from the administration's perspective. To everyone's surprise, Violeta de Chamorro and the National Opposition Union (UNO) won. Ortega, *sandinismo*, and Marxism-Leninism were defeated. Communism and Castroism were repudiated. In this way not only were U.S. security concerns in Central America resolved but, more important, the congressional democrats had been mollified, and domestic conservatives could also claim that the Reagan policies of supporting the Contras as a way of putting pressure on the Sandinistas had finally paid off. From the administration's perspective, the outcome was far better than could possibly have been expected. The election result, which was entirely unanticipated, solved both a foreign policy and, even more essentially, a domestic policy problem. The United States had basically lucked out. And with that, Nicaragua and the rest of Central America virtually disappeared from the headlines, the television sets, and U.S. policy consciousness in subsequent years—precisely the outcome that Secretary Baker had sought.

Panama and Operation Just Cause

During the same year, 1989, that the Nicaragua issue was moving toward resolution, Panama under Gen. Manuel Noriega continued to heat up. It is not my purpose here to review the entire history of the United States's Panama operations, only to indicate some of the more salient features.[14]

First, no one doubts that General Noriega was a brutal, corrupt, and undemocratic leader. He had been an informer, a drug agent, a double dealer. He was gross and coarse. His human rights record was awful and he had stood against the emergence of democracy in Panama. In the U.S. press Noriega had been portrayed in truly villainous terms, but in Latin America his reputation was not much better. That made it easier for the United States to justify its actions when it eventually went in militarily to get Noriega; it also explains why the reaction against the U.S. intervention was so muted.

Second, Noriega was the victim of one of the most interesting campaigns ever launched by the United States to get rid of a "friendly tyrant."[15] By this time the scenarios in such a campaign to rid ourselves of the Somozas, Marcoses, Stroessners, Duvaliers, Pinochets, and so on of this world are largely familiar. First we try friendly low-level persuasion: a meeting with the U.S. ambassador in which he tries to get the dictator to hold elections, to share power more broadly, to improve human rights, maybe to step aside and enjoy a comfortable retirement in Geneva or Miami. Then we may send a special presidential emissary or a private communication from the president himself. If these steps fail, coercive diplomacy will usually do the trick: diplomatic isolation, an economic embargo, sanctions of various kinds. But in Noriega's case the United States went far beyond the usual levers of diplomacy employed in such circumstances: it sought to ruin the domestic Panamanian economy (made easier by the fact that Panama's economy is largely based on dollars); it brought in a major Washington law firm (Arnold and Porter) to escalate the campaign; it brought pressure to bear on Panamanian banks and commercial enterprises; it tried to foment an internal military coup against Noriega; and eventually it sent U.S. military forces to Panama to capture Noriega and bring him to trial in the United States, meanwhile installing in power a government that had earlier been elected but now had to be sworn in at night on a U.S. military base. The U.S. actions in Panama went far beyond anything the United States had ever attempted before to get rid of an inconvenient dictator.

Third, we must ask what the motives were for the U.S. invasion. The answer is, when we scratch away all the other justifications offered and get to the heart of the issue, presidential pique and impatience. My view of how this operation should have gone is very close to that of former U.S. ambassador to Panama Ambler Moss.[16] That is, it was appropriate for the United States to pressure Noriega to hold honest elections, to improve human rights, to stop the flow of drugs through Panama, even to step aside. However, once we had put the policy of opposition to Noriega in place, then we should have waited for the *Panamanian* political process to operate. We made clear our goals and even encouraged and aided those opposed to Noriega. But it should have been the Panamanians who overthrew Noriega, not the United States. The movement could have come from within the Panamanian armed forces, from a civilian movement, or, most likely, from a combined military-civilian movement. But for this policy to be successful, patience and restraint from Washington would be necessary—not exactly U.S. foreign policy character traits. The United States should not impose a solution, not engage in a quick fix, but it needs to be prepared to stay the course of pressure and diplomacy for weeks or even months.

To these arguments, the U.S. administration countered that it *had* tried to exercise patience and restraint. It *had* relied on the Panamanian political processes, it said; but after the failed coup attempt of October 1989 (which the United States had encouraged but then, inexplicably, had failed to support), there were no signs the Panamanians could or would take matters into their own hands. Everyone in Panama was waiting for the *United States* to oust Noriega, but no Panamanian was willing to lift a hand to initiate the process—especially after the United States failed to aid the plotters in the October coup attempt. Later, Noriega made a tactical mistake by stupidly declaring war against the United States and thus escalating the conflict. The imprisonment and mistreatment of a U.S. military officer stationed in Panama and his wife was, similarly, a move that could only provoke American officials.[17]

But the deciding factor, as in Nicaragua, was domestic political considerations. Noriega had become an embarrassment to the administration. He had defied the United States at every turn. His ability to stand up to the United States and survive was making him a folk hero in Latin America. Worse, from the administration's point of view, he was embarrassing President Bush, making him look inept. Our inability to "get" Noriega made Bush look like a wimp, thus reviving memories of Bush's earlier reputation, giving new credence to the Gary Trudeau, anti-Bush "Doonesbury" political cartoons, and making Bush appear to be a blundering incompetent rather than a decisive leader. The factors mentioned in the paragraph above were also important but they were not decisive; the decisive factor was Baker's and Bush's conclusion that Noriega was making Bush and the United States look bad in front of the electorate and therefore that he had to go.[18]

A fourth consideration involves the reaction to the U.S. military action. A reliable *Washington Post*/ABC poll done nationwide immediately after the intervention showed eight in ten Americans approved of Bush's action to send troops to Panama to capture Noriega, eight in ten characterized it as a "success" and five in ten as a "big success," and seven in ten approved of the idea of bringing Noriega back to the United States to stand trial on drug charges.[19] After the intervention, Bush's job approval rating went from 66 to 79 percent (higher than Reagan's after his first year in office), and more Americans now considered the Republican party as "best able to deal with the country's major problems." Panama helped Bush achieve these high ratings which Operation Desert Shield and Operation Desert Storm in the Middle East put at even more stupendous heights: 90 percent. Clearly the Panama invasion was popular with the American people.

The UN General Assembly condemned the invasion of Panama as a "flagrant violation of international law" by a vote of 75 to 20 with 40 abstentions. But in Panama itself, the U.S. action to rid the country of Noriega was strongly approved, by a margin of 85 to 90 percent. These figures, plus Noriega's dastardly reputation at a time when the rest of the hemisphere was becoming more democratic, undoubtedly had an effect on the rest of Latin America. Few anti-American demonstrations occurred as a result of the intervention, opinion polls showed that most Latin Americans understood the U.S. position and were sympathetic to it, and the OAS was unable to muster a vote that would condemn the U.S. action.[20] As one who has been strongly condemnatory of past U.S. military interventions in Latin America and roundly criticized the 1965 U.S. intervention in the Dominican Republic (and almost got fired as a result), I would normally be inclined to be strongly critical of the U.S. action in Panama. I still think the policy of assisting and waiting for a Panamanian political process to remove Noriega was the appropriate one. However, I am impressed by the overwhelming public support for the intervention in Panama itself and by the almost total absence of hostility toward U.S. actions in the rest of Latin America.

The real tragedy in Panama was not the intervention per se—although the civilian casualty loss was particularly worrisome—but the fact the United States did so little to assist in rebuilding Panama *after* the intervention. A pattern begins to emerge here that is repeated elsewhere in Central America. Once the crisis of the moment (Guatemala in 1954, Nicaragua, El Salvador, more recently Panama) eases, the United States quickly loses interest, even though it bears considerable responsibility for causing damage and has, in my mind, a moral obligation to say nothing of political responsibility to help rebuild a society it helped to shatter. In this regard the White House and the Congress share equal responsibility: the White House for not pushing harder for its social and economic agenda for the area, and the Congress for erratically jumping from one issue where the members gain political advantage to the next. For example, all during the 1980s the Democrats in Congress had been crying that the real problems in Central America were social and economic, not strategic; but when the political conflict over Nicaragua, El Salvador, and Panama began to be solved and it came time to assist them with some real economic aid, the Congress backed out.[21] Once it could no longer get political mileage out of it, the Congress was no longer interested in Central America; its members had already moved on to the next issue that got them headlines: Eastern Europe and the former Soviet Union.

The War on Drugs

In 1989–90, opinion surveys told us, the American public identified drugs as *the* number one foreign policy problem. Not Communism, the Soviet Union, or Japan, but drugs.[22] The source of most of the drugs in the United States is Latin America.

First, it is necessary to provide some historical context. Drugs began to become a serious issue in the United States during the first term of President Ronald Reagan. Drugs were then viewed primarily as a domestic problem—as indeed they were. So Reagan's first proposal was to deal with the issue at the domestic level through stricter law enforcement, random drug testing, and rehabilitation. But the proposal for random testing ran into so much political opposition—from the media, teachers' unions, the Teamsters, the AFL-CIO, and the American Civil Liberties Union—that the administration determined it could not win on that front and largely abandoned the effort. Hence, in a decision that was largely made by the president's *domestic* affairs advisers, the administration determined to focus on the supply or production side of the equation. That is essentially how the drug war came to Latin America. The decision was made by people who knew nothing about Latin America and almost nothing about international affairs. They simply assumed that there would be less grief in dealing with the drug issue on the international than on the domestic side, that there would be fewer political problems, that the issue could be solved internationally even if it could not be solved domestically.[23]

That explains the administration's focus first on Mexico, then on Colombia, as well as the militarization of the antidrug campaign in Operation Blast Furnace, directed at drug production in Bolivia. Only after the initial decision had been made did the administration begin to realize that the problems of the counter-narcotics campaign were at least as great on the international or production side as on the domestic or consumption side. The problems included the widespread use of drugs in Latin America for cultural or religious reasons, the absence of any stigma attached to such use, the perception that drug use was a U.S. problem, not a Latin American one, and had to be dealt with by the United States, the immense economic advantages to Latin American farmers in growing drug-producing plants, the similar advantages to Latin American GNP and government revenues, the low-level technology of drug production, which made it almost impossible to detect and eradicate, the involvement of many government and military officials in drug trafficking, the good relations that the U.S. State Department wished to maintain with these countries as contrasted with the "arrest-them-all" attitude of the

Drug Enforcement Agency, and so on. In short, the administration learned by experience what it should have known from the beginning: that the antidrug campaign was at least as problematic on the international side as it was on the domestic side.[24]

President Bush introduced a more complex strategy. He determined to focus on *both* the domestic and the international arenas. At the same time, the Bush administration introduced some new strategies that had not received much attention before: the trail of money that goes with the drug business and therefore the effort to clamp down on banks, couriers, and so on involved in drug money laundering operations; the use of American military high-tech surveillance techniques, which are in fact very good at tracking drug suppliers; a more sophisticated education campaign that showed the devastating medical and physical effects of drug use (under Reagan, drugs had still been seen largely as a lifestyle issue); and somewhat greater coordination among the forty-three agencies involved in combatting drugs. The Bush program was undoubtedly more effective than earlier efforts.[25] However, despite the strenuous interception activities, the price and availability of drugs on the street were largely unaffected.

Meanwhile, political considerations (as we have seen, never far from the forefront in any of the policy considerations) reentered in new ways the calculus concerning drugs. Those advertisements on television portraying your brain frying like an egg under the impact of drugs, as well as the testimonials of prominent sports figures against drug use, undoubtedly had a strong effect. Drug imports in general only went down slightly if at all, but among white, suburban youth and young people usage was dramatically down. Drugs were no longer viewed by these potential users as a lifestyle issue as they had been earlier but as causing serious, long-term medical debilities. That meant that drugs were becoming less of a problem to society as a whole and were, instead, concentrated in the inner city among ghetto youth. That is still a problem, but, viewed cynically, since these are people who seldom vote, it is less of a problem because it is no longer such a strong political issue for the administration. The drug problem can still command some resources because it is viewed in part as a national social problem and because the violence associated with it also spills over sometimes into white, affluent neighborhoods. But by the political calculus by which Washington deals with such issues, drugs are now viewed as a declining issue—maybe even a problem that has been "solved." It has not been really solved, we know, just as Central America or the debt issue have not been "solved," but it has been *politically* solved, and therefore political Washington need not pay it as much attention as in the past.

The Enterprise for the Americas Initiative and the North American Free Trade Agreement

President Bush's Enterprise for the Americas Initiative (EAI, not to be confused with a famous think tank that has the same letters but in a different order) grew out of the meetings held at the Hemispheric Summit in San José, Costa Rica, in October 1989; and out of the Andean Drug Summit in Cartagena, Colombia, in February 1990. At these meetings the Latin American presidents told Bush that while they welcomed resolution of the several Central American problems, they also needed a long-term program for the region as a whole. Specifically, they said that more than traditional aid they wanted the opportunity to sell their products in the U.S. market. Hence, on the way back from Cartagena, Bush instructed treasury secretary Nicholas Brady to review U.S. economic policy toward Latin America and come up with some new initiatives.

As announced four months later, in June 1990, the EAI rests on three main pillars.[26] The first is *trade:* to expand trade between the United States and Latin America through the Uruguay round of the General Agreement on Trade and Tariffs (GATT) and by entering into free trade agreements with individual countries or regional blocks to create a hemispherewide free trade zone. Mexico under the North American Free Trade Agreement (NAFTA) would be the first country with whom the United States would try to reach such a trade agreement. The second pillar was *investment:* to promote investment in the region and help the Latin American countries compete for capital through reform efforts (privatization, lowering of tariff barriers, streamlining of inefficient practices) that would encourage new investment, both foreign and domestic. The third pillar was *debt relief:* to build on the earlier Baker and Brady Plans to ease the debt burden of the Latin American countries and to increase the incentives for further reform by promising additional debt relief. For example, debt relief could be tied to environmental programs: Latin

American policies to protect the environment could result in further debt forgiveness.

The EAI was at first expressed in terms of high-flown rhetoric rather than specific programs. The result was some confusion in both Latin America and Washington as to what the initiative meant. Latin American leaders expressed vague and general support for the program while also waiting for the details. In the United States, congressional staffers as well as executive agency bureaucrats searched for ways to fill in the specifics of Bush's lofty proposal.[27]

In September 1990, Bush sought to fill the blanks in the program with a specific legislative program. On debt, the first pillar, he proposed reductions in the amount owed to the U.S. government (approximately 3 percent of the total Latin American debt), eligibility being determined by the secretary of the treasury and an interagency committee whose approval would be contingent on satisfactory agreements being negotiated between the country in question and the International Monetary Fund (IMF), the World Bank, and the private commercial banks. To bolster investment, the president sought $100 million per year for five years to establish a multilateral fund at the Inter-American Development Bank (IDB); the fund would be supplemented through donations from Japan (also $100 million per year for five years) and Western Europe. The trade pillar of the EAI would be based on continued U.S. commitment to GATT, supplemented by separate trade agreements reached with individual countries or regional blocks. Reflecting that country's importance to the United States as well as newfound fears for its stability, Mexico was chosen to be the first country with which to negotiate such a trade treaty; other countries could sign "framework agreements" that could later be converted into full trade agreements.

These proposals were warmly praised in Latin America as the most forward-looking and progressive U.S. initiative since John F. Kennedy's Alliance for Progress. However, they were only weakly implemented. The problems included the U.S. budgetary crisis, election year politics in 1992, the absence of a Cold War threat in Latin America, which made the area seem a less immediate strategic interest, the drug problem, which gave Latin America a bad reputation, and election-year fears of the economic and employment ramifications of the proposals in the United States.[28] As a result, Congress has been very slow to act and as of 1992 has only approved a reduction in concessional debts under Public Law 480 (food aid) as well as fast-track negotiating authority for the NAFTA with Mexico.[29] Additional attempts to move these cumbersome processes along by increasing funding or extending the provisions for another fiscal year were stalled because of executive-legislative struggles over a new, greatly reduced foreign aid bill.

With the languishing of the legislative proposals, most of the movement under the EAI came from the executive branch and the Latin American countries. By the end of 1991 twenty-nine countries (all but Cuba, Haiti, and Surinam) had signed framework agreements with the United States either individually or as members of blocs such as CARICOM or MERCOSUR. New integration efforts were under way either to revive existing but largely moribund trading blocks or to create new ones. But debt reduction agreements had been signed with only three countries, Chile, Bolivia, and Jamaica, each of which contained a provision for environmental protection. The EAI had also sought to accelerate market-based reforms by encouraging free trade, enhancing growth, streamlining bloated bureaucracies, and privatization. Some progress had occurred in all these areas, and Latin American growth in 1991 was 2.4 percent—not fantastic but solid, particularly after a decade of economic decline. Investment, both foreign and domestic, also increased in 1991, resulting in about $10 billion in new capital; U.S. exports to Latin America also increased in 1990 and 1991. However, these indicators of progress were often stymied because of the executive-legislative deadlock in the U.S. government and because the economic reform efforts in Latin America, while welcome and certainly impressive in some countries, were often seen as a shell game or a smokescreen: the public firing of excessive public employees and their quiet rehiring shortly thereafter, the "selling" of one state-owned company to another state-run agency, the cleaning up of one patronage or sinecure network while others are created to replace them.[30]

Part of the reason for the EAI's (as well as other programs') languishing is that there were too few people at high enough levels in the Bush administration to push for Latin American programs. Latin America's importance to Washington policy makers is not self-evident, and there are competing programs and areas that also demand attention at high levels. Hence the importance of having strong advocates at high levels: a Nelson Rockefeller or a Jeane Kirkpatrick, for example. But under Bush the secretary of state was not much interested in Latin America and preferred to dispose of it, and his assistant secretary was selected for political reasons and did not have a strong background in the area; the Department of Defense had little interest in the region aside from the drug issue; and the NSC did not have members strong on Latin America. The Departments of Commerce and Treasury were principally responsible for the EAI, but their Latin Americanists were at very low levels and had limited experience in the area. One of the problems for Latin America programs in Washington under Bush was that there was no one at the secretary, deputy secretary, or undersecretary rank who was a champion of the region. Vice President J. Danforth Quayle had traveled to Latin America several times (the only place where Secretary Baker let him go, since presumably he could do little harm there), and his staff was considering picking up the Latin America portfolio; but when Chief of Staff John Sununu left the White House, conservatives came to rely more on Quayle for access to the administration on other issues, which meant that the vice president had a full plate and could not also take on Latin America. Only Bush had an interest in the area, and of course that was often fickle and, given the press of other issues, hard to sustain.

The EAI is a far-reaching proposal—at least on paper. In the aftermath of the Cold War and the absence of any alternative models, Bush was able to take advantage of a unique and rare opportunity when the United States and Latin America were actually in considerable agreement on political and economic goals. His vision was of a stable, democratic, free market, free trade area from Alaska to Tierra del Fuego. But the framework agreements remained still only vague promises, NAFTA was viewed with suspicion and hostility in many domestic quarters, debt reduction went very slowly, and the three IDB agreements were in countries that had undertaken drastic economic reforms *before* the EAI was proposed. There was in fact in many areas a tendency to credit the EAI with accomplishments in trade, economic recovery, debt lowering, and investment that had in fact occurred earlier. The EAI remained a useful vision with only modest implementation.

The El Salvador Accords

El Salvador has long been one of the most strife-torn and brutal countries in Latin America. It is riven by immense economic, social, and racial gaps; it is the second most overpopulated country in Latin

America; its class relations are tense and bitter; and until the 1980s it had virtually no democratic experience. Its brutal civil war from the late 1970s until recently was also intensively divisive in U.S. domestic politics. The United States devoted more attention to El Salvador and Nicaragua during the course of the 1980s than to any other countries in Latin America—often to the detriment of good relations with the larger and arguably more important nations. But now, with the signing of the historic peace accords between the government and the guerrillas, El Salvador may at last be poised to embark on a new course. Both sides—government and guerrillas—in the long conflict were exhausted by the war and ready to negotiate a settlement or to advance their ends and other needs.

The accords provide for the demobilization of the Faribundo Marti National Liberation Front (FMLN) and its reconstitution as a legitimate political force openly contending in a democratic political system. The government's concessions to reach this agreement were also significant—at least on paper. The armed forces are supposed to be reduced in size by half, from 60,000 to 29,000; the army gave up some control over the curriculum and admissions policy at the military academy; intelligence functions are supposed to be transferred to a civilian authority. A civilian review board has been established to weed out corrupt, violent, and inept officers; another panel made up of foreign dignitaries is supposed to probe the past human rights offenses of both guerrillas and soldiers; and the National Police, Treasury Police, and National Guard are scheduled to be disbanded and replaced by a new police force that will also include some former guerrillas.[31] The FMLN as well as the government were both to qualify for foreign financial assistance.

The peace process in El Salvador provides a fascinating glimpse of the "new" post–Cold War diplomacy. All the overblown rhetoric and verbal overkill by several parties aside, U.S. policy in El Salvador spanning at least three presidencies has had three basic purposes: to weaken and isolate the guerrillas; to pressure the Salvadoran Right and military into accepting some reforms; and to encourage a moderate, democratic political opening, process, and system. The costs were significant but, with patience, blandishments, and what we now call "coercive diplomacy"[32] (together with about $5 billion in assistance, one-fourth of it military, over the last decade), U.S. policy succeeded in achieving all three goals. Even the *Washington Post*, long a critic of the policy, was obliged to admit editorially that the

"United States did what it had to do to help a small, vulnerable friendly neighbor fend off a foreign-assisted revolutionary assault."[33] The accords may yet turn out to provide only the semblance of peace, but at least they gave El Salvador a chance at national reconstruction.

A second important factor was the role played by regional governments and, ultimately, the peace formula devised by President Oscar Arias of Costa Rica. Arias brought some moral authority to settling the conflict; his proposals also served as a framework and a political lever enabling all sides to move closer together. The Arias plan, worked out in several incarnations, involved pressuring the Sandinistas in Nicaragua to hold elections, end the civil war, and reintegrate the Contras into society while also terminating U.S. military pressure.[34] As applied to El Salvador, the Arias plan similarly involved ending the civil war, pressuring both the Salvadoran government and the guerrillas into peace negotiations, and reforming the military while also reintegrating the FMLN into society as a legitimate political party. The problems were to get the United States to accept the Arias intermediation and Central Americans to recognize legitimate U.S. security interests in the region. Essentially, both goals were achieved in the Reagan–Jim Wright accord of 1987, in Secretary Baker's "deal" with the congressional democrats in 1989, and finally in the peace accords brokered by the UN in 1991–92.

The disintegrating Soviet Union also put pressure on the FMLN in 1990–91 to settle the conflict and carry on the struggle through other, presumably democratic means. Without the Sandinistas in power in Nicaragua and with Cuba facing hard times, it would become more difficult for the FMLN to secure arms, find safe havens, and secure the backing it needed. The guerrilla movement would likely atrophy and decline. In the end, both the U.S.S.R. and the United States made it clear to their respective Salvadoran clients that they were tired of the conflict, tired of their costly involvement in this and other Third World struggles, unwilling to commit many additional funds to "black holes" (everything gets sucked in, nothing ever comes back in return) like El Salvador, and eager to see the conflict resolved.

Fourth, the UN, along with the so-called four friends (Colombia, Mexico, Spain, Venezuela; with Spain now in place of Panama, the group was very similar to that comprising Contadora), whose UN ambassadors prodded and cajoled the Salvadoran parties during the negotiations in New York, also played a constructive role in helping solve the crisis. The UN's role in El Salvador was in some ways comparable to its role in the Persian Gulf. By itself, in a world of sovereign nations, the UN cannot resolve very many problems, but as an instrument for ameliorating conflict, when the parties are agreed that is what they want, the UN can be very useful (unlike the UN involvement in Yugoslavia in early 1992, when one of the protagonists clearly did not want UN peacekeeping). In the Salvadoran case, the peace accords agreed to on New Year's Eve, 1991, were the last major accomplishment of outgoing Secretary General Javier Pérez de Cuellar and the capstone of his career. The United States had also been instrumental in cajoling the Salvadoran parties involved, working with the four friends and supporting Pérez de Cuellar. More than negotiating the settlement, the UN also sent police and observers to help monitor the cease-fire.

Immediately after the signing of the UN accord, euphoria and celebration reigned in El Salvador. Even the guerrillas, who had lived in clandestinity for a decade or longer, went out into the streets to celebrate. But El Salvador is a severely fractured country—like Lebanon —and the problems are immense, including severe demographic problems, a devastated economy that in 1992 began to show signs of recovery, pervasive violence not all of which is political, deep class divisions, and a weak democracy whose new institutions have not yet been consolidated. More immediately, it seems unlikely that the guerrillas will be integrated into a reformed Salvadoran armed forces, or that they will surrender all their weapons, or that the military will be fundamentally restructured—all of which are called for in the accords. Thanks to Secretary Baker's finessing of the area, El Salvador is out of the headlines, but its problems have been by no means solved. Nevertheless, there is considerable dynamism and energy in the Salvadoran economy and people that may help the country to recover.

The U.S. role in El Salvador, frequently controversial, was surprisingly steady, pragmatic, and consistent. In terms of the goals of U.S. policy, it may also have been successful: the guerrillas were denied power, a democratically elected government was put in place, and the extremist military and civilian elements were also successful. Congress ceased berating the president over El Salvador, the religious and human rights lobbies were pacified and moved on to other issues, Central America and its divisive political fallout went off the television screens, and President Bush was able to gain time and political space for dealing with bigger issues such as NATO, China, Japan, and the breakup of the Soviet Union. One can say that American constancy in Central America was crucial in the last decade both in helping to resolve major issues in that area and in moving the foreign policy agenda on to other, larger matters. In "solving" the Central American conflicts, however, it is to be hoped that the United States will not abandon the area and allow the nascent democratic institutions to disintegrate—although, as with Panama and Nicaragua, once the issue of the moment (the civil war in El Salvador) is settled, it becomes very difficult to sustain congressional and executive interest in continued support for the country.

Supporting Democracy: Haiti and Peru

Assistant Secretary Aronson was selected for his position by Secretary Baker for one reason only: because as a Democrat he was acceptable to the congressional Democrats and would hence be able to implement the deal that Baker had worked out with Congress on Central America to solve the problems of Nicaragua and El Salvador and go on to other issues. Aronson succeeded well in this task because his role required no knowledge of Latin America; rather, political acceptance by the Congress and the ability to negotiate were the traits and skills required. Subsequently, when issues arose that did require sophisticated knowledge of Latin America, Aronson proved to be far less effective. Such was the case with regard to the U.S. response to challenges to democracy in Latin America, especially in Haiti.

The administration made the fundamental mistake of conceiving of Haiti as a test case of U.S. support for democracy in Latin America. If the overthrow of Haitian democracy were allowed to stand, the argument was, then U.S. credibility and policy in support of democracy elsewhere in Latin America would be seriously compromised. A wave of antidemocratic movements might ensue, it was feared, that would propel U.S. policy back to the dead-ends of the 1970s, when, without a broad democratic center, the only choices appeared to be a Marxist-Leninist guerrilla triumph or a rapacious military regime.[35]

But in many respects Haiti is not a Latin American country, as almost all Latin Americans know, even if this is not recognized at the highest levels of the inter-American bureau at the State Department. Haiti is an economic basket case: its topsoil has been eroded over the centuries, it has almost no resources or democratic infrastructure (political parties, trade unions, peasant associations, pluralist interest groups, functioning governmental institutions), it has no democratic tradition. Geographically it is located *in* Latin America but it is not *of* Latin America in terms of its social, political, or cultural traditions or history. Haiti is a case all by itself and is not a test of democracy's survivability in Latin America—or at least that is what Latin Americans think, even if the State Department does not.

Latin America lamented the overthrow of Jean-Bertrand Aristide by a military junta, but to the Latin Americans that was politics as usual in Haiti. Haiti lacks the institutional foundation that most of the rest of Latin America has; and while everyone recognized the immensely popular support that Aristide had, no one in Latin America was entirely surprised when he was ousted. Haiti's case, they reasoned, was sad, but it had little relevance to the rest of Latin America. Hence, while the Latin American members of the OAS were willing to vote sanctions against Haiti's military regime, they did not want to see that become a cause célèbre nor did they see Haiti's unfortunate situation as affecting them in any meaningful way.

When Haitian democracy, only eight months old, was overthrown on 30 September 1991, the reaction was rapid. The OAS voted to impose sanctions and an economic embargo on Haiti.[36] But the embargo proved to be a very blunt instrument: it hurt the already long-suffering Haitian people but it had seemingly no effect on the military regime in power. In addition, the United States continued to insist, futilely, that Aristide be returned to full power as constitutional president, even in the face of the adamant opposition of the military and civilian elites in Haiti and of repeated revelations, which the State Department should have been more fully cognizant of earlier, of inappropriate actions by Aristide during his short presidency. These included inflammatory speeches, the creation of a presidential militia to offset the power of the army, death threats against his political foes, ineffective administration, provocative challenges to the Haitian military and the business class, and inappropriate provocations of the United States. Long before he was overthrown and despite his popular support, Aristide was widely thought of by people who know Haiti as a rabble-rousing but largely ineffective and possibly dangerous demagogue who might well trigger or himself initiate civil war.

It is important for the United States to support democracy but not necessarily Aristide in Haiti. At the same time, since Aristide received such a large mandate initially and was the constitutional president, it is probably important to maintain at least the semblance of constitutionalism. The question is, can a formula be found to accomplish this? Probably it can, even in several situations. For example, Aristide could be brought back as constitutional president for a short time to preserve face and constitutionality, but all would understand that he would go quickly into exile and a vice president would take over or new elections would soon be scheduled. Alternatively Aristide would return, but he and the army would agree to share power in a broadly based civil-military junta until new elections could be held. A third option would be for Aristide to return as a largely honorary or ceremonial president but for real executive power to be exercised by a prime minister. A fourth possibility is to let the Haitian political process proceed without Aristide until a semblance of democracy is restored and the former president can be permanently shunted aside and largely forgotten. All these proposals preserve democratic continuity and constitutionalism to some degree while also recognizing that someone besides Aristide ought to run the country. These proposals have the added advantages of solving the U.S. domestic conflict over Haiti policy, which has taken on racial overtones, and of solving the problem of the Haitian boat people, since, with a constitutional government in place in Haiti, there could be no legitimate reason under U.S. law for the continued emigration of Haitians for political reasons.

Whereas U.S. policy toward Haiti had often been naive, ill-informed, and misdirected, U.S. policy toward Peru has been far more nuanced and sophisticated. In this case the key actors were persons at the State Department and the OAS who actually know Peru, as distinct from the situation in the Haitian case. In Peru, elected president Alberto Fujimori staged an internal or self-coup on 5 April 1992 in which he sent the Congress packing, restricted press freedom, and suspended the constitution. This is quite different from the Haitian situation: first, the elected government is still in power; second, Peru is much more important to the United States than Haiti because of Peru's drug policy coupled with the challenge of a strong left-wing movement in the form of Sendero Luminoso; and third, because the armed forces are not actually in power. In addition, unlike Haiti, Peru is very much a Latin American country and what happens there does have an impact elsewhere; for example, in Venezuela, where constitutionalism is also threatened and where the Peruvian case, as well as the reaction of the international community to it, are being scrutinized very carefully. A further difference is that Peru's problems have had fewer domestic reverberations in the United States.

In Peru, in response to Fujimori's actions, foreign assistance was suspended by Bush (and continued into the Clinton administration), but there have been no sanctions nor has an embargo been imposed. Moreover, there is considerable evidence that Fujimori miscalculated the international community's reaction to his actions, now understands the error of his ways, and is ready to make some amends. So the policy issue here for the United States is how to allow Fujimori to back away from his earlier actions without losing credibility (in Peru, his action of proroguing the Congress was supported by 80 percent of public opinion), restore the constitution, and at the same time continue to pursue the U.S.-favored counter-narcotics and counter-guerrilla campaign. The policy put in place of gently pressuring Fujimori to accomplish these aims through the use of both carrots (restored aid) and sticks (coercive diplomacy) seems to be far more sophisticated than the trap the United States fell into over Haiti policy.

Conclusion

The Bush administration has some major accomplishments to its credit in terms of Latin America policy, not all of which can be fully analyzed here. These include the strengthening of the OAS and the increased use of this regional multilateral agency, the Enterprise for the Americas Initiative, the resolution of the contentious Nicaragua and El Salvador problems (solved politically for the United States but not of course solved in terms of underlying social and economic problems), the free trade agreement with Mexico, and the ouster of Noriega (although at major human and economic costs). Certainly as compared with other presidencies, it is a quite impressive list of accomplishments.

At least as impressive as these concrete policies is the change in the hemispheric mood. The entire political culture of U.S.–Latin

American relations has been altered. In part this is due to U.S. policy such as the emphasis begun under Carter and continued under Reagan and Bush on human rights and democracy, but in large part it is due to the absence of any other alternative. The Soviet Union and Eastern Europe have collapsed, Cuba is no longer a model to emulate, and the Marxist-Leninist guerrilla movements (with the exception of the Sendero Luminoso) are atrophying and drying up. Authoritarianism and corporatism are no longer acceptable. A nearly continentwide consensus on the value of democracy, human rights, and open markets has emerged that makes relations far more amicable than in the past. Bush's EAI helped cement a relationship that has provided a mechanism for helping to resolve the lingering debt problem, aiding the hemisphere economically, and especially helping Latin American goods find access to U.S. markets. These intangible changes in perception regarding how the two parts of the Americas view each other are every bit as important as the more concrete manifestations of policy and have led many observers to comment that relations between the United States and Latin America are better than at any time since the Alliance for Progress.[37]

Numerous problems, nevertheless, remain. First, while the Bush administration's rhetoric was often noble, implementation lagged behind in terms of real funding, particularly in countries like Panama, Nicaragua, and El Salvador, where the United States owes a certain debt but has provided no real follow-through. Second, issues were too often dealt with politically and bureaucratically for the sake of solving a U.S. *domestic* problem rather than with much thought of Latin America in mind. Third, the infrastructure, located at subcabinet levels, was not in place to carry out a serious program to assist Latin America; there were too many weak staff appointments. Fourth, other areas (the former Soviet Union and Eastern Europe) kept getting priority over Latin America even when the logic for continuing to focus so heavily on these other areas seemed rather thin. And fifth, there simply is no money for very many Latin America programs, as domestic considerations, a weak U.S. economy, and election-year politics ruled out the possibilities for the Congress or the president to do more for the area. The result, once again, was benign neglect with regard to Latin America.

We all know that what Latin America needs is a multipronged program that will truly assist the area. Furthermore, there is growing evidence that even with all the congressional indifference and the

public's hostility toward Latin America, the area's growing importance to the United States, particularly economically, is being recognized. As other areas (Europe, East Asia) form their own trading
blocs and put barriers in the way of U.S. commerce, Latin America
begins to look better and better,[38] an idea recognized in Bush's EAI
and in the notion of a hemispherewide free trade zone. It is likely
that the realities of these new economic requirements and market
forces will do more to cement better U.S.–Latin American relations
than the rhetorical flourishes of any recent American president.

Notes

The views expressed in this chapter are the author's own and not necessarily
those of the Department of Defense or the National Defense University.

1. The best, most balanced study is by Lou Cannon, *President Reagan*
(New York: Knopf, 1990); my own impressions of Reagan from serving as an
occasional adviser may be found in Howard J. Wiarda, *American Foreign Policy towards Latin America in the 80s and 90s: Issues and Controversies
from Reagan to Bush* (New York: New York University Press, 1992).

2. On Bush's "vision problem," see James David Barber, "George Bush: In
Search of a Mission," *New York Times*, 19 January 1989, p. A31. The *Washing-
ton Post* has run numerous articles on this theme, and the Democratic Study
Group has a computerized listing of all references to it.

3. The position papers drafted, agendas, lists of participants in these
panels, summarizes of discussions, etc. are drawn from my own files as a participant in the process. For elaboration on these differences as well as on the
context, see Howard J. Wiarda, *Foreign Policy without Illusion: How Foreign
Policy Works and Fails to Work in the United States* (New York: Scott, Fores-
man/Little, Brown, 1990).

4. *Time*, 1 August 1988, p. 22.

5. *The Report of the President's National Bipartisan Commission on
Central America* (New York: Macmillan, 1984).

6. Based on personal interviews with Dukakis campaign officials.

7. The documents here and in the preceding paragraph are based on my interviews with many of the participants in these events and on my participation in the campaign; see also Howard J. Wiarda, "United States Policy in
Latin America," *Current History* 89 (January 1990): 1–4, 31.

8. For an analysis of these negotiations, see Georges A. Fauriol, "The
Shadow of Latin American Affairs: America and the World 1989–90," *Foreign
Affairs* (January 1990): 116–34.

9. The issue can be followed in the *Washington Post*, November 1988–
April 1989. The text of the bipartisan accord and the Central American peace

plan can be found in U.S. Department of State, Bureau of Public Affairs, "U.S. Support for Democracy and Peace in Central America," Selected Documents No. 36, March 1989.

10. *New York Times*, 24 August 1989, p. B10.

11. Ibid., p. A25.

12. Wiarda, *American Foreign Policy*, chap. 7; and W. Raymond Duncan, "Superpower Cooperation in the Caribbean and Central America," in Roger E. Kanet and Edward A. Kolodziej, eds., *The Cold War as Cooperation* (London: Macmillan, 1991, pp. 224–51.

13. *New York Times*, 18 February 1990, p. A14.

14. For the background, see Kevin Buckley, *Panama: The Whole Story* (New York: Simon and Schuster, 1991).

15. Daniel Pipes and Adam Garfinkle, eds., *Friendly Tyrants* (New York: St. Martin's Press, 1991).

16. Ambler Moss, *New York Times*, 21 May 1989, sec. 4, p. 2.

17. See the account in Bob Woodward, *The Commanders* (New York: Simon and Schuster, 1991).

18. Based on interviews with U.S. government officials.

19. *Washington Post*, 18 January 1990, p. A9.

20. The UN vote was on 20 December 1989 and was amply reported; see also U.S. Department of State, Bureau of Public Affairs, "Panama: A Just Cause," Current Policy No. 1240.

21. See the comments of Senator Patrick Leahy (D-VT) in the *Washington Post*, 23 March 1990.

22. John E. Reilly, ed., *American Public Opinion and U.S. Foreign Policy: 1991* (Chicago: Chicago Council on Foreign Relations, 1991).

23. Based on author interviews and participant observation in some areas of this decision-making process.

24. Howard J. Wiarda, ed., *On the Agenda: Current Issues and Conflicts in U.S. Foreign Policy* (New York: Scott, Foresman/Little, Brown, 1990), chap. 10.

25. U.S. Department of State, Bureau of International Narcotics Matters, *International Narcotics Control Strategy Report* (Washington DC: Department of State Publication 9948-B, March 1992).

26. See *Enterprise for the Americas Initiative: A Vision for Economic Growth in the Western Hemisphere* (Washington DC: White House, February 1992).

27. An excellent analysis is Donald B. Harrington, "Enterprise for the Americas Initiative (EAS)." Paper presented at the National Defense University, 1992.

28. Howard J. Wiarda, "The United States and Latin America: Toward the 1990s," *Five College International Forum* 2 (fall 1988): 24–31.

29. M. Delal Baer and Sidney Weintraub, eds., *North American Free Trade* (Washington DC: Center for Strategic and International Studies, 1992).

30. A balanced but more optimistic view is Peter Hakim, "President Bush's Southern Strategy: The Enterprise for the Americas Initiative," *Washington Quarterly* (spring 1992): 93–106.

31. An early assessment is Howard J. Wiarda, "El Salvador: Can the Wounds Be Healed?" *World and I* 7 (April 1992): 86–91.

32. Gordon Craig and Alexander George, *Force and Statecraft* (New York: Oxford University Press, 1990), chap. 14.

33. *Washington Post*, 19 January 1992, editorial page.

34. Mary K. Meyer, "Latin American Diplomacy and the Central American Peace Process: The Contadora and Esquipulas II Cases" (Ph.D. diss. University of Massachusetts/Amherst, 1992).

35. For a general discussion of the policy stakes involved, see Howard J. Wiarda, *The Democratic Revolution in Latin America* (New York: Holmes and Meier, 1990).

36. *Washington Post*, 9 October 1991, p. 1.

37. For example, Peter Hakim, "The United States and Latin America: Good Neighbors Again?" *Current History* 91 (February 1992): 49–53.

38. See my article, "Seeing Latin America in a New Light," *North/South* 2 (April–May 1993): 8–9.

Michael J. Kryzanek

The Grenada Invasion:
Approaches to Understanding

The invasion of the tiny eastern Caribbean island of Grenada by nineteen hundred U.S. Marines and Army Rangers on 23 October 1983 took the American public and indeed the American political system by surprise. Not since 1965 in the Dominican Republic had the United States used military force to advance its foreign policy objectives. The intervention in Grenada was thus an important step for this country and for the administration of President Ronald Reagan.

The Grenada invasion initiated the expected wave of analysis, criticism, and second-guessing.[1] In the post-Vietnam political environment where restraint, if not paralysis, had been the operating guidepost, the decision to employ intervention as a means of solving a problem in the region was a significant departure from policies of previous administrations, in which negotiation and accommodation had been emphasized. One invasion does not produce a trend, but in the context of the U.S. response to crises in the past, the Grenada invasion took on a meaning beyond the decision to intervene in the affairs of a neighboring nation-state.

Looking back over the official pronouncements, the newspaper accounts, and the expert assessments of the Grenada operation one is struck by the importance attached to the intervention. The Reagan administration declared the invasion a "success" and our objectives of protecting American citizens and restoring order to a chaotic internal political situation accomplished. Official accounts of the Grenada invasion were marked by a renewed sense of confidence, pride, and euphoria as policy makers and the American people alike expressed relief that the United States had achieved a victory. President Reagan told the country after U.S. forces secured the island that "our days of weakness are over. Our military forces are back on their feet and standing tall."[2] Reagan's pleasure in the outcome of the invasion was reinforced by public opinion surveys that showed support for the decision increasing from 53 percent shortly after the intervention to 71 percent at the conclusion of the first week of the operation.[3] Even the Grenadan people seemed to be swept up with emotion over the U.S. invasion as residents of the island painted messages on walls declaring "God Bless Ronald Reagan."

However, an examination of many journalistic and scholarly analyses of the invasion paints a much different picture. Charges were made that the Reagan administration rushed into war with little interest in diplomacy, overstated the danger to American medical students on the island, fashioned a highly questionable regional alliance with eastern Caribbean ministates, and then nearly bungled the invasion despite the use of overwhelming force.[4] Representative Edward Markey from Massachusetts, one of the more outspoken opponents of the invasion, asked the question, "where does all this military intervention end? Are the Marines going to become our new Foreign Service officers?"[5] Although Markey's comments and those of other liberal Democrats in the Congress were overshadowed by strong bipartisan support for the invasion, the debate over the intervention continued long after the operation was completed.

The contradictions in how the Grenada invasion was viewed raise the question of how to properly assess this intervention and place it in the context of our long-standing penchant for influencing events in the circum-Caribbean region. The vast amount of information, opinion, and evaluation surrounding the invasion requires that this military operation and its diplomatic antecedents be studied in a more systematic manner in order to better organize the vast amount of official justification and critical analysis. The best method is to discuss the invasion through a series of analytic approaches that provide the means to understand the objectives of the operation, assess the performance of the key players and institutions, and comment on the implications, both foreign and domestic, of the intervention. When a president defines a political and military action as a success, it is essential to determine how the administration arrived at that position. When critics of the invasion describe the invasion as "illegal," "unnecessary," and a modern-day version of "gunboat diplomacy," it is important to delve further into the reasons why the intervention fostered such controversy. And when analysts describe the invasion as an important step in redirecting U.S. foreign policy, it is necessary to explore the implications of this extraordinary use of American power.

Sorting out the pros and cons of the Grenada invasion and assigning meaning to this intervention is an important part of reaching conclusions about the appropriateness of the U.S. action. In many respects this discussion will contribute to what has commonly been termed by analysts of political systems as the feedback process of policy making. By viewing the complex of decisions and events that made up the Grenada invasion, the intervention becomes more than a litany of political, diplomatic, and military maneuvers. The Grenada invasion instead becomes an operation that can be assessed from a number of different angles to determine not only why we acted but also how we performed the action and what impact that action had on our political system and on our region.

The Cost-Benefit Approach

The Grenada invasion, or, as it was termed by military planners, Operation Urgent Fury, has been viewed as falling within the general category of a Caribbean-style intervention. All the elements were present for the United States to follow an oft-used script for invading a neighboring nation: American citizens apparently in some danger, internal political unrest after the assassination of Prime Minister Maurice Bishop, an unpopular governing regime with ties to our adversaries, shipments of arms entering the country from Eastern Europe, and the construction of an airport by Cuban engineers that raised the suspicions of the Pentagon. Each one of these developments in Grenada linked up with established national security and national interest objectives that in the past had pushed the United States to either take military action or implement some form of destabilizing operation.

But Grenada not only fit into the traditional mold of a Caribbean hot spot that required U.S. intervention, it also offered the Reagan administration the prospect of a diplomatic and military success. Grenada fulfilled President Reagan's expectations perfectly as the U.S. military and its Caribbean allies defeated a surprisingly stubborn Cuban and Grenadan opposition in three days, sustained nineteen deaths and eighty-seven casualties, and remained for a few weeks as the country returned to normal under a government supportive of the United States. The Reagan administration fashioned one of its more effective public relations campaigns to tout the heroism of the armed forces. The Pentagon awarded 8,633 service medals to the 7,000 participants in Operation Urgent Fury and used every media opportunity to emphasize the importance of this victory in its challenge to Communist expansionism in the hemisphere.[6]

The link between invasion and success is not unique to Grenada. Pronouncing a U.S. military action initiated to achieve U.S. foreign policy objectives a success has become part of the lexicon of presidents eager to justify intervention. President Lyndon Johnson and his foreign policy team boasted in 1965 that they had successfully staved off a leftist revolution in the Dominican Republic and in the process showed the Communist world that the United States would not tolerate a second Cuba in the hemisphere.[7] Ronald Reagan faced what he felt was an even greater threat to the hemisphere as the prospect of a third base of Marxist revolution loomed large in Grenada, laying the groundwork for what one journalist described as a "Coconut Curtain." For Reagan it was essential to make the stand against expansionism and to do it in a convincing manner for all the world, in particular the Communist world, to see.[8]

The Grenada invasion was declared a success by the Reagan administration largely because interventions are often evaluated from a cost-benefit perspective. In the minds of presidents such as Johnson and Reagan, the standards for evaluating a military intervention are rarely connected to issues related to international law, world opinion, and long-term political or economic development. Rather, evaluating intervention becomes associated with factors such as the unity and decisiveness of the policy makers, the speed of the victory, the loss of life, and the time necessary to place the invaded nation on the correct track, or what has come to be called normalcy. The attainment of short-term goals and the smooth operation of the invasion process become the key criteria for judging success. Quite simply, the prevailing logic is that if we can get into a country, achieve our goals, and get out quickly with little or no loss of life, then the intervention can be placed in the category of "success."

Under these circumstances it is well-near impossible to describe the Grenada invasion as anything but a success. The Reagan administration had computed the cost-benefit relationship quite accurately: the invasion removed the Marxists, returned the island to a pro-U.S. stance, and instilled a general spirit of pride among the American people. As Eldon Kenworthy states,

Grenada . . . had all the makings of an ideal setting for a successful yet inexpensive display of American military prowess. The Cuban-Soviet presence on the island did not entail a commitment to defend Grenada. After Bishop was assassinated the Grenadian regime was as unpopular with its own people as it was with its Cuban allies. These factors, along with the island's size—there would be one U.S. soldier for every 18 Grenadians—promised a U.S. military operation that could be a fait accompli before critics at home and abroad even had time to react.[9]

It is important to stress, however, that although invasions like that in Grenada are discussed and evaluated in terms of costs and benefits, they are often officially connected to noble or humane causes. In Grenada the focus of the Reagan administration's justification for the invasion was the presence of over a thousand American citizens, particularly a large contingent of medical students at the St. George's Medical School. On 27 October President Reagan stated that his "overriding" and "paramount" concern was "to protect innocent lives."[10]

As events unfolded and the record of the invasion became public it appeared that the medical students were in no real danger from the internal turmoil in Grenada. In fact, when U.S. forces came to rescue the students they went to the wrong campus center and needed nearly two days to find the Americans, time enough for the Grenadan rebels to use them as hostages or worse.[11] Nevertheless, when the students were filmed kissing the ground upon arrival home from Grenada, the Reagan administration had garnered its greatest benefit from the invasion. As one Democratic congressman from California stated, "We have heard the terms 'warmonger' and 'gunboat diplomacy' used. Well last night we saw the results of that action. Students were getting off the plane. They were kissing the ground. They were saying 'God Bless America.' They were thanking the President for sending in the marines and the rangers."[12]

If the rescue of the medical students was used to bolster support for the invasion by appealing to a noble cause, the description of the airport the Grenadans were building with Cuban engineers and construction workers raised questions about the motivations behind the decision to intervene. The construction of a 9,800-foot airfield at Point Salines was officially described as a crucial step in enhancing

Grenada's tourist industry. International agencies along with financial assistance from fifteen non-Communist countries provided the support for the project. Canada also was committed to building a $16 million tourist hotel nearby so that Grenada could compete more effectively with island tourist centers.[13]

But for the Reagan administration the Point Salines airport was a major threat to national security and another opportunity to lay the groundwork for future action against the governing regime of the New Jewel Movement in Grenada. In a nationwide address on 23 March 1983 Reagan stated, "On the small island of Grenada . . . the Cubans with Soviet financing and backing, are in the process of building an airfield with a 10,000 foot runway. Grenada doesn't even have an air force, who is it intended for? The Caribbean is a very important passageway for our international commerce and military lines of communication. . . . The rapid buildup of Grenada's military potential is unrelated to any conceivable threat to this island country."[14]

President Reagan continued this linkage between the airport and national security throughout the crisis despite the fact that there were no signs the Grenadans were seeking to militarize the project or that the Cubans and Soviets intended to use the airport as another strategic base of operations for the Caribbean. In fact, documents captured after the operation point clearly to the government of Grenada holding to the view that the airport would only be used to attract tourists. Yet President Reagan constantly stressed the military value of the airport as he termed Grenada "a Soviet-Cuban colony being readied as a major military bastion to export terror and undermine democracy."[15] Thus when the invasion was completed President Reagan praised the operation as ridding the hemisphere of a potentially dangerous base of Communist influence. The irony of defining the airport as a military project and then using it as one of the justifications for the invasion is that in April 1984, some six months after the invasion, the Reagan administration provided $40 million in aid to Grenada of which $19 million was to finish the Point Salines airport. In February 1986 President Reagan dedicated a plaque at the newly completed airport. What started out as a strategic threat was transformed into a regional asset, a clear benefit of the invasion.

Viewing an intervention in terms of cost benefit can strip the operation of all the less-appealing facets of using force to achieve a foreign policy goal. An invasion becomes a kind of sterile bureaucratic decision rather than an action where people are killed or wounded and the invaded nation and its political system is torn asunder. Yet by analyzing the Grenada invasion from a cost-benefit perspective it is possible to more clearly examine the decision-making arena in which officials operate. Faced with a crisis that is perceived to threaten national security and national interests, policy makers rely on costs and benefits to fashion a response. Those outside the decision-making chain of command often prefer that other approaches and values be used, or more important that decision makers refrain from relying on questionable motivations for their actions. But in most instances crisis response is grounded in the belief that the only practical approach is to define the costs and gauge the benefits and if necessary wrap the costs and benefits in an attractive package of public justifications.

The Efficient Crisis Management Approach

Cost-benefit analysis of the U.S. intervention in Grenada is not the only approach that can be used to shed light on this important foreign policy and military exercise. Another approach that was employed primarily by the critics of the invasion was efficient crisis management or, in more simple terms, evaluating what worked and what did not work as the United States moved through the process of decision making and policy implementation. Much of efficient crisis management analysis was reserved for the diplomatic and military phases of the intervention. From the perspective of those critics of the invasion it was because of diplomatic insensitivity that the crisis escalated, and it was because of military unpreparedness that the invasion was a logistical failure.[16]

One of the turning points in the preinvasion period that widened the gap between Grenadan leaders and Washington was the meeting between Prime Minister Maurice Bishop and U.S. Ambassador to the Eastern Caribbean Frank Ortiz. Ambassador Ortiz in a 10 April 1983 meeting assured Bishop that deposed Grenadan prime minister Eric Gairy would not be permitted to mount a counterrevolution from the United States. Ortiz then read a statement warning Bishop not to seek assistance from Cuba. The statement by Ortiz hit a sensitive nerve with Bishop and his associates, who felt that the United States was dictating the foreign relations of a sovereign nation.

While Ortiz felt that he was presenting the position of the United States to a group of Marxist revolutionaries who had made up their minds in advance, Bishop and his eventual successor, Bernard Coard, described Ortiz as an "arrogant racist" who "did everything possible to arouse a black man."[17]

From this failed encounter with the U.S. ambassador the Grenadan leadership was determined to present themselves as standing firm against the dictates of the United States and openly supportive of their Cuban allies. As Robert Pastor remarks on the impression left on Bishop and Coard and in Washington policy centers by the U.S. ambassador's visit, "Ortiz's demarche . . . served to reinforce their image of the United States as an imperialist monster, bent on destroying their young revolution. And their response, in turn, confirmed the impression in Washington that these young Marxists wanted to provoke the United States to justify their militarization and alliance with Cuba."[18]

The decision to lecture Bishop coupled with a general lack of interest in addressing the concerns of the Grenadan leadership at the highest policy-making levels throughout the crisis period quickly widened the gulf between the two governments and made the prospects for confrontation inevitable. The rhetoric on both sides reached a fever pitch as President Reagan and Prime Minister Bishop traded verbal salvos about Communist expansionism and American imperialism. It is important to stress, however, that the diplomatic problems between Washington and the Bishop government may have been unavoidable. The New Jewel Movement in Grenada was becoming increasingly radicalized and aggressively seeking to heighten the tensions between the two countries. But as the tensions mounted and the rhetoric on both sides continued, the diplomatic option diminished in importance. The Grenadans decided they were going to place their confidence in the Cubans, while Washington was looking for ways to remove a government that was posing a new threat to U.S. security interests in the region.

If the diplomatic interchange between Washington and the New Jewel Movement in Grenada broke down irreparably, the development of a more prominent relationship with the ministates of the eastern Caribbean was certainly one of the critical ingredients in gaining domestic support for the invasion. From virtual anonymity the Organization of Eastern Caribbean States (OECS) vaulted to the forefront of the Grenadan crisis. The arrest and eventual murder of

Prime Minister Bishop prompted the leaders of neighboring island nations to inform the Reagan administration that they feared the unrest and radicalism in Grenada would spill over into their countries. Prime Ministers Tom Adams of Barbados, Eugenia Charles of Dominica, and John Compton of Saint Lucia led the movement at an October meeting of the OECS to establish a peacekeeping force and seek help from friendly countries, that is, the United States.[19]

The Reagan administration did not immediately respond to the pleas from the OECS, but the murder of Maurice Bishop and the increased unrest in Grenada spurred the United States to pursue the intervention option under the auspices of the OECS. The invasion that followed was a multilateral venture as troops from Jamaica, Barbados, Antigua, Dominica, Saint Kitts-Nevis, Saint Lucia, and Saint Vincent and the Grenadines joined U.S. forces in invading Grenada. The United States immediately categorized the invasion as a response to the "urgent request" of the OECS and in accordance with security clauses in the UN Charter and relevant articles of the OAS Charter.[20]

The Reagan administration's defense of its actions using the OECS treaty and UN and OAS security articles created the grounds for criticism by opponents of the invasion. Article 8 of the 1981 treaty forming the OECS stated that collective action could only be taken by unanimous decision of all seven member states. Only four of the member states voted to request intervention. More important, the United States was not a party to the OECS treaty nor was the treaty registered with the UN. Finally, the intervention of the United States violated Articles 15 and 17 of the Rio Pact, which prohibits intervention in member states affairs.[21]

But if the legal standing of the United States and the OECS in the intervention is questionable, the ability of the Reagan administration to present the invasion as a multilateral action taken at the request of neighboring states was instrumental in justifying the decision to intervene. Officials in Washington recognized the importance of collective military action as a way of defusing congressional opposition and justifying what could easily stimulate a new round of anti-Americanism in the region. There are those who still hold to the view that the request of the OECS was orchestrated by the Reagan administration and the legal basis for the invasion was fabricated.[22] These views, however, were quickly dismissed as the debate over Grenada shifted away from the issues of international law and treaty prohibitions.

Perhaps the most vivid example of examining the Grenada invasion in terms of what worked and what did not is with respect to the performance of the U.S. military. Much has been written about the inadequacies of the invading forces from outdated maps to communication snafus to interservice rivalries. As Richard Gabriel states: "The Grenada operation was carried out with a large number of blunders. Had the operation met a slightly larger force that was more determined to fight and slightly better armed, the United States would have had much greater difficulty subduing the defenders."[23]

The logistical and institutional inadequacies of U.S. invading forces led to a series of mistakes, some near-comical, others tragic. There were reports of ground forces using AT&T long-distance credit cards to call in air strikes. Nearly two-thirds of the reported 19 American deaths were caused by so-called friendly fire. Although U.S. casualties were low due in large part to the shortness of the skirmishes with the Cuban and Grenadan forces, civilian casualties were placed at 45 killed and 358 wounded. Reports of indiscriminate shootings and misdirected helicopter gunship missions were common during the invasion.[24]

What was most bothersome to Pentagon officials, however, were the intelligence failures. Advance intelligence reporting stated that there were "an estimated 50–60 Cubans present in Grenada" when in fact there were nearly 800.[25] The failure to acquire adequate intelligence was attributed to the speed with which Operation Urgent Fury was developed and executed. Nevertheless, the inability of the invading forces to benefit from accurate data on the enemy and on the terrain led to numerous delays, aborted landings, and most important a surprising casualty count.

The aftermath of the Grenadan invasion became a time of extensive internal review and introspection on the part of the U.S. military. The "learned lesson" procedures of the various military units involved in Operation Urgent Fury pointed to the need for reforms beyond the gathering of accurate intelligence. More effective command-and-control procedures were targeted by Pentagon planners as high priority so that units at various positions on the battlefield would in future operations be able to communicate with each other and with headquarters. Better cooperation among the various services was viewed as essential to avoid what many both in and out of the armed forces felt were military decisions made to assuage the egos and the political interests of the Joint Chiefs of Staff. Finally, greater attention was placed on improving the rapid deployment capabilities of the United States.[26] What was intended to be a lightning strike to liberate Grenada turned out to be a rather disorganized and cautious venture that relied on more traditional battlefield tactics.

Despite the glowing praise of President Reagan and the awarding of medals to the participants in Operation Urgent Fury, the Grenada invasion was not the U.S. military's finest hour. As one observer mentioned at the time, "but for a lot of luck . . . [the invasion] could have been a disaster." [27] The invading forces did accomplish their objectives of securing the island, rescuing the medical students, and removing from power an unpopular regime and its Communist allies. Furthermore, the uncovering of huge stockpiles of weapons from Eastern Europe, North Korea, and Cuba provided the Reagan administration with further evidence that the invading forces arrived "just in time."[28] Yet the fact that the Grenada invasion became more of a case study on how not to use military force to achieve a foreign policy objective calls into question the official claim of success.

Relations with neighbors are never going to be completely smooth nor are large military operations always going to be marked by optimum implementations, but the Grenada invasion did raise serious questions about whether the United States could manage crises efficiently. Although the Reagan administration was able to mount a multilateral operation and was able to use this spirit of cooperation as a key stepping-stone to intervention, what happened before the request for assistance and after the decision to invade again raises the issue of using force as a tool of American foreign policy. The cursory and arrogant manner in which the Reagan administration conducted relations with the Bishop government and the serious deficiencies of the U.S. invading forces are facets of the Grenada intervention that have stimulated extensive debate over the quality of diplomatic representation and the preparedness of our front line troops.

The Intervention Approach of the 1980s

Operation Urgent Fury ushered in a new era of intervention. Although little had changed with respect to American interests in the circum-Caribbean region, the Grenada invasion did afford the Reagan administration an opportunity to use the political instability and ideological divisions on the island to modernize the process of using American power. Interventions are not freestanding actions with no connections to the governmental systems that devise them; rather, they are reflections of the political conditions that existed at the time of the intervention.

The Grenada invasion was an intervention of the 1980s. Much had changed in the United States since the election of Ronald Reagan as president. Not only was the mood of the country different in terms of its view of America's place in the world, but there was also a discernible need to expunge the failures of the Vietnam and Iran eras. Political leaders like Ronald Reagan, along with State Department officials and military commanders, were determined not to commit the errors of past administrations. In particular, the Reagan administration wanted to be certain that it was not constricted by congressional maneuvering and partisan criticism or incapable of shaping public opinion by controlling the images arriving from the battlefield. Most important, the Reagan administration wanted to make certain that the military came away from the invasion with not just a victory but with its morale and its prestige enhanced.

The Reagan administration had seen what the Vietnam War and the Iran hostage crisis had done to the president's powers as commander in chief. The War Powers Resolution pushed through the Democratically controlled Congress in the waning days of the Nixon administration had given the legislative branch the opportunity to demand an equal voice in the use of American military force outside U.S. borders. Although the War Powers Resolution was always embroiled in controversy and was never viewed as a hindrance to a president anxious to employ military force abroad, the days of congressional acquiescence in foreign policy were over. Congressional oversight committees, appropriations battles, and outspoken representatives seeking to compete with the White House as foreign policy experts became common occurrences after 1973.

Not surprisingly, the decision by the Reagan administration to invade Grenada resuscitated the War Powers Resolution and served as the basis of congressional opposition. Senator Gary Hart of Colorado said early in the invasion debate, "The War Powers Act is still the law of the land, is still in full force and effect. It still binds all citizens of our country up to and including the President of the United States. And we expect the President, absent a change or repeal of that law, to obey it."[29] But from the beginning of the Grenada crisis, many members of Congress were deeply displeased with the Reagan administration's adherence to the letter and the spirit of the War Powers Resolution. Specifically, Democratic representatives felt that the administration had not solicited the opinions of Congress as required in Section 3 of the resolution. Instead, members of Congress were brought into the White House to be informed about the invasion and not to seek their advice.

But the Reagan administration's point of view was that it had fully complied with the War Powers Resolution and was not required to base its decision to intervene on prior consultations with leaders in Congress. Moreover, the Reagan administration was concerned about the possibility of leaks resulting from extensive discussions with members of Congress. The focus was on maintaining secrecy and allowing the military to prepare for the assault without interference. From the perspective of the administration, Congress had become an unreliable player in foreign policy making.

Thus despite heavy criticism from Democratic leaders in the House and Senate, the Reagan administration was able to weather the storm of criticism for its alleged failure to consult Congress. The popularity of the president coupled with the apparent agreement of the American public that the use of force was appropriate created too much of a counterweight to congressional legalism. But the real impact of the decision to permit only marginal involvement in the preinvasion policy-making process was the further strengthening of the president's decision to use force as a tool of foreign policy and the eroding of Congress's role in this area of exclusive decision making. As Michael Rubner states, "The Grenada episode makes perfectly clear that it is not the absence of constitutional or legal powers that presents effective enforcement of the War Powers Resolution. Rather . . . Congress was unwilling to secure strict compliance with the law because it was severely constrained by political circumstances over which it had very little control."[30]

Constitutional squabbles between the executive and the legislative branches were not the only sources of conflict on the domestic scene. The Grenada invasion also created controversy in the journalistic community. As George H. Quester observed, "The October 1983 intervention in Grenada might just illustrate the deepest and most explicit tension between the press media and the U.S. government for all of our history."[31] This is certainly a strong statement, but Quester's analysis is supported by many newspaper editors, reporters, and television executives who experienced the restrictions placed on them by the Reagan administration.

Once the invasion began, representatives from the press and the media sought entry to the battlefield. Their requests were denied by military commanders who threatened to arrest them if they violated the news blackout. In one instance reporters were fired upon by U.S. Navy aircraft as they approached the island.[32] It was only after the island had been secured by American troops that members of the press were permitted access to Grenada and then were treated to a series of military-controlled public relations excursions to see captured eastern bloc arms, Cuban prisoners, and grateful citizens.

The control of news from the invasion scene unleashed a storm of controversy in the United States as major newspapers such as the *Washington Post* and the *New York Times* as well as the Big Three television networks complained that the blackout violated basic tenets of freedom and openness that had been recognized by the government and the military during wartime. But from the perspective of the Reagan administration and the field commanders it was time to place limits on battlefield access and allow the invasion to reach its conclusion without the interference, the instant analysis, and the visual images that in the past were perceived as limiting the effectiveness of military operations.

Military commanders were especially concerned about allowing the press the same freedom and influence that they had enjoyed during the Vietnam War. The need for secrecy was paramount, but there was also a clear antipathy between the Vietnam-era commanders and a press that was viewed as partially responsible for failure and embarrassment, the watchwords of the last U.S. intervention.[33] Furthermore, the military commanders were fully supported by the Reagan administration, which in the words of Quester, "treated the press with greater callousness than is the norm for the U.S. executive branch."[34] Together the military and the administration set a new tone for government-press relations during times of crisis that was designed to shift the pendulum away from First Amendment freedoms and toward national security.

Just as the Grenada invasion weakened the War Powers Resolution, the traditional influence of the press during wartime was limited. The Reagan administration, sensing the public mood, was critical of press power and increasingly anxious (especially in light of the Beirut massacre) to achieve a military victory, capitalizing on this shift in opinion to change the rules of press and military operations. From the administration's point of view the Grenada operations allowed it the opportunity to regain control of the battlefield and avoid the endless stream of self-analysis that press reporting created during the Vietnam War. But for proponents of freedom of the press and the people's right to know, the Grenada invasion signaled a sad and dangerous departure from past practice, a departure that would allow future presidents and commanders to conduct war free of visual images and critical reporting.

The final ingredient in the new approach to intervention that the Grenada invasion created was the validation of what has come to be called low-intensity warfare. As defined by James Motley, low-intensity warfare is a "range of activities and operations on the lower end of the conflict spectrum involving the use of military force on the part of the United States to influence and compel an adversary to accept a particular political-military condition."[35] Operation Urgent Fury fits securely in the definition of low-intensity warfare, but more important, Operation Urgent Fury convinced military planners and foreign policy makers that the United States must further intensify its efforts to expand and modernize its capacity to engage in this new kind of warfare.

With the Grenada invasion terms such as "quick strike," "rapid deployment," and "light infantry forces" entered the language of warfare and presidential discourse. In the view of the Reagan administration, the circumstances in which military force would be employed in the international arena were undergoing significant change. Conflict involving the United States was increasingly being defined as taking place outside the European theater and directed at small regional wars or Grenada-type "rescue missions." Much of this thinking was presented in the army's "Strategic Requirement for the Army for the Year 2000," a document that emphasized the value of preparing U.S. forces for "quick strikes," low-intensity warfare.[36]

The Grenada invasion therefore was a test case of an emerging theory of modern warfare. As has been shown earlier, transferring theory into practice in Grenada was a near disaster as the concepts of quick strike and rapid deployment ran up against delays, intelligence failures, and communication problems. Nevertheless, the military commanders who evaluated the Grenada operation were pleased with the overall performance of the troops and urged further development of these new modes of warfare. As Gen. John A. Wickham stated after the invasion, "initial conclusions from the operation in Grenada suggests that this new direction for the army light forces is sound and timely."[37]

The Reagan administration agreed with General Wickham's assessment as it pushed through a defense budget for fiscal year 1984 that emphasized the importance of the new techniques of low-intensity warfare. As described by James Motley, the budget proposal stressed the importance of "restructuring of army and marine forces, increasing commando type units, purchasing intercontinental cargo planes and constructing faster ships." The objective of these changes was to create a military force that was flexible and capable of being deployed with great speed to carry out the foreign policy objectives of the United States in Third World settings.[38]

Viewing the Grenada intervention as a test case of low-intensity warfare and as a stimulus for further expansion of the military's capacity to engage in new forms of intervention is important, because the invasion of Panama to remove Manuel Noriega was not without its ties to Operation Urgent Fury. Joint Chiefs of Staff chairman Colin Powell and Gen. Maxwell Thurman, commander of the invasion forces, were, in the words of Bob Woodward, "haunted by the criticism of the 1983 Grenada invasion" and determined not to repeat the failures of the past.[39] In particular, General Powell wanted to ensure that the invading forces honed their skills of surprise attack using the latest in night-vision equipment. Thurman, for his part, developed a minutely detailed communications instruction manual that when completed was three feet high and thorough in its description of how units were to be linked up with command headquarters.

The impact that the Grenada invasion had on validating low-intensity warfare and improving the capability of the United States to respond to crises around the world must also be included in the debate over whether the intervention was a success. By using its new style of warfare in Grenada, evaluating its performance, and making critical adjustments, U.S. military gained valuable lessons for the future, lessons that would be applied in Panama and ultimately in the Persian Gulf.

The Superpower Approach

The decision to invade a country, no matter how justified or necessary it may be in terms of national security or regional stability, forces a nation to look at itself and explore what the operation revealed about the broader or long-term goals of intervention. The Grenada invasion, despite the fact that it involved a ministate and was of short duration, was a significant event in contemporary U.S. foreign policy making. The importance that can be assigned to Grenada is that the invasion served as a catalyst for intensifying the movement to reassert U.S. preeminence in the Caribbean Basin region. Through the Grenada operation the Reagan administration was able to show its adversaries and indeed the world that American superpower status was not confined to nuclear arsenals but could swiftly be applied to localized conflicts that threatened the interests of the United States.[40]

President Reagan gave a hint of the underlying objectives of Operation Urgent Fury when he stated, "The events in Lebanon and Grenada, though oceans apart, are closely related. . . . We're a nation with global responsibilities. We're not somewhere else in the world protecting someone else's interest; we're there protecting our own."[41] Having been stung by the loss of 243 marines in the Beirut terrorist explosion, President Reagan was conscious of American credibility in the world. Entering the presidency as someone who would not vacillate or be intimidated by threats to the United States, Reagan seized upon the unrest in Grenada as a challenge to America's position in the hemisphere and its responsibility to lead the free world against the apparent onrush of revolutionary Marxism.

The guiding force or perhaps subtext of the Grenada invasion was the need on the part of the Reagan administration to prove that the United States was not reeling from its tragedy and embarrassment in Lebanon. Instead, President Reagan wanted to emphasize that this country was in control of events, willing to come to the aid of desperate allies, anxious to save the lives of fellow citizens, and adamant in its desire to rid the hemisphere of Communist influence. The Grenada invasion validated a fundamental characteristic of foreign policy decisions, namely, that governmental responses to particular problems or threats are often shaped by an agenda of broader objectives. In the case of Grenada, the resurgence of American military power and the enhancement of American prestige as the leader of the free world made for a perfect match.

What is perhaps most interesting about the Grenada invasion is the conflict between the stated objectives of the operation and what can be termed the superpower objectives. The reasons most often given for the intervention (saving the medical students and stopping the construction of the airport at Point Salines) are filled with inconsistencies and exaggerations. Yet if the short-term goals of the invasion were questionable, the unstated or less-emphasized reasons for the action (using force to send a signal to the Communists, stimulating popular opinion and national will, and regaining the initiative in the region) can be viewed as normal responses of a superpower seeking to rebound from a series of setbacks.

What the conflict between the stated and superpower objectives points to is not that the Reagan administration was cynically pursuing humanitarian and strategic goals while all along holding to a hidden agenda, but rather that the Grenada intervention was more than the simple little Caribbean invasion that captured U.S. attention for a week in October 1983. Grenada was both a challenge and an opportunity—a challenge brought on by another Marxist government in the region and an opportunity to respond to that Marxist government in ways that fulfilled larger international and domestic objectives. Moreover, the fact that neighboring Caribbean countries sought out U.S. involvement further enhanced the opportunity to present the invading forces as not merely more modern representatives of Pax Americana but partners in regional peacekeeping working on behalf of grateful nations.

There of course will continue to be critics of the invasion who feel that the Reagan administration ignored other foreign policy objectives in Grenada such as respect for the principle of nonintervention, development of a positive image in Latin America, and greater concern for the economic development of less-developed ministates. As the *New York Times* editorialized, "pacifying Grenada will prove only the obvious about American power. The enduring test for Americans is not whether we have the will to use that power but the skill to avoid having to. A President who felt he had no other choice last Monday night should not be celebrating a victory, he should be repairing the prior political failures and forestalling the bitter harvest to come."[42]

But from the perspective of the Reagan administration, Grenada offered too much of an opportunity to make the point to our adversaries and to the nation that the United States was on the offensive in the Caribbean Basin and capable of responding to threats in its traditional sphere of influence. As the *Jacksonville Journal* (and many other newspapers from the South and Midwest) stated, "let the critics rave: Reagan has sent two clear messages to the Kremlin this week that he will not be content with mere U.S. handwringing while the Soviet Union uses every form of brutality to advance its imperialist policies."[43]

The *Jacksonville Journal* may have been overly zealous in its analysis of the impact of the Grenada operation on superpower relations, but it nonetheless hit on a key function of the invasion. The decision to use force over diplomacy in Grenada was an international attention-getter that sent a clear message: the United States was once again willing to assert its power in the hemisphere and reassert its dominance in the region closest to its borders.

Conclusion

Intervention in Latin American affairs has been such a consistent part of the U.S. policy that when it does occur, as in Grenada, the tendency is to approach the action as just another example of American hegemony in the face of instability and/or Communism. The invasion of Grenada, coming as it did twenty years after the Dominican intervention, served as a reminder that the use of force by the United States is much more than Uncle Sam carrying a big stick. Invasions are calculated maneuvers designed to attain short- and long-term objectives; they often introduce new strategies and tactics and send signals to adversaries and allies alike. Most important, invasions are not encased in molds to be brought out when crisis appears. The act of invasion experiences transformations over time as governmental leaders and military strategists seek to address changing political and geopolitical condition.

The Grenada invasion was an example of a foreign policy action that was more than a brief military operation in the Caribbean. From protecting stranded citizens, to pushing Marxists out of power, to reminding the Communist world of U.S. power, to purging the domestic scene of the Vietnam paralysis, the Grenada invasion can be seen as being played out on a number of levels and with a number of objectives. As the Reagan administration moved on from Grenada to more critical engagements with Communism in Central America, the ability to act decisively against a Caribbean ministate strengthened its resolve and intensified its efforts to rid the hemisphere of Marxist influence.

Notes

1. See, for example, Gordon K. Lewis, *Grenada: The Jewel Despoiled* (Baltimore, Md.: Johns Hopkins University Press, 1987), Reynold A. Burrowes, *Revolution and Rescue in Grenada: An Account of the U.S. Caribbean Invasion* (Westport, Conn.: Greenwood, 1988), and Jorge Heine, ed., *A Revolution Aborted: The Lessons of Grenada* (Pittsburgh, Pa.: University of Pittsburgh Press, 1990).

2. U.S. Department of State, President Reagan's Address on Lebanon and Grenada, 27 October 1983, repr. in U.S. Department of State Bulletin, December 1983.

3. *Washington Post*/ABC poll data as reported in *Washington Post National Weekly Edition*, 21 November 1983.

4. See, for example, the critique of the invasion in Wendell Bell, "The Invasion of Grenada: A Note on False Prophecy," *Yale Review* 75 (Summer 1986): 564–86.

5. As quoted in Kai P. Schoenhals and Richard A. Melanson, *Revolution and Intervention in Grenada: The New Jewel Movement, the United States and the Caribbean* (Boulder, Colo.: Westview, 1985), p. 154.

6. Richard Gabriel, "Scenes from an Invasion," *Washington Monthly* (February 1986): 41.

7. Isaak I. Dore, "The U.S. Invasion of Grenada: Resurrection of the 'Johnson Doctrine,'" *Stanford Journal of International Law* 20 (spring 1984): 173–89.

8. For a discussion of some of the positive results of the Grenada invasion in terms of U.S. foreign policy objectives, see D. Brent Hardt, "Grenada Reconsidered," *Fletcher Forum* (summer 1987): 305–58.

9. Eldon Kenworthy, "Grenada as Theater," *World Policy Journal* (spring 1984): 650.

10. Text of President Reagan's Announcement on the Invasion of Grenada, 25 October 1983, repr. in U.S. Department of State Bulletin, December 1983.

11. See Robert A. Pastor's analysis of the medical student rescue in "The Invasion of Grenada: A Pre- and Post-Mortem," in Scott B. MacDonald et al., eds., *The Caribbean after Grenada: Revolution, Conflict and Democracy* (New York: Praeger, 1988), pp. 88–92.

12. As quoted in Schoenals and Melanson, *Revolution and Intervention*, p. 155.

13. See Bell, "The Invasion of Grenada," pp. 579–82.

14. U.S. Department of State, President Reagan's Address.

15. Televised Presidential Address, 23 March 1983.

16. See "Grenada: Critical Questions," *Washington Post*, 31 October 1983.

17. See Robert Pastor, "The United States and the Grenada Revolution: Who Pushed First and Why?" in Heine, ed., *A Revolution Aborted*, p. 193.

18. Ibid., p. 194.

19. Jacqueline Anne Braveboy-Wagner, *The Caribbean in World Affairs: The Foreign Policies of the English Speaking States* (Boulder, Colo.: Westview, 1989), pp. 179–94.

20. See U.S. Ambassador to the UN Jeane Kirkpatrick's defense of the invasion in "The U.N. and Grenada: A Speech Never Delivered," *Strategic Review* (winter 1984): 11–18.

21. Pastor, "The Invasion of Grenada," p. 88.

22. W. Frick Curry, "Grenada: Force as First Resort," *International Policy Report*, Center for International Policy, Washington DC (January 1984).

23. Gabriel, "Scenes from an Invasion," p. 41.

24. "Reports Cite Lack of Coordination during U.S. Invasion of Grenada," *New York Times*, 4 December 1984.

25. See Dorothea Cypher, "Urgent Fury: The U.S. Army in Grenada," in Peter M. Dunn and Bruce W. Watson, eds., *American Intervention in Grenada: The Implications of Operation "Urgent Fury"* (Boulder, Colo.: Westview, 1985), pp. 99–108.

26. See Gerald Hopple and Cynthia Gilley, "Policy without Intelligence," in Dunn and Watson, eds., *American Intervention*, pp. 55–71.

27. *Washington Post*, 24 November 1983, p. A23.

28. Nicolas Dujmovic, *The Grenada Documents, Window on Totalitarianism* (Cambridge, Mass.: Institute for Foreign Policy Analysis, 1988). See also *Grenada Documents: An Overview and Selection*, released by the U.S. Department of State and the U.S. Department of Defense, September 1984.

29. *Congressional Record*, 98th Cong., 1st sess., 28 October 1983, pp. 129–14869.

30. Michael Rubner, "The Reagan Administration, the 1973 War Powers Resolution and the Invasion of Grenada," *Political Science Quarterly* 100, no. 4 (winter 1985–86): 643.

31. George H. Quester, "Grenada and the News Media," in Dunn and Watson, eds., *American Intervention*, p. 109.

32. Henry E. Catto Jr., "Dateline Grenada: The Media and the Military Go at It," *Washington Post*, 30 October 1983, p. C7.

33. See the comments of Adm. Joseph Metcalf, the overall commander of the Grenada operation, in the *Washington Post*, 19 December 1983, p. 10.

34. Quester, "Grenada and the News Media," p. 125.

35. James Berry Motley, "Grenada: Low-Intensity Conflict and the Use of U.S. Military Power," *World Affairs* (winter 1983–84): 221.

36. See Capt. John J. McIntyre, ed., *The Future of Conflict* (Washington DC: National Defense University Press, 1979).

37. As quoted in *U.S. News and World Report*, 29 December 1983, p. 47.

38. Motley, "Grenada," p. 225.

39. Bob Woodward, *The Commanders* (New York: Simon and Schuster, 1991), p. 141.

40. See, for example, Dov S. Zakheim, "The Grenada Operation and Superpower Relations: A Perspective from the Pentagon," in Jiri Valenta and Herbert J. Ellison, eds., *Grenada and Soviet/Cuban Policy: Internal Crisis and U.S./OECS Intervention* (Boulder, Colo.: Westview, 1986).

41. U.S. Department of State, President Reagan's Address.

42. *New York Times*, 30 October 1983, p. D18.

43. As quoted in Schoenhals and Melanson, eds., *Revolutions and Intervention*, p. 160.

Steve C. Ropp

The Bush Administration
and the Invasion of Panama:
Explaining the Choice and Timing
of the Military Option

Throughout the post–World War II period, the United States has intervened in the internal affairs of various Latin American countries on numerous occasions. The general forms that such intervention has taken have been diplomatic, economic, and military in a wide variety of sequences and combinations.[1] For example, in Nicaragua the United States used a combination of diplomatic and economic pressure combined with direct support for irregular Nicaraguan military forces (the Contras) to pressure the Sandinista government. In El Salvador, the Reagan and Bush administrations supplied massive amounts of economic aid, together with military arms and advisers, to a series of Salvadoran governments they supported in order to prevent Marxist guerrillas from coming to power.

In spite of the fact that U.S. intervention has been a constant of Latin American political life during the post–World War II period, the *direct* combat involvement of U.S. troops has been rare. While the United States has frequently used military measures to supplement its economic and diplomatic strategies, these measures have generally stopped short of the direct insertion of U.S. military forces. Since World War II, the United States has only directly committed its troops to combat in Latin America on three occasions: the Dominican Republic in 1965, Grenada in 1983, and Panama in 1989.

Even more uncommon have been instances where the United States has inserted its military forces in a *unilateral* fashion without some form of support from other hemispheric nations. The Dominican intervention was supported by an Inter-American Peace Force (IAPF) that was patched together under the auspices of the Organization of American States (OAS). The Grenada operation was backed by the Organization of Eastern Caribbean States (OECS). Only the Panama invasion lacked even such symbolic support, thus constituting the first unilateral use of direct U.S. military force in more than sixty years.

Given the relative infrequency of direct combat involvement as a form of U.S. intervention during the post–World War II period and the singularity of such unilateral involvement in the Panamanian case, this chapter will attempt to answer several interrelated questions. Why did the U.S. government choose the option of direct unilateral military intervention when it had not been used in the past sixty years? And why did the government wait until late 1989 to choose this option given that it had been available since early 1988 during a period of equally intense crisis in U.S.-Panamanian relations? In other words, how does one explain both the *choice* of the unilateral military interventionist option and the *timing* of intervention?

Some observers (including myself) have argued that the choice and timing of the military invasion are partially explained by the specific nature of the crisis situation that faced members of the Bush decision-making team in the fall of 1989. After several years of unsuccessful attempts to remove Gen. Manuel Antonio Noriega from power through various indirect means, including support for a military coup, U.S. decision makers finally concluded that the Panamanian military itself was a large part of the problem. Once this conclusion had been reached, the decision to remove not just Noriega but also the Panamanian military from power virtually dictated the decision to mount a massive military invasion.[2]

While the specific nature of the crisis facing the Bush decision-making team no doubt played an important role in determining both choice and timing of the military option, I argue that the decision to use unilateral military force for the first time in sixty years cannot be understood exclusively in these terms. It cannot be understood apart from a variety of additional factors that expanded the parameters within which the choice of an appropriate means of dealing with the concrete situation was made and influenced the timing of the decision to use force.

I begin with a short background section detailing the pattern of deteriorating relations between the United States and Panama as well as general U.S. policy responses during 1988 and 1989. I pay particular attention to the secret development of a military option for removing Noriega that paralleled the more overt use of economic and diplomatic approaches. I then discuss the impact on the decision-making process of three broad "environmental" factors: changes in international opinion, domestic public opinion, and domestic electoral contexts. Finally, I examine the influence on choice and timing of several unique aspects of the foreign policy decision-making process itself.

Deteriorating Relations and U.S. Policy Responses

In 1968 a military coup in Panama produced a new regime that was destined to endure until destroyed by a U.S. military invasion in 1989.[3] After a somewhat troubled start, the U.S. government was able to establish good working relationships with the regime's strongman, Gen. Omar Torrijos. Although prone to the use of radical populist rhetoric in his efforts to gain leverage in canal treaty negotiations with the Nixon, Ford, and Carter administrations, he managed to maintain generally good relations both with key members of these administrations and with Congress. Development and cultivation of these relationships culminated in 1977 with the successful negotiation of two new canal treaties.

The death of General Torrijos in 1981 brought this relatively long period of stable U.S.-Panamanian relations to an end. Working relationships between the two countries began to slowly deteriorate in the 1980s, partially as a result of leadership changes within the Panamanian military. Although a group of high-ranking officers concluded an agreement providing for an orderly succession of command, this agreement masked an ongoing power struggle between Col. Rubén Darío Paredes, Roberto Díaz Herrera, and Manuel Antonio Noriega. Colonel Noriega, long-time head of the powerful G-2 intelligence branch of the military, used the 1984 presidential elections to force Paredes's retirement and quickly consolidated his position as commander in chief.

As the 1980s progressed, relationships between the Noriega regime and the U.S. government further deteriorated for reasons that are still being heavily debated.[4] From the standpoint of the Reagan and Bush administrations, such deterioration occurred due to a number of specific transgressions by the military regime. General Noriega expanded the institutional role and power of the military by creating the Public Defense Forces (PDF) and extending their reach to include control over transportation, customs, and immigration services. U.S. officials were later to allege that such expansion allowed the military to more fully participate in the region's growing arms and drug trades. Noriega was further accused of having held fraudulent presidential elections under military auspices in 1984 and of having authorized the murder of a leading opposition figure in 1985.

From Noriega's standpoint, this determination in relations was due to unjust accusations that were increasingly being made by members of Congress and the press. Senator Jesse Helms (R-NC) called for hearings in early 1986 to investigate charges of drug trafficking, electoral fraud, and murder. Journalist Seymour Hersh wrote a series of articles for the *New York Times* that addressed some of these same issues. Noriega was later to claim that the deterioration in relations between his government and the Reagan administration was largely due to his unwillingness to allow Panama to be used as a platform for U.S. operations to overthrow the Sandinista government in Nicaragua.

Regardless of how one explains the deterioration of U.S.-Panamanian relations, the crisis entered a more intense phase in the spring of 1987. In June, an officer who had been forcibly retired from the PDF by Noriega publicly accused him of a variety of illicit and criminal acts. As a result, the Panamanian civilian opposition became more active, as did the U.S. Senate, which passed a resolution calling for Noriega's ouster.

By early 1988, relationships between the two countries had deteriorated to the point that the Reagan administration was willing to consider any and all means for getting rid of Noriega. Economic sanctions were imposed in March that dramatically affected the performance of the Panamanian economy. Two federal indictments that had been handed down against Noriega for drug trafficking were used as diplomatic leverage by the administration in an attempt to force him to step down as commander in chief. In the end, all these measures came to naught, leaving the problem for the Bush administration to handle.

Little U.S. foreign policy attention was devoted to Panama by the Reagan administration during the summer and fall of 1988 for reasons that will be discussed below. When attention was resumed following the election of George Bush, it publicly continued to focus on economic and diplomatic means for effecting change. Teams of U.S. observers closely monitored Panama's May 1989 elections and duly noted their annulment by the military. Following failure to influence Panama's elections, the policy focus shifted toward support for efforts by the OAS to encourage a mediated settlement. This effort also ended in failure.

In early October 1989, an unsuccessful coup was attempted by midlevel Panamanian officers. Although U.S. troops provided some support to the coup makers by blocking access roads available for the reinforcement of Noriega's forces, this support was not sufficient to prevent the uprising from being crushed. The fact that the October coup was led by officers who appeared to have no interest in restoring democratic government in Panama helped to create a decision-making context in which selection of the military interventionist option became more appealing. It was increasingly apparent that democratic government could not be restored unless both General Noriega and the Panamanian military were removed from power.

In mid-December, a U.S. Marine lieutenant was killed by Panamanian soldiers. This was the most visible precipitating event for the 20 December invasion. Operation Just Cause, launched in the early morning hours, constituted the largest U.S. military operation since the end of the Vietnam War. The entire exercise lasted for four days, during which time 20,000 troops destroyed the main combat units of the PDF and routed the organized paramilitary resistance.

Development of a "Parallel" Military Option

In order to be able to more fully discuss the Bush administration's eventual choice of the military option in December 1989, it is first necessary to describe how this option developed and evolved. At first glance, it might appear that the policy responses of the Reagan and Bush administrations during 1988 and 1989 to deteriorating relations with the Noriega regime were created in sequential order. From this perspective, the Reagan administration first developed a set of economic and diplomatic policies that failed to remove Noriega. President Bush then tried some further economic and diplomatic measures that also failed. Having failed to accomplish its goal of removing Noriega by economic and diplomatic means, the Bush administration then turned to its only remaining option, the use of military force.

Viewed in this light, the use of force was largely the result of a single decision reached by President Bush and his closest advisers on 17

December to authorize an invasion in response to a specific situation. This decision was made at the end of a much longer series of decisions that sequentially authorized other methods for removing Noriega.

While there may be some merit in viewing the decision to invade Panama from this perspective, it ignores the fact that the military interventionist option had been developed and to some extent implemented under President Reagan in 1988. Rather than viewing the decision-making process as one in which a set of decisions sequentially authorized economic, diplomatic, and finally military intervention, it is better viewed as one in which a military interventionist option was designed and implemented through a "parallel" decision-making process.

Although major turning points leading in the direction of armed intervention are sometimes difficult to specify, there are a number of decisions that have to be made before such intervention can occur. These include the point at which the national leadership begins to pay serious attention to the problem and to the development of military contingency plans. Such contingency plans then have to be staffed and refined, followed (if there is sufficient time) by a period during which they are practiced. The final point in this decision-making process comes when the full-scale use of combat troops is authorized by the top leadership.

Serious contingency planning for an invasion of Panama can be traced back to the early months of 1988, when a feud erupted between the Department of State and Department of Defense concerning the possible use of military force. In personal terms, this feud pitted Elliott Abrams, assistant secretary of state for Inter-American Affairs, against Adm. William Crowe, chairman of the Joint Chiefs of Staff. Abrams argued that the United States should consider any and all means (including military force) to remove Noriega, while Crowe adopted the position that use of U.S. bases in Panama for such military action would seriously affect base agreements around the world.[5]

Admiral Crowe authorized the revision of the existing Pentagon contingency plans following a contentious meeting on 29 March 1988 of the National Security Planning Group during which President Reagan considered but did not adopt five separate military and paramilitary options for removing Noriega. A broad series of plans called "Prayer Book" were developed that contained a "Blue Spoon" option for a full-scale invasion to be launched from U.S. bases in Panama.[6] Development of these plans coincided with the movement of an additional thirteen hundred U.S. troops to the canal area to improve base security and security for U.S. civilians living in Panama.[7]

While the seeds of military invasion can thus be traced back to the Reagan years, it is important to note that none of these early measures really moved U.S. policy from the planning to the implementation stage. Measures that did in fact move U.S. policy in this direction were delayed for a full year until the spring of 1989, when the Bush administration took a number of dramatic new steps. Beginning in May, the U.S. Southern Command (SOUTHCOM) began to implement a "triad strategy," which added a military threat component to the economic and diplomatic interventionist means already being employed to pressure Noriega. President Bush authorized new high-level military exercises to "assert U.S. treaty rights," and a brigade-size force (together with Delta Force and SEAL units) was dispatched to Panama.[8]

During the summer of 1989, a further important step was taken in the direction of eventual intervention. President Bush began installing the group of general officers who were to become his war-fighting commanders. In addition to Gen. Colin Powell, who was tapped to succeed Adm. William Crowe, Gen. Maxwell R. Thurman was chosen to replace Gen. Frederick F. Woerner as SOUTHCOM commander. A new command structure was quickly assembled that was designed to effectively wage war against the PDF by marrying conventional military capabilities to those of the newer special operations forces.[9]

In the months just prior to the invasion, the "Blue Spoon" option was further specified and refined to include the complete integration of conventional and special operations forces and a forty-eight-hour time frame for implementation. This updated version of the plan was signed by General Thurman on 30 October and then extensively practiced both in Panama and the United States. Military equipment was also prepositioned during November.[10]

The final step in this long process came at a White House meeting on Sunday, 17 December. This meeting between the president and nine key members of his administration lasted for nearly two hours. Following discussion of the killing of Marine lieutenant Roberto Paz, various options were reviewed. The president finally settled on that of a military invasion through implementation of "Blue Spoon."

Impact of the International and Domestic Decision-Making Environment

The pattern of U.S. policy responses to the Panama crisis detailed above indicates that although some serious thinking about the military interventionist option took place during the final year of the Reagan administration and the first five months of the Bush administration, no major steps were taken to actually implement such measures. This raises questions concerning the various factors that may have inhibited implementation of this option during 1988 and early 1989 and accelerated the process thereafter. The search for answers to these questions must begin with some discussion of the general causal factors that have been used to explain the foreign policy behavior of nation-states and the level at which these factors are deemed to operate. At the most general level, such behavior can be attributed to the international operational environment of national decision makers, an environment that includes the global system and any regional subsystems in which the particular nation-state may participate.[11] A second level of explanation involves factors operating within the domestic foreign policy environment. Finally, one must examine the characteristics of specific national decision-making institutions and of the individual decision makers who utilize them.[12]

The International Environment

What impact might changes in the U.S. global operational environment have had on the decision to use direct military force in Panama? Beginning in 1984 with the accession to power of Mikhail Gorbachev, it became increasingly clear that the pattern of relationships between the United States and the Soviet Union was beginning to change in ways that would affect the operation of the entire global system. The bipolar world was coming to an end and being replaced by a much more complex and amorphous pattern of new multipolar relationships.[13] A number of dramatic developments in U.S.-Soviet relations directly paralleled the growing crisis in U.S.-Panamanian relations, developments that could be interpreted as signaling the end of the Cold War. Three U.S.-Soviet summits were held, the first coinciding with the effort in May 1988 to negotiate Noriega's departure. The second was held in December 1988 during a lull in the crisis, and the third in Malta during December 1989.

One conclusion that can be derived from the literature on foreign policy decision making is that changes in perceptions concerning the distribution of global military resources may give leaders whose nations are favorably affected by these changes increased confidence in the use of military force.[14] During an address in December 1988 to the United Nations, Gorbachev announced plans to drastically reduce the size of the Soviet armed forces and to reduce Soviet tank deployments in Central Europe by at least 50 percent. This raises the question of whether these dramatic developments at the level of the global system may have affected U.S. perceptions of military resource distribution within the Latin American regional subsystem and hence indirectly the propensity to give more serious consideration to military options.

Political scientist Jorge Dominguez argues that this was in fact the case: "The structural change in the international system stemming from the internal and international changes in Eastern Europe and the Soviet Union freed the United States from the old Cold War framework in the conduct of its foreign relations. And, for this reason, *it allowed for a broadening of the possibilities for the use of force*" (italics mine).[15] To elaborate further on Dominguez's argument, he suggests that the Cold War strictly limited the situations in Latin America where the United States would be willing to use highly interventionist means up to and including direct combat involvement.[16] Prior to the end of the Cold War, such means were used only in cases where there was a clear perception of "linkage" between the target regime and the forces of international Communism. When the Cold War ended, the United States was free to apply force in less ideologically charged situations such as Panama and the Andean "drug wars."[17]

Although a strong prima facie case can be made that the end of the Cold War may have affected U.S. perceptions of military resource distribution and hence have heightened the propensity to intervene militarily in Panama, it is difficult to prove the point. A major problem with this line of argument is that Latin Americanists have traditionally used the Cold War to explain U.S. military intervention. Now, the end of the Cold War is being used for the same purposes.

The end of the Cold War certainly must have heightened the general perception among U.S. decision makers that military resources could be brought to bear in Panama without endangering resource availability worldwide. But it is far from clear that such a perception would have been a *necessary* military condition for selection of the invasion option in either 1988 or 1989. By way of contrast, the end of the Cold War was clearly a necessary condition for the United States to adopt an offensive military posture toward Iraq in 1990 following its invasion of Kuwait. Offensive military action would have been extremely difficult had not the end of the Cold War made the VII Armour Corps available for deployment from Western Europe to the Middle East.[18]

While military force might have been used in Panama by either the Reagan or Bush administration even in the absence of concrete signs that the Cold War had ended, these events probably boosted confidence in the successful outcome of an invasion. This must have been particularly true in the concrete situation that existed in December 1989, when the recently installed members of the Bush administration's foreign policy team faced their first major foreign policy crisis (see part 3).

In addition, certain specific international events that occurred in October and November 1989 do appear to have served as accelerators for military intervention. Within the Central American regional subsystem, Nicaragua's Sandinista government suspended its cease-fire with the U.S.-backed Contras, and the guerrillas in El Salvador mounted a major military offensive against the U.S.-backed government there. Since the failed October military coup in Panama was widely viewed as reflecting a failure of U.S. policy, these developments in Central America were interpreted as being international responses to U.S. weakness and timidity.[19] Although such an interpretation of regional events was no doubt erroneous, it placed additional pressure on the Bush administration to quickly find a solution to the Panama problem.[20]

The Domestic Public Opinion Environment

In addition to the effect that international factors may have had on the U.S. decision to use military force in Panama, we also need to look closely at several changes in the domestic foreign policy environment.[21] One of these changes related to the partial reestablishment during the 1980s of a consensus about the use of force abroad.

Following World War II, a broad public consensus developed concerning the needs and means of foreign policy that in turn supported a high degree of bipartisan consensus in Congress. Such public support and bipartisanship made decisive military action possible in situations such as that that existed in 1965 in the Dominican Republic.

Eugene Wittkopf has convincingly argued that the Vietnam War was a critical event that negatively affected this post–World War II disposition to use military force: "The evidence based on mass public attitudes that best supports the view that Vietnam was a causal factor as well as a watershed in American foreign policy is that regarding the use of force. It is comparatively clear that in the immediate post-Vietnam years the disposition to use force in a broad range of overseas conflict situations was severely restricted."[22] This shift in attitudes during the Vietnam years translated into a dramatic change in the extent to which the public would support military intervention in Central and South America. In a number of specific situations between 1947 and 1965 involving a perceived external or internal Communist threat, 65 percent of the American people were willing to use armed force in the region. However, similar questions asked about the possible use of force in 1982 and 1983 elicited only a 16 percent favorable response rate.[23]

What is important here for our purposes is the extent to which this crumbling domestic consensus concerning the use of military force in Central and South America may have been partially restored by the late 1980s. Certainly, the evidence does not suggest that a public consensus concerning the use of force was completely reestablished during the Reagan years. For example, only 56 percent of the American people supported the invasion of Grenada, even after having been supplied by the administration with considerable evidence of Communist influence.[24] And bipartisan support within Congress for Ronald Reagan's broad array of foreign policy initiatives was hardly greater than that afforded Jimmy Carter.[25] Issues involving even indirect forms of military intervention, such as in Nicaragua and El Salvador, were particularly contentious. Lack of bipartisan agreement concerning the appropriate role of force led to the Iran-Contra affair, which threatened to bring down the Reagan administration.

Still, it can be argued that a *limited* foreign policy consensus was reestablished during the 1980s around issues such as the need for a stronger defense posture and for a more hardheaded approach toward dealing with international "troublemakers." In the wake of the disastrous Iran hostage crisis, the American people were clearly in the mood for assertive national leadership. President Reagan used these broadly based public sentiments as a platform for his efforts to relegitimize the use of force in American foreign policy.[26]

In spite of the absence of a broad new foreign policy consensus, this more limited consensus appears to have allowed both the Reagan and Bush administrations to carve out a certain decision-making "space" for the use of military force abroad. While the *general* constraint against the use of force remained in place because of the public's continued concern with "another Vietnam," this did not prevent its selective use in certain limited circumstances. As Richard Melanson puts it, "The Grenada 'rescue mission' and the April 1986 bombing of Libya demonstrated that the public would support low-risk, ends-specific, limited-cost military operations."[27]

During the late 1980s, a limited consensus also appears to have developed concerning the major problems affecting U.S. national security and the regions of the world where addressing these problems was most important. Public opinion surveys taken during the 1987–88 presidential campaign revealed that a large percentage of the American people were concerned with combating international drug trafficking. They were also very concerned with the threat of Communist governments appearing in Central America. This limited consensus concerning problems and the importance of various regions in finding solutions for them pointed the nation's attention toward the deteriorating situation in Panama.[28]

As with the end of the Cold War, the reestablishment of a limited public consensus concerning situations where the use of military force was appropriate probably boosted the confidence of officials in the Bush administration in the probabilities of success if force were to be used in Panama. There was an expectation of sufficient public acceptance based on past experiences with the public's response following similarly limited military operations during the early 1980s. (see part 3).

The Domestic Electoral Environment

Another change in domestic foreign policy making that may have had a more immediate and direct impact on decisions about Panama was the approach of a U.S. presidential election. Although foreign policy events do not normally determine the outcome of presidential elections, decisions about foreign policy tend to be made with an eye to the effect they are likely to have on voters' choices. It can be argued that George Bush and his key advisers were even more inclined to view foreign policy decisions through the prism of electoral politics than were their predecessors. As reported by Bob Woodward, Adm. William Crowe is said to have worried about the degree to which political perspectives colored discussion in meetings of the NSC. "Decisions were made based on their likely impact on the Congress, the media and public opinion, and the focus was on managing the reaction."[29]

Public opinion polls taken in May 1988 showed that Democratic presidential candidate Michael Dukakis had a 10 percentage point lead over Vice President Bush and that the primary foreign policy concern of the American people was drug trafficking. Furthermore, there was a perception that Bush did not speak with an independent voice on foreign policy matters but merely echoed those of President Reagan.[30] Equally troubling to Bush's supporters was the fact that Dukakis was beginning to raise questions concerning his past ties to Noriega. Bush had met with Noriega on several occasions, and it was asserted that he must have known about Noriega's drug dealings in his former capacity as director of the CIA.

For these reasons, Bush's campaign managers became increasingly concerned about the impact that the Reagan administration's policy for dealing with Noriega might have on the upcoming elections. Negotiations were being conducted by the State Department to drop the indictments in exchange for Noriega's retirement as commander in chief. Lee Atwater and Robert Teeter, key members of the campaign team, worried that these negotiations could result in Noriegas removal as commander in chief but that he might be allowed to remain in Panama,[31] raising questions in the electoral context as to whether Noriega had information that he was using to blackmail the administration.

The political imperatives of the electoral campaign led Vice President Bush to break in mid-May with the Reagan administration's policy for dealing with Noriega. Shortly thereafter, the State Department terminated negotiations for his removal. From May until the November election, political considerations prevented implementation of any effective policy toward Panama. As Bush's chief of staff put it: "Noriega was one of those things that fell into the category of the less you had to say about it, the better. . . . There was almost nothing you could say that could help. If you suggested that you should find another way to get rid of him, that conjured up in people's minds American troops and Panama, and that scared them more than Noriega."[32] The lingering American fear of military intervention thus served as a partial constraint on such action prior to the election.[33] The U.S. ambassador in Panama and military commander of the Southern Command headquartered there were informed that they were to avoid inflammatory measures that might antagonize Noriega. Panamanian opposition groups were told that the United States would not support their efforts to remove him and that no direct U.S. military action should be anticipated.

The U.S. presidential elections thus partially explain why the invasion option was not exercised in 1988 despite growing tensions with Noriega. It is even more important to note that their conclusion with a victory for George Bush removed a major domestic constraint to consideration of a military solution. Bush now had a full year in office during which he could contemplate interventionist military measures without having to give much thought to the impact the implementation of such measures might have on presidential or congressional elections.

In sum, changes in the international and domestic decision-making environment may have had important if countervailing effects on the decision concerning the use of military force to deal with the Panama crisis. The end of the Cold War and the reestablishment of a limited foreign policy consensus increased confidence in the probable success of an invasion. At the same time, the electoral context seems to have been one of the factors that played an important role in delaying implementation of this option until 1989.

Impact of the Foreign Policy Decision-Making Process

So far, we have emphasized changes in international and domestic foreign policy making that affected decision making concerning the choice and timing of a military option. However, there is a risk that our analysis may become overly deterministic if we rely exclusively on such changes to explain the decision to invade Panama.

In order to more fully account for the choice and timing of military intervention, we must also examine the impact of additional factors operating at the level of the decision-making process itself to include changes that took place over time in government bureau-cracies and individual decision makers who dealt with the Panama issue. Traditionally, we have tended to minimize these factors and rely to a greater extent than is probably warranted on international and domestic "structural variables" to explain decision-making out-comes. According to Charles Kegley,

We have been asked to believe that foreign policy behaviors are influenced al-most exclusively by the internal characteristics of nations or the attributes of those nations' external environments. . . . The foreign policy-making pro-cess . . . has been discounted. . . . We have often dealt with these secretive features and functions by ignoring them or failing to incorporate them into our models, forgetting that the absence of evidence is not evidence of absence.[34]

Bureaucratic Stalemate and Delayed Intervention: 1988

Bureaucratic politics has long been recognized as an important com-ponent of the foreign policy decision-making process. Thus, it is not unusual to find that many analysts of the Panama crisis have stressed this factor in attempting to determine what happened and why.[35] What impact did such factors as bureaucratic infighting and organizational change have on the decision not to implement the military option in 1988 and to do so in 1989? Here, we will stress the process of consensus building as it involved key individual players in the Department of State, the Department of Defense (DOD), and the CIA.

When the crisis began to intensify during 1985 and 1986, CIA di-rector William Casey, Assistant Secretary of State Elliott Abrams, and the DOD's Nestor Sanchez formed a "troika" whose support for the Noriega regime was based on Panama's support in the effort to aid the Contras in Nicaragua. Peripheral players opposed to existing U.S. policy of support for Noriega included Senator Jesse Helms, Constantine Menges of the NSC, and Seymour Hersh of the *New York Times*. Given the overwhelming bureaucratic power and for-eign policy interests of the central players, there was a consensus during this period not to do much about the Noriega problem.

During 1987, this old consensus began to break down in the wake of the Iran-Contra affair and growing public concern about drug traf-ficking. As a result, more individual and bureaucratic players were added to the mix so that the decision-making process became increasingly complex. The Senate as a whole began adopting tougher positions on Noriega, and committee hearings on drug trafficking were initiated by Senator John Kerry. The Department of Justice also devoted more attention to Panamanian issues as indictments were handed down against Noriega by grand juries in Miami and Tampa.

By 1988, the list of players and bureaucracies devoting some attention to Panama had become even longer as the issue of what to do about Noriega became increasingly politicized within the context of the upcoming U.S. presidential elections. The Department of State, initially one of Noriega's strongest supporters, was now calling for paramilitary or military action to remove him. Within a post-Iran-Contra context that reduced the institutional need for close working relations with Noriega, the DOD had also shifted its position. Although not supportive of military action, it sent an organizational representative to Panama in an attempt to persuade Noriega that it was time to step down.[36]

During 1988, this expanded combination of policy makers, organizational players, and issues failed to produce a decision to implement the military option. One of the explanations for exclusion of this option has already been alluded to—the 1988 election campaign. A further important factor was the role played by various key U.S. military leaders in opposing the use of military force and the bureaucratic stalemate that resulted.

Much of the academic discussion of the policy-making stalemate that prevented serious consideration being given to the military option during 1988 has correctly focused on the personal conflict between Assistant Secretary of State Elliott Abrams and Adm. William Crowe, chairman of the Joint Chiefs of Staff. While Mr. Abrams believed that all means, including military force, should be considered in order to remove Noriega, Admiral Crowe represented those in the Pentagon who had been convinced by their Vietnam experiences of the adverse consequences of ill-conceived interventions. There was a strong belief among many of Crowe's military generation that politicians and their organizational supporters in other Washington bureaucracies were all too willing to initiate conflicts for which the nation's soldiers would be blamed if they failed.[37]

The position adopted by U.S. military leaders regarding Noriega and the potential use of force against him during 1988 largely contradicts conventional assumptions about the military's institutional aggressiveness. In other words, while they might have been expected to back military solutions more readily than their civilian counterparts, this was not the case. The reasons for this hesitancy on the part of military leaders to support the use of force varied from individual to individual. Admiral Crowe had been affected by the Vietnam experience. Gen. Colin Powell was also opposed to the use of force during this period but appears to have been more heavily influenced by his position as a "political general" temporarily serving as Reagan's national security adviser.[38] In this capacity, he made sure that Secretary of State George Shultz's calls for a cabinet-level discussion of the Noriega problem did not reach the president's desk and personally informed the U.S. military commander in Panama that no provocative military actions were to be taken.[39]

Although the Abrams-Crowe debate was an important factor inhibiting the emergence of a consensus concerning the use of force during this period, there has been a tendency to trivialize the issue as nothing more than a personal conflict between two powerful bureaucratic players. Admiral Crowe did manage to prevail, and force was not used during this period. But his "victory" had more to do with organizational changes within the DOD than with his personal powers of persuasion. Prior to passage of the Goldwater-Nichols Act in 1986, the chairman of the Joint Chiefs of Staff had very limited influence in the highest decision-making circles. Unless unanimous agreement could be reached among the individual chiefs concerning an issue such as Panama, advice was likely to be diluted and articulation of a military position postponed. Crowe was the first chairman who could speak for the professional soldier with the full authority of a single voice.

Admiral Crowe's influence with regard to the decision not to use force in Panama during 1988 was further reinforced by several other factors. The history of American foreign policy decision making suggests that presidents normally will not recommend the use of force when it is opposed by the nation's top military professionals.[40] With regard to this particular decision, the U.S. military was also in a very strong position "on the ground." Because of its historical role in Panama and the large American troop presence there, the military had a larger direct voice in policy formulation than did the U.S. Embassy.[41]

The military's powerful new institutional role in the formulation of U.S. foreign policy following passage of the Goldwater-Nichols Act thus created something of a paradox. Increased military influence in the decision-making process did not lead to a "militarization" of U.S. policy toward Panama. Rather, this powerful new institutional role, coupled with the domestic electoral constraint, resulted in a general avoidance of military solutions during the period prior to mid-1989.

Personality and Prior Experience in the Decision to Use Force: 1989

In the final analysis, decisions to use military force are usually made by small coteries of top national leaders that comprise the critical element within the policy-making "black box." Thus, in order to fully explain the choice and timing of the U.S. invasion, we must also examine the changes in national leadership that took place following the 1988 presidential elections. These changes produced the Bush decision-making team that authorized the military invasion.

The formal decision to intervene militarily in Panama was made in a hastily called meeting at the White House on 17 December 1989 following the murder of a marine lieutenant and the serious maltreatment of several other Americans by members of the PDF. The meeting was attended by the president and nine members of his inner circle including Vice President J. Danforth Quayle, Secretary of State James Baker, Secretary of Defense Dick Cheney, National Security Adviser Brent Scowcroft, Deputy National Security Adviser Robert Gates, White House Chief of Staff John Sununu, Press Secretary Marlin Fitzwater, Chairman of the Joint Chiefs of Staff Colin Powell, and Gen. Thomas Kelly.[42]

Although the formal decision to use force was made by President Bush following consultation with those in attendance at this December meeting, the final outcome was more heavily influenced by the nature and predispositions of the key group of foreign policy advisers that had been in place since October 1989. Dick Cheney and Colin Powell assumed their new positions in the fall and were added to the core group within the administration that already included James Baker and Brent Scowcroft. Advanced planning for the invasion was managed by a subgroup within the Pentagon that included Cheney, Powell, and Kelly.

Decisions are the product of the specific decision-making units that produce them and can be affected in major ways by the general nature and structure of these units.[43] For example, some national leaders assemble teams of foreign policy advisers that consist of delegates from highly autonomous organizations. Because of their loyalty to these organizations, the issue positions of these advisers are unlikely to change. Under such circumstances, it is difficult to build coalitions across the team, so there is a tendency for decisions to be oriented toward preservation of the status quo.[44]

By the fall of 1989, George Bush had assembled a foreign policy decision-making team that can be best described as a "predominant leader with a staff of advisers." Unlike the type of team mentioned above, the primary characteristic of this particular configuration is that members of the team have no strong association with nor loyalty to the organizations to which they are formally attached. Team members may alternate in a variety of high-level organizational positions at the discretion of the president.[45]

The core foreign policy decision-making unit (Bush, Baker, Scowcroft, Cheney, and later Powell) included players who had served a number of presidents in a variety of capacities. Their previous positions had often been political in nature (outside the executive bureaucracies), giving them a finely honed sense of the impact that foreign policy decisions can have on electoral politics and public opinion. Baker had managed both Gerald Ford and Bush's presidential campaigns, while Cheney had served as White House chief of staff and in Congress. Colin Powell was a "political general" who had past experience within the office of the secretary of defense and as President Reagan's national security adviser.

This team was also an extremely harmonious one, consisting of players with long-standing personal ties, respect, and affection for each other. Cheney had been White House chief of staff for Gerald Ford, while Scowcroft served as his national security adviser. Baker and Cheney also had similar ties dating back to the mid-1970s. It is no coincidence then that both Scowcroft and Baker pushed hard for Cheney as secretary of defense when it became clear that John Tower's nomination was in trouble.[46] It is also no coincidence that team player George Bush picked a group of kindred spirits who worked well together.

Margaret Hermann has noted that certain processes and patterns of behavior are associated with decision making by a predominant leader operating with such a staff of advisers. Very little attempt is made to gather information unless the leader's personality characteristics suggest that this be done. There is a tendency for members of the team to reinforce the predispositions of the leader. Efforts may be made to persuade the leader that he has embarked on the wrong course of action, but they are generally muted and little dissent is tolerated. Leaders who rely on such a team have the advantage of being able to make bold decisions quickly but at some risk of doing so without full consultation.[47]

Given that the organizational affiliations of key players are normally not a major determinant of decisions that emerge from such a unit, it is unlikely that they were important in the decision to use military force in Panama. Where organizational affiliations are not important, we have to look at other factors that are known to influence decision makers operating in small closed groups under crisis conditions. Such factors include personality, personal interests, prior experience, and the nature of the crisis situation itself.[48]

Even before the Panama invasion, a close observer of the American presidency had argued that Bush's personality and background would lead him to view military force as a legitimate tool of diplomacy.[49] He had been raised in the austere tradition of public service of former Secretary of State and Secretary of War Henry L. Stimson. Like Stimson, Bush was steeped in the values of a militant Republican internationalism that traced its origins to the foreign policies of President Theodore Roosevelt.[50] The president's views concerning the use of force were further shaped by his own generation's experience with world affairs during the 1930s and 1940s. Leaders had a right, indeed a duty, to use force against international aggressors, a perspective that led Bush to enlist in the military when World War II began and to become the navy's youngest fighter pilot. James Baker and Brent Scowcroft were of the same generation, and it can be presumed that they were considerably influenced by these same experiences.

Baker and Scowcroft were both key members of Bush's foreign policy team. But the fact that the division of labor among its members exempted them from a central role in the Panama decision means that an assessment of their personal perspectives with regard to the use of military force is not terribly important. Baker wished to wash his hands of Central America as a regional concern so that he could concentrate on broader global problems. As for Scowcroft, he had been schooled in the Europocentric foreign policy perspective of Henry Kissinger. Intellectually and emotionally committed to questions of strategic arms control, he had little reason by background or inclination for wanting to involve himself deeply in the Panama decisions.[51]

By a process of elimination, we are led to the conclusion that the personalities, personal interests, and prior experiences of three men—Bush himself, Cheney, and Powell—played a critical role in the choice of the force option in Panama. The unique organizational position of the U.S. military in Panama, the lack of interest on the part of Baker and Scowcroft, and the definition of the situation after the failure of the October coup all contributed to their paramount role in this particular decision.

There is no question that Dick Cheney was an advocate of assertive national leadership and military preparedness. While in Congress, he strongly supported the Contras in the belief that Nicaragua could easily become "another Cuba."[52] With regard to his thinking concerning the various options for dealing with Panama, it is also important to note that Cheney was the ranking Republican on the House Select Committee to Investigate Covert Arms Transactions with Iran. Although a strong supporter of paramilitary and covert activity, he had the opportunity in this capacity to think long and hard about the high domestic political costs of such alternatives to the direct use of military force.

As for General Powell, his views concerning Panama seem to have been heavily colored by his keen sense of domestic political costs and benefits. Having served previously as military assistant to the secretary of defense and as national security adviser, he was well aware of the U.S. domestic dimensions of the Noriega problem. That Powell did not view Panama and Noriega as terribly important foreign policy matters in their own right is demonstrated by the fact that he used his former position as Reagan's national security adviser to dampen presidential enthusiasm for dealing forcefully with the issue prior to the 1988 election.

Following the failed October coup, Bush and his two top military advisers had strong personal motives for advocating military intervention in Panama. At the time of the coup, both Cheney and Powell were new to their jobs, and its failure was erroneously attributed by the media and the public to their personal ineptness. Even worse, the "wimp factor" had emerged once again to affect perceptions of the president's job performance. Conservative Republicans were particularly harsh in their judgments, accusing Bush of following a course of action toward Panama "marked by incompetence and timidity bordering on appeasement."[53]

Because many of the key players in the Bush administration had been members of the Reagan foreign policy team, their views concerning what worked and what didn't in crisis situations such as Panama must have been heavily shaped by their experiences during the Reagan years. There seems to have been an important learning curve associated with these previous experiences with regard to the appropriate and inappropriate uses of force. Some of the lessons they learned were positive and some were negative, but all seem to have had an impact on the decision to invade Panama.

During the Reagan years, Bush and his future team of advisers learned to use force in a limited and carefully calibrated way. They learned when force was likely to be effective, as well as what kind of force was most appropriate in a variety of situations. Most important, they learned how to use it effectively without exceeding the boundaries imposed on such use by the public fear of another major overseas involvement such as Vietnam.

Many of the lessons concerning what would not work from a domestic point of view came from Lebanon, Nicaragua, and El Salvador. The short but disastrous intervention in Lebanon demonstrated the high cost of direct military involvement in situations where there was no clear delineation of goals and hence no clear time frame for the removal of U.S. troops. Nicaragua and El Salvador provided valuable lessons concerning the difficulties associated with covert and indirect combat operations. In providing aid to the Contras, the Reagan administration deeply offended the moral and legal sensibilities of a large portion of the American public as well as the sensibilities of many within Congress. The result was the Iran-Contra affair and major problems with attempts by the administration to restore bipartisanship in American foreign policy.

On the other hand, Libya and Grenada taught Bush and his team of advisers that both the American public and Congress would support military interventions when they were swift, when vital national interests were perceived to be at stake, and when they were conducted on a pragmatic "one time only" basis. A majority of the American people approved of both actions, and congressional criticism was muted after the fact. In the case of Grenada, the goal of protecting American lives was viewed as legitimate by a public that was demonstrating increasing resistance to interventionist exercises based on the more generalized ideological principle of fighting Communism.[54]

Although a definitive conclusion must await further evidence, there is good reason to believe that the Grenada invasion provided the critical analogy for key decision makers as they struggled with the case of Panama. Analogical thinking is known to play an important role in crisis decision making, and we can note the broad similarities between the two cases.[55] In both, the decision-making time frame concerning how to react to a hostile government was quite long, spanning two presidential administrations. The United States had overwhelming military superiority in both cases, so that the probability of dire adverse consequences resulting from military intervention was quite low. The military option was clearly available and feasible due to geographical proximity.

The Grenada analogy is also compelling as a potential source of influence because two of the central participants in the decision to use force against Panama (Bush and Cheney) had considerable experience with the Grenada operation. Bush chaired two sessions of the White House Special Situations Group, which, in President Reagan's absence, made a number of key recommendations concerning the goals to be pursued and the most appropriate methods for achieving them.[56] Cheney was involved with Grenada as a member of the House Intelligence Committee and as a participant in a fourteen-member postinvasion congressional delegation.[57]

Most likely, there was little discussion of Grenada during the high-level debate that took place in the White House on 17 December 1989 concerning what to do about Noriega. If the above-mentioned hypothesis concerning the influence of the Grenada analogy is correct, such discussion would not have taken place because key decision makers had deeply internalized the lessons they learned during the Reagan years. In the final analysis, the domestic fallout from an invasion of Panama would be positive as long as military victory came quickly, there was little loss of life, goals were stated in narrow pragmatic terms, and U.S. troops withdrew quickly.

Conclusion

The United States has intervened in the affairs of Latin American countries on numerous occasions since World War II, but there have been few instances when U.S. troops became directly engaged and none in the past sixty years involving unilateral U.S. military action. The fact that the Bush administration chose to use military force against the Noriega regime in December 1989 thus raises a number of interesting questions. How does one explain the fact that the military option was used at all? How does one explain its use during late 1989 rather than earlier?

As the Panama invasion fades from public view, it becomes easier to portray the decision to use direct military force as having resulted from a rational and calculated series of decisions during the Reagan and Bush years that were guided by the changing nature of the situation itself and by the progressive elimination of options to the use of force. According to such a view, the Reagan and Bush administrations first attempted to encourage Noriega to leave power by economic and diplomatic means, with the Bush team finally concluding in late 1989 that Noriega's removal required an invasion in order to simultaneously eliminate his power base in the military and establish a democratic government.

Upon closer scrutiny, this model of sequential decision making appears to obscure as much as it illuminates. By early 1988, the Reagan administration had developed a military option that paralleled its existing economic and diplomatic strategies. Explaining why the administration chose not to exercise this option during 1988, as well as why a decision to do so was reached late in 1989, requires looking beyond the exhaustion of options and the situation as it existed in late 1989 for explanations.

The dramatic changes in East-West relations, which closely paralleled the Panama crisis, certainly must have removed any lingering doubts among both Reagan and Bush administration decision makers concerning the favorable international context for military intervention. Feelings of confidence must have been heightened by the understanding that a new foreign policy consensus had been established concerning the limited use of force in well-defined situations. These factors operating at the international and domestic levels to boost confidence in a successful outcome in Panama were reinforced yet again by the fact that Bush himself and key members of his foreign policy team had personally experienced the success of the earlier Grenada operation.

At the same time, other factors operating at the domestic level and within the foreign policy decision-making process delayed actual implementation of the military invasion option until 1989.

Most important, the upcoming presidential elections forced the Reagan administration to put this option on the back burner. The fact that the military voice in decisions to use force had been increased by passage of the Goldwater-Nichols Act allowed Admiral Crowe as chairman of the Joint Chiefs to further ratify the appropriateness of this politically generated decision.

The U.S. decision-making process that led to the Panama invasion thus operated in fits and starts rather than in the form of a smooth sequential progression. This is largely explained by the variety of often conflicting and countervailing factors operating at the international, domestic, and decision-making levels. Because of these countervailing factors, the Reagan administration seemed to be pushing on the accelerator of policy and stepping on the brakes at the same time during 1988. Changes in these factors in 1989 allowed the Bush administration to reverse this process. As a result, a group of war-fighting commanders was installed during the summer who further specified and refined the military plans that had been developed in 1988. The broadened parameters of decision making that had been created by favorable changes in the international and domestic environments thus allowed the Bush decision-making team the widest possible latitude for choice and implementation of the military invasion option.

Notes

An earlier version of this chapter was given as a paper at the 1991 annual meeting of the American Political Science Association in Washington DC. I am indebted to Robert Pastor for his insightful comments on that earlier draft.

1. Alex Hybel has developed a convenient classification system for types of foreign intervention, including four basic subcategories for forms of military intervention. Alex Hybel, *How Leaders Reason: U.S. Intervention in the Caribbean Basin and Latin America* (Cambridge, Mass.: Basil Blackwell, 1990), pp. 37, 304.

2. See Steve C. Ropp, "Panama: The United States Invasion and Its Aftermath," *Current History* 90 (1991): 114; and Margaret E. Scranton, *The Noriega Years: U.S.-Panamanian Relations, 1981–1990* (Boulder, Colo.: Lynne Rienner, 1991), p. 3.

3. For a theory as to why this military regime endured, see my "Explaining the Long-Term Maintenance of a Military Regime: Panama before the U.S. Invasion," *World Politics* 44 (1992).

4. Useful general sources on the Noriega years and the pattern of deteriorating U.S.-Panamanian relations include Frederick Kempe, *Divorcing the Dictator* (New York: G. B. Putnam's Sons, 1990); John Dinges, *Our Man in Panama* (New York: Random House, 1990); R. M. Koster and Guillermo Sanchez, *In the Time of the Tyrants* (New York: W. W. Norton, 1990); and Kevin Buckley, *Panama: The Whole Story* (New York: Simon and Schuster, 1991). The best treatment of U.S.-Panamanian relations during the Noriega years from a theoretical and analytical standpoint is Scranton, *The Noriega Years.*

5. Kempe, *Divorcing the Dictator*, pp. 293–97.

6. Bob Woodward, *The Commanders*, (New York: Simon and Schuster, 1991), pp. 85–86.

7. *Christian Science Monitor*, 4 April 1988.

8. Gabriel Marcella and Gen. Frederick F. Woerner (retired), "The Road to War: The U.S.-Panamanian Crisis, 1987–1989," unpublished manuscript, 6 May 1991, p. 48; and Woodward, *The Commanders*, p. 99.

9. Other key members of this war-fighting team were Gen. Thomas Kelley, J-3 Operations of the Joint Staff, and Gen. Carl W. Stiner, commander of the Joint Task Force. This new group of military commanders was disparagingly referred to within the Pentagon as the "Neanderthals" by those opposed to the use of force in Panama. They were believed to be, by training and inclination, too quick to use force and adhering to old negative stereotypes about Latin Americans. Privileged interview, 6 November 1989, Washington DC.

10. Woodward, *The Commanders*, pp. 133–39, 141.

11. Michael Brecher, Blema Steinberg, and Janice Stein, "A Framework for Research on Foreign Policy Behavior," *Journal of Conflict Resolution* 13 (1969).

12. For a good general overview of these different perspectives, see Maurice A. East, Stephen A. Salmore, and Charles F. Hermann, eds., *Why Nations Act: Theoretical Perspectives for Comparative Foreign Policy Studies* (Beverly Hills, Calif.: 1978). Scranton also uses these three levels of analysis to examine the broader pattern of U.S. policy responses to Panama from 1981 to 1990. Scranton, *The Noriega Years.*

13. See James N. Rosenau, *Turbulence in World Politics: A Theory of Continuity and Change* (Princeton, N.J.: Princeton University Press, 1990); and Kenneth A. Oye, "Beyond Postwar Order and New World Order: American Foreign Policy in Transition," in Kenneth A. Oye, Robert J. Lieber, and Donald Rothchild, eds., *Eagle in a New World: American Grand Strategy in the Post-Cold War Era* (New York: HarperCollins, 1992), pp. 18–21.

14. Charles W. Ostrom and Brian Job, "The President and the Political Use of Force," *American Political Science Review* 80 (June 1986): 546.

15. Jorge Dominguez, "La política de la administración Bush hacia Amér-

ica Latina," Center for the Study of the United States, National Autonomous University of Mexico (UNAM), forthcoming.

16. Such situations included Guatemala (1954), Cuba (1961), the Dominican Republic (1965), Chile (1973), Grenada (1983), Nicaragua (1983–89), and El Salvador (1981–91).

17. Dominguez, "La política," p. 2. Further discussion about the end of the Cold War and unilateral-multilateral policies can be found in Abraham F. Lowenthal, "U.S. Policy in Latin America," in Robert J. Art and Seyom Brown, eds., *U.S. Foreign Policy: The Search for a New Role* (New York: Macmillan, 1993), p. 359.

18. The VII Armour Corps was a central and critical component in NATO's plans to defend Europe. Gen. Norman Schwarzkopf requested that it be released for use against Iraq's forces in Kuwait in October 1990, when it became clear that President Bush wanted to go on the offensive. Such a request would have been unthinkable before the collapse of the Warsaw Pact. Woodward, *The Commanders*, pp. 309–10.

19. Marcella and Woerner, "The Road to War," p. 52. For further analysis of system-level factors relating to U.S. security interests in the region, see Scranton, *The Noriega Years*.

20. The guerrilla offensive in El Salvador did begin several weeks after the failed coup in Panama, but the FMLN appears to have spent several months planning for it. The timing of the offensive was more closely tied to the end of this planning phase and to right-wing attacks in October on labor union leaders. Jose Z. Garcia, "Tragedy in El Salvador," *Current History* 89 (January 1990): 12.

21. The reason for devoting considerable attention to the domestic environment is that much of the recent theoretical literature suggests that domestic factors may be more important than international ones with regard to presidential decisions to use force. See Ostrom and Job, "The President"; and Patrick James and John R. O'Neal, "The Influence of Domestic and International Politics on the President's Use of Force," *Journal of Conflict Resolution* 35 (June 1991): 307.

22. Eugene R. Wittkopf, *Faces of Internationalism: Public Opinion and American Foreign Policy* (Durham: Duke University Press, 1990), p. 191.

23. Ibid., p. 182. It has also been convincingly argued that the Vietnam War put an end to the broad bipartisan consensus existing in Congress. According to Wittkopf, who used a wide variety of foreign policy issues to measure bipartisanship, "the Congress Index peaked at 75 percent in the 80th Congress (1947–48), and it reached a low point in the 96th (1977–78) Congress, when President Carter received bipartisan support just over one-quarter of the time." Ibid., p. 199.

24. Ibid., p. 229.

25. Ibid., p. 200.

26. Richard Melanson argues that foreign policy consensus needed to be reestablished at three distinct levels. There was need for a new *policy consensus* built around some grand strategic design. There was also need for a *cultural consensus* concerning the values that the United States should project abroad. Finally, a new *procedural consensus* had to be established, allowing Congress to work effectively with the Executive Branch. Richard A. Melanson, *Reconstructing Consensus: American Foreign Policy since the Vietnam War* (New York: St. Martin's Press, 1991), p. 3.

27. Ibid., p. 190.

28. The data came from twelve public opinion surveys of the Americans Talk Security Project taken during the 1987–88 presidential campaign. Data are summarized in Wittkopf, *Faces of Internationalism*, pp. 222–37.

29. Woodward, *The Commanders*, p. 81. Jorge Dominguez has gone even further to suggest that *all* the major Latin American initiatives of the Bush administration were rooted in political logic and in the administration's reading of various domestic imperatives. He cites U.S. policy on Nicaragua, Latin American debt, and drug trafficking as examples of this linkage and suggests that the Panama invasion resulted from the administration's need to address domestic political concerns about leadership style. Dominguez, "La política," pp. 4–7.

30. Kempe, *Divorcing the Dictator*, p. 336.

31. Ibid., pp. 336–37.

32. Ibid., p. 333. James Baker, Bush's campaign manager, is reputed to have remarked following the election that "if we had known we would win the election by so much . . . we would not have dug ourselves so deep a hole [with Noriega]." Quoted in Woodward, *The Commanders*, p. 86.

33. There have been surprisingly few studies of the impact that elections and electoral cycles have on decisions to use military force. However, one such study suggests that democratically elected governments are statistically more likely to wage war soon after an election than they are immediately prior to one. Kurt Taylor Gaubatz, "Election Cycles and War," *Journal of Conflict Resolution* 35 (June 1991): 212.

34. Charles W. Kegley Jr., "Decision Regimes and the Comparative Study of Foreign Policy," in Charles F. Hermann, Charles W. Kegley Jr., and James N. Rosenau, eds., *New Directions in the Study of Foreign Policy* (Boston: Allen and Unwin, 1987), p. 248.

35. See, for example, Scranton, *The Noriega Years*, pp. 45–47.

36. During this phase, the policy-making process was further complicated by the fact that some of the most important players were private parties or individuals with quasi-official status. The strategy of denying economic resources to the Noriega regime by freezing Panamanian assets in the United States was designed and implemented in March 1988 by the Washington law

firm of Arnold and Porter. And, as noted above, critical policy recommendations were made in May and June by Bush's campaign managers.

37. Kempe, *Divorcing the Dictator*, p. 293.

38. Richard Betts classifies previous chairmen of the JCS as falling into three categories according to the criteria used for presidential selection: routine-professional, professional-political, and exceptional-political. Because of his close ties to the administration, Powell clearly fits in the exceptional-political category. Richard K. Betts, *Soldiers, Statesmen, and Cold War Crises* (Cambridge: Harvard University Press, 1977), pp. 58–67.

39. Kempe, *Divorcing the Dictator*, p. 347.

40. In his careful study of military advice and the use of force since World War II, Richard Betts finds that "the only cases in which military recommendations on the use of force were considered irresistible were the instances in which they opposed intervention." Betts, *Soldiers*, p. 6.

41. In this regard, the balance of bureaucratic forces was very similar to that existing on issues related to the Philippines.

42. *New York Times*, 24 December 1989; and Woodward, *The Commanders*, pp. 167–71. Noticeably absent from this meeting was Director of the CIA William H. Webster.

43. For an excellent study of various types of decision-making units, see Margaret C. Herman, "Foreign Policy Role Orientations and the Quality of Foreign Policy Decisions," in Stephen G. Walker, ed., *Role Theory and Foreign Policy Analysis* (Durham, N.C.: Duke University Press, 1987).

44. Ibid., p. 130.

45. Ibid.

46. Woodward, *The Commanders*, pp. 62–63.

47. Hermann, "Foreign Policy Role Orientations," p. 130.

48. Charles A. Powell, Helen E. Perkitt, and James W. Dyson, "Opening the Black Box: Cognitive Processing and Optimal Choice in Foreign Policy Decision Making," in Hermann, Kegley, and Rosenau, eds., *New Directions*, p. 212.

49. James Barber, "George Bush in Search of a Mission," *New York Times*, 19 January 1989, p. A31. See also Charles W. Kegley Jr., "The Bush Administration and the Future of American Foreign Policy: Pragmatism or Procrastination?" *Presidential Studies Quarterly* 19 (fall 1989): 723–24.

50. *The Nation*, 21 January 1991, p. 41.

51. Woodward, *The Commanders*, pp. 50–51.

52. Ibid., p. 67.

53. *Human Events*, 14 October 1989, p. 3. For further discussion of Bush's personal motivations, see Robert Pastor, *Whirlpool: U.S. Foreign Policy toward Latin American and the Caribbean* (Princeton, N.J.: Princeton University Press, 1992), p. 93.

54. Kai P. Schoenhals and Richard A. Melanson, eds., *Revolution and In-*

tervention in Grenada: The New Jewel Movement, the United States, and the Caribbean (Boulder, Colo.: Westview, 1985), pp. 168–69.

55. Dwain Meffort, "Analogical Reasoning and the Definition of the Situation: Back to Snyder for Concepts and Forward to Artificial Intelligence for Method," in Hermann, Kegley, and Rosenau, eds., *New Directions*, pp. 221–44.

56. In Bush's own words, "As chairman of the White House Special Situations Group, I helped coordinate plans to send American forces to Grenada after neighboring Caribbean countries called on the United States to prevent a Castro-inspired Marxist takeover of the island." George Bush, *Looking Forward* (New York: Doubleday, 1987), fn. p. 243; see also Maj. Mark Adkin, *Urgent Fury: The Battle for Grenada* (Lexington, Mass.: Lexington Books, 1989), pp. 118, 120.

57. Participation in the congressional delegation to Grenada appears to have been a formative experience for Cheney in terms of orienting him more toward international affairs. Although long destined to play a prominent future role in national politics, his goals prior to 1983 related more to leadership within the House of Representatives or possibly a cabinet position such as secretary of the interior. Cheney claims to have learned a number of valuable lessons from the Grenada invasion that probably had an impact on his thinking about Panama. The international image of the United States would be bolstered when we demonstrated a willingness to support our allies through the use of military force. We would be welcomed with open arms by the local population following such an invasion, and the global spread of Communism would be stopped. *Casper Star Tribune*, 6 November 1983.

Part Two

Bilateral Relations

George W. Grayson

U.S.-Mexican Relations:
The Challenge of NAFTA

Mexico's president Carlos Salinas de Gortari shattered one taboo after another upon taking office on 1 December 1988. He ousted "untouchable" labor barons, slashed tax rates and threw tax cheats behind bars, reprivatized the banking system, and sold the state-owned airlines, telephone company, and steel mills. He also launched a reform of once-sacrosanct communal farms known as *ejidos*, invited a Texas oil firm with an all-foreign crew to drill in Campeche Sound, reorganized Petróleos Mexicanos (Pemex), the state oil monopoly, and normalized relations with the Roman Catholic Church, long reviled as part of the exploitative, prerevolutionary social order by intellectuals, union leaders, leftist politicians, and activists in his own Institutional Revolutionary party (Partido Revolucionario Institucional—PRI).

In contrast to Mikhail Gorbachev, who simultaneously promoted *glasnost* and *perestroika*, Salinas stressed economic liberalization over a political opening to avoid generating demands that could not be satisfied before robust, sustained growth was achieved. Nonetheless, he recognized the victories of opposition gubernatorial candidates over his own party's standard-bearers for the first time in sixty years. He also called for new elections in Guanajuato and San Luis Potosí states when losing nominees of the center-right National Action party (Partido de Acción Nacional—PAN) alleged fraud in August 1991. Later, he accepted the "resignation" of the newly inaugurated PRI governor of Michoacán when the nationalist-leftist Democratic Revolutionary party (Partido de la Revolución Democrática—PRD) staged aggressive demonstrations to protest his mid-1992 victory. In addition, Mexico's *jefe máximo* diminished the influence of the corporatist labor and peasant sectors as part of a reform of his own Tammany Hall–style PRI. And he lavished billions of dollars on a National Solidarity Program (Programa Nacional de Solidaridad—PRONASOL) designed to involve peasants and shanty-town dwellers in development projects that they, not self-serving party bosses, identified as crucial to their communities.

The most notable innovation of Salinas's administration, how-ever, involved a new relationship with the United States. The cen-terpiece of this relationship was the North American Free Trade Agreement (NAFTA), designed to spur the integration of Mexico's economy with those of the United States and Canada. Inherent in Mexico's diplomatic demarche was the chief executive's belief that continental interdependence would advance Mexico's national in-terests. Unlike many largely symbolic programs proclaimed by his predecessors (the New International Economic Order, the Charter of Economic Rights and Duties of States, the World Energy Plan, and the International Meeting for Cooperation and Development, for ex-ample), Salinas's commitment to economic liberalization repre-sented real, not rhetorical change.[1] This chapter (1) discusses the president's decision to pursue a free trade accord, (2) describes the proponents and opponents of NAFTA, (3) analyzes the transforma-tion of Mexico's lobbying efforts to generate support for the pact in the United States, (4) reviews the scope and rhythm of negotiations and NAFTA's key provisions, (5) evaluates the consequences of a con-tinental trade pact on bilateral affairs, and (6) examines the prospects for U.S.-Mexican relations in light of economic integration.

Salinas in Office

Salinas, as planning and budget secretary in the administration of President Miguel de la Madrid Hurtado (1982–88), spearheaded the dismantling of an import-substitution industrialization model. That development policy had impelled the country's "economic miracle" of the post–World War II period. Yet by the mid-1970s the spry, eager infant industries of the previous generation had grown fat, lethargic, inefficient, and whiny. Sheltered by import permits and formidable tariffs, many of these firms produced expensive goods of inferior quality that were uncompetitive in foreign markets. Worse still, im-port substitution spawned a huge bureaucracy renowned for feather-bedding, incompetence, delays, and surly officials who demanded under-the-table payments called *mordidas*.

De la Madrid and Salinas realized that Mexico had to break out of its protectionist cocoon to boost labor productivity, activate the domestic business community, promote exports, stimulate investment, obtain foreign loans, and attract state-of-the-art technology. As a first step toward integrating his nation into the international economic system, de la Madrid signed a Bilateral Subsidies Understanding with the United States in 1985. This accord stipulated that his country would phase out export financing within two years in return for receiving an injury test in countervailing duty litigation. To build on this important foundation, the two nations entered into a Bilateral Trade and Investment Framework Agreement in November 1987. Although appearing more symbolic than substantive, this pact created a consultative mechanism for resolving disputes in two often nettlesome areas. Two years later, the United States and Mexico reached a second trade and investment understanding that relied on the work begun under the earlier bilateral arrangement. In 1986, moreover, de la Madrid and Salinas championed their country's membership in the General Agreement on Tariffs and Trade (GATT), a move rejected by de la Madrid's predecessor as economically imprudent and a surrender of national sovereignty. In June of that year, Mexico also dropped the threat of joining a debtors' cartel to confront the United States over Mexico's $100 billion plus debt owed to private and public lenders. This action proved a critical turning point in bilateral relations.[2]

As chief executive, Salinas removed trade barriers and permitted imports to surge as part of a strategy to force internal corporations to compete with their foreign counterparts. "Our first challenge was privatizing the private sector," stated the country's finance secretary.[3] In the process, Mexico lowered its top tariffs from 100 percent to 20 percent and eliminated licensing requirements for 95 percent of the nation's goods purchased abroad. In the six years after joining GATT, Mexico achieved as much trade liberalization as the United States had attained in forty years after reaching its protectionist zenith in 1930.[4]

Even though the youthful president presented no blueprint for linking his country with the global economy, his enthusiasm for market principles and readiness to pay interest on his nation's mammoth international debt earned for Mexico the distinction of becoming the first beneficiary of the Brady Plan for reducing Latin America's commercial bank loans. This marked the first time since the debt crisis erupted in the early 1980s that the United States had backed relief for hugely overborrowed countries.[5]

Lest it chill ever warmer economic and diplomatic relations with its neighbor, Mexico's condemnation of the December 1989 U.S. invasion of Panama was one of the mildest in the region, even though the incident contravened Mexico's cherished principles of nonintervention, peaceful dispute settlement, and respect for sovereignty. As fervently as he desired a trade accord, Salinas could not refrain from excoriating the kidnapping from Guadalajara and trial in California of Dr. Humberto Alvarez Machain, who allegedly participated in the torture and murder of an agent of the U.S. Drug Enforcement Administration. For his part, President George Bush, who developed a close rapport with Salinas, also made a concerted effort to accentuate economic positives while downplaying political negatives. Thus, he handled discreetly such highly sensitive issues as drug trafficking, human rights violations, and electoral chicanery, the public condemnation of which had embittered U.S.-Mexican relations during the Reagan era.

Salinas's bold attempt to integrate Mexico's economy with that of the United States began in earnest after he failed to broaden Mexico's commercial and financial ties with Japan and Western Europe. In early 1990, Salinas spent ten days in Western Europe, where he met with the leaders of Great Britain, West Germany, Belgium, Switzerland, and Portugal. Although then–prime minister Margaret Thatcher encouraged him, the other hosts conveyed a disheartening message: "We admire your market-oriented strategy to open and modernize Mexico's hidebound economy, but Eastern Europe will be the target of our capital investment, finance, and commercial activities."

This polite rebuff reinforced Salinas's belief that Mexico must work with a dynamic partner to avoid becoming a stagnant backwater as trading blocs emerged in Western Europe, in the Pacific Rim, and between the United States and Canada, who entered into a free trade agreement (CFTA) in 1988. The United States was an obvious choice. Location, tradition, and multiple economic ties pointed Salinas northward. The bonds between Mexico and the United States were already impressive, as evidenced by the 1989 flow of exports ($25 billion), investment ($5.5 billion), and traveler expenditures ($5.7 billion) from the United States to its southern neighbor.[6] For their part, Mexican consumers purchased goods and services valued at $27.2 billion, making Mexico the third largest export market for the United States in 1989.[7] Some two thousand *maquiladoras*, or border assembly plants, employing half a million Mexicans fortified the bilateral linkage, as did the growing interrelationship between the New York and Mexico City stock exchanges. Other signs of mounting U.S.-Mexican interdependence included increasing migration, tourism, telephone calls, telegraph messages, and media contacts, items discussed later in the chapter. In addition, Pemex had furnished 43.5 percent of the almost 600 million barrels of oil stored in the U.S. Strategic Petroleum Reserve. Meanwhile, Pemex and private Mexican firms purchased upwards of $100 million worth of oil equipment and services from U.S. suppliers in 1989.

In early 1990 Salinas endorsed a free trade agreement with the United States. Just a few years earlier, this issue had been a political third rail in Mexico. Even publicly favoring such a scheme would have terminated the career of most politicians in this defensively nationalistic nation where the "colossus of the north" is frequently blamed for real and imagined evils afflicting Mexico. An example of this defensiveness occurred in mid-1980, when Mexican officials and newspapers had a field day accusing Washington of stealing rain by diverting hurricanes from Mexico's shores. The villain was the U.S. National Oceanographic and Atmospheric Administration, whose hurricane-hunter aircraft had supposedly intercepted a storm named Ignacio off Mexico's Pacific coast in October 1979, thereby contributing to the country's worst drought in twenty years. Mexican observers, including the director of the National Meteorological Service, apparently believed that Yankee ingenuity was so great that Uncle Sam could bend Mother Nature to his indomitable will.[8]

Reactive nationalism aside, Salinas committed himself to economic integration. Mexico's highly centralized political system, buttressed by ubiquitous official influence in the media, guaranteed broad acceptance of the presidential initiative. Taking their cue from the Los Pinos presidential palace, most PRI leaders applauded a free trade pact; the sixty-four-member Mexican Senate overwhelmingly embraced the proposal; many editorial writers wrote glowingly of the venture; and major business associations backed an accord. Even the Confederation of Mexican Workers (Confederación de Trabajadores Mexicanos—CTM), the 5.5-million-member trade union federation that forms part of the PRI's corporatist structure, threw its weight behind a bilateral economic agreement.[9]

On 21 September 1990 Salinas officially told President George Bush that he wanted to begin talks on NAFTA. Subsequently, Bush, who had praised the concept two years earlier, asked Congress to grant the administration "fast-track" authority to commence negotiations. Such authority would immunize any accord hammered out by U.S. and Mexican negotiators from legislative changes. The two houses of Congress would either accept or reject the proposal as a package after its negotiation, without the barrage of amendments that often delay and cripple controversial legislation. To facilitate harmonious bargaining, Mexico City removed migration from its negotiating list, while Washington agreed to refrain from pressuring Mexico to modify Article 27 of its constitution that reserves to the state petroleum ownership, exploration, and refining.

Friends and Foes of NAFTA

Opponents to fast-track quickly emerged on both sides of the Rio Grande. In Mexico a collection of intellectuals, journalists, ecologists, union activists, and leader of the PRD and other leftist parties formed the Mexican Action Network on Free Trade (Red Mexicana de Acción Frente al Libre Comercio—RMALC).[10] This group argued that a trade agreement would bankrupt less efficient firms, exacerbate unemployment in a nation where 1 million young people enter the workforce each year, exacerbate pollution, and compromise the nation's highly prized independence. Sergio Aguayo Quezada, a professor at the Colegio de México and a human rights activist, warned the United States might pressure Mexico to forge a military alliance, modify its nationalistic petroleum policy, and alter its treatment of foreign investment.[11]

The presence of pro-NAFTA legislatures in their own countries prompted Mexican and Canadian critics of the pact to take their case to the United States, whose Congress seemed more persuadable. RMALC spokesmen faced a Mexican Senate composed overwhelmingly of *priistas*. Thus, through speeches, news conferences, and participation in public forums, they tried to convince U.S. decision makers that the accord would exacerbate poverty, civil rights abuses, environmental degradation, and political corruption in Mexico. Canadian opponents to the agreement, many of whom belonged to the Canadian Action Network and the Canadian Labour Congress, also made their case in the United States because of the majority of seats held by then–prime minister M. Brian Mulroney's pro-NAFTA Progressive Conservative party in their country's parliament. They insisted that the CFTA had wiped out some 500,000 manufacturing jobs in Canada—a contention vigorously rejected by both the Mulroney and Bush administrations.[12]

In the United States, a plethora of groups railed against NAFTA. The most politically potent was the American Federation of Labor–Congress of Industrial Organizations (AFL-CIO) and several of its constituent unions with large memberships in the Midwest, Northeast, or border states—specifically, the United Auto Workers, the International Ladies Garment Workers Union, the International Brotherhood of Electrical Workers, the International Union of Electrical Workers, and the American Federation of State, County and Municipal Employees. The AFL-CIO made opposition to fast-track and a ban on employers hiring permanent replacements for strikers its top legislative priorities in the early 1990s. One especially virulent union newspaper advertisement warned that approval of fast-track would worsen diseases arising from polluted water and food in border towns because of the dearth of sewage treatment and other health precautions.[13] Equally harsh was labor's criticism of corruption and lax work standards arising from the Confederation of Mexican Workers' coziness with the government. "[CTM Secretary-General] Fidel Velázquez is the Al Capone of Mexico's labor relations," averred the spokesman for one U.S. worker rights group.[14] Above all, unions argued that a free trade agreement would spur the relocation of U.S. factories to Mexico to take advantage of sweatshop conditions, depress wages north of the Rio Grande, and spark unfair competition with domestic producers of footwear, textiles, autos, and electronic goods.

The AFL-CIO found itself in the unusual position of being on the same side of an issue as a majority of environmental groups with whom it often crossed swords, including the Sierra Club, Friends of the Earth, and Greenpeace. Labor and environmental organizations frequently joined religious, consumer, agricultural, and human rights groups in one of three anti-NAFTA coalitions: the fifty-member Mobilization on Development, Trade, Labor and the Environment (MODTLE) that spearheaded cooperation with Mexican and Canadian foes of the trade pact; the Ralph Nader–inspired Citizen

Trade Watch; and the San Francisco–based Fair Trade Coalition. In addition to espousing "bread and butter" issues articulated by trade unions, these coalitions condemned the fast-track process as undemocratic, claimed it would vitiate the Clean Air Act, the Clean Water Act, and other environmental legislation, insisted it would devastate Mexico's natural resources, and decried torture, electoral fraud, and human rights abuses in Mexico.[15] Critics of fast-track took advantage of a prolonged recession and high unemployment, NAFTA foe Harris Wofford's victory in a Pennsylvania U.S. Senate race, and the Bush administration's preoccupation with Operation Desert Storm/Desert Shield to press their case with Congress. At the same time that UN forces were routing Saddam Hussein, the anti-fast-track coalition attempted to vanquish NAFTA through lobbying on Capitol Hill.

Nearly two months after Iraq's defeat, President Bush began his counterattack. In this battle, he enjoyed enthusiastic backing from the Coalition for Trade Expansion (later to become USA*NAFTA Inc.), which constituted a veritable Who's Who of major business interests.[16] The chief executive and his business allies argued that, since 1986, U.S. exports to Mexico had doubled to $28.4 billion, creating 315,000 export-related jobs in the United States, and that NAFTA would generate 113,000 new trade-focused jobs in Texas alone.[17] "If Americans are honestly concerned about the environment, the standard of living in Mexico and about democratization," contended a leading academic proponent, "they cannot escape the recognition that a thriving, open market economy will raise living standards, foster individual freedom, decentralize political power and allow people to organize around local issues."[18]

Fearful of losing fast-track authorization, Bush announced bilateral discussions keyed to the concerns of labor and environmental groups. These talks produced a memorandum of understanding on worker health and safety signed by U.S. Labor Secretary Lynn Martin and her Mexican counterpart. This document provided for the exchange of information on worker health and safety, working conditions, labor standards enforcement, resolution of labor-management disputes, collective bargaining agreements, social security, credit institutions, labor statistics, labor quality, and productivity. NAFTA would make it possible "to move earnestly with our neighbors to the south to address child labor and safety and health concerns and improve the lives of our working men and women," Secretary Martin said.[19] Furthermore, in a 1 May 1991 "action plan," the president assured Congress of his commitment to strict health and safety standards for agricultural imports to prevent Mexican products that do not meet U.S. health or safety requirements from entering the United States; transition periods of more than ten years for reducing U.S. tariffs in certain sectors and industries; worker adjustment programs for workers who may lose their jobs as a result of an agreement with Mexico; and exclusion of labor mobility and immigration laws from the negotiations.

At the direction of Bush and Salinas, environmental authorities in both countries crafted an Integrated Environmental Plan for the Border. Following seventeen public hearings, the United States ($384 million in 1992–93) and Mexico ($460 million in 1992–94) pledged substantial resources to implement the 1992 to 1994 phase of this program. The highest priority was wastewater treatment projects for twin cities along the border (San Diego/Tijuana, Imperial Valley/Mexicali, Nogales/Nogales, and Laredo/Nuevo Laredo). Monies were also promised for enforcement, environmental health, emergency planning and response, and the monitoring and mitigation of transboundary air pollution.[20] This initiative was designed to blunt the charge that Mexico would be a "pollution haven" for unscrupulous foreign firms if NAFTA were approved. In March 1991 Salinas emphatically raised his profile on the ecology by closing the aged, sulfur-belching Azcapotzalco oil refinery in Mexico City, which employed five thousand workers. Between 1989 and 1991, the environmental and natural resources budget for Mexico's Ministry of Ecology and Urban Development (Secretaría de Desarrollo Urbano y Ecología—SEDUE) shot up from $6 million to $36 million, and the agency closed twenty-eight border businesses for environmental infractions in 1991.[21]

The Bush and Salinas administrations' attentiveness to ecological issues helped to split the labor-environmental axis aligned against free trade negotiations. With the promise that environmental organizations would be represented on panels advising U.S. Trade Representative Carla A. Hills, the National Wildlife Federation (NWF) expressed support for fast-track. The organization's president, Jay D. Hair, stated in a *New York Times* column: "While Mr. Bush's position is not all that many environmentalists might want, the ideal should not be the enemy of the good. His word is his marker. The job ahead is to forge environmentally sound free-trade agreements, beginning with Mexico. We should not obstruct a path that can lead to significant international benefits."[22]

Enhancing the prospect for obtaining fast-track authorization was the resolute backing that NAFTA enjoyed from key U.S. policy makers, many of whom were Texans. In addition to President Bush, Secretary of State James A. Baker, commerce secretary Robert A. Mosbacher, Senate Finance Committee chairman Lloyd Bentsen, Senator Phil Gramm, and Representative Bill Archer, ranking minority member of the House Ways and Means Committee, knew first-hand of Mexico's crucial importance to the United States. House Speaker Thomas S. Foley, House Majority Leader Richard A. Gephardt, and Ways and Means Committee chairman Dan Rostenkowski also cast their lot with fast-track proponents, although Gephardt reserved judgment on the final agreement.

Ultimately, the president succeeded in elevating fast-track approval to a referendum on protectionism. "Having already opposed Bush on the use of force in Iraq, many Democrats fear[ed] a vote that would be portrayed as economic isolationism."[23] In mid-May 1991, the House and Senate voted overwhelmingly to defeat House and Senate resolutions to reject fast-track authority.[24] These votes followed strong endorsements for fast-track by the House Ways and Means Committee (27 to 9) and the Senate Finance Committee (15 to 3)—bodies that have principal jurisdiction over trade legislation.

Once the fast-track prerogative was secure, negotiations began in mid-1991, with completion anticipated within a year. The struggle over fast-track had strengthened the bonds between Hills and her Mexican counterpart, Jaime Serra Puche, head of the Ministry of Commerce and Industrial Development (Secretaría de Comercio y Fomento Industrial—SECOFI). The process was complicated only slightly by Canada's formal request, in late 1990, for inclusion in an accord that would create the world's largest free trade zone, stretching from the Yukon to Yucatán, composed of 360 million consumers who produce more than $6.2 trillion in goods and services. In response to fears from its negotiating partners that Canada might impede the deliberations, Ottawa pledged that it would excuse itself from the talks if it proved an obstacle to concluding a free trade accord. Canadian participation did assuage some Mexican fears that their country—with one-twentieth the gross domestic product of the United States—would be overwhelmed if it entered the proposed trade configuration alone with an economic giant.

NAFTA Negotiations

Once the U.S. Congress granted the Bush administration fast-track authority, formal negotiations began on 12 June 1991. These talks focused on six issue categories that were negotiated in nineteen working groups: (1) market access that covers topics such as tariffs, rules of origin, and government procurement; (2) trade rules; (3) services; (4) investment; (5) intellectual property rights; and (6) dispute settlement. The U.S. government assigned several officials to each working group; the Canadians assigned at least one; and the Mexicans, with markedly fewer personnel, generally assigned one official to cover several groups. Seven private sector advisory groups provided a bridge between the negotiators and the U.S. business community. Another advisory group linked organized labor to the negotiators.

The first four months of negotiations concentrated on determining the scope of the agreement and exchanging detailed information on each nation's impediments to the free flow of trade, services, and investment. On the average, each working group met once a month for one to three days. On 19 September 1991, the three countries exchanged tariff offers. Five weeks later, Ambassador Hills met with her Mexican and Canadian counterparts, Commerce Secretary Serra Puche and Trade Minister Michael Wilson, in Zacatecas, Mexico, to review the progress of the working groups. For most working groups, this 25–28 October Third Trilateral Ministerial Oversight session marked the completion of the fact-finding stage of the NAFTA talks.

The negotiations then entered the second stage, during which representatives to most working groups crystallized their positions in concept papers and exchanged them with each other. In early January 1992, ten "compositors" from the three countries met at Georgetown University in Washington to organize the material from the working groups in a consistent manner, ensure that key words employed in the different drafts conveyed the same meaning, and combine the papers with a view to narrowing the differences among them. Finally, the drafters crafted chapters that conveyed the consensus of the negotiators, with key unresolved issues highlighted in brackets. In several working groups, bracketed areas consumed more space than points of agreement. Groups responsible for five controversial subjects (agriculture, energy, textiles, automobiles, and antidumping rules) failed to produce even bracketed chapters.

The bracket reduction stage started in early 1992. U.S. negotiators pressed hard for across-the-board concessions, including such sensitive areas as energy, investment, and government procurement. Three factors accounted for their assertiveness: the greater importance of NAFTA to the relatively underdeveloped Mexico, where it commanded twice the support found in the United States;[25] the fact that Mexico's tariffs were, on average (10 percent), at least twice as high as those of the United States (4 percent) and Canada (5 percent); and the possibility that Congress might reject any pact that failed to contain conspicuous benefits for the United States. Lending credence to the last point was Representative Gephardt's mordant observation that the U.S. trade representative was keeping the public "in the dark" about the negotiations. "This secret process, I believe, could seriously undermine the ability of Congress to affirm an agreement at the end of the day," he told Ambassador Hills.[26] In view of the continual briefings provided by USTR staff and working group members to representatives and their aides, Gephardt's conclusion appeared unfounded. Later, Chairman Rostenkowski contradicted this charge when he praised USTR for its "relentless" efforts to keep Congress informed.

The chief negotiators made a crucial breakthrough at a 17–22 February 1992 session in Dallas called a "jamboree" because all working groups were present. At that meeting, the Mexicans finally realized that one-for-one trade-offs were unacceptable to the United States and Canada. Mexico, as the most protectionist of the three countries, would have to give more than it received if an agreement were to be achieved. Within six weeks, notable progress had been made on such questions as intellectual property, textiles, standards, sanitary practices, customs administration, financial services, other services, banking, and surface transportation. In July the endgame commenced as negotiators, chief negotiators, Hills, Serra Puche, and Wilson held marathon sessions in Washington's Watergate Hotel devoting even more than the customary 90 percent of their time at this point to the most controversial subjects. During the endgame, working groups met more often and for longer periods. They also referred an increasing number of politically sensitive items to superiors—at times, even to chiefs of state—for resolution. Ultimately, deals were struck in such contentious areas as agriculture, automobiles, energy, government procurement, and rules of origin. These accommodations permitted Bush to announce completion of a NAFTA accord at an early morning ceremony held in the White

House's Rose Garden on 12 August just before the Republican party opened its national convention in Houston. Five weeks later, on 18 September the White House notified Congress that Bush intended to sign the pact in ninety days. Presumably, only minor changes would be made to the text during that period. The private sector and labor advisory groups were also given an opportunity, as required by the U.S. Trade Act, to review the text and submit reports. Then, on 7 October, candidate Bush invited the trade ministers of the three countries to gather in San Antonio to initial the agreement with the chief executives serving as witnesses.

Reelection politics rather than the conclusion of negotiations inspired Bush's 12 August and 7 October actions. In several controversial areas, negotiators remained at the bargaining table after the president had announced the completion of the talks. Indeed, the early August text only embraced the essence of what the country teams had agreed to, often condensed into several pages. It remained for the working groups and their legal advisers to flesh out the language into full-blown chapters—and, in some cases, agree upon common definitions on crucial concepts. The country representatives continued to wrestle over substantive matters, although the public was told they were engaged in mere fine-tuning or "legal scrubbing." As one participant expressed it, the "devil was in the detail." Among the issues resolved were devising formulas for phasing out Mexican restrictions on auto imports, clarifying the breadth of the government procurement coverage, and reaffirming the inclusion of services in the energy chapter. With respect to the latter, the Mexicans apparently sought to renege on services they had originally agreed to include in the pact.

NAFTA's Key Provisions

Key provisions of the two-thousand-page accord include the following.

Agriculture

In recent years, Mexico has imposed import permits on one-quarter of U.S. agricultural goods entering its country, as well as tariffs—ranging from 15 to 20 percent—on vegetable oils, processed meats, tree nuts, and other commodities. NAFTA converts nontariff barriers to tariffs ("tariffication") and phases out, over fifteen years, these levies on orange juice, melons, certain vegetables, and other sensitive items.

Automobiles

Mexico has applied tariffs of up to 20 percent and nontariff barriers to virtually prohibit imports of parts and assembled vehicles into the world's fastest growing auto market. NAFTA would immediately halve Mexican tariffs and eliminate them over five years for light trucks and over ten years for cars. It further stipulates that these vehicles must contain at least half North American content—rising to 62.5 percent over eight years—to qualify for duty-free treatment.

Dispute Resolution

The pact employs a three-tiered mechanism for resolving disputes: consultation, a trade commission composed of the top trade official from each country, and, if necessary, a decision made by a panel of trade experts.

Energy

NAFTA opens all but eight petrochemicals in Mexico to foreign investment, permitting private electricity production, authorizing direct sales of natural gas between U.S. and Canadian suppliers and Mexican customers, and allowing Pemex to pay "performance" bonuses to successful oil exploration firms while still barring foreign ownership of oil reserves. An important breakthrough lies in greater opportunities for U.S. and Canadian companies to boost sales to Pemex and the Federal Electricity Commission, which have followed a "buy-Mexico" policy. After nine years, these two monopolies, which buy more than $8 billion worth of goods and services annually, must permit open bidding by all North American suppliers.

Financial Services

NAFTA opens Mexico's $330 billion financial services market, which has, with one exception, been closed for more than fifty years to foreign firms. The agreement removes by 1 January 2000 virtually all limitations on U.S. and Canadian banks, financial service providers, and insurance companies that want to establish subsidiaries in Mexico, with limits on aggregate and individual market shares during the transition.

Intellectual Property

The pact ensures a higher standard of protection for patents, copyrights, trademarks, and trade secrets than any other bilateral or international accord. The three signatories must provide rigorous protection of intellectual property rights based on national treatment. They are committed to enforce rights effectively against infringement, both domestically and at the border. As in the CFTA, Canada has retained its "cultural exemption" to free trade in films, recordings, books, and other cultural industries.

Investment

NAFTA grants national treatment to North American firms in any of the three signatory nations. Should a host country breach the agreement's investment rules, a NAFTA investor—at his or her option—may pursue remedies available either in the host nation's courts or monetary damages through binding investor-state negotiations.

Tariffs

The agreement provides for the progressive elimination of all tariffs on goods meeting the pact's rules of origin criteria. For most items, existing customs duties will be removed at once or phased out in five or ten annual stages. For certain sensitive products, tariffs will be gradually eliminated over a period of up to fifteen years.

Textiles

NAFTA eliminates in six years or less Mexican tariffs (10 to 20 percent) on more than 80 percent of U.S. textile and apparel exports. A rigorous rule of origin ensures that third countries will not use Mexico as an "export platform" to sell to the United States. During the ten-year phase-out period, a special safeguard mechanism will apply to textile products. During that transition, quotas may be imposed on imports of non-NAFTA goods in the event of import surges. There is also a tariff "snap-back" provision to redress surges in imports of NAFTA-produced apparel.

Transportation

Nearly 90 percent of U.S. trade with its neighbors—$210 billion worth of goods—travels overland. Mexico has impeded such transport by requiring that trucks and buses transfer their cargoes and passengers at the border. NAFTA provides for open roads for railroads (1994), buses (1996), and trucks (1999).

Clinton and NAFTA

Three days before the San Antonio meeting, Democratic nominee Bill Clinton endorsed NAFTA with the proviso that adequate safeguards be adopted to toughen environmental and worker-safety standards in Mexico and allow the president to establish a commission to monitor the agreement's impact. "There are apparel workers, fruit and vegetable farmers, electronic workers, auto workers who are at risk not only of short-term dislocation, but of permanent damage if this agreement is not strengthened and improved," he said. NAFTA supporters throughout North America breathed a sigh of relief when the Democrat added, "I believe we can address these concerns without renegotiating the basic agreement."[27] Even as Clinton proved conciliatory toward the pact, independent candidate Ross Perot lambasted it as a scheme to send millions of jobs south of the Rio Grande. His presidential debate reference to "a giant sucking sound"—the alleged noise made by jobs moving south—emerged as the most memorable sound-bite of the 1992 campaign season.

Following his victory over Bush, the president-elect evinced little public interest in NAFTA. Youthful advisers on Clinton's transition team and, after the 20 January 1993 inauguration, on the White House staff went so far as to recommend jettisoning the pact. They argued that it was a Bush hand-me-down certain to engender friction between the new chief executive and traditional Democratic constituencies: the AFL-CIO, environmental groups, consumer activists, and African American organizations. In fact, these NAFTA adversaries took advantage of Clinton's early inaction on trade issues to mobilize opposition to the pact. The new president was slow to name as his U.S. trade representative Mickey Kantor, a partner in a

Los Angeles law and lobbying firm who had little experience in trade matters. By mid-March, however, Kantor began negotiating parallel agreements with Mexico and Canada on labor issues, the environment, and import surges in hopes of blunting opposition to the pact. Five months later, the three governments unveiled these side deals. At their heart were trilateral environmental and labor commissions to monitor each country's compliance with its own laws in these particular areas. Ultimately, these commissions could levy fines of up to $20 million on Mexico or the United States for failure to resolve conflicts. Canada won exemption from such commission-imposed sanctions, relying instead on its own courts.

NAFTA supporters hoped that, just as a staunch anti-Communist like Richard M. Nixon could renew diplomatic relations with China and a southerner like Lyndon B. Johnson could obtain passage of civil rights legislation, President Clinton would have more success than Bush in persuading a Democrat-dominated Congress to approve NAFTA. While most senators proved congenial to the accord, Clinton ran into a buzz saw of opposition in the House of Representatives. Gephardt greeted the Kantor-inspired embellishments to the accord as inadequate. "Although progress has been achieved," he stated, "the announced side agreements fall short in important respects and, taken alone, are not supportable. I am not optimistic that these deficiencies can be successfully resolved."[28] House Majority Whip David E. Bonior (D-MI) expressed his dissent even more caustically. "What we are exporting to Mexico is our factories—and our jobs," he thundered. "Rather than reversing this trend, NAFTA rolls out the red carpet for multinationals who want to move to Mexico. That's why NAFTA must be defeated."[29]

In many ways, the NAFTA debate focused less on economics than on a power struggle within the Democratic party. Traditional constituencies—organized labor, consumer groups, militant environmentalists, and African American leaders (including the Congressional Black Caucus)—bemoaned their party's shift to the center and Clinton's refusal to give them a dominant voice over policies in their interest areas. By defeating the trade pact, they hoped, the president would appreciate their enduring political muscle and return them to the position of influence they had enjoyed before the New Deal coalition began crumbling in the late 1960s and early 1970s.[30]

As late as August 1993, many senior White House staff members believed that the chief executive should abandon NAFTA, making the best effort possible "to cover his tracks."[31] By early October Clinton began to see NAFTA as more than a free trade pact. It loomed as the possible Waterloo of his administration: a resounding defeat after he had retreated or suffered setbacks on gays in the military, an economic stimulus plan, and Bosnia. To avoid this outcome, he invited former presidents to the White House for a joint endorsement of the plan, dispatched Vice President Al Gore to vanquish Perot in a televised debate on "Larry King Live," recruited Deputy Minority Whip Newt Gingrich (R-GA) to round up GOP votes, and personally drummed up support with favors for lawmakers representing interests ranging from broom makers to citrus growers. What observers called "a full court press" paid off handsomely when the House approved the pact 232 to 202 on 17 November and the Senate gave its thumbs up by a 61 to 38 vote three days later.

De Facto Integration

Congressional passage of NAFTA will accelerate North America's inexorable economic integration evinced in the flow of goods, people, vehicles, and communications across the border. This process is reflected in the data on trade, investment, migration, travelers' expenditures, visitors, and telephone and telegraph messages that appear in tables 1 through 6.

If integration was inevitable, why did President Salinas place his reputation on the line for an initiative that the U.S. Congress could have killed? To begin with, Mexican chief executives cannot succeed themselves. Salinas saw NAFTA as a means to consolidate his market-oriented reforms and obviate the likelihood that his successor, who will take office in late 1994, would dismantle them. An agreement would also enhance Mexico's appeal to foreign and domestic private investors. The accord would be particularly helpful in attracting provincial U.S. corporations whose officers still regard Mexico as a modern version of the Wild West, overrun by pistol-packing desperados sporting Pancho Villa mustaches. In addition, many Far East firms, especially those in Hong Kong, were inclined to delay investing in Mexico until the U.S. Congress placed its imprimatur upon the initiative. Finally, although continental linkages would have increased regardless of what politicians did, a free trade arrangement would minimize dislocations resulting from the ad hoc economic merger of North America's economies. Safeguards include tariff phase-outs, snap-backs, and a simplified dispute resolution process.

U.S.-Mexican Prospects

Whether de jure or de facto, North American integration profoundly affects U.S.-Mexican relations. First, a successful trade pact enhanced the standing of Salinas, his PRI, and their *perestroika*-style reforms. The chief executive's success came at the expense of the anti–United States Democratic Revolutionary party, which excoriated NAFTA even as it championed a return to a large, highly protected welfare state. Washington policy makers viewed the free trade accord as a means to promote Mexico's economic progress while lofting the ruling party's electoral prospects in the August 1994 presidential contest. U.S. policy makers believed that market-impelled development combined with continued PRI governance offered the best prospect for sustained growth in a less-developed country with which the more-developed United States shares the longest border in the world.

Second, Congress's approval of NAFTA may well have affected the selection of Luis Donaldo Colosio Murrieta as the PRI's presidential standard-bearer. Salinas handpicked the forty-three-year-old secretary of social development because he expected him to pursue Mexico's economic changes. In Colosio, the PRI also boasted a man who combined technocratic credentials with a remarkable political résumé: congressman, senator, party president, and, as chief of social development, head of the ever larger and more politically significant Solidarity Program. An assassin's bullet removed Colosio from the race in March 1994. In his place, Salinas selected Ernesto Zedillo Ponce de León, a forty-two-year-old, Yale-trained technocrat. As secretary of planning and budget, Zedillo had played a key role in promoting economic liberalization. In mid-1994, it remained to be seen whether he could develop the political skills required to manage both the multiple, acute dislocations arising from an ever more open Mexican economy and the political challenges that Cuauhtémoc Cárdenas's Democratic Revolutionary party will present in the August 1994 election. To protest its likely loss, the PRD is expected to engage in demonstrations, sit-ins, and protest marches of the kind seen in major gubernatorial elections in the early 1990s. Zedillo's challenge will be to run a sufficiently clean campaign so that protest

Table 1
Bilateral Economic Relations: U.S.-Mexican Trade, 1970–1993

	Mexican Exports to U.S. ($ millions)	Percentage of all Mexican Exports	Mexican Imports from U.S. ($ millions)	Percentage of all Mexican Imports
1970	839	65.3	1,568	62.7
1971	911	65.1	1,479	61.6
1972	1,288	75.8	1,745	58.2
1973	1,318	58.8	2,277	54.2
1974	1,703	58.7	3,779	62.2
1975	1,668	53.8	4,113	57.9
1976	2,111	60.9	3,774	62.5
1977	2,738	59.5	3,493	58.2
1978	4,057	68.1	4,564	60.4
1979	6,252	69.6	7,563	62.6
1980	10,072	63.2	11,979	65.6
1981	10,716	55.3	15,398	63.8
1982	11,887	52.0	8,921	59.9
1983	13,034	—	4,958	—
1984	14,612	60.4	6,695	59.3
1985	15,029	68.6	11,132	69.1
1986	17,600	61.7	12,400	61.9
1987	20,500	66.6	14,600	61.9
1988	23,500	65.5	20,600	66.7
1989	27,200	65.5	25,000	70.8
1990	30,900	69.8	28,400	64.6
1991	31,200	69.6	33,300	62.0
1992 (estimated)	40,600	69.7	35,200	62.1
1993 (projected)	46,700	70.0	40,500	62.5

Sources: U.S. Department of Commerce (1970–85) and U.S. Department of the Treasury (1986–93).

tactics will not undermine his legitimacy if he defeats Cárdenas and Diego Fernández de Cevallos, the attractive and articulate PAN candidate whose popularity soared following a strong performance in a mid-May televised debate. The 1 January 1994 launching of a rebellion in Chiapas by the Zapatista National Liberation Army may find Mexico's conservative electorate opting for continuity over change. There is, however, virtually no difference in the platforms of the

Table 2
Bilateral Economic Relations: U.S. Direct Investment in Mexico, 1970–1991

	Investment in Mexico	Investment in All Countries	Percent in Mexico	Investment in Developing Countries	Percent in Mexico
1970	1,786	78,178	2.3	21,448	8.3
1971	1,838	86,198	2.1	25,358	7.2
1972	2,025	94,337	2.1	25,235	8.0
1973	2,379	103,675	2.3	25,266	9.4
1974	2,825	118,613	2.4	28,479	9.9
1975	3,200	124,212	2.6	26,222	12.2
1976	2,984	137,224	2.2	29,050	10.3
1977	3,230	149,848	2.2	34,462	9.4
1978	3,690	167,804	2.2	40,339	9.1
1979	4,490	186,750	2.4	44,525	10.1
1980	5,989	215,578	2.8	53,277	11.2
1981	6,977	226,359	3.1	56,182	12.4
1982	5,544	221,512	2.5	52,441	10.6
1983	4,999	226,117	2.2	50,978	9.8
1984	4,568	212,994	2.1	50,131	9.1
1985	5,087	232,667	2.2	54,474	9.3
1986	4,826	259,980	1.9	60,609	8.0
1987	4,913	314,307	2.0	73,017	7.0
1988	5,712	335,893	2.0	80,060	7.0
1989	7,341	372,491	2.0	90,374	8.0
1990	9,938	424,086	2.2	102,360	9.2
1991	15,570	450,196	3.4	111,608	14.0

Sources: U.S. Department of Commerce and U.S. Department of State.

PRI and PAN, except that the latter carries little of the baggage of corruption and economic sacrifice associated with the ruling party.

Third, *perestroika* may contribute to *glasnost*. Economic progress expands the size of the middle class, which in turn serves as a powerful advocate for civil liberties and democratic choice. Free trade–inspired contacts with democratic trading partners in North America and Europe should diminish authoritarianism in Mexico, just as Spain and Portugal's entry into the European Economic Community fostered democracy in those erstwhile dictatorships. Experience in making economic decisions generates demands for greater choice in the political marketplace. Moreover, market-oriented pol-

Table 3
Bilateral Communications: U.S.-Mexican Telephone and Telegraph
Messages, 1970–1991

	Mexico to United States			United States to Mexico		
Telegraph Messages	No. of Messages	Total Minutes	Cost $	No. of Messages	Total Minutes	Cost $
1970	11	361	32	37	1,467	83
1971	334	334	34	50	2,406	123
1972	1	46	4	17	1,281	75
1973	1,798	81,152	3,334	12,712	612,735	47,407
1974	1,824	81,313	3,062	12,228	572,735	47,407
1975	2,115	84,636	3,177	12,710	657,612	26,368
1976	4,730	185,814	7,361	14,551	803,462	34,893
1977	4,146	148,151	8,615	11,114	653,198	36,212
1978	4,348	149,550	9,332	12,138	737,895	43,187
1979	4,419	153,407	9,826	16,333	1,025,249	60,693
1980	4,401	153,779	9,556	16,146	1,046,064	62,387
1981	4,613	165,175	10,853	27,803	1,073,928	123,094
1982	3,409	115,588	7,688	25,728	1,938,222	123,856
1983	2,083	69,083	4,235	18,027	1,454,007	101,131
1984				20,780	1,397,271	129,601
Telephone Calls (in millions)						
1978	10.7	—	69.9	17.0	—	122.2
1979	14.3	—	93.6	21.6	—	186.3
1980	18.4	—	126.4	26.1	—	220.7
1981	22.4	—	173.6	29.8	—	294.7
1982	25.8	155.6	175.0	36.4	251.8	317.0
1983	26.7	144.5	146.3	39.3	294.3	334.5
1984	25.9	187.1	149.4	41.7	307.0	361.4
1985	30.4	170.0	169.2	45.6	336.1	381.4
1986	34.1	185.7	179.7	52.2	392.8	442.4
1987	36.3	188.7	181.1	59.5	450.7	499.5
1988	47.7	239.4	233.1	77.0	561.9	639.4
1989	60.8	306.4	298.9	97.4	702.5	720.0
1990	72.5	361.7	366.8	114.4	823.6	837.5
1991	93.4	468.3	428.7	147.2	1,038.3	1,024.3

Sources: U.S. Federal Communications Commission and U.S. Department of Commerce.

icies stimulate decentralization, which curbs the government's ability to manipulate economic resources as a tool of political control. Additionally, such policies undermine the influence of heavy-handed labor chieftains, long accustomed to sweetheart contracts with the public and private sectors. The emphasis on market forces also diminishes the number of regulations and, concomitantly, opportunities for bureaucrats and politicians to exact bribes.

Table 4
Bilateral Communications: Foreign Visitors to the United States, 1970–1993

	Visitors from All Countries	Visitors from Mexico	Percent of Total
1970	12,362,299	1,058,772	8.6
1971	12,739,006	1,170,583	9.2
1972	13,057,119	1,377,143	10.5
1973	13,995,164	1,619,451	11.6
1974	14,123,253	1,840,849	13.0
1975	15,698,118	2,155,651	13.8
1976	17,523,239	1,920,509	10.9
1977	18,610,000	2,700,000	14.5
1978	19,842,000	2,100,000	10.6
1979	20,310,000	2,600,000	12.8
1980	22,300,000	323,000	15.0
1981	22,100,000	1,767,000	8.0
1982	18,600,000	1,548,000	8.3
1983	21,700,000	669,000	3.1
1984	20,800,000	823,000	4.0
1985	19,298,000	2,731,000	14.2
1986	22,003,000	3,900,000	17.7
1987	29,500,000	6,713,000	4.4
1988	34,100,000	7,900,000	4.3
1989	36,600,000	7,200,000	5.1
1990	39,500,000	7,200,000	5.5
1991	42,900,000	7,600,000	5.6
1992 (estimated)	45,900,000	8,258,000	5.6
1993 (projected)	49,400,000	8,700,000	5.7

Source: U.S. Department of Commerce.

Note: Except for Canadian visitors, arrival figures include persons traveling for business, pleasure, study, and transit. Arrival figures exclude Canadian and Mexican border crossings.

Salinas has responded to the forces unleased by his version of *perestroika* by reforming the electoral law, forging parliamentary alliances with the National Action party, recruiting more candidates who can win elections fairly, eroding the party's corporatist structures, and recognizing opposition victories in several fiercely contested contests. Still, Mexico remains a hierarchical, centralized, and authoritarian political system. The persistence of these traits

Table 5

Bilateral Economic Relations: U.S.-Mexican Travelers' Expenditures, 1970–1992 ($ millions)

	Mexican Travelers to the United States	U.S. Travelers To Mexico
1970	583	778
1971	565	959
1972	620	1,135
1973	830	1,264
1974	1,142	1,475
1975	1,490	1,637
1976	1,364	1,723
1977	1,316	1,918
1978	1,456	2,121
1979	1,975	2,460
1980	2,522	2,564
1981	3,775	2,862
1982	3,098	3,324
1983	1,951	3,618
1984	1,899	3,609
1985	2,130	3,552
1986	2,200	3,100
1987	2,400	3,241
1988	3,200	2,591
1989	4,300	3,659
1990	5,600	4,166
1991	5,900	4,788
1992	6,400	5,081

Source: U.S. Department of Commerce.

was revealed by Salinas's spurning intraparty primaries in favor of designating from Mexico City most gubernatorial candidates during his term. Charges of fraud in the December 1993 state elections in Yucatán, where ballot boxes vanished during a prolonged, mysterious power blackout, also cast doubt on the PRI's commitment to democracy. NAFTA will spur more intensive interactions between Mexico and its democratic North American neighbors. Such contacts may encourage top Mexican officials to speed PRI's modernization and seek more candidates who can win clear-cut victories. This

Table 6
Legal and Illegal Mexican Migration to the United States, 1970–1991

	No. of Legal Mexican	Illegal Aliens Apprehended	Total Apprehended	Percent Mexican
1970	44,469	277,377	345,353	80.3
1971	50,103	348,178	420,126	82.9
1972	64,040	430,213	505,949	95.0
1973	70,141	576,823	655,969	87.9
1974	71,586	709,823	788,145	90.1
1975	62,205	680,392	766,600	88.8
1976	57,863	781,474	857,915	89.7
1977	44,079	954,778	1,042,215	91.6
1978	92,400	976,667	1,057,977	92.3
1979	52,100	988,830	1,076,418	91.9
1980	56,680	817,381	910,361	89.8
1981	101,268	874,161	975,780	89.6
1982	56,106	887,457	970,246	91.5
1983	59,079	1,172,306	1,251,357	94.0
1984	57,557	1,170,769	1,246,981	93.9
1985	61,077	1,266,999	1,348,749	94.0
1986	66,533	1,671,458	1,767,400	95.0
1987	72,351	1,139,606	1,190,488	96.0
1988	95,039	949,722	1,008,145	94.0
1989	405,172	865,292	954,243	91.0
1990	679,068	1,092,258	1,169,939	93.0
1991	946,167	1,131,510	1,197,875	94.5

Source: U.S. Department of Justice, Immigration and Naturalization Service.

process could diminish complaints by U.S. authorities, journalists, and human rights activists about vote fraud and electoral corruption. On the other hand, Zedillo, worried about his prospects, has admitted to his campaign entourage old guard *priistas,* the infamous "dinosaurs," whom Colosio publicly avoided. It remains to be seen whether he will use them to mobilize votes only to spurn them if successful or whether he believes them necessary to ensure social control in a nation beset by turmoil.

Fourth, through the trade talks, the Mexicans learned a great deal about the U.S. political system while honing their lobbying skills. Even though Mexico focused its pro-NAFTA campaign on Washington, it developed a national network of supporters that includes Hispanic American civic, business, and professional organizations. Such groups could help influence U.S. policy on narcotics, law enforcement, immigration, and other sensitive subjects that were managed carefully by Washington and Mexico City during the free trade talks. The rapid growth in the number of Chicanos combined with their significant presence in the populous Sun Belt, as well as in states such as New York, New Jersey, and Illinois, makes them increasingly important because the Electoral College amplifies the influence of minorities in major states. Factors such as leadership conflicts, language barriers, relatively low income and educational levels, tensions with other Hispanics, and newness to the country will limit the short- to medium-term political impact that Chicanos can have compared to Jews and Greek Americans, who often help advance the policy goals of, respectively, Tel Aviv and Athens.

Fifth, immigration may emerge as an ever more prickly bilateral issue as a result of NAFTA's passage. Eventually, heightened investment in Mexico will create employment for more of the one million people who enter the workforce each year but cannot find jobs. But it may be generations—if ever—before opportunities arise for the 40 percent-plus of Mexicans who eke out a living at the margin of a distended social pyramid. The Solidarity Program offers hope to some, as does the PROCAMPO initiative, designed to assist farmers to diversify production. Still, hundreds of thousands, possibly millions, of deracinated peasants and workers will emigrate northward in quest of a better life. A continued diaspora of illegal aliens will elicit cries, foreshadowed in GOP presidential aspirant Pat Buchanan's 1992 "America First" platform and articulated by California governor Pete Wilson in 1993 and 1994, for more rigorous border management; others may demand that Mexico further reduce its birthrate. Perhaps contacts and bargaining mechanisms arising from the NAFTA negotiations will furnish channels for the United States and Mexico to engage difficult questions before they inflame passions on both sides of the frontier.

Sixth, economic integration will accelerate trilateral contacts among academic, religious, labor, environmental, human rights, and other nongovernmental organizations. Such activities will lead to publicizing real and perceived abuses throughout the continent. In 1990, for example, Roman Catholic bishops from the United States, Mexico, and Canada urged debt relief for Mexico and other Third World countries. They also insisted that any free trade pact contain safeguards against the exploitation and displacement of workers and farmers unable to protect their interests. A year later, the president of the United Auto Workers, anxious for Mexican wage rates to climb, lambasted the Mexican government's crackdown on a labor leader who had organized *maquiladora* workers in Matamoros. Although egregiously corrupt, the union chief garnered praise for obtaining for his members the highest wages in the assembly plant sector.

Seventh, to diversify its economic relations and defuse charges of unhealthy dependence on the United States, Mexico will pursue closer ties with Europe, the Far East, and Latin America. Even as the accord was being negotiated, European entrepreneurs increased investments in Mexico in the hopes of gaining easier entrée to the U.S. and Canadian markets. "As much as Mexico needs Europe to counterbalance U.S. influence in the region, Europe needs Mexico to ensure an ongoing presence in the same region."[32] In January 1990 Mexico signed a Cooperation and Friendship Agreement with Spain that set forth a blueprint for encouraging bilateral economic relations that could be emulated with other European states. This accord stipulated that between 1990 and 1994 Spain would provide $4 billion: $2.5 billion in joint ventures and $1.5 in export credits. Pemex's 5 percent equity ownership of the Spanish oil company Repsol constitutes another important link between Mexico City and Madrid.[33] Even more impressive, in early 1994 the European-dominated Organization for Economic Cooperation and Development, composed of industrialized nations, admitted Mexico as its first Third World member. With respect to Asia, Salinas has reiterated his belief that Mexico is a "Pacific nation," and Japan constitutes the country's second largest trading partner, largely because of Pemex oil shipments to Japanese energy and power companies. Even though far behind the United States, Japan is the second most important investor in *maquiladoras*. Moreover, Tokyo has made $3.65 billion in export credits and investment loans available in recent years. These funds have helped finance pollution control in Mexico City, electricity generation for the Sicartsa steel complex in Michoacán, and other high-priority projects. On the heels of the U.S. Congress's approval of NAFTA, Asia-Pacific Economic Cooperation (APEC), the economic coordinating body for nations of the region, accepted Mexico as a member. To burnish his Luso-Hispanic credentials, Salinas convened the first Ibero-American Summit Conference in Guadalajara in July 1991. This unprecedented conclave attracted twenty-three heads of state and government from Latin America, the Caribbean, and Iberia. The officials discussed how best to promote Latin American integration, foster cooperation, and attack poverty. They also reviewed ways for Spain and Portugal to represent Latin American interests within the European Economic Community. In mid-1992, Salinas took an active part in a second summit held in Spain.

Eighth, a completed NAFTA endowed Mexico with a key role in Bush's vaunted Enterprise of the Americas Initiative (destined to be renamed by the Clinton administration), conceived to promote free trade from the Arctic Circle to Tierra del Fuego. At the beginning of the decade, Mexico conducted only 4 percent of its foreign commerce with Latin America. Mexico has already signed a framework agreement with Central America to stimulate trade, entered into a free trade agreement with Chile in 1991, and laid the groundwork for a trilateral commercial accord with Colombia and Venezuela. Formal economic integration with its North American neighbors highlighted Mexico's remarkable market-focused reforms, making it a showcase for free trade schemes between North America and Latin American states. As such, Mexico has attained the indisputable status of a middle-level power that eluded it when past efforts at regional leadership were predicated on diplomatic hostility toward, rather than economic cooperation with, Washington. Possessed of greater knowledge of the United States and more tools with which to manage disputes, future Mexican leaders may be more likely than Salinas to voice publicly their differences with Uncle Sam, either as a spokesman for Latin America or as an interlocutor between the region and Washington.

Finally, despite all the expectations that NAFTA has aroused in Mexico, it must be remembered that the pact is an extremely attractive agreement for the United States and Canada. Arguably, Washington and Ottawa negotiated too favorable a deal for themselves, with the result that Mexico will have to rewrite twenty-one economic-financial laws even as its business community faces increased competition from north of the Rio Grande amid social and political effervescence. Salinas deserves enormous credit for his unswerving commitment to change. Yet in many ways he was sedulously adhering to an orthodox blueprint for reforming a hugely statist and inefficient economy. No similar prescription exists for the twin challenges that face his successor: implementing widespread,

NAFTA-impelled changes in the economy and legal system while opening up Mexico's authoritarian political system under ever more aggressive pressure from domestic and foreign interest groups.

Notes

Segments of this chapter appeared in George W. Grayson, *The North American Free Trade Agreement* (New York: Foreign Policy Association, 1993).

1. Roberta Lajous, "Mexico's European Policy Agenda: Perspectives on the Past, Proposals for the Future," in Riordan Roett, ed., *Mexico's External Relations in the 1990s* (Boulder, Colo.: Lynne Rienner, 1991), p. 81.

2. Laurence Whitehead, "Mexico and the 'Hegemony' of the United States: Past, Present, and Future," in Roett, ed., *Mexico's External Relations*, p. 256.

3. Pedro Aspe Armella, speech delivered at the Center for Strategic and International Studies, Washington DC, 22 September 1992.

4. Sidney Weintraub and M. Delal Baer, "The Interplay between Economic and Political Opening: The Sequence in Mexico," *Washington Quarterly* 15, no. 2 (spring 1992): 187.

5. Peter Hakim, "President Bush's Southern Strategy: The Enterprise for the Americas Initiative," *Washington Quarterly* 15, no. 2 (spring 1992): 94.

6. U.S. Department of Commerce, *Survey of Current Business* (September 1990): 41.

7. *Wall Street Journal*, 22 October 1990, p. B6.

8. The U.S. embassy claimed that flights into the storm, which had been authorized by the Mexican government, were made only to record Ignacio's temperature and other vital signs. Without contradicting this explanation, Foreign Minister Castañeda barred U.S. hurricane hunters from Mexican airstrips during the summer until a thorough investigation of the matter was completed. See the *Washington Post*, 7 July 1980, pp. A1, A12.

9. For example, CTM Secretary-General Fidel Velázquez and the body's secretary of education and social communication, Senator Arturo Romo Gutiérrez, contributed pro-NAFTA essays to the *Wall Street Journal* (3 May 1991, p. A11) and *Washington Post* (19 May 1991, p. D7), respectively.

10. Founded in April 1991, the RMALC claimed to embrace eighty organizations, including the Authentic Labor Front (Frente Auténtico del Trabajo—FAT), unions representing workers in telecommunications, the National Autonomous University of Mexico, the Ministry of Fishing, and the Assembly of Neighborhood Associations; see *Proceso*, 30 March 1992, p. 7.

11. *El Financiero*, 18 January 1991, p. 25.

12. In fact, Canada's exports to the United States during the CFTA's first three years of operation performed better in sectors (particularly non-resource-based manufacturing) that were liberalized by the accord; see Dan-

iel Schwanen, "Were the Optimists Wrong on Free Trade? A Canadian Perspective," *Commentary* 3, C. D. Howe Institute (October 1992).

13. *Wall Street Journal*, 22 May 1991, p. A16.

14. Daniel La Botz quoted in the *Wall Street Journal*, 12 February 1991, p. A10.

15. See, for example, Lori Wallach and Tom Hilliard, "The Consumer and Environmental Case against Fast Track," Public Citizens' Congress Watch, May 1991 (mimeo.).

16. The coalition was made up of the American Electronics Association, the American League for Export and Security Assistance, the American Farm Bureau Federation, the Business Roundtable, the Chemical Manufacturers Association, the Computer and Business Equipment Manufacturers Association, the Computer and Communications Industry Association, the Coalition of Service Industries, the Corn Growers Association, the Consumers for World Trade, the Council of the Americas, the Emergency Committee for American Trade, the National Association of Manufacturers, the National Foreign Trade Council, the National Electrical Manufacturers Association, the Pharmaceutical Manufacturers Association, the Pro Trade Group, the U.S. Chamber of Commerce, the U.S. Council for International Business, and the U.S. Council of the Mexican-U.S. Business Committee; see *Inside U.S. Trade*, special report, 28 February 1992, p. S5.

17. Such data appear in the *NAFTA. Review* 1 (January 1992): 2–3. This is a publication of the U.S. trade representative.

18. Rudiger Dornbusch, "If Mexico Prospers, So Will We," *Wall Street Journal*, 11 April 1991, p. A14.

19. The *Wall Street Journal*, 6 May 1991, p. C9.

20. Office of the Press Secretary, White House, "Integrated Environmental Plan for the Mexico-U.S. Border Area," news release, 25 February 1992.

21. Congressional Research Service, "North American Free Trade Agreement: Issues for Congress," Library of Congress, Washington DC, 25 March 1991, updated 12 July 1991, p. 48 (mimeo.); *Congressional Quarterly*, 18 May 1991, p. 1258.

22. *Congressional Quarterly*, 19 May 1991, sec. 4, p. 17.

23. David S. Cloud, "Bush's 'Action Plan' May Be Key to Approval of Fast Track," *Congressional Quarterly*, 4 May 1991, p. 1120.

24. On 23 May 1991, the House of Representatives voted 231 to 192 against a resolution sponsored by Representative Byron Dorgan (D-ND) to deny fast-track authority; the next day the Senate turned thumbs down, by a 59 to 36 vote, on a similar measure proposed by Senator Ernest F. Hollings (D-SC). The overwhelming majority of opponents to fast-track extension in both houses were Democrats (170 of the 192 "no" votes in the House; 31 of 36 "no" votes in the Senate). In the main, opponents came from states with heavy industries and strong unions (the Northeast and the "rust belt"), large textile in-

dustries (the Carolinas), and large agricultural subsidies (the Dakotas). Most supporters came from border, Sun Belt, and coastal states or philosophically supported free trade; see the *Wall Street Journal*, 24 May 1991, p. A4.

25. Mexican pollster Miguel Basañez found that 71 percent of Mexicans, desperate for change after a decade of economic crisis, favored unrestricted continental trade, twice the support expressed in the United States; see the *Wall Street Journal*, 13 May 1991, p. A11.

26. Quoted from a letter written to Carla Hill on 24 February 1992 and published in *Inside U.S. Trade*, special report, 28 February 1992, p. S6.

27. *New York Times*, 5 October 1992, pp. A1, A16.

28. *Facts on File*, 19 August 1993, p. 607.

29. *Washington Post*, 17 September 1993, p. A21.

30. For a trenchant exposition of this thesis, see J. W. Anderson, "Sore Losers," *Washington Post*, 1 October 1993, p. A25.

31. *New York Times*, 18 November 1993, p. A1.

32. Wolf Grabendorff, "Mexico and the European Community: Toward a New Relationship?" in Roett, ed., *Mexico's External Relations*, p. 18.

33. Roberta Lajous, "Mexico's European Policy Agenda: Perspectives on the Past, Proposals for the Future," in Riordan Roett, ed., *Mexico's External Relations*, p. 87.

Eul-Soo Pang

Brazil and the United States

Brazil did not take dollars to throw them away.
The country went into debt to grow.
    Antônio Delfim Netto, 1982[1]

The 1980s will be remembered as the decade that changed irrevocably bilateral relations between the United States and Brazil. If the so-called lost decade symbolized economic and social retrogression for Latin America, it was also the most contentious decade for the two giants of the Western Hemisphere, ushering in the end of the era of "special relationship" and the beginning of a new era of "autonomous solidarity" (*autonomia solidária*) in which Brazil pursues an independent approach to foreign policy.[2] While the relative importance of the United States as a model for Brazil's political redemocratization, economic growth, and trade strategies decidedly waned during the decade, Brazil as a newly industrialized country (NIC) posed a new set of problems and issues in international and hemispheric relations for the United States that the two Republican administrations of Ronald Reagan and George Bush failed to address. The metamorphosis of this relationship can serve as a warning of what might occur in U.S. relations with other NICs in the years to come. Brazil has gone through a dynamic period of growth and development during the preceding three decades, emerging as the world's eighth largest economy by the 1980s and then slipping to eleventh by 1990. In 1968, over 56 percent of Brazil's exports were raw materials and other primary goods; in 1985, over 67 percent of the exports came from the manufacturing sector.[3] It is this economic and social transformation—both growth and retrogression as well as diversification and verticalization of the economy—and the accompanying political and social upheaval that forced a fundamental transformation of the extraordinary U.S.-Brazilian partnership that had endured for over seven decades.

A recent publication by a research institute at the Brazilian Ministry of External Relations identifies the country's principal interests and preoccupations: foreign trade, nuclear research, relations with the Third World and with Eastern Europe, and the future of Brazil's role in the Río de la Plata.[4] The book's contributors are the pacesetters of Brazil's foreign policy thinking. On the topic of bilateral relations, the United States is not included, but relations with Asia, Western Europe, and Argentina are analyzed in depth. Although they represent a partial view of what the country wants, this and other official Itamaraty publications proffer clues to policy directions, sending both covert and overt messages on how Brazil views the outside world, especially the United States. Brazil's foreign policy establishment is a tightly knit collegial group of highly independent-minded and even inbred ideologues who often chart and sort out the country's priorities without societal consensus or censure, especially during a time of crisis or rapid change such as the 1980s. The omission of U.S.-Brazil bilateral relations from the book is an indication of how bad they have become.

Bilateral relations also have been tempered by the interests of other branches of the government. Unlike the U.S. Congress, the Brazilian National Congress boasts no single senator or deputy who specializes in foreign affairs.[5] Former speaker of the Chamber and long-term president of Brazil's largest party, PMDB (Partido Movimento Democrático Brasileiro), Ulysses Guimarães long served as chair of the Foreign Relations Committee. Throughout his political career, which spanned nearly fifty years, the man never showed any interest in foreign relations.[6] During the twenty-odd years of military rule, he was Mr. Opposition. Equally, the Brazilian senate has no foreign policy specialist. But the army produced a renowned strategic thinker, Gen. Golbery do Couto e Silva, who outlined Brazil's place in the modern world system and who ponderously argued that because of unique geopolitical endowments (among other things, he viewed his country as the center of Western civilization, if not of the universe) Brazil had an ineluctable contribution to make to the salvation of the West in its life-or-death struggle against international Communism.[7] He also argued that Brazil was destined to emerge as the authority of the (South) Atlantic because of its membership in the Luso-Brazilian, Latin, and Catholic communities and its position as one of the most developed NICs of the underdeveloped South.[8] These windows of opportunity must be exploited. Not coincidentally, much of Brazil's foreign policy concentration on the Mediterranean world, the Middle East, Asia, and sub-Saharan Africa during the 1970s and 1980s reflected Golbery's geopolitical convictions, which compelled Brazil first to challenge and then to diverge from the United States in the world arena.

To be historically accurate, however, it must be stated that the divergence between the two countries began well before President Ernesto Geisel unilaterally canceled the U.S.-Brazil military accord in 1977, the most often cited beginning of the U.S.-Brazil diplomatic fallout. This era of independent foreign policy was phased in during the early 1960s under the Jânio Quadros (1961) and João Goulart administrations (1961–64), which called for a new course for Brazil by modifying the country's role in the Cold War as a subservient follower of the United States.[9] Politically, the late fifties and early sixties were the heyday of the "positive Left," a concept further modified by the nationalistic military and refined by Itamaraty officials. Soon after 1964 it became the cornerstone of the military regime's foreign policy. Ironically, President Geisel, having broken off the traditional subservient ties with the United States, pursued the same foreign policy objective of President Goulart, whom he and his colleagues in the army had overthrown in 1964.[10] The faculty of both the Superior War College and the Rio Branco Institute enthusiastically espoused theories of independent foreign policy, the doctrine of security and development, and the quest for the hegemony of the primus inter pares in the Third World as the legitimate military-industrial power. The claim of territorial rights extending two hundred miles into the sea, for instance, began in the Superior War College as a student research project in the 1950s, but when Brazil proclaimed it in the early 1970s as an official policy, Itamaraty and the Rio Branco Institute wholeheartedly embraced it. Also embraced by the foreign policy establishment was Brazil's right to attain the status of a nuclear power.

Brazil has also steadfastly refused for over twenty-five years to sign the Nuclear Non-Proliferation Treaty, a perennial sore point between the United States and Brazil. Even before 1964, Itamaraty was concerned with the freezing of the Cold War status quo by the two superpowers, the Soviet Union and United States, thus denying Brazil access to nuclear technologies. The author of this thesis was José Araújo de Castro, one of the proponents of the positive Left, foreign minister of the Goulart administration, and ambassador to the United States under the Geisel government. Hence, it was no mystery that Geisel endeavored to build a self-sufficient armament industry and actively sought to establish a nuclear bridge with West Germany when the contract with Westinghouse (to build nuclear power plants near Rio) was not honored by the United States. Geisel found a way to diversify Brazil's access to additional sources of high technology.[11]

Brazil and the United States diverged on other issues in the world arena. In southern Africa, Brazil found itself supporting MPLA (Popular Movement for the Liberation of Angola) guerrillas, who eventually came to power, while the United States bankrolled their rival, UNITA (National Union for the Total Independence of Angola), which waged guerrilla wars against the winning faction (later the government of Angola) until 1991.[12] In South Africa, Brazil was also at loggerheads with the United States because Brazil condemned apartheid first, while the United States wavered for another decade. In the United Nations, Brazil voted against U.S. proposals 70 percent of the time.[13] In retaliation, the United States frequently vetoed Brazil's requests for funding from multilateral banks. By the mid-1980s, it was widely perceived that the United States was in a full decline as the world's premier economic and military power. Brazil was cognizant of the transmutation: in 1950, the United States had held a 50 percent share of the world GNP; in 1989, it held about 25 percent.[14] This perception, whether correct or not, guided Brazil's policy makers in the conduct of bilateral relations during the 1980s, and this attitude has irked U.S. officials.

A Defiant Brazil

What contributed to the rapid deterioration of bilateral relations? How did it affect Brazil's debt negotiation strategies? What was at stake for the United States and Brazil in such important trade issues as subsidies, nontariff barriers, and flagrant protectionism? And why was Brazil so adamant about gaining foreign policy independence from the United States decades before the Cold War ended? There have been several factors—internal, bilateral, and global—that have played a role.

The post–Vietnam era changes wrought into American society and economy injected little or no new thinking into U.S. policy toward Latin America. The decline of the United States as the world's major power riled American conservatives. The United States was used to trading economic concessions for geopolitical advantages and obedient diplomatic support for its objectives. For decades U.S. foreign and military assistance programs paved the way for securing trade and investment advantages for America's multinationals, but by the mid-1970s, this approach by and large failed to yield results. As the Third World's most advanced NIC, Brazil became self-sufficient in its arms requirements and did not need to parrot anti-Communism or pro-Americanism to sustain the status of a respectable industrial-military power. To do so in fact would have been antithetic to its budding global trade interests in Africa, the Middle East, Asia, and even throughout Eastern Europe. In brief, the U.S.-Brazil military cooperation program became an anachronism. In the 1977 confrontation with the Carter administration over human rights questions, an irritated Geisel sent U.S. military advisers packing. The nuclear accord with West Germany signaled to the Carter administration that Brazil no longer considered the United States the sole source for the most advanced military technologies.[15]

The Reagan and Bush administrations relished the free market economic doctrine, or laissez-faire principle, as the foundation for a new global economy. Gone was the lavish praise under the Nixon and Ford administrations, also Republican, for Brazil's economic performance. Around the globe, U.S. diplomats pushed economic liberalism as the true religion, and those resisting this proselytization of free market principles were regarded as unfriendly and even hostile to the United States. As a waning hegemonic power, the United States became less tolerant and even brusque in dealings with Brazil, insisting that the two countries must live by the same economic system and values. Such a policy position was unwise, for it fundamentally ignored the cultural differences between the Latin nation and the United States. Brazil went along with the United States as long as it had no choice.

Brazilians have always distrusted U.S. policies in view of the history of the northern colossus: historically, the United States had been a bully in inter-American relations, and it resumed that role again under Reagan in Central America. The U.S. role in the April 1964 coup was not universally appreciated by Brazilians; Brazil's participation along with Somoza's Nicaragua in the 1965 Dominican intervention was disparaged at home, even by military men and Itamaraty officials, and its subtle opposition to U.S. involvement in the Southeast Asian war became more apparent soon after the 1968 Tet offensive. These anti-U.S. attacks flourished in spite of the fact that the United States put together an aid program for Brazil second only to that for South Vietnam. By the late 1960s, Brazil was well on its way to a decade of heady economic growth that made it surpass Argentina as the continent's largest economy.[16] One USAID report to Congress under the Ford administration praised Brazil's impressive economic achievement, concluded that the country no longer required aid from the United States, and recommended that Brazil pay its debt to the U.S. government before the note was due. The U.S. military hegemony began to founder in the Pacific, coupled with the crescendo of U.S. domestic economic and political crises. Such changes further reinforced Brazil's desire to pursue an independent, nonaligned (to the United States) policy in a newly emerging international order wherein the United States could yield its premier position in the world economy to Japan and Germany at any time.[17] The demise of the United States would not sadden Itamaraty, the military, and Brazil's nascent industrial elite in the least.

The phenomenal economic growth of Brazil during the late sixties and early seventies (the "Brazilian miracle"), along with the blossoming nationalistic independent foreign policy, granted a renewed confidence among military and civilian technocrats as rulers by the early 1970s but with a different slant. The difference was that the earlier policy of the 1950s and early 1960s had been formulated by the positive Left of Brazilian politics, who had sought socially equitable reforms within the law at home and pursued neutral, nonaligned foreign policy objectives abroad.

The post-1964 independent foreign policy has a different etiology, however. This new policy was ensconced in a geopolitical view of Brazil as a South Atlantic power allied to the West but not as a subservient junior partner of the United States. Such nationalistic officers as Gen. Orlando Geisel, Gen. Golbery do Couto e Silva, as well as equally nationalistic, if not xenophobic, Itamaraty diplomats advocated an independent foreign policy. No less important in the consolidation of this independent foreign policy process was the desire of the armed forces to become self-sufficient in military supplies, logistics, and finally doctrines.[18] "Ninguem vai segurar o Brasil" (No one is going to hold down Brazil) a popular official slogan during the apogee of the miracle years. Brazil emerged as the Third World's largest manufacturing economy, aggressively implementing its export-promotion policy. Its import-substituting industrialization development and growth performance were so impressive that even international and domestic detractors of the regime praised the success of the Brazilian statist model. It was during this period that the country diversified considerably its economic ties worldwide and reduced its dependency on the United States. In this relentless pursuit of a "greater Brazil," the close and subservient alliance with the United States became a liability.

The growth of Western European and Japanese economies in the global arena offered an alternative to Brazil: the need to forge new ties and reform old ones. Since the early 1980s, the United States has sustained the position of Brazil's largest trading partner, buying a quarter or more of its annual exports. U.S. purchasing power was equal to that of all of Europe and in some years surpassed it. But its political clout in Brazil has failed to match the position commensurate to the largest trading partner. The deteriorating diplomatic and political relationship with Brazil was therefore the function of the changing world's economic and trade patterns, the declining importance of the Cold War posture to Brazil, the readjusted position of Brazil in the global arena as the premier Third World NIC, and the perceived decline of the United States as the world's economic and political superpower.[19] In this global matrix of the power curve, Brazil saw itself on the ascent and the United States on the descent. There is a newly emerging international economic order in which Brazil must find a proper place. This view is shared pervasively by the Left and Right alike.

The U.S. Agenda in Latin America

There were more issues pitting the United States against Latin America during the 1980s than at any other time in history: the debt crisis, the wars in Central America, drugs, migration, and Reagan's push for the democratization of Latin America.[20] The issues and problems that prompted Brazil to distance itself from the United States, however, are not the same as those general concerns the United States exhibited toward Mexico, Central America, the Caribbean, and the Spanish-, English-, and Dutch-speaking parts of South

America. The issues of illegal immigrants and drugs were and still are important but have been subordinated to other problems unique to U.S.-Brazil bilateral relations. The tension-ridden issues of the 1980s were (1) external debt, including Brazil's unwillingness to negotiate since 1985; (2) excessive statization of the economy and Brazil's protectionist and subsidized trade policies; (3) domestic market reserve for Brazilian-made personal computers and peripherals and state-condoned wanton piracy of information technologies; (4) the lack of guarantee for intellectual property rights, especially for fine chemicals, pharmaceuticals, and computer hardware and software; (5) Brazil's arms trade with Middle Eastern countries hostile to the United States; (6) Brazil's (or more precisely Itamaraty's) penchant for linking the country's interests to those of the Third World, while basking in the glory of being the eighth largest economy in the world; (7) Brazil's nuclear policy; and finally (8) environmental concerns about arresting the deforestation of the Amazon. These specific issues were intermingled with the broad but immediate policy objective of the Reagan and Bush administrations in Latin America, namely, to push democracy and liberal market economic reforms on Brazil.[21] At times, the desire to implement both the long-term and immediate agenda at once confused Brazilians.

In July 1988, the Reagan administration imposed surcharges on sixty-six Brazilian products in retaliation for the country's failure to introduce corrective measures to protect U.S. pharmaceutical patents. The official condemnation from Brasília was both swift and undiplomatic. One high-ranking official of the Bank of Brazil condemned the retaliation as a "terrorist action." A month earlier, in anticipation of such an action on the part of the Reagan administration, Itamaraty's number-two man lashed out against "foreign press, business, and banks" at the U.S.-Brazilian Business Council luncheon by accusing them of turning Brazil into an international pariah. While the Constituent Assembly was considering the most restrictive and regressive measures for international capital in the world, the official dared to claim that Brazil had "legislation on foreign capital that is the most stable in the world."[22] The previous year the state-owned steel mill, Siderbrás, threatened U.S. coking coal exporters: if the United States imposed sanctions against the computer market reserve, Brazil would stop importing American coal altogether. In 1987, Brazil imported $250 million worth of American coal, mostly from West Virginia and Virginia. Senators Jay Rockefeller and Robert Byrd of West Virginia immediately pressured their colleagues in the Senate and White House officials to retract the sanction.[23]

In view of these troublesome issues, Secretary of State George Shultz's August 1988 visit to Brazil was most ill-timed. He was in Latin America to drum up support for Reagan's anti-Sandinista Central American policy. The administration wanted to trade economic concessions for Brazil's diplomatic support for the Reagan objectives in Nicaragua and El Salvador and presumably was willing to ease pressure on the pharmaceutical question. Brazil was not interested. Neither Foreign Minister Roberto de Abreu Sodré nor Itamaraty secretary general Paulo Tarso Fleicha de Lima was at the airport to receive the U.S. secretary of state; instead, the foreign ministry sent out its protocol chief. This chilly reception was followed by an inconclusive talk between Sodré and Shultz on the disputes over the infringement of U.S. pharmaceutical patent rights. Central America was discussed, but Brazil was not willing to support the United States unconditionally. By the time Secretary Shultz met with President Sarney, neither one was willing to bring up any or all of the contentious bilateral issues. The traditional coupling of arm twisting and trading concessions for politicodiplomatic support for U.S. policy simply did not work. Shultz also learned that anti-communist rhetoric was not sufficient to move postmilitary Brazil to the U.S. side in Central America. The local press noted that Brazil treated Bolivia, a $240 million trading partner, better than the United States, which bought $8.7 billion worth of products from Brazil.[24] By February 1989, President Sarney publicly admitted that bilateral relations were at the lowest ebb in history.[25]

For the purpose of this chapter, the following four issues will be analyzed in depth: the external debt, contending commercial relations, market reserve for computers and patent rights, and arms industry and trade with those countries hostile to the United States.

The External Debt: Saving Banks or the Country?

In more than a decade of searching for a satisfactory solution to its gargantuan debt of over $120 billion (the Third World's largest), Brazil has unsuccessfully pursued a strategy consistent with its macroeconomic objectives of recovery and growth. The result has been disheartening. Brazil has gone through five phases of debt negotiation: subservient accommodation (1982–85), xenophobic confrontation (1985–88), accommodation under duress (1988–March 1990), confrontation again (March 1990–June 1991), and again accommodation by necessity (since June 1991). In this arduous period of negotiations and renegotiations, Brazil has also pursued in vain the support of the U.S. government. On at least three occasions, the U.S. government has directly involved itself in arranging short-term bridge loans from its treasury but has steadfastly refused to become a partner in debt negotiations with commercial banks. For the decade-long trade disputes with Brazil, it has also imposed severe restrictions on Brazil for its access to funds from such multilateral financial entities as the International Monetary Fund (IMF) and the World Bank. As the holder of a fifth of the total operating capital shares both in the IMF and the World Bank, the United States has a virtual veto over all financial transactions of the two institutions.

Between 1964 and 1984, the penultimate year of military rule, the country's external debt galloped from $3.5 billion to over $100 billion, a mind-boggling 28.5 times increase, or 13 percent of the entire world debt. Brazil's per capita income, however, increased only 2.8 times.[26] During the decades of the 1960s and 1970s, industrial output of such NICs of the Third World as Brazil, Korea, Taiwan, Singapore, and Mexico was doubling every six years. It was also during these decades of growth that Third World countries became heavily indebted as they pursued debt financing for their economic development. Of some $1 trillion of the Third World's external debt, three-fourths are held by twelve countries—five in Latin America, five in Asia, and two in the Middle East. Their combined gross domestic products leaped from $130 billion in 1967 to over $1 trillion in 1981.[27]

Brazil's external debt has fluctuated between $100 billion in 1983 and $121 billion in 1991. During the same period, Brazil has paid out close to $40 billion in interest alone. Brazil also has declared a moratorium on interest payments four times: 1982 and 1983 (involuntary), 1987 (declared by Sarney), and 1989 (also declared by Sarney and continued by Collor).[28] When Collor made his state visit to the United States as president in June 1991, Brazil was still in its fourth moratorium, eighteen months behind its last payment. Brazil's overdue interest alone ballooned to $8.5 billion.[29]

The debt management strategy employed by the three different Brazilian governments (Figueiredo, Sarney, and Collor between 1982 and 1991) has been remarkably inflexible, xenophobic, overcautious, and even phlegmatic, vacillating between confrontation and accommodation: turning to the IMF, reaching an agreement of adjustment programs, accepting stand-by loans, and then negotiating with commercial banks for rollover and/or fresh credit. IMF conditionality has severely restricted Brazil's ability to achieve economic recovery, frustrated growth objectives, and imposed austerity programs so harsh they often provoked social unrest and hardship.

The difficult process of Brazil's democratization, the less than clearly outlined debt resolution strategy (the Baker and Brady Plans) of the Reagan and Bush administrations for developing countries, and the protean and graphic modifications in the global financial markets also preempted possibilities in finding solutions acceptable to Brazil and its commercial creditors. The largest investor in the global capital market has been pension funds. General Motors pioneered a pension fund that is not tied to its own corporate stocks but is free to be invested in any equity and soon in any part of the world. Not only did workers receive profits from their own company, but they also benefited from diversified portfolios. Peter Drucker called it "pension fund socialism." Brazil incurred its debt when commercial banks reigned as the chief dispensers of credit. No longer does Brazil live in a world where banks are the only dispensers of capital; over 75 percent of all fresh credit comes from capital markets. But Brazil's debt negotiation strategy has failed to reflect this important structural and functional change in the global financial community.[30]

Brazil also signed six letters of intent to impose austerity programs on itself, but none was fulfilled. Each time, the Brazilian government sought a waiver, which the Brazilian press has harshly translated as a "pardon" and "forgiveness," thus fueling strong anti-IMF popular resentment. Each time banks granted even less credit to Brazil. In the mid-1980s much of the available money was going to the bond markets in Western Europe, Japan, and the United States.[31] It became a joke among top Brazilian policy makers that such agreements were signed to accommodate the demands of the U.S. Treasury, to satisfy the whims of technocratic managers of the multilateral banks, and to allay the commercial creditors' fear of default. It served no other purpose. Gilson Funaro unceremoniously broke off with the IMF and led Brazil on a different path to recovery.

The Road to Sarney's Moratorium

Funaro's approach to the debt problem was populist, nationalistic, and reflective of the times. His first policy priority was to put the national finances in order and to resume economic growth. The minister and his top aides ambitiously targeted 6 percent growth per annum as the absolute necessity to turn the recessive economy around. To grow 6 percent per year, Brazil must invest capital equivalent to 20 percent of its GDP: "Brazil wants and is going to pay what it owes, but without subjecting itself to asphyxiating measures." Also unlike his predecessors in the military governments, Funaro was known for his unequivocal empathy for the poor. To Funaro, the poor came before international bankers, and one of his policy goals was to disperse national wealth to them. It was this aspect of his social democratic disposition, in spite of his background as a bourgeois toy manufacturer, that rallied PMDB leaders around Funaro.[32]

The Cruzado Plan of March 1986, the first of six "economic shock" packages to be introduced between 1986 and 1991, was designed to dampen inflationary fevers by freezing both wages and prices; the old 1,000 cruzeiros were devaluated to 1 cruzado. The inflation rate during the first few months of 1986 hovered at less than 3 percent. But the economy soon began to stagnate. Exports declined, and Brazil had little foreign reserve with which to service its debt. Funaro and Sarney agreed that when reserves fell below $5 billion, the country would have no choice but to suspend its interest payment, never exceeding 2.5 percent of its GDP, however. By the end of 1986, the reserve level had fallen below $3.5 billion.[33]

The question was, To whom should the moratorium be directed? To target the entire universe of the international financial community—the IMF, World Bank, Paris Club, and private banks—would have been suicide. Funaro's advisers told Sarney that if a moratorium (the expression of which Sarney assiduously avoided) was aimed at a historically unpopular segment of the community, private banks, there would be no risk. Sarney gambled, hoping that Brazil would gain sympathy if not support from the Third World, the multilateral agencies, and some European governments when the Third World's largest debtor refused to pay interest on $67 billion of commercial debt. None of these happened. Banks reacted by cutting Brazil's short-term credit (mostly used for trade) and raising spread points for new borrowing. But Brazil was not prepared to repudiate its debt. A month and a half after the February 1987 moratorium, Sarney banished Funaro from the Ministry of Finance.[34]

Why did the moratorium fail? The answer can be found in several places: the miscalculation of the banks' positions by Funaro; the increase on banks' reserves for Third World debt exposure; Funaro's self-righteous style of negotiation; the U.S. government's steady refusal to be a negotiation partner; and, not least, deteriorating bilateral relations with the United States. However, Funaro and his economic team justified their somewhat messianic approach in their dealings with high officials at the U.S. Treasury, IMF, World Bank, and commercial banks. First, Funaro thought, and rightfully so, that the bank creditors' committee, consisting of sixteen representatives from Brazil's major creditors, was dominated by American bankers, particularly Citibank's William Rhodes. Second, U.S. banks collectively held about a third of Brazil's total commercial debt and yet had half the committee votes. Finally, Funaro was offended by the way the committee conducted its business. By agreement, the proper function of the committee was to advise Brazil how to service its debt. However, in reality the committee was being used by U.S. banks to dictate bank terms to Brazil, instead of accommodating the country with satisfactory solutions to its crisis. Brazil paid all the expenses incurred by committee activities.[35] Funaro's constant harping and his uncompromising negotiation tactics rattled the bank committee, U.S. Treasury officials, and IMF–World Bank mandarins.

In April 1987, Sarney changed his economic team for the third time in two years. His first choice for minister of finance was Brazil's ambassador to Washington, Marcílio Marques Moreira, who was much liked by international bankers and Brazilian businessmen but lacked political support from PMDB, the largest party in the country. Instead, Sarney caved in under PMDB pressure and appointed Luiz Carlos Bresser Pereira, a party militant.[36] Like his predecessor, Bresser is from São Paulo, where he worked as a university professor and was serving as president of the state bank (Banespa) when appointed to the ministry. His domestic policy was a moderate success in reducing the public deficit, implementing wage and price control by stages, and resorting to a selective application of indexation.

Bresser's external debt strategy, however, was different from that of Funaro. When he took office, the Brazilian debt dollar was being traded in the secondary market at about 50 cents, or half the nominal value. Bresser offered to buy back from the banks at the market price half Brazil's commercial debt, or roughly $34 billion (the total being a little over $67 billion), with thirty-five-year bonds at 6 percent interest. These Brazilian bonds would carry no U.S. Treasury guarantee. Both U.S. government officials and private bankers dismissed the Bresser proposal as "crazy." If the Bresser offer had been accepted, the banks would have lost over $16 billion of the nominal value in one transaction.[37] The flip side of such a deal would have been the increased value of the remaining debt portfolios. When Collor took office in mid-March 1990, the Brazilian debt dollar was at its all-time low of 22 cents. When Collor's negotiators sat down to talk with bankers in October, the value inched up slightly to 24 cents. By the summer of 1991, the debt dollar was still negotiated at less than 30 cents.[38] In hindsight, the banks should have taken the Bresser tender.

A Latin American Collective Default

When the bankers did not accept his offer, Bresser had Brazil conspire with Argentina to proclaim a joint default. Previous attempts to bring together all Latin debtors into a collective default had not worked. Mexico, Chile, and Venezuela preferred to deal with banks directly and separately, while Colombia never declared insolvency and never defaulted. Furthermore, Caribbean and Central American countries owe more to the multilateral agencies and official entities of the Organization of Economic Cooperation and Development (OECD) than to commercial banks, while Brazil, Mexico, Argentina, and Venezuela owe more to commercial banks than to multilateral entities. Therefore, a collective Latin default could not be fashioned to suit Bresser.

In his third year of office, Raúl Alfonsín saw the Austral plan collapse and made strenuous efforts to manage the economy. Like Sarney, Bresser, and Brazil's leftist and center-leftist parties, he considered the IMF and international banks' conditionality a hindrance to his recovery program. At the 1985 annual World Bank–IMF meeting in Seoul, Argentina's economy minister, Juan Sourrouille, flatly refused to sign on with the Baker Plan. At last, Argentina and Brazil agreed on something. The combined external debt of the two countries reached $175 billion, or a full 40 percent of the entire Latin American debt. Alfonsín dispatched his finance minister, Mario Brodersohn, to Brasília to hold a strategy session with Sarney and

Bresser. Joint action could have had seismic consequences. By bringing banks to their knees they would have sent a strong message to
Washington that the two Southern Cone nations effectively seized
the day to control their own destiny without fear of retaliation from
the United States and its global financial bogeymen, the IMF and the
World Bank. But at the last minute, Argentina backed out of the
scheme. It was a daring thought, but Brazil did not care to risk it by
going solo.[39] By late December 1987, Bresser was out of a job.

From Accommodation to Moratorium

Bresser's successor in January 1988 was Mailson da Nóbrega, a conservative economist and taciturn Finance Ministry official. Mailson
did a public mea culpa on the Sarney moratorium and regained Brazil's membership in the international financial community. He willingly agreed to pay a portion of the interest in arrears ($510 million)
as a readmission fee and to sit down with the IMF and work out an
accord. Mailson asked for a package of fresh money totaling about
$12 billion from the multilateral and private banks; they granted
$5.4 billion to be dispersed over three years. Citicorp's John Reed
pointed out that Mailson was able to persuade banks to loan money
to Brazil, for he was willing to work with them.[40] In spite of criticism at home against Mailson's accommodation strategy, it was the
first time commercial banks had loaned fresh money to the Brazilian
government since 1982. But by July 1989, the economic situation
had worsened and inflation continued to gallop in triple digits. Sarney and PMDB incessantly spent funds on pork barrel projects and often checkmated Mailson when the minister attempted to cut federal
spending and subsidies. To the dismay of bankers, Brazil once again
had to cease its payment of interest.

During the rancorous presidential campaign in 1989, Collor made
it clear that he would "negotiate the debt with honor." Brazil should
not kowtow to bankers. The debt negotiation policy pursued by Collor's first economy minister, Zélia Cardoso de Mello, was patterned
in part after Funaro's and in part after Bresser's. However, her tactics
were considered too intransigent and even abrasive by her own
countrymen so no progress was made on this front. By May 1991, she
was forced out of the ministry. Her successor, Ambassador Marcílio
Marques Moreira, who had spent five years in Washington and who
had close ties to international bankers, set a conciliatory tone by ac-

cepting the IMF recommendation of economic and fiscal reforms and seeking better terms from commercial creditors than all his predecessors had been able to extract. By December 1991, the managing director of the IMF had visited Brazil and the Brazilian government had offered a blueprint for another letter of intention.[41]

From the Baker Plan to the Brady Plan

From the outset, Brazil was unwilling to adopt the Baker Plan, unveiled at the 1985 IMF–World Bank annual meeting in Seoul. The core of the plan was to restructure or reschedule the debts of the fifteen most indebted countries, also known as "Baker's fifteen," by having the IMF and the World Bank jointly put up as much as $9 billion for dispersement. At the same time, commercial banks were pressured into increasing their credit to the fifteen up to $20 billion. The debtors in turn would accept IMF-imposed austerity measures and would restructure their domestic economies so that they could grow. Baker understood that without growth, none of the fifteen could pay off their debt. For the first time, the United States tied the debt issue to economic growth prospects. But not everyone saw in the Baker Plan viable solutions. Commercial banks were reluctant to loan more money to Third World governments; the IMF resisted the idea of turning the debt issue (a short-term liquidity crisis) into a long-term development issue by lending money for economic growth. And the debtor countries had had enough of austerity measures that begat nothing but political and social hardships. There were few takers of the Baker Plan. But it served as a harbinger of U.S. debt reduction policy.[42]

The Brady Plan of 1989 was the Bush administration's response to the failed Baker Plan. Recognizing that some of the debts could never be paid in full, the administration introduced a debt reduction plan with limited participation of the U.S. Treasury but still tied to the restructuring of economies and long-term growth policies. The IMF and the World Bank would put up $20 billion and Japan would provide $10 billion. Each debtor country would meet certain conditions, adopting liberal economic measures such as opening up markets, deregulation, and privatizing state-owned enterprises, or SOEs. In return, the World Bank and the IMF would grant such loans to carry out structural economic reforms, the commercial banks would grant a reduction of debt, and the remaining portion would be restructured and converted into U.S. Treasury zero coupon bonds, which the debtor nation would purchase. The interest, whose rate was set by the U.S. government, would be paid upon the maturation of the Brady bonds with the principals. Mexico, Venezuela, Costa Rica, and the Philippines so far have accepted the plan. Both the Baker and Brady Plans were criticized by Brazilians as veiled interventionist attempts by the United States to salvage commercial banks at the expense of debtors. European governments were lukewarm at best. Japan worked against the Brady Plan. The president of a major Japanese bank in Brazil warned a federal deputy that if Brazil signed on with the plan, Japan would cease to extend any more credit to Brazil.[43] The Brady Plan became a U.S. foreign policy instrument but not a concerted debt solution supported by OECD countries. Argentina and Brazil have resisted the politically unpopular Brady Plan but of late are reevaluating their positions.[44]

The Statization of the Economy and Commercial Relations

It was under Getúlio Vargas in the 1930s that Brazil began to build in earnest capital-intensive industries, owned or operated by the state. By 1945, the country boasted 33 state-owned enterprises (SOEs); by 1960, when Juscelino Kubitschek completed implementing his Fifty Years of Progress in Five program of heated economic expansion, the total number of Brazil's SOEs had grown to 55. During the short years of ultranationalism of the Quadros and Goulart administrations, however, the state expanded its control over the economy by creating some 120 new SOEs. When the military seized power in 1964, the country had 180 public enterprises. The heyday of real growth of the state and all its accompanying interventionism, however, took place under the right-wing military regime that ruled the country between 1964 and 1985. During those two decades, the generals and their civilian technocratic allies established over 500 new SOEs under federal, state, and municipal ownership and management. In the penultimate year of military rule, Brazil boasted 683 SOEs.[45] Heavy protection, subsidized credit (or negative interest rate loans), hefty subsidies catering to special interests, and state-sponsored monopolies and cartels in all sectors had by then four decades of history. Between 1940 and 1980, Brazil was growing at the rate of 7 percent per year; between 1967 and the 1973 oil crisis, Brazil was one of the fastest growing economies in the world, averaging 10 percent per annum. State sponsorship, financing, and protection worked well. Its vehicles, SOEs, came to dominate the economy at an unprecedented level. During the early 1980s, the public sector enterprises came to represent somewhere between 60 and 70 percent of the country's production.[46]

In the statization process of the Brazilian economy, the interests of the private sector became intertwined with those of the public sector. Excessive protection and subsidies after 1974 became entrenched and institutionalized. At the center of the public trough were major contractors and suppliers (*empreteiros*) who developed cozy relationships with public officials and SOE managers. National content laws, import quotas, price fixing, conditional import authorization, prior consented import, special exchange rates for import-exporters, surcharges, and similar legislation kept foreign competitors out and gave *empreteiros* near monopolies as purveyors to the state. Pharaonic public work projects like Itaipú and Tucuruí (the largest and second largest hydroelectric dams in the world, respectively), the Rio-Niterói bay bridge, the Transamazonic highways, public housing projects, the huge Carajás mine complex in the Amazon, and infrastructure building created an unprecedented boom for private engineering and supply companies but at the same time turned *empreteiros* into semipermanent denizens of the public coffers, as inefficient and bloated as SOEs. The United States protested against Brazil's increasing protectionist policy of excluding foreign competition in engineering services at home. Abroad, U.S. contractors learned that Brazilian counterparts often received hefty state subsidies and government support in their overseas bidding.[47]

The public sector's domination of the economy did not end here. In the financial sector, the state expanded its position from 50 percent of the market share in 1975 to near 80 percent by 1988. Private banks were squeezed out of the market. In addition to various federally controlled banks such as the Bank of Brazil (established in the early nineteenth century), Federal Savings Bank (CEF), National Economic and Social Development Bank (BNDES), and the Federal Housing Bank (BNH, now defunct), each state has one or more of its own banks. Many of them have been money losers and principal sources for politically motivated loans, frequently bailing out the state finances and failing SOEs. The Collor government shut down state banks in three northeastern states—Piauí, Rio Grande do Norte, and Paraíba. Bank officials, who were political cronies of governors and federal politicians, often lacked the professional competence to operate banks profitably. These banks chronically turned to the Central Bank for additional infusions of capital. The Brazilian states owe their national government a whopping $53 billion, over half the country's internal debt. One recent study by the Central Bank shows that of the twenty-six state banks, only eight are profitable, and all the profits came from the loans to private enterprises, while the portfolios to SOEs and state and municipal governments were either defaulted or performing poorly. The rest (eighteen) are financial indigents, stretching out their hands to Brasília for more money.[48] Both the Reagan and Bush administrations have encouraged Brazil to liberalize and deregulate its banking industry and financial markets.

Periodic Economic Reforms

The price that Brazil had to pay during the second half of the 1980s was a pernicious galloping inflation that reached over 3,000 percent by the end of the decade. In five years, Brazil went through six economic reforms, or shock packages, and four currencies—cruzeiro in 1985, cruzado in 1986, cruzado novo in 1987, and back to cruzeiro in 1990; each time one thousand units of the old currency were converted into one new unit, except in 1990. This meant that Cr $1,000,000 in 1985 was equivalent to 1 cruzado novo of 1987 and 1 cruzeiro of 1990.[49] The government's monetary reforms, part of its excessive and repetitive economic shock packages, alone were responsible for institutionalizing inflation. The economic shock treatments—freezing wages and prices, temporary cuts in public spending, suspension of public works, reducing imports, overvaluing exchange rates, currency reforms, and other draconian measures—turned out to be short-term panaceas and failed to lay the groundwork for long-term solutions. In fact, they worked contrary to plan; instead of arresting inflation, the economy was subject to chronic hyperinflation. The political democratization did not help. To sustain themselves in power, Gen. João Figueiredo, the last military president (1979–85), and his accidental successor, José Sarney (1985–90), became populists by necessity. Both indulged politicians, catered to special interests, and pampered public sector enterprises by overspending and expanding public payrolls.

Pursuing an unintended populist policy at home also meant taking an unduly ultranationalistic posture abroad in international trade and bilateral relations with the United States. Big and generous export subsidies and easy credit policy continued. Trade and nontrade barriers abounded. So-called laws of similarity often subjected foreign products to exorbitantly high import duties, a nightmarish bureaucratic maze of customs clearance procedures, product registration and packaging rules, and even outright exclusion from the Brazilian market.[50] At one time, over two thousand items could not be imported into Brazil, until the Collor government tore down barriers in 1990 and 1991.[51] The laws governing international capital inflow and outflow, at one time competitive enough to have attracted $34 billion (the largest in the Third World), became anachronistic. The government predictably ignored international patent rights, forcing multinational corporations to keep most sophisticated products out of the Brazilian market; even worse, some foreign corporations "disinvested" by leaving the country. Companies working in fine chemicals, biotechnology, information, and high tech fields refused to do business in or transfer technology to Brazil. By the end of the decade, Brazil had little access to vital high technologies to make its economy globally competitive and no new capital to expand it.

While the U.S. administration saw such a tangle of laws and regulations as detrimental to American business interests in Brazil, its pressure tactics to liberalize and deregulate the Brazilian economy have not been productive. Many Brazilian products, ranging from orange juice concentrate to shoes to steel to airplanes, are blatantly subsidized by a series of Byzantine fiscal incentive measures and export bonuses. It bears repeating that Brazil was not the only country to practice such measures. However, it was one of the few countries in Latin America that made the importing of U.S. products very difficult and at times nearly impossible. The Reagan administration strove to loosen Brazilian regulations and to eliminate state subsidies by retaliating against them.

From Antidumping and Super 301 Retaliation

Two important changes in the 1970s were the higher cost of energy for industrialized economies and the highly subsidized export policies of NICs. The consequence of these two developments was an increasing competition in international trade and rising protectionism. European, Japanese, and American governments began to

impose gradual restrictions on foreign access to their markets. Between 1973 and 1980, world trade grew by 4.6 percent yearly, while
GDP grew only 3.3 percent. The first half of the 1980s saw a real decline of international trade as protectionism throughout the world
rebounded. By one Brazilian count, the United States charged 532
antidumping and compensatory duties on imports during the first
half of the 1980s.[52] During the 1970s and early 1980s, the United
States preferred to use voluntary export restraint (VER) mechanisms,
typically negotiated with each country and on each item. There are
some three hundred VER agreements in the world, of which eighty-
five apply to Japanese and Korean products. In practice, it is difficult
to enforce VER agreements, and the U.S. Trade Act of 1974 became
ineffective in protecting U.S. interests.

In 1988, Section 301 of the Trade Act was invoked to deal with imports worth $4 billion. The gentlemen's agreement of VER failed to
protect U.S. manufacturers. A frustrated Congress enacted and Reagan signed that year the Omnibus Trade and Competitive Act, turning Section 301 of 1974 into Super 301 and giving discretionary
power to the president. Unlike Section 301, Super 301 could cite a
country or countries for unfair trade practices instead of focusing on
specific goods. Once a country is cited, the U.S. trade representative
requires the accused to offer solutions within twelve to eighteen
months and insists on reciprocity, nondiscrimination, and transpar-
ency in trade practices, although GATT and other agencies have
pointed out that the United States itself has not lived up to these
stated goals. In 1989, Brazil, Japan, and India were cited by Super 301
for unfair trade practices and high import duties for American goods,
failing to protect U.S. firms' intellectual property rights, and other
restrictive measures. Brazil was soon taken off the Super 301 citation
but was instead placed on a watch list.[53]

After the ill-fated August 1988 visit to Brazil by Secretary Shultz,
the U.S. government imposed 100 percent surcharges on several Brazilian products for Brazil's negligence in protecting U.S. pharmaceutical patents and trademarks. Brazil countercharged the
United States with violating GATT rules. Since GATT has no provisions regarding protection of intellectual properties, its panel heard
the case and ruled that Brazil did not violate GATT rules.[54]

The Collor government, after it came to power in mid-March
1990, removed trade barriers and proposed major revisions in the
Brazilian Industrial Property Law, which regulates patent rights and

trademarks. Brazil opened its market to foreign products ranging from toys to automobiles, one of the major contributions of the Collor government in its first two years in power. Collor did more in one year to liberalize the trade structure than all his predecessors together since 1945. In May and June 1991, the Brazilian Congress debated the revision against stiff resistance from the alliance of right-wing businessmen and left-wing organized labor, with the military also championing the nationalistic cause in the background. Before the patent rights were overhauled, however, the Congress preferred to look at the Information/Communications Computer ("Informatics") Law (Lei Informática) of 1984.[55]

Informatics Law and Market Reserve

The Brazilian computer market reserve policy was based on two considerations. First, by the early 1970s, Brazil had become an important computer market. Its big and small businesses, especially banks, had begun to computerize their operations. Such major multinationals as IBM, Olivetti, Hewlett-Packard, DEC, Burroughs, and Texas Instruments became major players in the domestic market. The idea that computer technology would be critical for the modernization of the economy was widely accepted, and those in the scientific community, including universities, the armed forces, and business, came to realize that Brazil must seize available opportunities to develop its home-grown computer industry so that it could gain informatics independence. Multinationals traditionally did not carry out basic research and development of hardware and software technologies in Brazil, except those relating to customer services such as installation, repairs, and networking. Hence, officials in Itamaraty, the armed forces, the nascent computer sector, and the scientific establishment advocated a policy that would give Brazil opportunities to engage in R&D and informatics independence.[56]

In 1971, the Brazilian Navy and then National Economic Development Bank (BNDE—later the word "social" was added to the name, becoming BNDES) funded $2 million for two universities to begin basic R&D of a microcomputer G-10. The following year, the armed forces established Coordenação das Atividades de Processamento Eletrônico (CAPRE), which was charged with the development of domestic computer technology by assisting existing companies and establishing new informatics SOEs. As in the past, when there was a vacuum the state moved in to seize the opportunity to develop a new industry. By the late 1970s, CAPRE had emerged as the guiding light for Brazilian computer development as well as the agency that held veto power over activities of multinationals in importing and manufacturing computers, thus launching inadvertently the market reserve policy for those companies that the government, or more precisely the armed forces, favored. The quality of technology was never an issue.

By 1979, the National Intelligence Service (SNI), Itamaraty, and the National Council on Scientific Research (CNPq) had formed a screening agency that had complete authority over all aspects of computer technology development, import, and marketing. In fact, the trio, along with the Central Bank and the patent office (INPI— National Institute of Industrial Property), vetoed all product development proposals made by IBM and other international companies on the grounds that the plans did not include the transfer of technology to Brazil, acceptable overseas marketing strategies, and sufficient Brazilian capital participation. CAPRE instead actively encouraged Brazilian companies and SOEs to develop domestic technologies, and the government granted liberal credit to redouble R&D efforts.[57]

Second, given the enormous size of the Brazilian computer market, the notion of "dependency theory," or the antidependent objective of acquiring self-sufficiency in computer technology, played a decisive role in the formation of market reserve policy. In 1978, two multinational companies imported 77 percent of all microcomputers. The domestic market was growing so fast that the Brazilian computer industry feared multinationals' monopoly of the market, leaving little or no room for them. Such dependency would condemn Brazil to a permanent status of informatics underdevelopment. Exhorting economic nationalism and self-sufficiency in informatics technology and supporting excessive protection for the infant domestic industry from foreign competition, the armed forces, especially those in the National Security Council (CNS) and the SNI, began to institute restrictive decrees against multinationals. In 1983, the computer market stood at $1.5 billion, and Brazil imported over $400 million worth of computers and peripherals.[58]

In 1979, those officers active in the National Security Council adopted the next logical step in computer policy: introduction of the Informatics Law. To effectively enforce this law, a strong entity had to be created. CAPRE reported to the Ministry of Planning and had no direct access to the armed forces high command. A new enforcement organization, SEI (Special Secretariat for Informatics), would report directly to the president and the CNS. The law also expanded the power of SEI substantially, making it the absolute czar in matters of computer policymaking and enforcement. Those who favored this domestic market reserve sought to emulate the Japanese model. In the early years of its computer industry, the Tokyo government had dragged its feet deliberately on granting patent rights and permission to American companies to operate in Japan. This delay (which was perfectly legal in Japan) gave Japanese competitors time to develop their own products with government subsidies and support, typically from the Ministry of International Trade and Industry (MITI). Texas Instruments, the pioneer in semiconductor manufacturing, took over twenty years to secure a Japanese patent. By then MITI had made sure Japanese companies had established their foothold in the domestic and world markets. Those who pushed for this Japanese model as Brazil's policy foundation came from all sectors of the country: SEI (which also means "I know"), the Left, organized labor, universities, the armed forces, the scientific community, and the small but growing domestic computer industry. Brazil would do anything it took to keep international competition out while domestic manufacturers illegally copied American computers and software. SEI even vetoed IBM's request to continue to produce the existing personal computer Model 36, although production had begun well before the market reserve practice was in place. The agency also rejected Apple's and Hewlett-Packard's proposals to establish plants in Brazil to build PCs and export them.[59]

It bears repeating that the market reserve policy was established in a series of SEI-issued decrees and regulations (*actos*), not by law. The process was not reviewed by Congress; rather, it was an executive act. In September 1980, SEI decreed that the domestic market for hardware and software would be "guaranteed" to domestic private companies and encouraged SOEs and other government organs to use Brazilian computers. This policy was followed by another regulation in 1982 that SEI would have complete authority to grant or deny permission to import computer systems into the domestic market. Many Brazilian SOEs became victims of this regulation, which routinely denied the import of cutting edge technologies. In 1983, SEI was granted more sweeping power to oversee the introduction of all computer instrumentation into the country. No fewer than thirty organizations expressed their support, including the Brazilian Society for Scientific Progress (SBPC), the nation's main congregation of university scientists that carried political prestige and influence as a chronic critique of the military regime. This time the SBPC endorsed strongly the SEI market reserve policy.[60]

The United States vigorously protested this informatics authoritarianism. Congress considered retaliatory legislation against Brazil. SEI operated as an arm of the military but with strong support from the traditional opponents of the regime, making the market reserve policy viable and emboldening SEI. An unlikely political alliance was formed: the ideological Left of the country found one policy that they could support coming from the military. The business community was split. The nation's largest industrial association, FIESP, publicly denounced the market reserve policy. But many right-wing businessmen saw an opportunity to profit from the protectionist policy and rushed into the computer business.[61] Further, in the late 1970s and early 1980s, the military pumped a generous amount of money into higher education with the result that university professors were making as much as, if not more than, their European and American counterparts. The co-opted university scientists enjoyed generous research grants from the CNPq and other similar funding agencies and enthusiastically supported an independent computer development policy. They justified this as a patriotic action, not necessarily as support for the authoritarian regime.

U.S. protests fell on deaf ears. Those criticizing the SEI's informatics policy were branded as unpatriotic, favoring multinational interests, and, worse, condemning Brazil to eternal underdevelopment. Much like the McCarthy era in the United States, the Xiitas, or Shiites, as the ultranationalists of both the extreme Left and Right were called, went on massive witch hunts. Roberto Campos, the most articulate and outspoken opponent of the informatics policy, was ridiculed as a sellout to foreign interests. Campos, like other critics, deplored the extremes of the reserve policy but not always the "buy Brazilian" aspect of it. No foreign participation was allowed in the personal computer business—importing, manufacturing, distribution, and marketing. The critics saw such a comprehensive policy as equally unpatriotic.[62]

The biggest irony was that the Informatics Law (Lei no. 7232 of 29 October 1984) did not impose a market reserve. The purpose of the law was to promote and develop domestic technological capabilities, and it empowered sei to control the import of hardware and software for eight years, or to 1992 (article 4, section 8). As the U.S. ambassador judiciously pointed out, it was extremely confusing to have the law read in one way and see the enforcement of it in another.[63] Periodically, the United States refused to sell computer technology to Brazil. In June and July 1991, after emotional debates in the Congress, the Collor government signed a compromise bill into law that ended the market reserve in late 1992. As of late 1990, sei had still prohibited the import of some three hundred computer components and peripherals. The 1991 law allowed foreign computer companies to enter Brazil and manufacture hardware and software, but only under the condition that they would be a minority partner to a joint venture, guarantee the transfer of technology to Brazilian partners, and pay a surtax that went into the country's R&D funds. Domestic companies did not have to pay.[64]

Why did Brazil acquiesce to this pressure and abandon the market reserve? First, it was not voluntary. Brazil was isolated by international computer makers who denied its access to new and high technology. This boycott was effective. The market reserve policy made half a dozen companies rich, but they spent precious little in original R & D. Copycatting or piracy of trademarks, computers, and software was fought by U.S. and European firms in the Brazilian courts and at times they won. By the end of the 1980s, Brazilian computer technology had fallen so far behind international standards that exports never materialized, to the chagrin of the ultranationalists and the government. sei even denied Embraer (the Brazilian Boeing), Petrobrás (the national oil and gas monopoly), Telebrás (the national telecommunications monopoly), and other major soes permission to import advanced computer technologies. Their competitiveness and success as global companies depended on such imports.[65] By the time the Collor government came into office, a national consensus had developed: the excessive market reserve hurt Brazil more than it helped.

The Arms Industry and Trade

The development of Brazil's military enterprises in the 1960s and 1970s was an impressive feat. Brazil emerged as the world's sixth largest arms exporter, averaging $3 to $4 billion in sales per year. The global arms market was worth $50 billion, of which Brazil garnered a 6 to 8 percent share.[66] In 1985, Brazil ranked thirty-eighth in military expenditure among the seventy-two countries monitored by the U.S. Arms Control and Disarmament Agency. Its armed forces (496,000) ranked thirteenth of the seventy-two countries, ahead of then West Germany's (fourteenth) but behind Italy's (twelfth). Of the thirty-six Third World countries with sophisticated defense industries, only Brazil and India (not even Israel) appeared as the economies capable of manufacturing all nine categories of weapons systems that the U.S. government monitored.[67] The industry could not grow while it counted solely on the consumptive capacity of the Brazilian armed forces, which bought less than 5 percent of the total output; rather, it had to rely on exclusively overseas markets for operation.

There were several reasons why Brazil entered the competitive field of arms manufacturing. First, Brazil's independent foreign policy would be hollow as long as the country depended on the United States for military hardware and components. Second, the internal industrial economy was so diversified, often with participation of multinationals as a source of advanced technologies, that manufacturing arms and weapons systems became the next logical step to growth once the civilian market began to exhibit signs of saturation. Third, both the United States and the Soviet Union in the sixties began to specialize in high-tech weapons, leaving conventional weapons manufacturing to advanced NICs. Fourth, ongoing civil wars, insurgencies, and regional conflicts throughout the Third World expanded markets, especially in Africa and the Middle East. In spite of ideological allegiance to the superpowers, African and Middle Eastern countries were unable to import low-tech weapons from the United States and the Soviet Union. Instead, they found ready suppliers among leading Third World NICs such as Brazil to satisfy their own needs.

The military enterprises in Brazil were the composite result, therefore, of several factors. The country's advanced industrial economy helped; the presence of diversified multinationals in the country provided access to new technologies; several regional wars in the Middle East and Africa created new markets; and the state engendered a policy of building the military-industrial complex by the generous infusion of capital, fiscal incentives, credit, and subsidies. The military-dominated government was able to refrain from the complete statization of the armament industry, as in the Soviet Union, while it also refused to relegate complete control of the industry to the private sector, as in the United States. By maintaining a fine balance, the state used patronage and financial resources to stimulate the expansion of military enterprises. In the process, the state set the export policy of armament. Itamaraty exploited in full the arms trade as a versatile diplomatic weapon in its relations with Third World countries.[68]

Brazil adopted the principle of interchangeable parts; Brazilian armored cars, for instance, use the same chassis that GM, Ford, Mercedes-Benz, and other major transnationals produce for their passenger cars and trucks. Hence, parts and service pose no problem to Third World users. In eight years (1977–85), Brazil emerged as Latin America's biggest arms exporter (three-fourths of the total), making one aircraft every twenty hours, one armored personnel carrier every eighteen hours, and one thousand weapons systems every week. There were five hundred companies supplying components and parts to Brazil's aircraft industry, Embraer, alone, and over one thousand companies were devoted full time to the arms industry. Its twenty shipyards with some four hundred suppliers made Brazil the world's major shipbuilder. In this foray into military enterprises, Volkswagen, GM, Ford, Alcoa, Du Pont, Dow, Volvo Scandia, Telefunken, Mercedes-Benz, GE, and other companies forged alliances with the military-industrial complex of Brazil. Private firms, or *empreteiros*, key SOEs, and transnationals turned their excess industrial capacities into this export sector.[69]

Conflict with the United States began as Brazil indiscriminately exported its arms and weapons systems to anyone willing to pay. Brazil soon developed a monopsony relationship with anti-U.S. states. The initial major buyers of Brazilian arms were Iraq, Syria, Iran, and Libya. After the two oil shocks (1973 and 1979), Brazil designed a series of countertrade agreements with Middle Eastern and African countries to exchange arms for oil. The Iran-Iraq War of the 1980s also created new demand. Saudi Arabia and Egypt became convenient conduits to Arab countries hostile to the United States and also became licensed manufacturers of Brazilian arms. Between 1980 and 1982, Saudi Arabia spent $62.5 billion for arms transfer. Libya in particular bought more than it could use, serving as a go-between for Iraq, Nicaragua, and terrorist groups.

Such military SOEs as Embraer, Arsenal, and Imbel and such private firms as Engesa and Avibrás worked hand in hand under state patronage and grew to become the Third World's leaders in the arms trade. None required end-user licenses, making it easy for those buying Brazilian arms to resell them to anyone who could pay without reporting to the Brazilian manufacturers. This also became a bone of contention, as far as the United States was concerned.[70] The United States came to consider Brazil's unregulated arms exports as a destabilizing factor in the Middle East and Africa, where the United States sought to maintain its hegemony. The United States was increasingly concerned with Libya's role outside the region as an arms supplier. In 1982 alone, Libya spent over $200 million to purchase 150 Tucano airplanes, designed as trainers but capable of being used in low-intensity wars. By the mid-1980s, Qaddafi was supplying arms to the Sandinistas. Libya requested permission from Brazil to refuel four transport planes that Qaddafi claimed carried humanitarian medical supplies to Nicaragua. The U.S. government, with secure information that the planes carried military matériel, persuaded the Brazilian military to intercept the transports. Over Itamaraty's vehement protest, the military seized the planes and inspected them. They were carrying military cargoes, not medical supplies. The U.S. government continued to remain wary of Brazil's arms trade with Libya and other hostile anti-American Arab countries, although it recognized that Brazil's oil-import needs alone called for such a trade structure.[71] Despite such misgivings, the United States sought to condone the Brazilian–Middle Eastern arms-for-oil trade until the 1991 Gulf War.

There were many Brazilian contractors, mostly civil engineering firms, that worked in the Middle East, including Iraq. In 1985, Brazil sold $1.1 billion worth of arms to Iraq, making it the fourth largest supplier to that country. Part of the sales agreements required Brazilian engineers and technicians to stay in Iraq. One retired air force general (Hugo Piva) was working as a high-level technical adviser to the Iraqi military in the area of missiles. When the Gulf War broke out, the Brazilian engineering firms withdrew their crews from Iraq, while Piva and his staff, known as HOP, remained in that country and were said to be working on the problem of improving the targeting accuracy of Soviet and North Korean missiles. When the United States protested, Itamaraty first denied the presence of the Piva group in Iraq and then shrugged it off by coyly asserting that the group did not represent the Brazilian government; hence, Itamaraty could not interfere. President Collor was more forthcoming and co-operative. He assured the U.S. government that Brazil would enact a law that would prohibit retired officers from providing military services to foreign governments. The HOP mission was withdrawn.[72]

To say the least, Itamaraty was short-sighted. A willing response to U.S. protests could have gone far toward ameliorating soured bilateral relations. Argentina, for instance, while historically not friendly to the United States, chose to dispatch a small naval squadron to the Gulf at the insistence of its Foreign Ministry. The grateful Bush administration reciprocated. Washington assisted Argentina in renegotiating its debt with bankers; it facilitated loans from the Inter-American Development Bank and World Bank; it granted generous funding to develop mining resources as a new economy; and the Bush administration encouraged U.S. businessmen to invest in Argentina under the protection of a U.S. government insurance company. Itamaraty's ultranationalism gave Brazil the immediate gratification of being "independent" in its conduct of foreign policy, but the country's long-term interests were not protected. The Piva incident offered an opening, but Itamaraty failed to turn it to the country's advantage. It was an empty show of Brazil's diplomatic independence.

Conclusion

It is an understatement to say that relations between the United States and Brazil became "contentious" (which is the most favored word used by Itamaraty in describing bilateral relations) during the 1980s. In fact, there are some fundamental and irreversible changes taking place in the global, regional, and bilateral arenas of the United States and Brazil that will have grievous consequences, if mismanaged, for the whole of Latin America and the United States. The relative economic stature of the United States in the global arena vis-à-vis Japan and Germany deteriorated and will continue to decline before it can recover. Still the holder of a quarter of the world's entire GNPs, the United States has fallen behind Switzerland, Japan, Norway, Finland, and Sweden in per capita terms.[73] Attention to internal issues such as national health insurance and viable industrial and energy policies, reshaping foreign trade policy (including a successful conclusion of the negotiation with Mexico for the North American Free Trade Agreement), and dealing with the yawning deficit and ballooning national debt will further divert the United States from its Latin American policy.

During the 1980s, the national debt of the United States almost quadrupled; its trade balance has consistently remained in the red, averaging over $80 billion and in some years exceeding over $100 billion. Only in the last two years has the deficit begun to slide down. The Cold War had run out of gas by 1985, when Mikhail Gorbachev came into power, and in six years the dissolution of the Soviet Union became the most historic development during the second half of this century. American politics took a turn to conservatism under the two Republican administrations, and their free market economic liberalism came to serve as the linchpin of U.S. foreign policy toward Latin America, Eastern Europe, Asia, and Africa. More unrealistically, the conservative Republican administrations sought to persuade the Third World and former Eastern Europe to live under American economic systems and political values.

These momentous changes at home and abroad left the United States seemingly unprepared to cope with its pivotal relations with the rapidly emerging Third World's NICs in general and with Brazil in particular. Newly gained wealth and its status as the Third World's largest economy gave Brazil confidence and an opportunity to pursue independent, and often anti-American, foreign policy objectives on the global and inter-American stages. It could afford to behave less subserviently toward the United States; in the Middle East and Africa, Brazil replaced both the United States and the Soviet Union as a major conventional arms dealer; in international trade, Brazil pugnaciously expanded its market share around the world, challenging, and often pitting itself against, the United States. Unabashedly seeking the Third World's leadership position with India on the council of GATT, Brazil staked out positions on such key trade issues as agriculture, services such as civil engineering and financial markets, and telecommunications that are diametrically opposed to U.S. positions. The fact is that the two countries have different interests to defend and promote.

As the Third World's largest debtor, Brazil needs U.S. support to carry out successful negotiations with banks and the IMF. The United States has consistently refused to be party to direct negotiation, although from time to time Washington made special efforts in facilitating Brasília with short-term bridge loans. Yet its independent foreign policy stressing so-called Third Worldism stood in the way of persuading the United States to be helpful. This was changing, however, under Collor's emphasis on becoming part of the First World. The United States chronically demanded geopolitical concessions, and during the 1980s, Washington was tireless but less than successful in obtaining Brazilian support for its interventionist policy toward Nicaragua. At most Brazil was a reluctant but autonomous supporter of the United States, when such support justified Brazil's global, regional, and bilateral interests. Brazil will insist on retaining the autonomy of granting or withholding U.S. policy support (or diplomatic solidarity) as part of its foreign policy objectives through the 1990s.

The decade of the 1990s does not bode well. The rapidly unfolding regionalized markets of Europe, North America, and potentially the Pacific Rim could leave Brazil behind in the forthcoming global economic realignments. Its computer policy has left Brazil behind Korea, Singapore, and Taiwan in new technologies; its heavy reliance on statism in economic development has exhausted the so-called developmentalist model, and the country is forced to seek an alternate model of development and growth. Its antiquated laws, which treat international capital and technologies as threats rather than positive forces, so clearly shown in the Constitution of 1988 and subsequent laws, have forced domestic capital to leave or international capital to disinvest. And worse yet, access to high-tech industries such as fine chemicals, pharmaceuticals, and biotechnology has been barred and will continue to be difficult until Brazil modifies its policies on intellectual properties. One high-ranking Itamaraty official accused the international (read U.S.) media, banks, and business of having turned Brazil into a pariah. Since 1982, no real foreign direct investment came to Brazil, although recently Brazil's financial market has been open to the participation of international capital.

The Brazilian government is determined to open up, liberalize, deregulate, and privatize the ossified statist economy but has been confronted with formidable opposition from all quarters. In 1990, over $18 billion were invested in Latin America; almost all of it went to Chile, Argentina, Mexico, and Venezuela. Brazil received less than $100 million. The government faces the daunting task of turning Brazil around economically and, more important, changing the country's attitudes toward statism, foreign capital, and external debt issues. It will take a Herculean effort to accomplish this. Unless

Brazil and the United States set a meaningful and frank agenda that fosters cooperation within and out of the hemisphere, neither of the two titans of the New World will come out ahead.

Notes

1. Presidência da República, Secretaria de Planejamento, Delfim: 'Não olhe só a dívida: veja o que ela representa: Itaipu, Tucurui. . . .' (Brasília, 1983). Delfim defended the debt policy by stating that Brazil either needed to print more money or borrow from overseas sources (pp. 1–5, 14–15).

2. "Relações Brasil-EUA I: 7 de outubro de 1987," in *Seminários do IPRI (1987 a 1989)*, Cadernos do IPRI, no. 1 (Brasília, 1989), pp. 15–19. IPRI stands for the Instituto de Pesquisa de Relações Internacionais. It publishes a variety of works, but two key items merit attention: the Coleção Relações Internacionais and Cadernos.

3. FIESP (Federação das Indústrias do Estado de São Paulo), *Livre para crescer: proposta para um Brasil moderno* (São Paulo, 1990), pp. 135–40.

4. *Temas de política externa brasileira,* ed. Gelson Fonseca Júnior and Valdemar Carneiro Leão (Brasília, 1989).

5. Interviews with João Ricardo C. de Souza and Marco Antônio Damasceno Vieira, Assessoria Legislativa, Câmara dos Deputados, Brasília, 14, 17, and 19 June 1991. Souza and Vieira are foreign affairs staff for the Chamber. Neither could identify a single deputy with a profound appreciation of Brazil's foreign affairs. In fact, Souza has written speeches for both leftist and rightist deputies on foreign policy issues, often reflecting what he perceived to be their ideological bias on the issues. Unlike their American counterparts, these staff members on the Foreign Relations Committee are hired by public examinations (*concursos*), not by deputies for their political leanings.

6. Interview with Federal Deputy Diogo Nomura of São Paulo, Chair, Subcommittee on External Debt, Foreign Relations Committee, Chamber of Deputies, Brasília, 18 June 1991. When asked why Guimarães is the chair of the committee, Nomura stated that it is an honorary position for all former speakers of the Chamber; the committee hearings often include foreign dignitaries, and hence the chair should be a recognized person of political prominence.

7. Golbery was many things to many people. One of his books that has become required reading for Itamaraty officials is *Geopolítica do Brasil* (Rio de Janeiro, 1967, and subsequent editions). The best edition is the fifth in the general's collective work, *Conjuntura política nacional, o poder executivo & geopolítica do Brasil,* 3d ed. (Rio de Janeiro, 1981), pp. 170, 176.

8. *Conjuntura política,* p. 198.

9. Vice President Goulart was in China when Jânio Quadros resigned in August 1961. Officials in Itamaraty recall that San Thiago Dantas was the

philosophical father of Brazil's "positive Left" and independent foreign policy, thus moving away from the United States, while José Araújo de Castro was the father of Brazil's Third Worldism. Vera Cíntia Alvares, "Reflexões sobre o surgimento da Política Externa Independente na gestão de Jânio Quadros," in *Ensaios de história diplomático do Brasil (1930–1986)*, Caderno do IPRI, no. 2, ed. Sérgio França Danese (Brasília, 1989), pp. 79–87. Oliveiros S. Ferreira, "A rocada geoestratégica," *O Estado de S. Paulo*, 12 July 1989.

10. "O Itamaraty, como Carolina, não viu o tempo passar," *Jornal da Tarde*, 6 June 1988. The title of the article is a paraphrase of Chico Buarque's song: like Carolina, Itamaraty was at the window, seeing the world and time go by. The newspaper also criticized both Figueiredo and Sarney for using the Third World language of the North's exploitation of the South. Brazil would be better off squarely in with the Third World community. It urged Itamaraty to end the voluntary isolationism and return to the real world.

11. Ambassador Araújo de Castro made this famous speech on 11 June 1971 in Washington before the visiting group of Brazil's National War College students: "Congelamento do poder mundial." Guido Fernando S. Soares, "O acordo de cooperação nuclear Brasil–Alemanha Federal," *Revista Forense* (January–March 1976): 210.

12. Júlio Glinternick Bitelli, "A política brasileira para a Africa e a descolonização dos territórios portugueses," in *Ensaios*, pp. 177–91. Fred Bridgland, *Jonas Savimbi: A Key to Africa* (New York, 1987).

13. Ambassador Vernon Walters made this observation. See "Programa de verão," *Veja*, 31 August 1988, and *Jornal do Brasil*, 30 April 1988.

14. World Bank, *World Development Report 1991: The Challenge of Development* (New York, 1991), p. 209, table 3. As of 1989, the world GNP was assessed at $19,981,540 billion.

15. Geraldo Miniuci Ferreira Júnior, "O acordo nuclear Brasil-Alemanha," in *Ensaios*, pp. 153–64, esp. 156–57.

16. By the 1990 World Bank figures, Brazil has been losing its venerable place since 1989 and 1990. Brazil slipped to ninth place in 1989 and then to eleventh in 1990. See "Brasil perde terreno na economia mundial," *Folha de S. Paulo*, 9 June 1991.

17. Comptroller General of the United States, Report to Congress, *The Brazilian Economic Boom: How Should the United States Relate to It?* (Washington DC, 1974), pp. i–ii. After 1974, Brazil did not receive USAID funds. Robert J. S. Ross and Kent C. Trachte, eds., *Global Capitalism: The New Leviathan* (Albany, N.Y., 1990), pp. 82–100. When Brazilians use the expression "international order" now, it has a connotation different from that of the 1970s. See Paulo Nogueira Batista, "Nova Ordem Mundial," *Folha de S. Paulo*, 12 June 1991, and Almirante-de-Esquadra Mario César Flores, Ministro da Marinha, "A inserção da Marinha no cenário brasileiro atual," testi-

mony before the National Defense Committee, Chamber of Deputies, Brasília, 16 May 1991, pp. 2–3.

18. *O Estado de S. Paulo*, 12 July 1989, and *Folha de S. Paulo*, 30 July 1989.

19. The U.S. government was so concerned with such a view (Paul Kennedy's book being the focal point of criticism) that it published a series of rebuttals: Robert Heilbroner, "Is America Falling Behind?: An Interview with Paul Kennedy"; Samuel P. Huntington, "Decline or Renewal?: A Rebuttal to Paul Kennedy"; Joseph S. Nye Jr., "New Dimensions of Power"; and Joel Kotkin, "The Emergence of a 'World Nation,'" *Dialogue* (April 1989): 32–52.

20. Kevin J. Middlebrook and Carlos Rico, "The United States and Latin America in the 1980s: Change, Complexity, and Contending Perspectives," in Kevin J. Middlebrook and Carlos Rico, eds., *The United States and Latin America in the 1980s: Contending Perspectives on a Decade of Crisis* (Pittsburgh, 1986), pp. 3–7. For the failure of Reagan's Latin American policy, see Linda Robinson, "Playing by Our Rules," *New York Times Book Review*, 29 December 1991, or Thomas Carothers, *In the Name of Democracy: U.S. Policy toward Latin America in the Reagan Years* (Berkeley, 1991).

21. The list is compiled from statements, interviews, and testimonies of key U.S. and Brazilian officials: Paul E. Boeker, *Lost Illusions: Latin America's Struggle for Democracy, as Recounted by Its Leaders* (La Jolla, 1990), pp. 275–89. In his interviews with Sarney and Ulysses Guimarães, Boeker reports that debt was named first and foremost when the two Brazilian leaders were asked for the most critical issue on which they would like to see the Reagan administration change its policy. Fleicha de Lima, Itamaraty's number two man, listed the following three issues as the most contentious between the United States and Brazil: (1) piracy of patents and trademarks, (2) drug trafficking, and (3) the destruction of the environment in the Amazon. "Fleicha de Lima pretende reverter o negativismo nas relações Brasil-EUA," *Folha de S. Paulo*, 25 August 1988. U.S. Ambassador Harry Shlaudeman identified the following issues that made the bilateral relations "difficult": (1) Brazil's excessive identification with the Third World, (2) the market reserve policy of computers, (3) the rising tides of U.S. protectionism, (4) Brazil's strengthening ties with Latin America, (5) Brazil's position on GATT, (6) the lack of confidence among U.S. businessmen in Brazil, and (7) subsidies. "Shlaudeman diz que investor perdeu confiança," *Jornal do Brasil*, 24 April 1987, "Shlaudeman alerta para retaliações contra o Brasil," *O Estado de S. Paulo*, 24 April 1987, and "Novo relacionamento com EUA," *Gazeta Mercantil*, 27 March 1987. "Relações econômicas Brasil-EUA: 6 de junho de 1988," in *Seminários do IPRI (1987 a 1989)*, pp. 31–35.

22. "O Itamaraty, como Carolina, não viu o tempo passar"; "Programa de verão," pp. 50–52. The remark on the "terrorist action" was attributed to Itamaraty. A week later, Namir Salek, head of CACEX of the Bank of Brazil (its foreign trade licensing department), used the expression in public. See "Os

bons frutos da visita do secretário dos EUA," *Gazeta Mercantil,* 9 August 1988. FEISP, *Livre pare crescer,* pp. 131–32.

23. "Represália contra o carvão dos EUA," *Gazeta Mercantil,* 5–7 October 1987.

24. "Programa de verão"; "Conversa à toa," *Veja,* 19 August 1988, p. 50.

25. "'Relações com EUA não atravessão fase boa' diz Sarney," *Folha de S. Paulo,* 10 February 1989. Sarney also criticized Secretary of State James Baker's testimony before the U.S. Senate confirmation hearing, where he devoted many "pages" on Central America, Nicaragua, and the Caribbean but only "four lines" on South America.

26. Eul-Soo Pang, "Brazil's External Debt: Part I: The Outside View," *UFSI Report* 1984/no. 37, South America (ESP-1-1984), December 1984 (Hanover, N.H., 1984), p. 1.

27. Jeffry A. Frieden, *Banking on the World: The Politics of International Finance* (New York, 1989), pp. 128–31, and *Debt, Development, and Democracy: Modern Political Economy and Latin America, 1965–1985* (Princeton, N.J., 1991), pp. 106–35.

28. Ministério da Fazenda, *The Financing of Economic Development in the Period 1987–1991* (Brasília, 1987), pp. 3–4. Since 1983, Brazil paid $39 billion until Sarney's first moratorium. A good background to Brazil's moratorium is Eric Nepomuceno, *O outro lado da moeda: Dilson Funaro: histórias ocultas do Cruzados da Moratória* (São Paulo, 1990).

29. *Folha de S. Paulo,* 11 June 1991.

30. Roy C. Smith, *The Global Bankers* (New York, 1989). Brasil, Câmara dos Deputados, Comissão de Relações Exteriores, Comissão Parlamentar de Inquérito, Depoimento pelo Ambaixador Jório Dauster, Brasília, 19 June 1991. "The Ebb Tide: A Survey of International Finance," a supplement to *The Economist,* 27 April 1991, pp. 7–8.

31. On the Brazil-IMF relations, see Jackie Roddick, *The Dance of the Millions: Latin America and the Debt Crisis* (London, 1988), pp. 139–45; Smith, *The Global Bankers,* pp. 50–60, 151–74; Julian Weiss, *The Asian Century* (New York, 1989), pp. 24–25.

32. Nepomuceno, *O outro lado da moeda,* pp. 37–38, 60–61 (the quote), 72–73, and 144–45.

33. For the details of the Cruzado Plan, see Eul-Soo Pang and Laura Jarnagin, "Brazil's Cruzado Plan," *Current History* (February 1987): 13–16, 41–42; and Eul-Soo Pang, "Debt, Adjustment, a Democratic Cacophony in Brazil," in Barbara Stallings and Robert Kaufman, eds., *Debt and Democracy in Latin America* (Boulder, Colo., 1989), pp. 132–35; Ricardo Noblat, *Céu dos favoritos: o Brasil de Sarney a Collor* (Rio de Janeiro, 1991), pp. 66–67; Nepomuceno, *O outro lado da moeda,* pp. 76–89. Carlos Alberto Sardenberg, *Aventura e agonia: nos basitodres do Cruzado* (São Paulo, 1987) is a mix of political gossip and a journalist's observations on the ill-fated Cruzado Plan.

The initial evaluation of the plan was published in "O Brasil da moeda forte," *Conjuntura Econômica* (March 1986). A solid interim progress report on the plan is found in *Veja*, 24 September 1986. The best work on the plan was written by those economists who fathered it: André Lara Resende et al., *Os pais do Cruzado contam por que não deu certo*, 2d ed. (Rio de Janeiro, 1987).

34. *Gazeta Mercantil*, 20 February 1987. The original intent was to suspend the payment of interest for ninety days until Brazil could accumulate more foreign reserves. Noblat, *Céu dos favoritos*, pp. 87–88; Paulo Nogueira Batista Jr., *Da crise internacional a moratória brasileira* (Rio de Janeiro, 1988), pp. 83–91.

35. When Zélia and her debt negotiator, Jório Dauster, sat down with bankers between October 1990 and April 1991, they made the identical arguments that Funaro made on the pro-American bias of the committee. In fact, Brazil expanded the size of the committee and included more European bankers in the hope that the new group would be sympathetic to Brazil. None of this happened. See Nepomuceno, *O outro lado da moeda*, pp. 44–49; *O Estado de S. Paulo*, 6 October 1990; *Folha de S. Paulo*, 21 October 1990.

36. *Veja*, 15 May 1991.

37. *Wall Street Journal*, 4 September 1987; *Washington Post: National Weekly Edition*, 21 September 1987; *The Economist*, 19 September 1987.

38. Depoimento pelo ambaixador Jório Dauster. See Smith, *The Global Bankers*, pp. 124–27.

39. Nepomuceno, *O outro lado da moeda*, p. 67; "Mágica frustrada—Bresser revela que, ao sair, planejava novo congelamento e moratória conjunta com a Argentina," *Veja*, 16 November 1988.

40. Pang, "Debt, Adjustment," p. 138.

41. 'Nos braços do FMI," *Veja*, 11 December 1991, pp. 30–34.

42. "U.S. Will Seek to Slash Debt of Third World" and "Bush Aides Are Likely to Offer a Plan Soon on Third World Debt," *Wall Street Journal*, 8, 9 March 1989.

43. Interview with Federal Deputy Diogo Nomura. For the Mexican acceptance of the Brady Plan, see "Another Round of IMF Poison?" *Wall Street Journal*, 20 March 1989.

44. "Sisters in the Wood: A Survey of the IMF and the World Bank," a supplement to *The Economist*, 12 October 1991, pp. 17–18; Rudgier Dornbusch, "The Latin American Debt Problem: Anatomy and Solutions," in Stallings and Kaufman, eds., *Debt and Democracy*, pp. 11–14.

45. Renato Ticoulat Filho, "Apresentação e síntese," in Filho, ed., *A crise do "Bom patrão"* (Rio de Janeiro, 1984), pp. 13–22 provides a short but solid overview of the growth of *estatais*. Celso Furtado, *A fantasia organizada* (Rio de Janeiro, 1985), pp. 175–76; Brasil, Seplan/CNPq, */Setor produtio estatal: dispêndios em ciências e tecnologia 1978/82* (Brasília, 1982), pp. 7–8; Sérgio Henrique Abranches et al., *A empresa pública no Brasil: uma abordagem*

multidisciplinar (Brasília, 1980); Instituto de Planejamento Econômica e Social (IPEA) and Comissão Econômica para a América Latina (CEPAL), *Seminário sobre planejamento e controle do setor de empresas estatais: debates e refleões* (Brasília, 1983).

46. Celso Luiz Martone, "Expansão do Estado empresário no Brasil," in Filo, ed., *A crise do "Bom patrão,"* pp. 59–65. Former U.S. Ambassador to Brazil L. A. Motley estimates that as much as 60 percent of the country's GDP came from the SOES. See his comments in, "Protecionismo existe em qualquer país: entrevista [com] Anthony Motley," *O Globo*, 5 June 1988. *Jornal da Tarde*, 7 December 1973, 6 April 1974, and 11 April 1977 published articles on the etiology and growth of Brazil's public enterprises.

47. FIESP, *Livre para crescer*, passim. For the post-1974 trade policy, see Donald Coe, "Brazil: Precedents and Prospects in Foreign Trade," in Geoffrey Shepherd and Carlos Geraldo Langoni, eds., *Trade and Reform: Lessons from Eight Countries* (San Francisco, 1991), pp. 15–19. For the government's support in overseas business, see J. Carlos de Assis, *A chave do tesouro*, 11th ed. (Rio de Janeiro, 1984).

48. Assis, *A chave do tesouro*, pp. 25–26; "Rombo estadual," *Veja*, 18 December 1991, pp. 88–89.

49. For the economic reforms, see Pang and Jarnagin, "Brazil's Cruzado Plan," pp. 130–35, and "Brazil's Catatonic Lambada," *Current History* (February 1991): 73–75, 85–87.

50. Some examples of "laws of similarities": Lei no. 6.624, de 23 de Março de 1979 (compulsory registration of all foreign products packaged similar to those of Brazilians); Lei no. 7.646, de 18 de Dezembro de 1987 (granting intellectual property rights to software of foreign and Brazilian origins); Decreto no. 96.036, de 12 de Maio de 1988 (regulating Lei no. 7.646); and Lei no. 7.762, de 27 de Abril de 1989 (an extension of PLANIN [Plano Nacional de Informática e Automação] for six months).

51. FIESP, *Livre para crescer*, pp. 145–52.

52. Ibid., pp. 148–50. Some argue that had Geisel not taken the expansionist policy after the oil shock, Brazil could not have pulled itself so quickly out of the recession of the 1980s. For such views, see Antônio Barros de Castro, "Ajustamento x transformação: a economia brasileira de 1974 a 1984," in Antônio Barros de Castro and Francisco Eduardo Pires de Souza, eds., *A economia brasileira em marcha forçada* (Rio de Janeiro, 1985), pp. 27–47; Sebastian Edwards, "The United States and Foreign Competition in Latin America," in Martin Feldstein, ed., *The United States in the World Economy* (Chicago, 1988), pp. 15–20.

53. "A Survey of World Trade," supplement to *The Economist*, 22 September 1990, pp. 9–11.

54. Riordan Roett and Scott D. Tollefson, "The Year of Elections in Brazil," *Current History* (January 1990): 27.

55. "Propriedade industrial em questão," *Jornal do Brasil*, 9 June 1991.

56. Paulo Bastos Tigre, *Technology and Competition in the Brazilian Computer Industry* (New York, 1983), pp. 3–5; Emmanuel Adler, *The Power of Ideology: The Quest for Technological Autonomy in Argentina and Brazil* (Berkeley, 1991), pp. 181–97.

57. Tigre, *Technology*, pp. 66–67; Christina Tavares and Milton Seligman, *Informática: a batalha do século XXI* (Rio de Janeiro, 1984), pp. 66–69.

58. Tigre, *Technology*, pp. 53–55.

59. Roberto Campos, *Além do cotidiano*, 2d ed. (Rio de Janeiro, 1985), pp. 229–35; David C. Bruce, "Brazil Plays the Japan Card," *Third World Quarterly* (1983): 848–60.

60. Tavares and Seligman, *Informática*, pp. 78–86.

61. Even banks and civil engineering firms entered into the computer business. For example, the ItauTec, a subsidiary of the Itaú Bank, is one of the major makers of personal computers in Brazil today.

62. Campos, *Além do cotidiano*, pp. 241–50.

63. An excellent critique of the market reserve was published in "Confusão electrônica," *Veja*, 16 July 1986, pp. 96–103. *A informática e a Nova República*, ed. Claudio Mammana (São Paulo, 1985), lists the complete text of the Lei Informática, pp. 277–94.

64. On his June visit to Washington, Collor wanted to bring two "gifts" to Bush: the new informatics law and the industrial patent law. Neither was ready when the president was ready to leave for the United States. For the details, see "PMDB decide contra a reserva na informática," *Folha de S. Paulo*, 5 June 1991, "PMDB negocia fim da reserva na informática," *Folha de S. Paulo*, 6 June 1991, and "Informática continuará com incentivos," *Jornal do Brasil*, 14 June 1991. For the continued import ban, see "Fugindo do atraso," *Veja*, 19 September 1990.

65. In October 1990, Senator Karsten of Wisconsin added a rider to a budget bill that would have prohibited Embraer from purchasing IBM components to upgrade its supercomputer. Brazil dispatched two pro-American cabinet members to lobby the U.S. Congress and succeeded in killing the Karsten rider. For the details, see *Folha de S. Paulo*, 21 October 1990.

66. "Who Supplies the Matches?" *South* (November 1985): 15–16; *Wall Street Journal*, 4 January 1985.

67. The nine categories are small arms, artillery, light armor, heavy armor, light aircraft, jet fighters, tactical missiles, small warships, and large warships. See USACDA, *World Military Expenditures and Arms Transfer 1987* (Washington DC, 1988), pp. 5–30. Stephanie G. Neuman, "International Stratification and Third World Military Industries," *International Organization* (winter 1984): 167–97 argued that the Third World share of the global arms market would continue to be small, for over 90 percent of R&D was carried out by the two superpowers of the Cold War era.

68. Patrice Franko-Jones, *The Brazilian Defense Industry* (Boulder, Colo., 1992), p. 88.

69. *Istoé*, 26 June 1984. Joseph E. Clare Jr., "Whither the Third World Arms Producers?" in USACDA, *World Military Expenditures and Arms Transfer 1986* (Washington DC, 1987), pp. 23–28; *Folha de S. Paulo*, 6 February 1983; *Jornal do Brasil*, 7 July 1982. *Jornal de Brasília*, 25 July 1982, argued that the arms industry pulled many civilian industries out of the 1982 recession.

70. H. M. F. Howarth, "Brazil's Defense Industry—Ambitious and Growing Fast," *International Defense Review* (1985): 1413–27; *Jornal do Brasil*, 25 April 1974. *Latin American Weekly Report*, 16 April 1987 and 2 July 1987. *Defense & Foreign Affairs Weekly*, 18–24 November 1985. "Arab Petrodollars: Where Did All the Money Go?" *South* (September 1985); 10–11; Petrobrás, *Relatório anual consolidado '79* (Rio de Janeiro, 1980); *Resposta a "Os Mandarins da República": Interbrás, ficção & realidade* (Rio de Janeiro, 1984), pp. 204–55; Franko-Jones, *The Brazilian Defense Industry*, pp. 180–81.

71. Eul-Soo Pang and Laura Jarnagin, "Brazilian Democracy and the Foreign Debt," *Current History* (February 1984): 66–67.

72. Pang and Jarnagin, "Brazil's Catatonic Lambada," p. 86; "Cientista das Arábias," *Veja*, 3 October 1990, pp. 48–50. As it turned out, U.S. pressure was not necessary. Before the Allied bombing began in February 1991, the Brazilian government ordered all its citizens to quit Iraq.

73. World Bank, *World Development Report 1991*, p. 205. The per capital GNP of the United States is $20,910, while Switzerland and Japan, the richest and second richest countries in per capita GNP, boast $29,800 and $23,810, respectively.

John A. Booth

Central America and the United States: Cycles of Containment and Response

> The Americas are under attack. Latin America, the traditional
> alliance partner of the United States, is being penetrated by
> Soviet power. The Caribbean rim and basin are being spotted
> with Soviet surrogates and ringed with socialist states.
>   Committee of Santa Fe[1]

Geopolitics and crisis have occasionally forced Central America to
the center of U.S. interest but rarely so spectacularly as in the 1980s.
In the lull following Vietnam and Watergate, revolution in the isthmus and shifting worldviews in Washington suddenly and unexpectedly catapulted Central America to and kept it very near the top of
three successive U.S. administrations' policy agendas. Rarely had
debate over U.S. foreign policy making become as acrimonious or
partisan as it did over Central America in the 1980s. Rarely had a
U.S. administration encountered so much congressional resistance
to its foreign policy initiatives. Only rarely had so much U.S. energy
short of outright and overt war-making been expended to shape
events in any world region. This abrupt transformation was remarkable because it seemed so disproportionate to the tiny size, population, and modest resource base of Central America. It was even more
striking because during the two prior decades U.S. treatment of the
region had often seemed nearly indifferent.

   U.S. policy toward Central America is cyclical, and in the 1980s it
cycled through three quite different approaches to its central driving
force, the containment of Communism. In turn, the Central American states adapted rather quickly to these important shifts in U.S.
foreign policy. Several years of intense U.S. efforts to contain leftist
movements in Central America generated ever-growing strains

within the isthmus. In response, once-divided Central American leaders eventually drew together against the United States in an unprecedented regional peacemaking effort. The resulting Central American peace process gradually succeeded in diminishing conflicts within and among the nations of the region despite strong U.S. opposition.

Theoretical Considerations

To understand U.S.–Central American interaction in the 1980s one must be aware of certain constant and variable factors. One constant of the interaction between Central America is inequality. Even should all five Central American republics presently combine and act in harmony (quite rare in its own right) with regard to the United States, they would still command less than 10 percent of the population of the United States and only about 1 percent of its economic activity.[2] A second constant feature is that U.S. relations with Central America over nearly two centuries have been driven mainly by U.S. security interests. These have been shaped by the isthmus's critical proximity, its potential (in the nineteenth century) for the territorial expansion of the United States, and transisthmian transit routes.[3] For much of the twentieth century, and especially since World War II, these concerns have manifested themselves particularly as a desire to contain Communism and Soviet bloc influence in the region. U.S. administrations' styles of containment and levels of attention to Central America have varied over time, but the desire to contain Communism has remained stable. Among the variable factors in U.S.–Central American relations are policy-making processes, policy makers, and the dimensions, rules, and players of the global playing field. The interaction of these variable features helps account for some of the volatility in Central American–U.S. bilateral relations in the 1980s.

The United States in the 1980s was a great power, the head of a broad alliance network, and (though bound by many obligations imposed by its superpower status) relatively rich in capacity and in the autonomy to act in the international arena. In contrast, the Central American nations were small, weak states and clients in the U.S. hegemonic system, which markedly constrained their behavior and potential for action.[4] Other things being equal, the more tightly managed and more unified the hegemonic system within which weak states like those of Central America find themselves, the more militarized become hegemonic relations, and the greater the tensions between the great power and its rivals, the less autonomy and discretion weak states have. Weak states, however, are not powerless. Their autonomy vis-à-vis the great power may be enhanced by developing greater resource levels of their own, assistance from third parties (including a great power's rivals), cooperation with other states, or a weakening of the hegemon's capacity or resolve. Their policy and behavior, too, may be conditioned by the shifting makeup, perceptions, and alliances of subnational actors. They need not, thus, merely submit to the great power but may pursue in their national interest, as Rosenau points out, various strategies, including acquiescent, promotive, intransigent, and preservative adaptation.[5] We see examples of most of these strategies in Central America during the 1980s.

Despite a commonplace tendency to regard nation-states as unitary actors with relatively stable interests defined by presidents, other important elements within national governments, foreign policy bureaucracies, and larger civil societies may also affect policy and its implementation. Indeed, a dominant foreign policy in a particular moment may be the product of a coalition of state and nonstate actors and thus subject to change. Shifts in the relative importance and influence of nonstate actors within both the United States and Central America altered U.S.–Central American interaction in the 1980s.

History and Context of U.S.–Central American Relations

Central America

The five modern Central American republics—Costa Rica, El Salvador, Guatemala, Honduras, and Nicaragua[6]—have shared much history and have developed economically along quite similar lines. All eventually specialized heavily in export agriculture, and all became importers of oil, manufactured goods, and technology. Their most important recent mutual effort was to form the Central American Common Market (CACM) in 1960, which operated until around 1980. By the early twentieth century U.S. investments and loans were a major factor in each Central American economy, and from then until the formation of the CACM the United States was usually the principal trading partner and major source of foreign investment of each isthmian nation. The United States has flexed its diplomatic, economic, and military muscles in the Caribbean Basin to consolidate and maintain its hegemonic role. Indeed, between 1898 and 1933 the United States occupied Cuba, Nicaragua, the Dominican Republic, and Haiti, established military bases in Panama, and sent troops into Mexico and Panama. As a result, Central American governments have usually treated U.S. concerns and actions with considerable deference and followed generally acquiescent adaptive strategies.[7] Competing elites in Central America, in contrast, especially on the left, have criticized their nations' status as clients in this hegemonic system.

In the 1960s and early 1970s the five Central American nations almost simultaneously underwent socioeconomic transformations that first brought about political mobilization and then revolutionary upheaval in the late 1970s and the 1980s.[8] High growth rates almost doubled their populations between 1960 and 1980. The CACM stimulated an industrialization and agroexport boom in the 1960s and early 1970s that pushed peasants off the land and substantially increased both the number of people working in manufacturing and the industrial sector's share of gross domestic product (GDP; table 1).

The architects of the CACM successfully promoted rapid economic growth in the 1960s and much of the 1970s (table 1). They also assumed that some of the new wealth and income created would make the isthmus's working classes less susceptible to political radicalism from the left that might be spurred on by the Cuban revolution. In truth, however, only Honduras and Costa Rica made successful efforts to redistribute wealth and income or to attenuate poverty.[9] Indeed, the CACM industrialization and agroexport booms actually worsened income inequalities and unemployment and eroded the living standards of the working classes, especially in Nicaragua, El Salvador, and Guatemala. Real working-class wages eroded sharply in those three nations between 1970 and 1980. An ever more urban, literate, and organized—yet worse off—populace in each country (table 1) mobilized and demanded reform, but the Nicaraguan, Salvadoran, and Guatemalan governments resisted change and fiercely repressed such mobilization. By the late 1970s or early 1980s escalating regime violence and continued erosion of popular and middle-class living conditions had greatly broadened the size and resources of once-tiny rebellions led by Marxist guerrillas

Table 1

Selected Data by Country, Central America, 1960–1990

	Costa Rica	El Salvador	Guatemala	Honduras	Nicaragua
Population[a]					
1960	1,236	2,570	3,964	1,935	1,493
1980	2,284	4,525	6,917	3,662	2,771
1990	3,015	5,252	9,197	5,138	3,874
Mean annual population growth (percent)					
1961–70	3.4	3.4	2.8	3.1	3.2
1971–80	2.8	2.3	2.8	3.4	3.0
1981–90	2.8	1.5	2.9	3.4	3.4
Percent urban population					
1960	33.2	36.4	34.0	22.5	41.7
1990	47.1	44.1	39.4	43.7	59.8
Percent literate					
1960	86.2	41.6	40.0	29.7	31.8[b]
1980	89.8	69.8	47.3	59.5	50.6[b]
1985	91.8	68.8	51.9	68.0	78.0
GDP per capita[c]					
1960	1,332	772	1,020	575	879
1970	1,694	958	1,373	725	1,388
1980	2,222	1,044	1,732	886	1,065
1990	1,910	845	1,403	673	469
Real working-class wage index (1973 = 100)					
1970	96	92	109	96[d]	121
1980	129	82	84	97	64
1990	121	57[e]	60	76[f]	2[f]
Percent[g] employed in					
Agriculture					
1960	51.0	62.0	67.0	70.0	62.0
Agriculture					
1980	29.0	50.0	55.0	63.0	39.0
Manufacturing					
ca. 1950	11.0	11.0	12.0	6.0	11.0
Manufacturing					
1983	16.0	14.0	15.0	13.0	15.0
Percent GDP from manufacturing					
1960	14.0	15.0	13.0	12.0	16.0
1980	22.0	18.0	17.0	16.0	25.0
1990	20.9	17.7	14.9	13.7	17.2

Sources: Inter-American Development Bank (1988: tables A-1, A-2, B-1, B-9; 1991, tables A-1, A-2, B-2, B-10, and country profile tables); Torres Rivas (1982: vol. 4); Perez Brignoli and Baires Martinez (1983: table 9); Castillo Rivas (1983b: vol. 1); UN Development Programme (1991: table 1).

[a]Thousands.
[b]From Ministerio de Educación (1979: 140–41, 147).
[c]In 1986 U.S. dollars; 1990 figures estimated from GDP per capita growth rates.
[d]1972.
[e]1984.
[f]1988.
[g]Of economically active population.

and were winning them vital support from broad-front civilian opposition coalitions.[10]

The first of Central America's dictatorships to fall was that of the Somozas in Nicaragua, where the coalition led by the Sandinista National Liberation Front (FSLN) assumed power on 19 July 1979. The revolutionary ousted a perennially well-supported, vociferously anti-Communist, and presumably impregnable U.S. ally. The revolutionary government began a strategy of promotive adaptation to the United States by pushing its revolutionary policies while forging ties to Cuba and the Soviet bloc to counterbalance expected U.S. antagonism. This set off alarm bells in Washington and among conservative elites throughout Central America.

The Sandinista revolution profoundly altered U.S. policy toward Central America, especially toward the rising turmoil and growing insurgencies in El Salvador and Guatemala. In other Central American countries, Nicaragua's revolution made conservative forces anxious, encouraged both rebels and reformers, and raised the prospects of external intervention and increased intraregional conflict. Central America's other governments adopted two distinct strategies in response to the growing turmoil and leftist threat. Like Nicaragua's Somoza regime, Guatemalan and Salvadoran rulers adopted an intransigent strategy: they escalated repression of popular forces and opposition and rejected U.S. pressures to improve their human rights performance. In contrast, Honduras and Costa Rica remained acquiescent to the United States. Honduras even embarked upon gradual political reform. Within this context there began a decade-long scramble among subnational actors throughout the isthmus for space, alliances, and resources both domestic and foreign that would on several occasions produce dramatic shifts in adaptive strategies vis-à-vis the United States.

The United States

In the early twentieth century, the United States intervened politically, diplomatically, and militarily to consolidate its hegemonic role in the region and to pursue certain specific goals: to establish and maintain the U.S. monopoly of the transisthmian canal in Panama, contain German and other geopolitical and economic incursions into the isthmus, promote U.S. investment and trade, contain leftist regimes and movements, and promote political stability and constitutional rule.[11]

After 1945 there was an interlude of U.S. support for liberal democratic regimes, but that soon succumbed to the new geostrategic imperative to contain Communism and Soviet influence.[12] World War II–era U.S.–Latin American military and political cooperation schemes were updated into the new inter-American security system under the Rio Pact and the OAS Treaty in the late 1940s, and Central America was incorporated into the system. The degree to which containment would dominate U.S. relations with Central America in coming decades was soon made clear by U.S. intervention to topple the constitutional government of Guatemala in 1954 under the pretext that it was Communist influenced.

From 1959 on the Cuban revolution further energized U.S. efforts to contain Communism in Central America. The defection of Cuba from the U.S. hegemonic system to the Soviet Union brought major U.S. efforts to solidify and consolidate its influence in the region. In the 1960s the United States sharply increased direct assistance to Central America (tables 2 and 3), including beefed-up regional military cooperation. Despite U.S. rhetoric about democracy during the Eisenhower, Kennedy, and Johnson administrations, four of the five Central American governments receiving U.S. aid were military dictatorships. The flagship U.S. assistance program of the 1960s, the Alliance for Progress, assisted the CACM by using U.S. economic aid to promote rapid capitalist development. Annual average U.S. economic aid to Central America for 1962 to 1972 was double that for 1953 to 1961 (table 3). On the military side of containment, the average annual rate of U.S. military assistance programs for 1962 to 1972 grew twelvefold over the previous eight years. The United States mobilized Central American cooperation in the abortive 1961 Bay of Pigs exile invasion of Cuba and in the 1965 U.S. invasion of the Dominican Republic. Although U.S. military assistance to Central America shrank somewhat during the Nixon and Ford administrations (table 2) because of the war in Vietnam, economic assistance to the region grew in the early 1970s (table 3).

Jimmy Carter's efforts to reform and improve U.S. relations with Latin America introduced some instability into this system. Carter completed previous administrations' reassessment of the strategic importance and vulnerability of the Panama Canal in the nuclear era, signed the Panama Canal Treaty, and secured its ratification.

Table 2
Mean Annual U.S. Military Assistance to Central America, 1946–1990[a]

	Costa Rica	El Salvador	Guatemala	Honduras	Nicaragua	Region[b]
1946–1952	—	—	—	—	—	—
1953–1961	.01	.03	.19	.14	.24	.63
1962–1972	.16	.72	3.31	.90	2.36	7.45
1973–1976	.03	2.08	.83	2.23	.28	5.45
1977–1980	1.25	1.60	1.25	3.13	.85	6.98
1981–1984	3.95	98.85	.00	41.48	.00	144.28
1985–1988	3.93	112.78	5.20	57.73	.00	179.64
1989–1990	.20	81.20	6.35[c]	31.20	.00	115.95
Overall mean 1946–1990	.87	22.92	1.66[d]	10.93	.66	37.04

Sources: Based upon Atkins (1977: tables D and E; 1989: tables 10.2 and 10.4); OPB–US-AID (1981, 1984, 1986, 1988, 1991).

[a]Millions of U.S. dollars.
[b]Includes only Costa Rica, El Salvador, Guatemala, Honduras, and Nicaragua.
[c]The Bush administration canceled Guatemala's 1990 military assistance of $3.3 million for human rights reasons. That left the actual period average for 1989–90 at $4.7 million.
[d]Includes the 1990 $3.3 million that was later canceled.

More important than the modest increase in U.S. aid levels to Central America (tables 2, 3), the Carter administration also refined the U.S. approach to the containment of Communism. The idea was that the United States should accept or even encourage gradual domestic reform in the Third World because "social explosions leading to radical outcomes were less likely if tensions could be directed through open governments."[13] Congress in the mid-1970s had imposed certain human rights performance criteria on U.S. foreign assistance to curtail past abuses.[14] The Carter administration embraced and implemented these policies to facilitate controlled reform and improve long-term Third World political stability. Although there was debate within the Carter administration and the foreign policy bureaucracy over whether and how to press for human rights reforms,[15] the United States quickly cut off military aid to chronic human rights abusers Guatemala and El Salvador in 1977. It also pressed Nicaragua's Somoza regime to improve its human rights performance.[16]

As anticipated, the canal treaty and new human rights policy encouraged opposition groups and rebels to press harder for political change by signaling reduced U.S. willingness to intervene on behalf

Table 3
U.S. Economic Assistance to Central America, 1946–1990[a]

	Costa Rica	El Salvador	Guatemala	Honduras	Nicaragua	Region[b]
1946–1952	1.00	.40	1.65	.42	1.03	4.50
1953–1961	5.80	1.23	13.48	3.90	3.73	28.14
1962–1972	9.41	11.95	14.52	8.42	12.95	56.07
1973–1976	14.10	6.10	19.60	24.43	26.90	91.13
1977–1980	13.65	21.85	17.28	27.88	18.63	99.56
1981–1984	112.75	189.43	21.13	79.53	16.55	419.39
1985–1988	171.13	383.38	135.90	179.33	.10	869.84
1989–1990	108.65	276.85	139.95	140.35	113.60	770.40
Overall mean						
1946–1990	35.54	68.74	29.30	36.07	13.50	183.14

Sources: Based upon Atkins (1977: tables D and E; 1989: tables 10.2 and 10.4); OPB–USAID (1981, 1984, 1986, 1988, 1991).

[a]Millions of U.S. dollars.

[b]Includes only Costa Rica, El Salvador, Guatemala, Honduras, and Nicaragua.

of Central America's repressive regimes. The expected short-term improvements in human rights performance in El Salvador, Guatemala, and Nicaragua proved illusory, however, because of elite intransigence. Meanwhile, raised opposition hopes and spiraling anger about the brutality of their rulers accelerated turmoil in the isthmus much faster than Washington had anticipated.[17]

The International Environment

During the 1970s and 1980s the international geopolitical environment and U.S. foreign policy underwent remarkable transformations. Although the United States remained the world's strongest military power and its largest single economy, U.S. relative capacity and influence in the world community during the 1980s continued to decline while others rose, particularly those of Japan and Europe. Moreover, by the 1980s U.S. influence within the Western Hemisphere had also eroded noticeably as other regional powers gained in size, resources, self-confidence, and assertiveness.[18] Both European and Latin American nations eventually challenged U.S. policies in Central America during the 1980s. External actors provided new sources of support that partially reduced Central American nations' dependency upon the United States and encouraged them to follow promotive or preservative strategies of adaptation rather than the more traditional acquiescent strategy. "The United States continued to play the leading role in the area, but other nations and groups were also prominent. Far from being an exclusive U.S. preserve, Central America became an internationalized arena."[19]

Central to the debate over Central America in the 1980s were Soviet interests and goals in Latin America. One side perceived dire security threats from the U.S.S.R. and Central American revolutionary movements,[20] while the other saw relatively little of concern.[21] In the policy arena the darker view prevailed during the 1980s. Sharply intensified U.S. tensions with the Soviet Union and efforts to contain Communist influence in the Americas marked the early years of the decade,[22] with Central America a principal venue of the resultant geopolitical struggle. Soviet and Cuban assistance helped revolutionary Nicaragua maintain its path of promotive adaptation apart from the United States for several years. Yet as the decade ended, first the Soviet bloc and then the Soviet Union itself went into sharp decline, their aid to Nicaragua shrank, and East-West tensions diminished. The rapid evolution of U.S.-Soviet relations in the late 1980s would sharply alter the course of events in Central America—again, largely unexpectedly.

The Eighties Begin: The Carter Administration after July 1979

Before Anastasio Somoza Debayle fell, the Carter administration pressed the Nicaraguan dictator to improve his human rights performance as civil resistance and the Sandinista guerrillas escalated their campaigns against the regime. By mid-1978 the United States had decided that Somoza should leave power and actively sought, along with Nicaragua's Catholic Church hierarchy, to arrange for a civil opposition coalition—without the Sandinistas—to assume power. Somoza refused to cooperate, and his National Guard waged a bloody campaign against the growing insurrection in Nicaragua's cities. When the mediation effort collapsed in early 1979, the once-divided FSLN reunited and rallied the civil opposition into its corner.[23] Within the Carter administration, which badly underestimated the escalating strength of the Sandinistas, a debate raged over whether to employ U.S. force to oust Somoza or merely wait for events to overtake him. In early 1979 there was an abortive U.S. effort to persuade the Organization of American States (OAS) to intervene militarily to force Somoza out. While U.S. diplomats sought ineffectually to have the OAS remove Somoza and to negotiate some sort of post-Somoza government without the FSLN, the Sandinistas, benefiting from widespread popular support, rapidly prepared, launched, and successfully prosecuted their final offensive.[24] The National Guard effectively collapsed, and on 19 July the Sandinista-led rebel junta assumed power.

Having failed to prevent the Sandinistas from taking power, the Carter administration sought to moderate their government while encouraging centrist and moderate reformers to make progressive, prophylactic changes in policy elsewhere in Central America. Testifying before Congress, Undersecretary of State for American Affairs Viron Vaky summarized the policy: "Our task therefore is how to work with our friends to guide and influence change, how to use our influence to promote justice, freedom and equity to mutual benefits—and therefore avoid insurgency and communism."[25]

The FSLN quickly consolidated its hold on the revolutionary government and forged close ties to Soviet ally Cuba. The U.S. effort to moderate the Sandinistas, though at least partly successful, proved unsatisfactory to many inside and outside of Washington. Outside the White House, critics on the right, including soon-to-be Republican presidential nominee Ronald Reagan and many of Somoza's former supporters in Congress, stridently attacked Carter for "losing" Nicaragua and Iran, where another revolution was under way. Congress delayed a $75 million U.S. aid package for Nicaragua while the United States pressed the Sandinistas to desist from several policies it viewed as menacing, including support for Marxist rebels in El Salvador.

As the Nicaraguan revolution began to unfold, political unrest and violent repression in neighboring El Salvador escalated rapidly. There appeared to be "another Nicaragua" in the making. When a coalition of opposition party reformers and military figures overthrew the Salvadoran regime on 15 October 1979, Washington quickly backed the new junta in hopes of quick social reforms and curtailed human rights abuse that might head off a second revolution in the isthmus.[26] The Carter White House lifted its prior aid suspension and sent a $54.3 million aid package to El Salvador in late 1979 (including almost $5 million in military assistance).

The Salvadoran junta proved unstable and became rapidly more conservative and military dominated. Most reformers and moderates pulled out in early 1980, when human rights abuses increased, not diminished. Conservative forces that included the agrarian oligarchy and the armed forces sought to undermine the agrarian reform program that was a cornerstone of the U.S.-backed reform package. Archbishop Oscar Arnulfo Romero was assassinated by rightist elements in 1980, as were four U.S. nuns and religious workers. Despite the Salvadoran junta's failure to attend to the reformist side of the Carter agenda, U.S. support and assistance continued through 1980, and additional military funding was found in the waning days of the Carter administration. Those in the administration who advocated human rights and reform as an antidote to revolution were quickly overwhelmed by supporters of more traditional containment policies. Thus in the last months of Jimmy Carter's administration, revolutions in Iran and Nicaragua and the rising neoconservative tide of election-year U.S. politics undermined many of his foreign policy innovations.[27]

Elsewhere in Central America, the Nicaraguan revolution and the growing Salvadoran insurrection began to elicit reaction. In Honduras, where the armed forces had ruled since the early 1970s, the turbulence in neighboring Nicaragua and the formation in 1978 and 1979 of two Honduran Marxist guerrilla groups prompted the military regime under Gen. Policarpo Paz García to begin political liberalization. A constituent assembly was elected in 1980 to write a new constitution, congressional and presidential elections were set for 1981, and certain populist programs were touted to mollify the impoverished Honduran public.[28] On the southern end of the region in democratic Costa Rica, both President Rodrigo Carazo, once a supporter of the anti-Somoza rebel coalition in Nicaragua, and the press became steadily more critical of the revolutionary government in Nicaragua.

The Guatemalan regime elected a policy of repression. Gen. Romeo Lucas García, who had come to power in 1978 via electoral fraud, faced a resurgent Marxist guerrilla movement. Rebel elements that dated from the 1960s had rebuilt themselves, and new guerrilla groups rooted in Guatemala's majority indigenous population had also appeared.[29] Guatemalan security forces responded with escalated counterinsurgency in rural areas and increased state terror in the cities. Because of high coffee prices and a relatively strong economy, the Guatemalan regime felt free to ignore U.S. pressures to improve its human rights performance. Guatemala replaced U.S. military assistance with arms and advisers from Israel.

The Early Reagan Administration: 1981 to 1986

Ronald Reagan assumed the presidency intending to adopt a much more vigorous and traditional style of containment of Communism than Carter's.[30] Reagan speedily changed U.S. policy but, ironically, his very loose management style and lack of a coherent vision of policy for Central America first animated and then ultimately undermined many of his own policy preferences in the isthmus. Lax supervision of subordinates encouraged freewheeling entrepreneurship in foreign affairs and permitted arch-conservative ideologues to gain control of key foreign policy instruments affecting Central America. There followed a remarkable degree of partisan polarization of foreign policy.

The perception of Central America by candidate Reagan and many of his advisers was articulated in a report by the Committee of Santa Fe, several of whose members took positions in the Reagan administration foreign policy apparatus. "The young Caribbean republics situated in our strategic back yard face . . . the dedicated, irrepressible activity of a Soviet-backed Cuba to win ultimately total hegemony over this region, . . . the 'soft underbelly of the United States.'"[31] The report continued with an extremist interpretation of the Monroe Doctrine of the early Cold War variant[32] and interpreted Latin America as "part of America's power base. Any United States power base . . . cannot be allowed to crumble."[33] After listing alleged Soviet surrogates or near-surrogates in the hemisphere in addition to Cuba (Nicaragua, Guyana, Jamaica, Grenada, and Panama), the report recommended that the United States should use its aid and other policy instruments to (1) rebuild eroded hemispheric security cooperation and restore cut military assistance programs; (2) counter leftist propaganda and liberation theology; (3) accept non-Communist authoritarian regimes and cease misguided efforts to promote U.S.-style democracy and human rights in Latin America; (4) increase the access of Latin American products to U.S. markets and promote private capitalist development schemes and "free" (that is, nonleftist) labor unions; and (5) disseminate in the isthmus political values congruent with those predominant in the United States. Perhaps most to the point regarding Central America, the report advocated a new policy to "provide multi-faceted aid for all friendly countries under attack by armed minorities receiving assistance from hostile outsider forces. . . . Concurrently the United States will reaffirm . . . [that] no hostile foreign power will be allowed bases or military and political allies in the region."[34]

The Reagan doctrine, as it emerged in the early eighties, incorporated the worldview and many of the specific policy recommendations of the Santa Fe document. Reagan sharply escalated confrontation with the Soviet Union and strove to contain its perceived influence in Central America. There were three basic prongs to this highly escalated containment effort: Nicaragua, El Salvador, and elsewhere in Central America.

Nicaragua

The Reagan administration dedicated enormous energy, albeit not publicly admitted at the outset, to overthrow the Sandinista regime. U.S. policy largely eschewed diplomacy and quickly became confrontational and increasingly militarized. Within months of taking office, President Reagan suspended U.S. economic aid to Nicaragua and mobilized and funded an anti-Sandinista Contra army from the remnants of the Nicaraguan National Guard.

Among additional U.S. efforts to harass, contain, and overturn the Nicaraguan revolution from early 1981 through 1986 were diplomatic initiatives to discredit and isolate Nicaragua; a U.S. domestic, Central American, and worldwide pro-Contra and anti-Sandinista propaganda campaign; securing cooperation from Honduras and Costa Rica for Contra bases and operations on their soil; CIA attacks on Nicaraguan harbors and oil storage facilities; harassing supersonic overflights of Nicaraguan territory; heavy electronic and conventional intelligence collection in Nicaragua; financing anti-Sandinista domestic opposition and press; a massive forward basing and logistical operation in Honduras that could permit a direct U.S. invasion; continuous U.S. and Honduran joint troop maneuvers for a period of several years; an embargo on U.S. trade with Nicaragua; an embargo of U.S. credit to Nicaragua and, over time, successful pressure upon other Western and international lenders to cut off credit.[35] Although the administration harassed Nicaraguan diplomats and missions in the United States, formal diplomatic relations were never broken.[36]

President Reagan and his spokesmen energetically argued that the Nicaraguan revolution and the Sandinistas constituted a vital and direct threat to the security of the United States. Many ob-

servers view the 1983 invasion of Grenada and removal of its Marxist government as a direct message to Managua that the same might
happen to Nicaragua. Yet despite its denunciations, implicit threats,
and preparations, the Reagan administration never resorted to direct, overt military intervention against Nicaragua. That the United
States never directly attacked Nicaragua had several likely causes.
First, the administration failed to win public support for its policies.
Despite using domestic and external propaganda, presidential ad-
dresses, and even the Bipartisan National Commission on Central
America (Kissinger Commission), a fairly consistent two to one majority of the U.S. public opposed Ronald Reagan's policy toward Nicaragua throughout the administration.[37] One possible reason for
public skepticism about Reagan's policies in Nicaragua (and elsewhere in the region) was the availability of alternative interpretations of regional affairs in the U.S. press. The administration's view
of the area was consistently countered by media reports by professional journalists, academics, peace-oriented or anti-interventionist
private, nongovernmental, and religious organizations and activists,
and even former U.S. diplomats and public officials. Such forces labored assiduously throughout the 1980s to counter administration
alarmism and court public and congressional opinion.[38]

Second, key parts of the U.S. government itself opposed military
escalation. Elements within the State Department, at times including Secretary of State George Shultz, pressed for more diplomacy
and less confrontation with Nicaragua. Still smarting from lack of
public support in Vietnam, the U.S. military services also quietly
but steadfastly opposed undertaking an unpopular adventure ground
war abroad.[39]

The third reason was lack of reliable support in Congress. Many
members, in particular Democrats, never agreed with the administration's perception of the threat in Nicaragua or with the means being employed by the administration against the Sandinista regime.
Pressures by Reagan's advisers and his allies on Capitol Hill badly
antagonized many legislators and intensified partisan polarization
on Central American issues. To some extent influenced by the
forces of opposition to the administration's policies, Congress
passed several different restrictions (known collectively as the Boland Amendments) upon the use of covert funds against Nicaragua
and was inconsistent in funding the Contras. In order to skirt and
subvert these congressional obstacles, members of the president's

national security staff developed an illegal covert operation to supply the Contras.[40] By the late 1980s, Reagan's lobbying and the Sandinistas' own policies (human rights problems, press censorship, and public relations gaffes) eventually eked out more support for the Contras from congressional Democrats. Ultimately, though, Reagan was never able to count consistently upon congressional support for his efforts to topple the Nicaraguan government.

U.S. anti-Sandinista policies also met obstacles within Central America. The Sandinistas responded tenaciously, flexibly, and imaginatively (albeit making many mistakes along the way). They often shifted policies to cut losses or win vital resources with which to counter the United States; areas particularly affected included human rights and political space for their domestic opponents and economic, agrarian, and foreign policy. They skillfully worked with U.S. domestic opponents of Reagan's policies, the press, the International Court of Justice, European governmental opposition to U.S. policy, European and other foreign assistance, and international political party organizations. The revolutionary government called elections (1984 and 1990) and invited myriad international observers to witness their probity. It made unexpected deals with domestic enemies and with neighboring countries (most notably accepting two draft Contadora accords, though these ultimately failed due to U.S. pressures on other Central American countries). Such maneuvering for resources helped keep the Sandinista revolution going despite the Contra war and other pressures, and many of these policy shifts seemed to catch the Reagan administration unawares.

The Reagan administration never garnered the support it wanted for its anti-Sandinista enterprise from the international community. Although it convinced such nations as Saudi Arabia and Brunei to help fund and Costa Rica and Honduras to harbor the Contras, there was little other support even from traditional U.S. alliance partners. Most Western European governments expressly opposed U.S. policy toward Nicaragua and continued various forms of assistance to Nicaragua well into the late 1980s. Spain and the Scandinavian nations remained particularly loyal to Nicaragua. Soviet bloc aid and technical cooperation (especially from the U.S.S.R. and Cuba) supplanted Western assistance to Nicaragua by the mid-1980s and permitted the massive and largely successful military mobilization that kept the Contras at bay. The external assistance that perhaps proved most valuable to Nicaragua involved peacemaking efforts by the Contadora countries (Panama, Colombia, Mexico, and Venezuela) and their allied Support Group. The Contadora peace process failed to achieve an accord largely due to U.S. opposition but nevertheless helped constrain U.S. actions by expressing the Latin American powers' disapproval of U.S. intervention in the isthmus.

El Salvador

Responding to increasing state terror and lack of progress on reforms, in 1980 the five Salvadoran guerrilla groups joined forces to form the Farabundo Martí National Liberation Front (FMLN), several very large civic opposition coalitions joined together into the Revolutionary Democratic Front (FDR), and the FDR and FMLN formed an alliance. In early 1981 the guerrilla war intensified sharply. Using these developments and the evolution of the Nicaraguan regime as evidence of a growing Communist beachhead in the isthmus, Ronald Reagan won far more cooperation from Congress for his policy toward El Salvador than toward Nicaragua. However, the Reagan administration was also more pragmatic and flexible regarding El Salvador than Nicaragua.

Reagan built upon the foundation established by Jimmy Carter by sharply escalating U.S. military and economic assistance to El Salvador and its now openly rightist junta. U.S. economic assistance for 1981 to 1984 was over eight times greater than for 1977 to 1980, and military assistance was over sixty times greater (tables 2, 3). The United States became deeply involved in shaping the Salvadoran regime and armed forces. U.S. advisers and diplomats assisted with and reportedly even essentially directed many Salvadoran government agencies as they sought to forge a competent state.

The United States anointed Christian Democrat junta member José Napoleón Duarte as its best hope for building a political center in the highly polarized society. Human rights concerns were at first sharply deemphasized by the Reagan administration, and the Salvadoran military (despite massive amounts of U.S. advice and funding) continued its brutality albeit at somewhat reduced levels.[41] Human rights abuses, however, so aroused many members of the U.S. Congress that the administration feared that funding for El Salvador might be cut. The Reagan administration by 1982 thus reversed field and embraced both human rights and democratization (the holding of elections) as a means to help ensure continued U.S. financing of the Salvadoran government and to calm rising U.S. domestic fears of possible direct U.S. military intervention.[42] Human rights abuses began gradually to diminish in response to U.S. pressures, and carefully managed elections—held in 1982 and 1984 in the midst of civil war—helped build legitimacy for the Duarte government within both El Salvador and the U.S. Congress.[43]

The Rest of the Isthmus

U.S. policy toward other nations was largely a function of policies toward Nicaragua and El Salvador. The United States sought to turn Honduras into a forward base, avowedly to contain Sandinista support for El Salvador's rebels but also for possible U.S. military action in El Salvador or Nicaragua. Honduran goodwill and its transition to civilian rule were sought through Washington's massive foreign assistance. There was a thirteenfold increase in military assistance to Honduras during the first Reagan term, followed by another 40 percent increase in the second. Economic assistance to Honduras for 1981 to 1984 doubled over the Carter period, then redoubled for 1985 to 1988 (tables 2, 3). Honduras engaged in continuous, cooperative military exercises with U.S. forces, let the U.S. build extensive military facilities around Honduras, permitted the Contras to base, train, and operate along the Nicaraguan border, and supported U.S. policy toward Nicaragua. Honduran cooperation with El Salvador's armed forces proved more difficult for the United States to attain because of the lingering enmity between the two nations after the 1969 Honduras–El Salvador War.

Washington heavily pressured Costa Rica to support U.S. and Contra efforts against Nicaragua's revolutionary government. President Luis Alberto Monge (1982–86) did cooperate, and average annual U.S. assistance levels to Costa Rica rose more than tenfold over the levels of the Carter administration. Traditionally unarmed Costa Rica, however, partly resisted U.S. efforts to build its military capability. In contrast, Guatemala's violent military regimes and atrocious human rights record curtailed the Reagan administration's relationship with that country for several years. Beset by hard times and having lost some of its powerful economic allies because of this, the Guatemalan military decided to return nominal power to civilians. This elicited enthusiastic U.S. support for Guatemala's 1985 elections, the restoration of military aid, and a sixfold jump in U.S. economic assistance (tables 2, 3) despite continuing massive human rights violations.

The Later Reagan Administration: 1987 to 1989

The watershed of the Reagan administration's policies and performance in Central America was the revelation in late 1986 that National Security Council staff members had helped sell U.S. arms to Iran in an effort to secure the release of American hostages and had illegally diverted the proceeds to the Nicaraguan Contras.[44] As investigations by the attorney general, the Tower Commission, the press, and Congress exposed the scandal, there were marked changes in the administration's capacity to continue its Central American policies. These changes also brought sudden and dramatic alterations in the behavior of most of the actors within Central America.

The weak states of Central America, subjected for several years to direct and intense U.S. pressures, found themselves suddenly in a much altered world. They perceived instantly that the Iran-Contra scandal would sap the Reagan administration's ability to support the Contras against the Sandinistas, prosecute the war in El Salvador, and oppose regional peace efforts. Thus partly freed from U.S. pressure while confronted with the rapid political and economic deterioration of their societies, Central America's presidents seized the initiative to reduce the growing conflict and destruction within and among them. Presidents Oscar Arias of Costa Rica and Vinicio Cerezo of Guatemala, each a new actor with new allies and agendas, forged a historic regional accord that was signed by all five isthmian presidents in a summit meeting in Guatemala on 7 August 1987. The Central American Peace (Esquipulas) Accord recognized the legitimacy of all five regional governments, called for democracy, partly delegitimized rebel forces, and required each nation to seek reconciliation of its internal conflicts through negotiations with insurgent forces.[45]

In disarray over the Iran-Contra scandal and pulled momentarily off guard by its own maneuvering, the U.S. administration failed to prevent this historic agreement. Indeed, a striking blunder left the White House in a position of actually publicly endorsing a pact to which it strenuously objected. In the days before the accord was signed in Guatemala, the White House had proposed its own draft peace proposal, one quite hostile toward Nicaragua. This constituted an attempt to co-opt then speaker of the House of Representatives and critic of administration Central America policy, Jim Wright (D-TX) behind the president's position. Speaker Wright, however, turned the tables on the White House hard-liners. He had agreed to endorse a joint Reagan-Wright peace proposal just days prior to the Guatemala summit, all the while knowing that a more balanced accord might eventuate there. When the Esquipulas Accord was reached, Wright effectively trapped the administration into supporting the historic Central American presidents' peace agreement as if it were an extension of the Washington draft.[46] Subsequent White House efforts to undermine the Central American accord proved fruitless for three main reasons. First, support for the Esquipulas peace process in Europe, Latin America, and international organizations counterbalanced U.S. opposition. Second, rightist forces in Nicaragua, El Salvador, and Guatemala became uncertain of U.S. support and unsure that they would ultimately prevail and thus were gradually more prone to consider political rather than military solutions. Third, the political and economic decline of the Soviet bloc and fading popular support curtailed the resources of and disheartened El Salvador's FMLN and Nicaragua's Sandinista leaders, making them also more amenable to negotiations. The accord thus ultimately prevailed because it offered Central Americans of all ideologies vehicles for seeking an end to dangerous regional tensions and bloody but stagnated civil wars.

Hard-liners in the Reagan administration fought a failed rearguard action against Esquipulas. Their major successes were nevertheless confined to victories in Congress on funding for the Salvadoran regime and for the Contras. Despite such U.S. obstacles, the Esquipulas accord eventually brought about a cease-fire and peace negotiations in Nicaragua, followed by the 1990 election and eventual settlement of the Contra war. Esquipulas also led to the first negotiations between regime and rebels in El Salvador and Guatemala.

The 1980s End: The Bush Administration

The election of George Bush to succeed Ronald Reagan signaled significant changes in U.S. policy toward Central America. Through appointments and rhetoric the incoming Bush administration mod-

erated its predecessor's stridency on Central America and adjusted
its policies toward the isthmus to fit the perception of a generally declining Soviet threat. The new administration's management style
curtailed the foreign policy entrepreneurship of the hard-liners, in
part because it wished to defuse the deleterious partisanship and
tensions with Congress that pervaded Central American questions.
It also wished to promote a new trade agreement with Mexico and
worried that the United States had several potentially more serious
problems in Latin America—Mexico, Peru, narcotics smuggling—
than those lingering in Central America.[47]

These shifts in emphasis by the Bush administration may be seen
on several fronts. While many observers viewed the December 1989
U.S. invasion of Panama as a portent of military action elsewhere in
the isthmus, that fear proved misplaced. Indeed, action against the
Noriega regime may well have represented a sop to the U.S. far Right
that permitted a significant deemphasis of the overall importance of
Nicaragua and El Salvador to U.S. security. Outside of Panama, Bush
administration policy changes on Central America consisted of
pragmatic adjustments to new geopolitical circumstances, despite
maintaining some of the Reagan rhetoric and antagonism toward
Nicaragua. In foreign aid, for instance, there was a roughly one-third
reduction in mean annual military aid to the isthmus for 1989 and
1990 and a one-seventh cut in mean annual economic assistance (tables 2, 3). Against the background of the weakening Soviet bloc and
the U.S.S.R.'s expressed desire to reduce confrontation in the Third
World, the White House became somewhat more tolerant of the
Central American Left; that is, it was willing to accept negotiated
settlements or electoral outcomes involving newly more pragmatic
leftists. Given the course of events in Central America, such adjustments in U.S. policy permitted considerable change within the
region.

Nicaragua

George Bush assumed office after a cease-fire with the Contras had
been reached and elections had been scheduled in Nicaragua.
Avowedly to keep pressure on the Sandinistas, the administration
successfully lobbied Congress for continued funding for the Contras
until after the early 1990 election. This was done against the explicit
wish of the Esquipulas Accord and even though Nicaragua's civil op-

position had agreed with the Sandinista government on electoral rules and called for an end to Contra funding. While much of the U.S. rhetoric on Nicaragua sounded quite the same under Bush as under Reagan, in one highly significant policy adjustment the administration indicated that it would accept even a Sandinista victory in 1990 if the election were open and fair. Not content, however, to remain on the sidelines, the United States worked assiduously (both covertly and overtly) and spent several million dollars to forge the Nicaraguan Opposition Union (UNO) coalition, to get UNO to nominate Violeta Barrios de Chamorro to run against Daniel Ortega, and to fund, shape, and promote the campaign.[48]

The Sandinista government invited extensive external observation,[49] which caused an unprecedented effort by the United Nations, the Organization of American States, the Council of Freely Elected Heads of Government led by Jimmy Carter, and many nongovernmental organizations to monitor the campaign and February 1990 election. After the largely unexpected Sandinista electoral defeat and transfer of power to de Chamorro's UNO government, the United States supported the negotiations that ended the Contra war, helped demobilize the rebel forces, and restored U.S. economic assistance to Nicaragua at historically high levels (table 3). The Bush administration disliked the continued Sandinista domination of Nicaragua's armed forces, but accepted this arrangement as a short-term cost of political stabilization.

El Salvador

The stagnation of the Salvadoran civil war and increased signs that Congress might significantly curtail military assistance there led to another shift in U.S. policy—acceptance of the Esquipulas-mandated peace negotiations. Both the United States and the Salvadoran government were shocked by the ferocity of the late 1989 urban campaign by the FMLN, which for its part was disheartened by the failure of the Salvadoran populace to rally behind the rebels. The United States and both the Salvadoran Right and Left began to view the war as unwinnable. The Salvadoran litigants on both sides also saw looming ahead new limits on their resource flows from abroad, which enhanced the Right and Left's willingness to negotiate. These changes animated the previously halting Esquipulas negotiation process, which was aided by the good offices of UN secretary general

Javier Pérez de Cuellar. Rather than oppose and surreptitiously block peace talks, as had his predecessor, President Bush accepted President Alfredo Cristiani's negotiations with the FMLN. The efforts bore final fruit in January 1991 with the signing of the Salvadoran peace agreement, which provided for military reform and force reductions, guerrilla demobilization, resumption of abandoned agrarian reform programs, and a mechanism for the inclusion of the FMLN in a new national police force.[50]

Conclusion

From the standpoint of the Central Americans themselves, there was much to lament about the 1980s, especially in the economic and social areas. In addition to some 250,000 deaths, well over 1 million external refugees, and at least as many internal refugees, the Central American region had lost decades of developmental progress. Foreign debt had risen, investment and services deteriorated, and the social and economic problems that helped start Central America's insurgencies had intensified. For example, real working-class wages were from 6 to 30 percent lower in 1990 than in 1980 for four nations and had fallen by 96 percent in Nicaragua.[51] Per capita GDP had fallen between 14 and 56 percent over the decade of the 1980s, and manufacturing's share of GDP had deteriorated between 2 and 31 percent (table 1). The prospects for U.S. aid to help address these problems were limited: in order to assist the newly non-Sandinista Nicaraguan government and to help repair the invasion's damage in Panama, the United States in 1990 did not increase aid but effectively reduced its economic assistance to the other nations of the area by the amount newly programmed for those two nations. The probability of substantially increased European or U.S. assistance to Central America to accelerate economic recovery for the battered region seemed minimal in the early 1990s because of the collapse of the Eastern bloc and the Soviet Union and the resultant massive, higher-priority demands for aid from that region of the world.

On the positive side of the ledger, Central America's two worst wars had ended by late 1991, and negotiations were under way between Guatemala's government and the rebels. Armed forces, military spending, and deaths were reduced in El Salvador and Nicaragua. However, civil peace in Nicaragua seemed ever more fragile as the Chamorro government coalition split and violence between rightists and Sandinistas escalated. In the policy confusion and relaxation of U.S. pressure occasioned by the Iran-Contra scandal, Central American regimes of quite diverse ideologies had collectively developed an effective consultative process that contributed to intraregional and intranational reconciliation. This shift in adaptive strategies by the Central American states somewhat mitigated the deleterious effects of prior U.S. intervention upon the isthmian nations' sovereignty and nominally increased their freedom of action. Both the diplomacy and the increased mutual respect and collaboration of the Central American states—aided by the good offices of the OAS and UN—held forth the prospect for continued regional cooperation and integration.[52]

A final positive factor for Central America was that by 1991 electoral, constitutional regimes in Guatemala, El Salvador, and Honduras had each survived through at least two national elections and a change of ruling parties. This hardly meant the consolidation of electoral democracy in any of these nations, because in each nation the armed forces remained very powerful and politicized. Nevertheless, some progress had clearly been made. Electoral, constitutional rule, however, was generally encouraged and endorsed by popular preference within each nation and by other nations of the hemisphere, Europe, the OAS and the UN, and the Catholic Church, factors that could certainly assist in the consolidation of democracy.[53]

For the United States, despite its massive intervention in Central America during the 1980s, its accomplishments had remained modest by the early 1990s. Jimmy Carter had failed to promote local reform at a pace either sufficient to head off revolution or that would be acceptable to the United States. Ronald Reagan's attempts to defeat the FMLN and to roll back the Sandinista revolution failed. However, U.S. policy did create the conditions for the FSLN's electoral defeat in 1990. El Salvador's FMLN was held at bay but not defeated. Ultimately the Bush administration lowered its sights and pragmatically accepted the negotiated settlement of the Salvadoran conflict, thus quite paradoxically legitimizing both the FMLN and securing extensive reforms of the Salvadoran polity. U.S. pressures for political democratization and improved human rights in the region—implicit but fruitless under Carter; first deemphasized, then embraced by Reagan as a tool of his hard-line containment posture—actually paid some dividends under Bush's pragmatic, lower-key policy in the new post-Soviet era.

Finally, the $6.7 billion of U.S. economic assistance to Central America in the 1980s functioned largely as the handmaiden of U.S. security policy and the $1.8 billion in security assistance.[54] This economic aid arrived while the region's wars and recessions made it useful mainly to fend off economic catastrophe but certainly unable to promote development. A continuation of the decline of political conflict under way in the early 1990s in the region could, of course, make appropriate levels of U.S. economic assistance vastly more useful for promoting economic recovery for the benighted nations of the region in the 1990s. Yet in a cruel irony, the very diminution of world geopolitical tensions plus the erosion of the U.S. economy were rapidly shrinking American aid to Central America at just the moment when its continuation might have done the most good.

Does the cycling down of U.S. security concerns for Central America in the early 1990s presage a new era of inattention to the region? Does the disappearance of the Soviet bête noire lead to a nadir of U.S. interest in Central America? If so, it appears that the economic neglect of Central America by the United States would likely be anything but benign. While the region itself had emerged from the 1980s with new political and diplomatic resources with which to confront its difficulties, social and economic problems seemed in many ways to be equal to or worse than those that had spawned the prior decade of revolution and geopolitical conflict.

Notes

1. The Committee of Santa Fe, *A New Inter-American Policy for the Eighties*, Council for Inter-American Security, May 1980, reprinted in Bruce D. Larkin, ed., *Vital Interests: The Soviet Issue in U.S. Central American Policy* (Boulder, Colo.: Lynne Rienner, 1988), p. 15.

2. Based upon data from the UN Development Programme, *Human Development Report: 1991* (New York: Oxford University Press, 1991), table 1.

3. During the nineteenth century motives for direct U.S. intervention in the region included the U.S. desire to displace Britain as the preeminent military power in the Caribbean, conflict over transisthmian transit routes, and filibustering expeditions seeking new slave states.

4. Michael Handel, *Weak States in the International System* (London: Frank Cass, 1990); James N. Rosenau, "National (and Factional) Adaptation in Central America: Options for the 1980s," and James R. Kurth, "The United States and Central America: Hegemony in Historical and Comparative Per-

spective," both in Richard E. Feinberg, ed., *Central America: International Dimensions of the Crisis* (New York: Holmes and Meier, 1982), pp. 39–41, 47–56, 239–69. Other terms such as "sphere of influence" are often used to describe a hegemonic system but mean basically the same thing.

5. Rosenau, "National (and Factional) Adaptation," pp. 244–47.

6. Though part of the Mesoamerican isthmus, Panama was a province of Colombia until 1903 and has not shared the numerous common historical experiences of the other five countries. It is therefore not normally treated as part of Central America. Belize, a British colony until the 1980s, is not only historically but culturally distinct.

7. So in thrall to U.S. political and special economic influence (especially the great fruit-exporting companies) did some of the region's countries become during the heyday of the banana industry in the early twentieth century that they earned the sobriquet "banana republics."

8. For more detail, see John A. Booth and Thomas W. Walker, *Understanding Central America* (Boulder, Colo.: Westview, 1989), chaps. 3–4, 6–8.

9. John A. Booth, "Socioeconomic and Political Roots of National Revolts in Central America," *Latin American Research Review* 26, no. 1 (1991): 33–73; Booth and Walker, *Understanding Central America,* chaps. 6–8; Charles D. Brockett, *Land Power and Poverty: Agrarian Transformation and Political Conflict in Central America* (Boston: Unwin Hyman, 1990); James Dunkerley, *Power in the Isthmus* (London: Verso, 1988).

10. See, for instance, Booth, "Socioeconomic and Political Roots"; Dunkerley, *Power in the Isthmus;* and Booth and Walker, *Understanding Central America.*

11. The United States justified such political intervention in the name of democracy but defined democracy in particularly narrow terms—constitutionalism and holding of elections within elite-dominated polities. U.S. intervention on behalf of democracy in Latin America and Central America in this period was also often inconsistent or subservient to security or economic concerns. Woodrow Wilson used direct military intervention in Mexico and Nicaragua, invoking democracy, while Franklin Roosevelt refused to intervene in Nicaragua in the 1930s to salvage constitutional rule. See, for instance, Walter LaFeber, *Inevitable Revolutions: The United States in Central America* (New York: W. W. Norton, 1983), pp. 19–83; Thomas Carothers, *In the Name of Democracy: U.S. Policy toward Latin America in the Reagan Years* (Berkeley: University of California Press, 1991), pp. 1–11; Kurth, "The United States and Central America"; and Paul Drake, "From Good Men to Good Neighbors: 1912–1932," in Abraham F. Lowenthal, ed., *Exporting Democracy: The United States and Latin America: Themes and Issues* (Baltimore, Md.: Johns Hopkins University Press, 1991), pp. 3–40.

12. See Carothers, *In the Name of Democracy,* pp. 1–11; Kurth, "The

United States and Central America," pp. 39–57; Leslie Bethell, "From the Second World War to the Cold War: 1944–1954" and Laurence Whitehead, "The Imposition of Democracy," both in Lowenthal, ed., *Exporting Democracy*, pp. 41–70, 216–42.

13. Richard Feinberg, "The Recent Rapid Redefinitions of U.S. Interests and Diplomacy in Central America," in Feinberg, ed., *Central America*, p. 61.

14. Congressional investigations in the early 1970s had revealed U.S. complicity in toppling the Allende regime in Chile and supporting the violation of human rights there and elsewhere (especially Latin America and Southeast Asia).

15. See, for instance, Anthony Lake, *Somoza Falling: A Case Study of Washington at Work* (Amherst: University of Massachusetts Press, 1989), chaps. 3, 7; Robert A. Pastor, *Condemned to Repetition: The United States and Nicaragua* (Princeton, N.J.: Princeton University Press, 1987); and Dario Moreno, *U.S. Policy in Central America: The Endless Debate* (Miami: Florida International University Press, 1990), chap. 2.

16. Laurence Whitehead, "Explaining Washington's Central American Policies," in Larkin, ed., *Vital Interests*, pp. 201–4; Lake, *Somoza Falling*; Pastor, *Condemned to Repetition*; Feinberg, "The Recent Rapid Redefinitions," pp. 58–77; Barry Rubin, "Reagan Administration Policymaking and Central America," in Robert S. Leiken, ed., *Central America: Anatomy of Conflict* (New York: Carnegie Endowment for International Peace—Pergamon, 1984), pp. 300–302. Describing the same processes, Moreno (*U.S. Policy in Central America*, chap. 2) interprets Carter's policies as an abandonment of containment; I would argue that it was merely containment of Communism by more sophisticated, reformist means.

17. Lake, *Somoza Falling*; Pastor, *Condemned to Repetition*.

18. Michael J. Kryzanek, *U.S.–Latin American Relations* (New York: Praeger, 1990), pp. 213–24; Peter W. Schulze, "A West European View: Walking a Tightrope between Self-Assertion and Alliance Loyalty," in Larkin, ed., *Vital Interests*, pp. 251–56; Abraham F. Lowenthal, "Ronald Reagan and Latin America: Coping with Hegemony in Decline," in Kenneth A. Oye, Robert J. Lieber, and Donald Rothchild, eds., *Eagle Defiant: United States Foreign Policy in the 1980s* (Boston: Little, Brown, 1983), pp. 311–36; Nora Hamilton and Manuel Pastor Jr., "Introduction," in Nora Hamilton et al., eds., *Crisis in Central America: Regional Dynamics and U.S. Policy in the 1980s* (Boulder, Colo.: Westview, 1988), pp. 1–7; Atkins, *Latin America in the International Political System* (Boulder, Colo.: Westview, 1989), pp. 210–35, 320–26.

19. Atkins, *Latin America*, p. 320.

20. See, for instance, the Santa Fe Committee report cited above and Jeane Kirkpatrick, "U.S. Security and Latin America" (pp. 49–72), David Ronfeldt, "Geopolitics, Security, and U.S. Strategy in the Caribbean Basin" (pp. 73–90), Ronald Reagan, "Central America and U.S. Security" (pp. 113–21); and "Why

Democracy Matters in Central America," (pp. 121–30), all repr. in Larkin, ed., *Vital Interests*; Arturo Cruz Sequeira, "The Origins of Sandinista Foreign Policy," in Leiken, ed., *Central America*, pp. 95–110; and Bruce McColm, "The Cuban and Soviet Dimension," in Mark Falcoff and Robert Royal, *Crisis and Opportunity: U.S. Policy in Central America and the Caribbean* (Washington DC: Ethics and Public Policy Center, 1984), pp. 53–78.

21. See, for instance, Marc Edelman, "Soviet-Cuban Involvement in Central America: A Critique of Recent Writings" (pp. 141–68), Laurence Whitehead, "Explaining Washington's Central American Policies" (pp. 199–242), George Philip, "The Nicaraguan Conflict: Politics and Propaganda" (pp. 243–49), "Perspectives on the Soviet Presence in Central America" (pp. 269–88), C. G. Jacobsen, "Soviet Attitudes towards, Aid to and Contacts with Central American Revolutionaries" (pp. 289–320), and W. Raymond Duncan, "Soviet Interests in Latin America: New Opportunities and Old Constraints" (pp. 371–97), all in Larkin, ed., *Vital Interests*. See also G. Pope Atkins, *Latin America in the International Political System* (Boulder, Colo.: Westview, 1990), pp. 97–103; Morris Rothenberg, "The Soviets and Central America," and Joseph Cirincione and Leslie Hunter, "Military Threats, Actual and Potential," both in Leiken, ed., *Central America*, pp. 131–49, 173–91.

22. See, for instance, Oye, Lieber, and Rothchild, eds., *Eagle Defiant*.

23. John A. Booth, *The End and the Beginning: The Nicaraguan Revolution* (Boulder, Colo.: Westview, 1985).

24. Ibid.; see also Moreno, *U.S. Policy in Central America*, chap. 3; Lake, *Somoza Falling*; Pastor, *Condemned to Repetition*.

25. Testimony before the House Foreign Affairs Committee, 1979, quoted in Moreno, *U.S. Policy in Central America*, p. 61.

26. Tommie Sue Montgomery, *Revolution in El Salvador: Origins and Evolution* (Boulder, Colo.: Westview, 1984), chap. 1; John A. Booth, "The Evolution of U.S. Policy in El Salvador: The Politics of Repression," in H. Michael Erisman, ed., *The Caribbean Challenge: U.S. Policy in a Volatile Region* (Boulder, Colo.: Westview, 1984), pp. 117–41.

27. Moreno, *U.S. Policy in Central America*, pp. 75–82.

28. Richard Millett, "The Historical Setting," and Steve C. Ropp, "National Security," both in James D. Rudolph, ed., *Honduras: A Country Study* (Washington DC: American University Foreign Area Studies–U.S. Government Printing Office, 1983), pp. 48–51, 241–46; Booth and Walker, *Understanding Central America*, chap. 8.

29. Susanne Jonas, *The Battle for Guatemala: Rebels, Death Squads, and U.S. Power* (Boulder, Colo.: Westview, 1991), chap. 9; Booth and Walker, *Understanding Central America*, chap. 7.

30. Much has been written about the Reagan foreign policy team and Central America; see especially Roy Gutman, *Banana Diplomacy: The Making of American Policy in Nicaragua 1981–1987* (New York: Touchstone, 1988),

212 John A. Booth

chaps. 1–6; Feinberg, "The Recent Rapid Redefinitions"; Moreno, *U.S. Policy in Central America,* chap. 4; Rubin, "Reagan Administration Policy Making"; Atkins, *Latin America in the International Political System,* pp. 320–36; LaFeber, *Inevitable Revolutions,* chap. 5; Whitehead, "Explaining Washington's Central America Policies," pp. 199–243; H. Michael Erisman, "Contemporary Challenges Confronting U.S. Caribbean Policy," in Erisman, ed., *The Caribbean Challenge,* pp. 3–30; Saul Landau, *The Dangerous Doctrine: National Security and U.S. Foreign Policy* (Boulder, Colo.: Westview, 1988), chaps. 12–13.

31. Robert F. Docksai, "Foreword," in *A New Inter-American Policy for the Eighties,* Council for Inter-American Security, May 1980, reprinted in Larkin, ed., *Vital Interests,* pp. 11–48.

32. "The doctrine prohibited non-American powers from acquiring territory, introducing alien systems, or intervening in the Western hemisphere." Ibid., p. 16.

33. Ibid.

34. Ibid., p. 43.

35. Thomas W. Walker, ed., *Reagan versus the Sandinistas: The Undeclared War on Nicaragua* (Boulder, Colo.: Westview, 1987); Moreno, *U.S. Policy in Central America,* chap. 4; William I. Robinson and Kent Norsworthy, *David and Goliath: The U.S. War against Nicaragua* (New York: Monthly Review, 1987); Holly Sklar, *Washington's War on Nicaragua* (Boston: South End, 1988).

36. This was because the U.S. Embassy in Managua provided a valuable "intelligence platform" and easy contact with the internal opposition.

37. This was true of U.S. policy toward El Salvador, as well.

38. Perhaps the greatest success of the opponents of the administration's Central America policy involved the report of the Kissinger Commission. The anti-interventionist and peace forces successfully lobbied commission members to alter somewhat the content of the report as it was evolving in late 1983. More important, mobilization of critical commentary in the press helped neutralize the administration's intended impact for the commission's report by publicizing its ideological and interventionist biases.

39. Author's conversations with members of the Kissinger Commission, 1983.

40. John Tower, Edmund Muskie, and Brent Scowcroft (the Tower Commission), *Report of the President's Special Review Board* (New York: Bantam Books–Times Books, 1987).

41. Some observers noted that human rights violations in El Salvador after the early 1980s had an instrumental character. That is, rights abuses tended to fall when key aid votes were pending in the U.S. Congress and to rise in order to intimidate regime opposition prior to Salvadoran elections.

42. Carothers, *In the Name of Democracy*, chap. 1; Booth, "The Evolution of U.S. Policy toward El Salvador," pp. 136–37; Kryzanek, *U.S.–Latin American Relations*, pp. 172–86.

43. Edward S. Herman and Frank Brodhead, *Demonstration Elections: U.S.-Staged Elections in the Dominican Republic, Vietnam, and El Salvador* (Boston: South End, 1984); José García, "Recent Elections in Historical Perspective," in John A. Booth and Mitchell A. Seligson, eds., *Elections and Democracy in Central America* (Chapel Hill: University of North Carolina Press, 1989), pp. 60–92.

44. Tower, Muskie, and Scowcroft, *Report of the President's Special Review Board*.

45. Latin American Studies Association (LASA), *Extraordinary Opportunities . . . and New Risks: Final Report of the LASA Commission on Compliance with the Central America Peace Accord* (Pittsburgh: LASA, 1988).

46. Jim Wright, *Streams of Hope, Rivers of Blood: A Personal Narrative about Central America and the United States* (unpublished ms., photocopy, ca. 1990); Moreno, *U.S. Policy in Central America*, pp. 128–32.

47. Author's conversation with a high-ranking administration foreign policy official, September 1989, Atlanta, Ga.

48. Bill Robinson, *A Faustian Bargain: U.S. Involvement in Nicaraguan Elections* (Boulder, Colo.: Westview, 1992); Latin American Studies Association (LASA), *Electoral Democracy under International Pressure: The Report of the Latin American Studies Association Commission to Observe the 1990 Nicaraguan Election* (Pittsburgh: LASA, 1990).

49. The Sandinistas clearly expected to win and hoped that external observation would confirm the honesty of the 1990 election and legitimize their victory. International organizations such as the UN and OAS participated as monitors/observers to promote settlement of the Nicaraguan conflict and help curtail U.S. intervention.

50. "Peace!" *Mesoamerica* 11, no. 1 (January 1992): pp. 1–2; Norberto Svarzman, "Salvadorans Achieve Peace," *Times of the Americas*, 8 January 1992, pp. 1, 6.

51. Available statistical data probably modestly exaggerate Nicaragua's plight by being shaped heavily by exchange rates in a period of currency hyperdevaluation. Though strikingly deteriorated, real working-class living standards would not seem to have fallen quite so badly if one were to take into account bartered labor and food supplies and informal economic activity.

52. The Central American Parliament, to be composed of twenty popularly elected representatives of each nation, got off to a rocky start. Nicaragua's delegates were not elected, and Costa Rica had not even ratified the treaty at this writing.

53. See Booth and Seligson, eds., *Elections and Democracy in Central America* and John A. Booth and Mitchell A. Seligson, "Political Culture and Democratization: Costa Rica, Mexico, and Nicaragua," in Larry Diamond, ed., *Political Culture and Democracy in the Third World* (Boulder, Colo.: Lynne Rienner, 1992).

54. See table 2 for sources. The military assistance program figure includes some $300 million spent on the Contras.

Enrique A. Baloyra

Latin America, Cuba, and
the United States:
From the Eighties to the Nineties

This chapter examines the present state of relations between Cuba and the other American republics and its implications for the United States. In maintaining relations with Cuba, do the Latin Americans act out of solidarity or self-interest? Are they presently trying to somehow rescue Cuba from its conflict with the United States and are they likely to bail the Castro regime out, or are they simply trying to isolate that conflict and protect themselves from its fallout? Is Cuban antagonism toward the United States in any way useful to the other American republics?

I will argue that what has predominated is a Latin American desire to be unaffected by the conflict between Castro and the United States and, whenever possible, to minimize that conflict. In one view a more moderate Cuba would be a less disruptive influence in the hemisphere, but even absent any domestic changes Cuba could be left behind in an era of economic integration and democratic consolidation.[1] Well before the collapse of the Central European socialist regimes in 1989, Cuba was not exactly a beacon of hope to a generation of Latin American leaders tempered by the lessons of bureaucratic authoritarianism. Cuba's mediocre record in solving the problem of production is more familiar and unlikely to stir much interest when proffered as a model. Opposite this is the interpretation that a Latin America devastated by structural crisis and requiring new economic and social development strategies has shifted more toward Cuban than U.S. positions.[2] Eventually North-South conflict between the United States and Latin America will intensify as a result of the former's unwillingness to accommodate the demands of the latter, and the Castro regime will benefit from deepening contradictions between the United States and Latin America in a new international context dominated by economic conflict.

Regardless of who is right, U.S.-Cuban conflict affects the rest of the hemisphere. Traditionally, many Latin American countries have found much to criticize about American policies toward Cuba, particularly what they regard as counterproductive ideological initiatives, but this disagreement does not necessarily translate into Latin American solidarity with Castro.[3] Conversely, open criticism of Cuba is of more recent vintage but should not be equated with alignment with the United States.

A Brief Overview

It was only natural that the Cuban revolutionary regime would seek to multiply its relations with countries of the Western Hemisphere and largely inevitable that Latin American countries would be affected by the growing conflict between Cuba and the United States. The sixties and early seventies witnessed this conflict play itself out. According to Castro, "Relations were broken when other governments broke relations with Cuba. That left us with only one relation: that with the leftists. . . . All of Latin America combined with the United States against us, with the exception of Mexico. . . . We saw ourselves in conflict with all of Latin America."[4] The outcome was inconclusive: Cuban support for revolution angered the other American republics and failed to create "many Vietnams," as Che Guevara had hoped. The Castro regime found itself isolated. But neither diplomatic isolation nor an economic embargo brought the regime to its knees.

In the mid-1970s, following this period of isolation and conflict in its immediate area, bilateral relations began to improve between Cuba and some Latin American countries. Tensions diminished following the July 1975 lifting of the diplomatic and economic sanctions imposed by the Organization of American States on the Castro regime in July 1964. Gradually, as many of those countries underwent processes of transition to democracy, the regime normalized relations with the rest of the hemisphere.

In the 1980s, reestablishing relations with Cuba had very practical implications for these newly emerging democratic regimes. It enabled them to reaffirm their autonomy in front of the hegemonic foreign policies of the Reagan administration.[5] It helped them increase their domestic legitimacy and appease leftist domestic constituencies whose demands for redistributive policies and prosecution of military perpetrators of human rights abuses could not be met. Latin American opposition to U.S. motions to produce a condemnation of the Castro regime by the United Nations Commission on Human Rights (UNCHR) in the late eighties may be viewed in this light. Above everything there was a determination to avoid the rekindling of conflict between Cuba and Latin America at the instigation of the United States.[6]

In essence, the other American republics show little inclination to become hostage to this antagonism.[7] In the eighties the Cuban regime found little support for its positions on issues arrayed on the East-West continuum, while receiving a respectful, even sympathetic, response but little actual collaboration on many questions pertaining to the North-South conflict. In the nineties, the regime is badly out of tune with the rest of the hemisphere on matters of human rights, democratization, and economic integration. But several efforts have been made by other governments to help bring the crisis of Castroism to a peaceful resolution.

Parameters of Cuban Foreign Policy

Regardless of their own ideological convictions, most students of Cuban foreign policy agree that the main imperative of that policy is surviving the antagonism of the United States.[8] That imperative has led the Castro regime to confront American foreign policy objectives on a global scale.[9]

Cuban support for proletarian internationalism poses some concrete problems. In the Western Hemisphere Cuban objectives include achieving the full independence of Latin America and the Caribbean by abolishing the system of U.S. domination, achieving the greatest unity and political integration possible, setting Latin Americanism against Pan Americanism, including the region in a new international economic order, achieving profound transformations that may promote these objectives, and uniting all anti-imperialist and progressive forces in a broad front.[10] Latin American governments may overtly espouse these desiderata or simply harbor them in pectore, but they primarily follow their own interests and convictions in implementing them.

Interpreting Cuban foreign policy requires knowledge of several points. The imperatives of "never to surrender to the United States" and "pursuing normal relations among states as a basic historical necessity" have guided revolutionary Cuba's diplomacy and must be included in any attempt at understanding how Cuban foreign policy may complicate inter-American relations. Overlooking these imperatives has often led to confusion about whether Cuba has been primarily a responsible and predictable actor in world affairs or an incorrigible state engaged in fomenting terrorism and exporting revolution. The "implementation muddle" adds to this confusion because Cuban foreign policy directives and policy behavior have operated through a conundrum of state, party, governmental, and mass organizations.[11] From these there emerged more than one voice, and, analytically, the real issue is explaining how the interaction among state (Fidel Castro and his control group), Communist party departments, and government agencies (the Foreign Relations Ministry— MINREX; the Foreign Trade Ministry; the State Committee for Economic Cooperation—CECE; among others) has shaped that policy. Also, for the most part, Cubans do not act on impulse. This does not deny Fidel Castro's preponderant influence on Cuban foreign policy, only that he stands alone and can operate without intermediaries; it does not negate that he is the major decision maker, only that his actions are exclusively dictated by his legendary temper.[12] There has been, after all, a pragmatic side to Cuban foreign policy.

All the foregoing is relevant because, until recently, Cuba has had the foreign policy capabilities of a major international actor. The Castro regime has been an international activist operating with a generous margin of autonomy, designing and implementing policies on a global scale, mobilizing resources to project power overseas, and it has carved out a certain sphere of influence of its own.[13] Mistakes by or conflict with a regime with these attributes posed a dilemma to relevant others. For the Latin Americans the dilemma has been how to put in place a framework that Cuban policies, even when intending to, cannot easily disrupt. More recently, as Cuba lost means, opportunity, and justification to conduct an activist revolutionary foreign policy, the Latin Americans have been more concerned with avoiding a catastrophic outcome in Cuba.

Cuba and the Western Hemisphere, 1986 to 1993

Ideological Fraternalism

Cuban bilateral relations of ideological fraternalism with other revolutionary regimes in the Western Hemisphere included very close,
regular, bilateral contact between state, party, government, and informal organizations, regulated by covenants and agreements and
foreign policy alignment and coordination. In the eighties Cuba's
most fraternal relations in the hemisphere were with the Sandinistas, who, although not socialist in the eyes of Havana, had a regime worthy of unqualified fraternal support. No other regime in the
Western Hemisphere was as interdependent with Cuba's as that of
the Sandinistas. In February 1986, Nicaraguan president Daniel Ortega described these relations as "friendly, fraternal, respectful, un-
alterable and nonnegotiable." With the exception of Grenada's
Maurice Bishop, and to a much lesser extent Michael Manley in the
late seventies in Jamaica, no other head of state or foreign minister in
the hemisphere professed anything similar.[14] The downside was that
Nicaragua was the other state in the hemisphere whose rancorous
relation with the United States had a potential impact similar to
Cuba's.

Ideological fraternalism suffered a major blow with the electoral
defeat of the Sandinistas in the general election of 25 February 1990.
Cuban media lamented that eleven years of revolution had succumbed to unfavorable trends and described the election as a contest
between imperialism and the Sandinistas. Cuban grief contrasted
with a generalized sense of relief in the rest of the hemisphere that,
after one decade, Nicaragua would finally move off the front pages of
American newspapers. Reacting to the outcome of the election, Castro somehow managed to reverse the causality between elections
and civil strife: "An unreal and absurd situation has appeared in Nicaragua because of all the elements I have explained to you. That situation entails a high risk of conflict and civil war. . . . Now another
situation has come up: What should we do about our cooperation?"[15]
In Nicaragua for Violeta de Chamorro's inauguration in April 1990,
Cuban vice president José Ramón Fernández confirmed Cuban willingness to continue cooperation activities if the "new authorities"
requested it.[16] In June Nicaraguan foreign minister Enrique Dreyfus
could see no reason to break relations with Cuba. Even though the
Cubans criticized many of the initiatives of the new Nicaraguan

government, the latter found some value in the relationship given the Cubans' sustained criticism of the lack of any significant amount of U.S. assistance to the Chamorro government. In May 1991 the two governments renewed the protocol regulating bilateral trade. Nevertheless, the situation was different: the Sandinistas were in opposition, and the country was desperately short of foreign exchange. At home, the Cubans were coping with the disappearance of their major trading partner and embarking on a very severe program of economic austerity.

Ideological fraternalism also characterized socialist Cuba's relations with revolutionary nonstate actors. Paradigmatic of the latter were Cuban relations with the Farabundo Martí National Liberation Front (FMLN) of El Salvador, with the National Unity of Guatemalan Revolutionaries (UNRG), and, until late 1990, with the Manuel Rodríguez Patriotic Front (FPMR) of Chile. These contacts were the most visible and public among the regime's reputed links with guerrilla groups in the hemisphere.[17] In the past, these linkages had provoked friction and irritation; at present and in the future, they remain a concern to other American republics trying to evolve normal relations with Cuba. In the early nineties, there simply were no regimes in the hemisphere that revolutionary Cuba could engage in ideological alignment.

Nonaligned Fraternalism

Cuba's next most cordial level of bilateral relations in the hemisphere included Mexico and Guyana. This was bilateralism anchored in intergovernmental commissions of cooperation and numerous agreements for collaboration in an impressive number of areas.[18] Optimal as these relations may become, they have not, in the case of Mexico, delivered the economic benefits that the Cubans had anticipated nor did they turn Guyana into a client state similar to the Grenada of Maurice Bishop.

Mexico is the only Latin American republic never to have broken relations with revolutionary Cuba and to systematically oppose efforts to isolate and punish the Castro regime. This the Mexicans have done on grounds of nationalism, to underline their foreign policy autonomy from the United States, and out of their unshakeable belief in the ultimate efficacy of the Calvo Doctrine of nonintervention, incorporated as a clause in the Mexican constitution, and in their own Estrada Doctrine, extending automatic recognition to other governments. The Cuba policy of Mexico, therefore, has been and remains inspired by tradition, pragmatism, and nationalism.

Although usually circumspect about Mexican domestic politics, the Cubans have not been immune to foot-in-mouth gaffes. In July 1988, amidst the uproar of an ongoing furious dispute about the results of a general election, Fidel Castro chose to congratulate Carlos Salinas de Gortari, the PRI candidate. This annoyed the opposition to no end, not only the conservative PAN but, more important, the PRD and its candidate, Cuauhtémoc Cárdenas. Beginning in the summer of 1990 it was Salinas's turn to be annoyed. While the Mexicans were keeping their fingers crossed waiting for fast-track approval by the U.S. Congress of NAFTA, the Cubans found nothing better to do than parrot criticisms raised by North American industrial and labor interests. In late August and early September, they hosted Cárdenas, a NAFTA opponent, in Havana. All the while the Cuban media remained unalterably critical of the agreement. On 29 October, Mexican ambassador-designate Mario Moya Palencia tried to mollify Cuban critics by stating that the new agreement with the United States would not alter the "traditionally excellent level of relations" with Cuba.[19] In December, the Cuban media echoed Canadian apprehensions about the potential negative consequences of the pact in the form of loss of jobs. There were also indiscreet comments about the absence of electoral democracy in Mexico.[20]

In the summer of 1992 President Salinas de Gortari broke precedent by holding private meetings with Cuban exile groups. On 3 August, Salinas met with a delegation of the Cuban American National Foundation (CANF) led by its president, Jorge Más Canosa. CANF is the best-organized, best-financed, and most visible organization of the conservative exile mainstream. In addition, during the Reagan-Bush era, CANF operated like a very effective lobby, contributing to harden U.S. policy toward Cuba and tightening the U.S. economic embargo. On 13 September, Salinas received Carlos Alberto Montaner, a Cuban writer, president of Unión Liberal Cubana (ULC), and one of the leaders of the Cuban Democratic Platform (PLADECU), a coalition of liberal, Christian Democratic, and Social Democratic parties created in Madrid in August 1990. In meeting with the most effective conservative and moderate Cuban American organizations, Salinas not only acknowledged the existence of an opposition to Castro but also the need to find new ways to promote Mexican interests in the United States. In addition, he confirmed the realist and pragmatic orientation of his foreign policy. Visiting Mexico at the time, Roberto Robaina, secretary general of the Union of Communist Youth (UJC), reacted by saying that "Cuba respected the internal decisions of other countries." For the first time in five years, Castro did not attend the 15 September, Mexican Independence Day reception hosted by Ambassador Moya Palencia in Havana.[21]

A September 1993 incident involving eight boat people who were returned to Cuba after they had reached Yucatán and some of their companions had perished at sea illustrates the current state of affairs. While a clamor of protest was raised in Miami, accompanied by very virulent anti-Mexican rhetoric, Mexican consul Bulmaro Pacheco engaged in quiet and calm consultation with representatives of Cuban American groups. Not forty-eight hours after their repatriation to Cuba, the Mexican government announced its intention to receive the eight if the Cuban government allowed their departure. The Cuban government obliged. Pacheco explained the actions of his government at a press conference at CANF headquarters.

Has Mexico kept Castro afloat economically? From 1985 to 1990, Mexico was not Cuba's main trading partner in the Western Hemisphere. In recent years trade discussions between Cuba and Mexico have evolved from how to diminish trade balances unfavorable to Cuba to how to finance those balances. In June 1986 the Banco de Comercio Exterior (BANCOMEX) extended a credit line of $150 million to Cuba to finance bilateral trade. In January 1991 the amount covered by the bank was $100 million, and the Cuban debt with Mexico stood at approximately $250 million. That month, following a round of discussions on the Cuban debt in Havana, BANCOMEX director Humberto Soto disclosed that Mexico might begin to refine crude oil at the Cienfuegos refinery in southern Cuba. No major upgrade was announced at the signing of a new trade cooperation pact in April 1991. In October Soto announced that a more generous line of credit would be made available. In June 1991 Ambassador Moya Palencia summarized Mexican economic policies toward Cuba: commitment to improve trade, good disposition to enter joint manufacturing agreements, and assistance and support for a tourism infrastructure in Cuba. But Moya Palencia delicately reminded his hosts that third-country products could not circulate within the free trade area and enjoy customs and tax dispensations.[22] In February 1992 Cuban economic cooperation minister Ernesto Meléndez expressed satisfaction that much of the hotel industry infrastructure was being provided by Mexico. He also hinted that Cuba could buy Mexican crude on the open market. In any case, Cuban oil purchases from Mexico were but a tiny fraction of what was provided to Cuba by Venezuela under a quadripartite agreement—$478 versus $16 million in 1990, and $386 versus $24.5 million in 1991.[23]

Driven by necessity, the Cubans launched some trial balloons regarding Mexican oil. In September 1990 Luis Suárez Salazar, director of the Center for the Study of the Americas (CEA), told an audience at the Matías Romero Institute for Diplomatic Studies in Mexico City that Cuba would try joining the San José agreement or, in its stead, seek a provisional arrangement with Mexico. Cuban ambassador José (Pepé) Fernández de Cossío denied later that Cuba had sought alternative suppliers of oil. In October 1991 Cuban media cited Mexican foreign minister Fernando Solana saying that Cuba's entrance into the San José agreement could be discussed in August 1992.[24] However, a few days later, at the conclusion of an impromptu meeting of the presidents of the Group of Three (G-3) in Cozumel, attended by Castro, Venezuelan president Carlos Andrés Pérez stated that the San José oil agreement was inapplicable to Cuba.[25] For his part, Castro declared he had not brought up the issue of oil.

In essence, the Mexicans have been pragmatic and prudent, sensitive to Cuban demands, patient with Cuba's inability to pay, and opposed to pressuring or isolating the Cuban regime. But their policies have fallen considerably short of delivering assistance in the terms and amounts that the Castro regime would require to come out of the depths of political and economic crisis. Simply stated, Mexico does not have that capability. Mexican offers and actual delivery of assistance to Cuba have been designed to forestall a catastrophic collapse rather than to buttress a regime considered anachronistic. This is cooperation or, at best, fraternal assistance, not ideological alignment.

There seems to be a consensus among sympathetic observers and diplomats anxious to cooperate in a peaceful transition in Cuba that, given its traditional relations with the Castro regime and increasing business interests in the country, Mexico remains a key player in the dynamics of Cuban–U.S.–Latin American relations. But, while willing to play a constructive role in this regard, Salinas appeared in no mood to allow this to jeopardize NAFTA and the search for a new relationship with the United States.

In general, Cuban relations with Guyana owe their importance to their symbolism. Courting Guyana had its costs for the Cubans, particularly in the matter of the Guyanese territorial dispute with Venezuela, in which they sided with Guyana without major benefit to themselves. Intergovernmental commissions have regularly met and produced new bilateral agreements in a number of areas, but bilateral trade remains in a barter configuration in which the parties are often unable to deliver—cement in the case of Cuba, rice on the part of Guyana—and the value of total annual trade is almost negligible. In the early 1990s, as the Cuban regime desperately searched for sources of foreign exchange and new trading partners, it appeared to be giving more attention to the CARICOM bloc. In turn, Guyana appeared to be totally absorbed by its domestic problems, including a general election and a peaceful transfer of power to a new government headed by Cheddi Jagan.

Some elements in Cuba's bilateral relations with the Panama of Manuel Antonio Noriega strongly resemble those attributed to nonaligned fraternalism. Furthermore, Cuban activities in Panama spawned a web of political intrigue and a network of economic activities designed to circumvent the U.S. economic embargo. However, given the nature of Panama's bilateral relations with the United States, the issue of the security of the canal, and General Noriega's ambivalent attitude toward Cuba, Panama-Cuba relations during this period probably call for an analytic classification other than nonaligned fraternalism.

Operation Just Cause, the U.S. invasion of December 1989 and its aftermath, gave the Cuban government much scope to fulminate against American imperialism and Yankee prepotency but also forced it to recognize a lack of solidarity on the part of the major Latin American governments. While Cuba voiced its strongest condemnation of what it called a "genocidal action" and sensed "a decisive moment for Latin American unity," the OAS passed a resolution deploring U.S. military intervention and calling for an immediate end to the fighting and the withdrawal of the invading troops. The Group of Rio tried to convene but did not; it then prepared a resolution to be presented to the UN only to withdraw it after Brazil recognized the new government of Guillermo Endara. Havana finally exploded at the "miserable opportunists" and "sons of bitches who have not said half a word of condemnation against the invasion and demand plebiscites in Cuba."[26] But the Cubans had it both ways.

Despite the March 1990 expulsion of Cuban ambassador Lázaro Mora on grounds that he refused to recognize the legitimacy of the government of Guillermo Endara, whom he had called a puppet of the American invaders, the Cubans remained very much in business in Panama.[27] The embassy operated with a reduced staff and offered asylum to officials of the deposed Noriega government, who eventually left the country in May 1991. Despite Cuban criticism of practically everything in their country, Panamanian business interests defended the continued presence of Cuban firms.[28]

The Discreet Cordiality of Democracy

In the early and mid-eighties, Cuba made considerable diplomatic gains reestablishing or rekindling relations with a host of newly inaugurated democratic regimes in Latin America. At that time, the Cubans may have found this to be the most promising aspect of their foreign relations. Normalization with Cuba produced friction between the United States and some of these countries. The Reagan and Bush administrations viewed this as part of a multilateral effort at neutralizing their initiatives. But Reagan and Bush and their colleagues need not have worried or, better, should have worried about other problems confronting these new democracies, not about their supposedly idyllic bilateral relations with Cuba. Contrary to what Washington alarmists and Cuban propagandists would have us believe, these regimes did not trip over themselves to establish intimate relations with Cuba.

The pattern of normalization of Cuban bilateral relations with the Latin American democracies was very uneven. Those relations were not meant to balance disgust at U.S. policies toward Cuba with alliances with the Castro regime or to bring Cuba at full speed into the framework of Latin American integration. More specifically, the new democratic regimes have disagreed with Cuban positions on the Central American conflict, the foreign debt, and Latin American economic integration. Nor did their reluctance to support U.S. motions to condemn violations of human rights in Cuba, their criticism of Radio and TV Marti, and their sporadic appeals for the end to the U.S. economic embargo imply an endorsement of the Castro regime.

Apparently, Castro's democratic counterparts prefer to deal with him in a low-key and informal way, taking advantage of opportunities for contact provided by presidential inaugurations and multilateral gatherings.[29] Castro used those opportunities to defend his government, deny that Cuba was isolated, trumpet the exploits of the revolution, reiterate his faith in socialism and his refusal to surrender to the United States, blame the foreign debt and capitalist exploitation for the misery and poverty of Latin America, laud the alliance of Christians and Marxists, and expound on his ideas about Latin American integration.[30] Other heads of state utilized these brief informal encounters with Castro to privately encourage him to engage in domestic reforms. A notable encounter took place between Castro, Venezuelan president Carlos Andrés Pérez, and Spanish president Felipe González at the Fernando Collor de Mello inauguration in March 1990. Pérez described the encounter as "extremely pleasant, good, and positive."[31] But Castro saw things differently: "Recently, the president of Venezuela and the prime minister [sic] of Spain told me they are concerned. . . . They have said that Cuba's strategy must not be resistance. They speak of Sagunto and Numancia, of holocaust. . . . They cannot talk about Sagunto or Numancia to us because we would rather die than be slaves to be dominated by the U.S. again."[32] This is hardly a picture of unconditional support for the Cuban president or of confabulation against the United States. A quick review of a few bilateral highlights easily confirms this.

For example, the government of Brazilian president José Sarney did not agree to a formal exchange of ambassadors until October 1986, only after the Cubans agreed to submit to very strict ground rules.[33] Nevertheless, normalization got off to a fairly auspicious start. Brazil was interested in Cuban health and sanitation strategies, biotechnology, and biogenetics. Cuba was primarily concerned with computers, sugar technology, and alternative energy sources. But there were obstacles, like finding a currency of exchange and going beyond what could be afforded by barter schemes and the small amounts of credit available. What collaboration could be worked out under these conditions was rapidly put in place.[34] But nothing major transpired until June 1989, when the Health Ministry announced Brazil's interest in creating a joint enterprise to produce the antimeningococci vaccine and in sponsoring a joint study to determine the effectiveness of the Cuban type B vaccine. According to Cuban sources, total bilateral trade nearly doubled from $25 million in 1985 to $49 million in August 1989. In essence bilateral relations between Cuba and Brazil have become cordial and sensible but are short of providing what, considering Brazil's size and importance, Cuban foreign policy decision makers feel would be necessary to advance their strategic goals or offer a way out of the dramatic economic situation affecting Cuba in the early nineties. Brazil is unlikely to evolve bilateral relations similar to Mexico's, but Cuba could find considerable relief by developing better trade links with Brazil's aggressive entrepreneurs. Thus far Cuban efforts have yielded modest results.

Argentina had the mixed experience of warming up to Cuba at a time when the Cuban regime was preparing for economic austerity. Argentina provided generous credit to Cuba in the mid-eighties. With their government guaranteeing exports, Argentine businessmen did not care if the Cubans paid or not, but, by late 1986, when it became obvious that the Cubans could not, the government tightened the screws. Initially Cuba was allowed to only pay interest on its debt to Argentina, estimated informally at $600 million, and borrow the sum back immediately. In April 1988 an agreement on trade was subscribed at the conclusion of the second joint foreign trade commission meeting.[35] In January 1990 Argentine growers expressed their willingness to sell wheat to Cuba to cover the shortfall in Soviet deliveries. In September Cuban ambassador Miguel Brugueras put the figure of total annual trade at around $150 million per year and expressed hope that this could be widened. However, considering Cuba's debts to Argentina, the fact that during 1986 to 1989 Cuban exports to Argentina never exceeded $2 million and that the Argentine government was unwilling to guarantee payments to Argentine exporters to Cuba, it is hard to see how this could take place. Politically, the Cubans met Argentina's relative generosity only halfway. For example, Castro praised the performance of President Raúl Alfonsín in the military revolt of Easter 1987, but in February 1989 Castro equivocated in his appraisal of a leftist attack on a military barracks in Buenos Aires, which he merely described as "unfortunate," and he failed to join in with other heads of state gathered in Caracas for the Pérez inauguration who resolutely condemned the attack. Matters cooled considerably as a result of Argentina voting for a U.S. resolution condemning human rights abuses in Cuba in the 1991 session of the UNCHR, subsequent high-pitched Cuban criticism of President Carlos Saúl Menem's alignment with the United

States, and Menem's own frequent public and harsh criticism of the dictatorial nature of the Castro regime. Nevertheless, both countries vowed and managed to maintain relations.

At the conclusion of the July 1991 Guadalajara meeting of Ibero-American presidents, the announcement of a renewal of consular relations between Cuba and Chile was made. The Chilean chancery had been considering the question of reestablishing relations with Cuba, but Castro's continued support of the FPMR and the front's insistence on terrorist activities made the topic a nonissue. The principal problem with the Cubans was that since the overthrow of President Salvador Allende in September 1973, their nonrelation with Chile fell under the supervision of the PCC's Americas Department. Manuel Piñeiro Losada, the department's chief, remained wedded to the extreme Left and, as a result, Cuban perceptions of Chilean politics were colored by those of the FPMR, the Chilean Communist party, and its first secretary, Volodia Teitelboim. As a result, Cuban pronouncements about Chilean politics were incoherent and/or untimely, and the *fidelistas* were perceived in Chile as having little to contribute to national reconciliation and democratic consolidation.

From a Chilean standpoint relations with Cuba are simply a matter of propriety owed to another country that is willing to respect formal diplomatic channels and procedure. The Cuban demand for full diplomatic relations was only partially met. More important, the coalition government of Christian Democratic president Patricio Aylwin has not refrained from criticizing the Castro regime record in human rights, and it presented its own critical motion at the 1992 session of the UNCHR in Geneva.

Preventing Cuban interventionism has been a long-term desideratum of the Colombians. In July 1991 the government initiated a gradual and cautious normalization, announcing the restoration of consular relations with Cuba following the Guadalajara summit. The Cubans had worked long and hard to bring this about, but they only had themselves to blame for the 1981 break. In July 1987 a Colombian study commission recommended that relations be renewed but without haste. In 1989 the government and the guerrillas finally got around to serious negotiations; reportedly, Castro called President Virgilio del Barco to wish him well and offer his cooperation. In 1990, a presidential campaign year, not much attention was paid to the topic of relations with Cuba, and negotiations with narcotraffickers exhausted the government. All told, the Cubans had to wait ten years to normalize relations with Colombia. While President César Gaviria seemed willing to explore ways to increase trade and economic cooperation, he was also on record expressing his hope that Cuba would democratize.[36] When the Group of Three was charged by the Guadalajara summit with monitoring the Cuban situation, Gaviria shared this responsibility with Carlos Andrés Pérez and Carlos Salinas de Gortari. But with Salinas fully engaged in the politics of NAFTA and with the removal of Pérez, Gaviria became Castro's main interlocutor. In October 1993, when full diplomatic relations were restored, foreign minister Noemí Sanín took pains to emphasize that "Cuba no longer finances or trains Colombian guerrillas and Cuba no longer sponsors armed rebellion" and that a normalization of relations was not an endorsement of the Cuban regime.[37] By contrast, Roberto Robaina, who had replaced Ricardo Alarcón as Cuban foreign minister in the summer of 1993, described the renewal as "an extremely important link in what has always motivated Latin American countries and their governments—the integration of Latin America. We have always belonged to that Latin America and are proud to be part of it."[38]

In short, the evidence suggests that bilateral relations between the new Latin American democracies and revolutionary Cuba are based not on fraternal solidarity but on cooperation. While it is less than official Cuba had hoped for, it is certainly more than what it could count on at the beginning of the eighties. If Latin American diplomacy has excelled at anything it is in the art of being noncommittal, which exasperates Cubans and North Americans alike. Whether the Cubans correctly interpret the nuanced diplomacy of these democracies remains to be seen.

The Diplomacy of Business

In 1993 the most immediate economic riddle facing revolutionary Cuba was not so much whether to change the model but how to cope with the loss of the socialist market and U.S. attempts to tighten the economic embargo.

According to Cuban sources, during 1985 to 1990, trade with the Soviet Union represented about 70 percent of total Cuban foreign trade, or $55 of $79 billion (see table 1). By contrast, during the same period Cuban exports to the Western Hemisphere were slightly above 2 percent and imports were less than 5 percent of the total; to-

Table 1

Cuban Trade with the Western Hemisphere, 1984 to 1989: Cuban Version (millions of Cuban pesos)

			Exports (from Cuba to)				
	1984	1985	1986	1987	1988	1989	Total
Hemisphere	111.2	72.9	85.4	81.6	98.1	248.2	697.4
% of total	2.0	1.2	1.6	1.5	1.8	4.6	2.1
Canada	43.5	32.2	37.2	36.0	38.5	54.8	242.2
All other	67.7	40.7	48.2	45.6	59.6	193.4	455.2
Nicaragua	31.2	19.9	30.1	26.6	20.1	19.6	147.5
Venezuela	2.0	7.8	2.1	1.5	21.8	31.1	66.3
Mexico	10.7	1.9	1.7	2.0	4.9	17.8	39.0
Rest	23.8	11.1	14.3	15.5	12.8	124.9	202.4
Eastern Europe	4,686.4	5,161.5	4,627.2	4,689.2	4,518.2	4,069.0	27,751.5
U.S.S.R.	3,952.2	4,481.6	3,935.8	3,868.7	3,683.1	3,231.2	23,152.6
% of total	72.2	74.8	74.0	71.6	66.7	59.9	69.9
World Total	5,476.5	5,991.5	5,321.5	5,402.1	5,518.3	5,392.0	33,101.9

			Imports (to Cuba from)				
	1984	1985	1986	1987	1988	1989	Total
Hemisphere	318.6	379.5	297.4	294.3	360.4	514.8	2,165.0
% of total	4.4	4.7	3.9	3.9	4.8	6.3	4.7
Canada	56.5	58.8	53.4	33.0	28.5	37.1	267.3
All other	262.1	320.7	244.0	261.3	331.9	477.7	1,897.7
Argentina	149.9	193.3	162.2	124.3	127.5	179.2	936.4
Mexico	72.7	77.1	29.7	72.0	108.0	80.0	439.5
Venezuela	7.5	5.8	10.2	19.1	28.9	56.5	128.0
Peru	4.7	3.0	3.7	3.6	8.4	19.1	42.5
Rest	27.3	41.5	38.2	42.3	59.1	142.9	351.3
Eastern Europe	5,784.8	6,507.0	6,297.4	6,530.0	6,432.5	6,636.3	38,188.0
U.S.S.R.	4,782.4	5,418.9	5,337.6	5,446.0	5,364.4	5,522.4	31,871.7
% of total	66.2	67.4	70.3	71.8	70.8	68.0	69.1
World Total	7,227.5	8,035.0	7,596.1	7,583.7	7,580.0	8,124.2	46,146.5

Source: Computed from Dirección General de Estadísticas, Anuario estadístico de Cuba, 1989, pp. 253–61.

tal Cuban trade with the Western Hemisphere was about $2.9 billion. But Western Hemispheric trade did not make up for the loss of the socialist market. By 1990 Cuban trade with the area had reached historic highs, with almost 7 percent of all imports and almost 5 percent of all exports. This suggested that improvements in Cuba's commercial relations with Latin America cannot possibly outrun the need to find sufficient foreign exchange with which to trade, program exportable volumes of new products, find new lines of credit, and resolve other vicissitudes related to foreign indebtedness. Despite their larger size, trade with the South American countries has been modest and new lines of credit hard to come by.

To be sure, the figures presented in table 1 offer only an incomplete version of the picture of Cuban foreign trade with Latin America, particularly as more recent trade patterns may be camouflaged by aggregate figures. The data in table 2 are derived from reports by Cuba's trading partners.[39] Ranking Cuba's trade partners with the DOTS data, it is obvious that during 1985 to 1990 Venezuela was a much more important supplier than Canada, Mexico, or Brazil, the economic powerhouses in the area outside the United States. It is obvious that Cuba's strategy of import substitution had not served it well since cumulative Cuban export values to the rest of the hemisphere were a paltry $957 million.

All told, Cuba bought seven times more in value ($6.5 billion) from than it sold to the rest of the hemisphere and, as a result, ran a series of trade deficits.[40] Only Nicaragua had a trade deficit with Cuba during this period. Apparently, the most important export transaction came in 1990, when Brazil brought the Cuban anti-meningitis vaccine. With the exception of Canada, none of the larger economies of the area can be singled out as playing the role of a major trading partner with Cuba. How long can this pattern hold unless Cuba has trade surpluses with other countries and geographic areas? Trade and economic relations with the hemisphere are relatively modest at present and prospects are relatively good for the future, but these will be slow in coming and will be influenced by the patterns of economic integration that are now beginning to unfold. The bottom line here is that trade with Latin America has not reached a significant magnitude and therefore cannot be conceived of as a substitute for trade with other areas in the short run.

Multilateralism

Have Cuban efforts to uproot Pan-Americanism in all forms and to promote Latin Americanism been successful or has Pan-Americanism died of its own accord? Have the Cubans been able to orchestrate a joint front against the United States?

Judging from present trends, Cuban views and positions are far

Table 2

Cuban Trade with the Western Hemisphere, 1985 to 1990: Trading Partner
Version (millions of U.S. dollars)

	Exports (from Cuba to)						
	1985	*1986*	*1987*	*1988*	*1989*	*1990*	*Total*
Hemisphere	101.7	109.6	103.0	168.6	183.9	290.6	957.4
Canada	31.8	50.2	37.3	68.3	52.7	89.0	329.3
All other	69.9	59.4	65.7	100.3	131.2	201.6	628.1
Nicaragua	29.0	30.4	31.8	39.8	43.8	50.3	225.1
Venezuela	16.0	4.0	15.0	45.0	26.0	20.6	126.6
Brazil	—	3.2	3.3	—	26.0	90.5	123.0
Mexico	2.1	2.2	1.4	2.0	21.4	24.8	53.9
Rest	22.8	19.6	14.2	13.5	14.0	15.4	99.5
World Total	1,085.9	973.8	1,208.6	1,616.9	1,671.3	1,386.9	7,943.4
Hemisphere % of total	9.4	11.3	8.5	10.4	11.0	21.0	12.1

	Imports (to Cuba from)						
	1985	*1986*	*1987*	*1988*	*1989*	*1990*	*Total*
Hemisphere	1,301.5	987.9	553.7	1,073.2	1,268.4	1,346.0	6,510.7
Canada	270.8	287.8	225.5	199.2	143.0	149.7	1,276.0
All other	1,030.7	700.1	308.2	874.0	1,125.4	1,196.3	5,234.7
Venezuela	467.5	396.0	—	452.7	571.4	633.7	2,521.3
Argentina	311.8	200.0	147.0	215.3	205.7	179.8	1,259.6
Mexico	76.7	55.2	86.3	87.3	119.3	120.9	545.7
Neth. Ant.	159.5	37.6	53.3	46.2	50.8	58.4	405.8
Brazil	—	1.5	3.3	25.5	84.3	86.8	201.4
Colombia	5.1	2.4	1.0	10.2	29.3	32.4	80.4
Trin. Tob.	—	—	4.7	9.9	21.6	41.6	77.8
Peru	—	2.2	3.6	14.6	19.1	19.1	58.6
Rest	10.1	5.2	9.0	12.3	23.9	23.6	84.1
World Total	3,291.9	2,840.7	2,177.2	3,007.5	3,254.3	3,267.8	17,839.4
Hemisphere % of total	39.5	34.8	24.5	35.7	39.0	41.2	36.5

Source: Computed from International Monetary Fund, *Direction of Trade Statistics
Yearbook, 1991*, pp. 146–47.

from modal among the rest of the American republics. The rhetoric
and the emphasis could not be more different. A brief discussion of
the contrast between Cuban and other views on Central America,
economic integration, foreign indebtedness, and democracy and human rights will bear this out.

Central America

According to the resolution of the third congress of the Cuban Communist party (PCC) of 1985, Cuba's priorities in Central America were the survival of the Sandinista regime and the incorporation of El Salvador into the Contadora framework. Cuba's blueprint for a negotiated solution relied primarily on Contadora, since the Cubans doubted the sincerity and efficacy of Costa Rican president Oscar Arias, did not believe that bourgeois Central American regimes could defy the United States, and were distrustful of any proposal deemed contrary to their own interests or those of the FSLN and the FMLN.

Contrasting with Cubans doubting that Central Americans could initiate their own solutions was the evolving attitude of the Group of Eight (later known as the Group of Rio) toward that very possibility. For the better part of three years, countries behind the Contadora initiative promoted it as the best avenue for a diplomatic approach to resolving or at least containing the Central American crisis.[41] But, gradually, Guatemala's "active neutrality" under Vinicio Cerezo and Costa Rica's emergence as a credible and effective mediator established the Esquipulas framework as a viable homegrown alternative. The legitimacy of the effort was bolstered by the international acclaim (including the 1987 Nobel Peace Prize) given Arias as well as by the tacit opposition of the Reagan administration.[42] Eventually, the Contadora and support group countries came to regard their efforts as complementary and supportive, not preemptive of Esquipulas and other Central American initiatives. The Cuban position evolved from qualified praise for Esquipulas, to doubts about whether it might work, to the conclusion that it could not possibly work, to open criticism of Arias.[43]

Eventually, the beleaguered Arias took his gloves off. In May 1987 he suggested that Castro had acquired a personal stake in the overthrow of Salvadoran president José Napoleón Duarte. In February 1989, at the Pérez inauguration in Caracas, Arias asked both Castro and U.S. vice president Dan Quayle to give Esquipulas II a chance. He suggested that despite Cuba's public approval of the plan, continued Cuban logistical and military support to the FMLN was a serious obstacle to Esquipulas II.[44] Castro protested that the "premises on which [Mr. Arias] bases his arguments . . . are not exactly so. . . . I said he had overestimated my influence over the FMLN. He said that he agreed but that they would never do anything against a view that I had expressed."[45] The Cubans remained critical of Arias during the crucial months leading to the October 1989 presidential summit in San José.

Despite all the unctuous rhetoric about the importance of Cuba's participation in settling the crisis, there was irritation in the rest of the hemisphere at both the United States and Cuba for keeping Nicaragua at the top of the agenda and for their attempts at imposing their views on the situation—whether to provide for the collective defense of Nicaragua or keep Central America at the top of the agenda. That the Nicaraguan crisis was settled through elections, within the framework provided by Esquipulas, and with the deep involvement of the OAS was a victory for hemispheric peace, not for anti-imperialism or for Pan-Americanism. The Castro regime did not take the lead in any of this and certainly could not take the credit for itself.

Integration

The Cubans have made important inroads into multilateral institutions by being admitted into the Latin American Parliament and the Latin American Economic System (SELA) and being granted observer status before the Latin American Integration Association (ALADI). Their approach to integration has been to stall on rejoining the OAS, insisting on the need to strengthen SELA and convert it into a forum for joint political initiatives, and gain entry into the Group of Rio. Implicit here is a preference for a single common process of integration.[46] All along Cuban officials have insisted on integration without any discrimination based on ideological or political differences.

The Group of Rio has emphasized that Cuba rejoin the OAS, and the OAS has been emphasizing the need to establish the democratic credentials of its members. Without a change in the nature of its regime or a pragmatic decision to treat it as one of the democratic nations of the hemisphere, revolutionary Cuba is not likely to succeed at this, within or without the OAS or through the Group of Rio. As repeated a number of times by group presidents, full-fledged integration is not possible without democracy. In October 1988 foreign ministers of the group drafted a political declaration. The document, approved later at a presidential meeting at Punta del Este, Uruguay, sought to establish a political accord, define security in terms of democracy and development, and create a new integration mechanism. In June 1991 the third plenary session of a meeting of OAS foreign ministers held in Chile produced the Santiago Commitment to Democracy and to the Renewal of the Interamerican System. The commitment acknowledged that changes to a more open and democratic international system are not assured, that representative democracy is the form of government of the region, and that the OAS is the political forum for dialogue, understanding, and cooperation among all the countries of the hemisphere.[47] Separate resolutions called for recognizing that the OAS charter assumes that each member state is organized as a representative democracy, supporting the Initiative for the Americas, and strengthening OAS initiatives in the area of human rights.[48] Official Cuban media rejected the advice that Cuba change "in order to gain entry not only to the OAS but also to profitable markets," described the results of the meeting as "quite short of the expectations of some Latin American sectors," and alleged that the OAS had lost status in the hemispheric plans of the United States.[49]

Differences in substance and rhetoric between Cuba and the Latin American republics were plain at the Guadalajara summit of presidents. At the opening ceremony host Carlos Salinas de Gortari spoke of common tendencies acting independently of the ideological origins of the area governments: "economies are opening up, the state is being reformed, politics is democratized, justice is proposed explicitly, private investment is encouraged, we are integrated within and with the rest of the world, the productive sectors are being modernized."[50] Venezuelan Carlos Andrés Pérez saw a new beginning: "We seek convergence with the First World without resentment or sterile polemics. . . . Integration will no longer be the favorite rhetoric of Latin American discourse, we are building it. . . . The Group of Rio [is] the political expression of the inexorable will of Latin American integration."[51] Felipe González of Spain said, "In order to bring about any regional or subregional project of integration we have to reasonably homogenize institutions and behaviors. It is difficult for countries with antagonistic political or economic models to reach an understanding. . . . We want pluralism. But there are common bases, [and] that is why I have spoken of democratization."[52] By contrast, Castro painted a very pathetic picture of his version of integration: "We could be everything and we are nothing. There always is a siren song. . . . I am referring to . . . that latest fantasy, the Initiative for the Americas. . . . Never before has it been so important to proclaim . . . that the independence and sovereignty of each state are sacred. . . . Cuba is ready to belong to a united and integrated Latin America . . . even to shed its blood."[53] In the twenty-four-point Declaration of Guadalajara, the presidents pledged their support to regional and subregional processes of integration and proposed to continue moving along this path.[54]

If anything, Castro fared even worse at the second summit of Iberoamerican presidents that convened in Madrid in July 1992. He was hounded by the media and by a well-organized and strategically deployed contingent of activists of the Cuban Democratic Platform. His supporters in Spain could not summon any large crowds to express their solidarity with his regime. In private he was lectured by Manuel Fraga Iribaren, a frequent visitor to Cuba and president of the Galician autonomous region. In public he suffered the indignity of being seated at the end of the table at a state dinner, flanked on his left by Guillermo Endara. Reportedly, Spanish president González made no effort to notice him in any special way. He cut the visit short and went home to face a crisis involving Carlos Aldana, one of the senior figures of the regime.

The Foreign Debt

Beginning in 1985, the Castro regime convened a series of conferences to support the proposition that a cartel should be formed among debtors to promote the nonpayment of their debts—this at a time when it was negotiating its own debt with the Paris Club. But the Latin American governments' refusal to send any official delegations and the Cubans' failure to attract many luminaries prevented them from organizing a permanent forum on the debt that they could control.

Castro has not abandoned his views on the debt. If anything, the Cubans now believe that the rest of the hemisphere is coming around to their view and continue insisting that the only remedy is nonpayment. But the Latin Americans insisted on finding formulas to facilitate, not renege on, payment.[55] They remained skeptical of the benefits of a common approach to the problem based on a single strategy. Since October 1988 no meeting of the ministers and presidents of the Group of Rio has concluded with a declaration conforming to the Cuban view.

Human Rights

Repeated U.S. failure to obtain a condemnation of the Castro regime by the UNCHR in Geneva in the late eighties has been attributed to Latin American solidarity. The United States resented what it viewed as an attitude of appeasement and a lack of public courage. To be sure, there is truth to that assessment, but the strong-arm tactics and clumsiness of the Americans may have played a part in this. In addition, the Latins felt vulnerable before home leftist constituencies still clamoring for justice for the disappeared.

In 1987 the nations of the Group of Rio strenuously objected to voting for a general motion condemning Cuba. Vernon Walters, U.S. permanent representative to the UN, was himself sent to Geneva armed with a report that was included in a U.S. draft resolution on the human rights situation in Cuba. In response, the Cuban delegation introduced a resolution on alleged violations of the human rights of ethnic and racial minorities in the United States. To defuse the situation the delegation of India introduced a motion not to consider the U.S. resolution that passed in a vote of 19 to 18 with 6 abstentions along with a companion measure, which also carried, to table the Cuban motion. In 1988 the Reagan administration appointed Armando Valladares, a former Cuban political prisoner, ambassador representative to the U.S. delegation in Geneva and instructed Ambassador Walters to reintroduce the 1987 draft resolution as a motion to investigate. Initially the Castro regime launched a campaign to discredit Valladares. In February, as a number of European governments announced their intention to support the U.S. draft resolution, the Cubans dispatched emissaries to all member countries of the UNCHR. In early March, when Argentina announced that it could support the U.S. resolution, the Cubans sought a compromise. After a Cuban invitation to the presidents of the Group of Rio to visit Cuba and investigate was unanimously declined, frantic negotiations produced a compromise solution, and, despite U.S. opposition, the UNCHR accepted an official Cuban invitation to Chairman Alione Sene and five member countries—the Philippines, Bulgaria, Nigeria, Colombia, and Ireland—to visit. The Sene Commission visited Cuba in September and interviewed more than fifteen hundred Cuban citizens who made denunciations against the government— many were subsequently tried and incarcerated.[56] Their reports were compiled in a four-hundred-page volume issued by the commission, but no conclusion or recommendation came from this.

The Sene Commission report was discussed at the 1989 session of the UNCHR and, with Cuban concurrence, the commission approved a resolution (1989/113) presented by Panama instructing Secretary General Javier Pérez de Cuellar to maintain direct contact with the Cuban government, discuss with it cases brought to his attention, and give the results of such contacts appropriate treatment. The secretary general's report to the 1990 session of the UNCHR consisted of an exchange of letters between Pérez de Cuellar and Cuban authorities. However, he wrote to the new UNCHR president that he would be willing to report at greater length. The U.S. delegation introduced and obtained approval—19 to 12 with 12 abstentions—of a resolution (1990/48) requesting precisely that. Official Cuban reaction was vitriolic. Cuban foreign vice minister Raúl Roa Khouri called the document "totally unacceptable." On 5 March the government staged a "repudiation act" in front of the house of Sebastián de Arcos, where his brother Gustavo, a former Castro comrade and president of the Cuban Committee for Human Rights (CCPDH), was meeting with other prominent dissidents. On 7 March a defiant Castro stated: "Do not even dream that we are going to comply. That is it. Do not even dream that we are going to follow a single rule of that resolution. . . . I will now see who comes to request information. . . . They are mistaken if they think there is going to be impunity for those who betray the fatherland."[57] A wave of arrests of prominent dissidents followed in Cuba.

The 1991 session of the UNCHR received the secretary general's report of his confidential contacts with Cuba. Members of the Group of Rio presented a draft resolution for continuing these contacts. The U.S. delegation countered with a resolution calling for a special representative for Cuba to carry out the mandate of the Sene Commission in expanded form. In a procedural vote the Latins won precedent for their motion, but before the substantive vote on that motion Argentina withdrew as co-author and Brazil abstained. The United States then proposed an amendment to the Group of Rio resolution, introducing the proviso of the special representative. The Latin delegates repudiated the motion, and it carried by 22 to 6, with

Brazil, Colombia, Mexico, Peru, and Venezuela abstaining. However, Argentina broke ranks with a "yes" vote. More important, on 2 July Rafael Rivas Posada, a Colombian diplomat who represented Latin America in the Sene Commission, was named special representative. Cuban Ambassador to the UN Ricardo Alarcón promptly restated that his government would not allow Rivas Posada into Cuba. Unable to fulfill his mandate, Rivas Posada resigned quietly. Following a 1992 decision by the UNCHR to name a "special rapporteur" for Cuba, which was greeted with invective by the Cuban regime, the new UN secretary general Boutros-Ghali appointed Carl-Johan Groth, a former Swedish ambassador to Havana, to the position.

Whatever heavy-handedness may have been at work in Geneva, it will be increasingly difficult for the Latin American republics to continue granting the Castro regime an exception on the matter of scrutinizing respect for human rights in Cuba, particularly when European governments have decided to assume greater initiative in this matter. There is little to gain and much to lose if this issue heats up, but Cuba would probably lose most. The attitude of the Latin Americans has changed from opposition to abstention. The Cuban regime in effect lost these votes, and it may lose them again if it fails to submit to practices legitimized by their widespread acceptance.

Prospects

What is really the attitude of the Latin Americans? Do they play Cuba up as a diversion, to confound and harass the United States? The evidence reviewed here does not support this contention. To a certain extent, at the level of the Group of Rio, an attitude seems to prevail that Castro's Cuba and the United States really deserve each other. It is hard to avoid the conclusion that what passes for solidarity with Cuba in many superficial analyses is really nothing but a defensive reaction on the part of the Latins.

How will the Cubans react to the slow progress and limited gains in their bilateral relations? How are they likely to react to what they regard as obstructionism in terms of the role and space offered them in multilateral relations? Given the rapidly changing international context of the early nineties it is difficult to prophesize about the Castro regime, but, assuming its short-term continuity, revolutionary Cuba's foreign policy is not likely to roll over and play dead. Despite the dire economic conditions affecting Cuba at this time, the Cuban regime can continue practicing an international activism that does not consume an enormous amount of resources. In addition, the economic crisis has made the Cubans hyperactive; they are spending less time trying to organize conferences on the debt and more on trying to cut deals with foreign investors.

If precedent is any guide, the Cuban response to frustration in their bilateral and multilateral relations in the hemisphere will likely be disjointed. The Cubans will vent their displeasure at what they consider the offending countries while trying to maintain the high road in the multilateral framework, where they will continue to engage in lofty rhetoric. For now the Cubans appear content to continue promoting their own agenda of "unity" and criticizing the shortcomings of what is emerging as a consensus of the majority. To compensate for their exclusion from the Group of Rio they will continue insisting on the need for creating a permanent committee of the whole for consultation and concerted action. The Latin American republics, on their part, are likely to continue insisting on coordination but without abandoning the positions that each understands to be serving its national interest best, such as subregional schemes of integration, bilateral trade agreements, and national solutions to the question of economic stabilization. The leading voices among them seem to have found in integration through democracy not only a pragmatic solution to absorb the reincorporation of Cuba but, more important, a method for resolving the crisis of a system that begins to be theirs for the first time.

Finally, there will always be the United States. As usual some hackneyed initiative responding primarily to domestic electoral considerations can muddy the waters. The most recent example was in November 1992, following approval of the so-called Cuban Democracy Act, a bill instigated by the CANF in close collaboration with congressional Democrats, tightening the economic embargo.[58] On the very day that special rapporteur Groth released an official UN report critical of human rights violations in Cuba, the General Assembly voted 59 to 3, with 71 abstentions, in favor of a resolution asking for an end to the embargo. As has been the case before, the real victims were overlooked.

It will be difficult for history not to repeat itself unless the United States comes to realize that the cause of democracy in Cuba, the kernel of the issue of Cuba's full-fledged integration into the hemisphere, will receive a considerable boost when American politicians renounce their attempt at playing a protagonist role in democratizing Cuba from the outside. As long as the contradiction between nationalism and imperialism occupies center stage, the domestic struggle between democracy and dictatorship will be overshadowed. Whether this comes to pass, the prudence of Latin American diplomacy will continue to exasperate Cuba and the United States.

Notes

The author is grateful to Jorge Pérez-López for his valuable assistance in deciphering some contradictory figures and to William Smith for his careful reading of an earlier version of this manuscript.

1. Howard Wiarda, "Cuba and U.S. Foreign Policy in Latin America: The Changing Realities," in Jorge I. Domínguez and Rafael Hernández, eds., *U.S.-Cuban Relations in the 1990s* (Boulder, Colo.: Westview, 1989), pp. 170–73.

2. Juan Valdés-Paz, "Cuba's Foreign Policy toward Latin America and the Caribbean in the 1980s," in Domínguez and Hernández, eds., *U.S.-Cuban Relations*, pp. 200–201.

3. A view articulated by the author in "The Many Rooms of My Father's Mansion: Cuban Foreign Policy toward Latin America in the Early Nineties." Paper prepared for the Inter-American Dialogue, October 1988, pp. 7–12.

4. Cubana de Televisión rebroadcast of Castro interview with Nelson Bucaranda, *Foreign Broadcast Information Service, Latin America* (hereafter *FBIS-LAT* (89–032), 17 February 1989, pp. 1–15.

5. For more details, see Heraldo Muñoz and Boris Yopo, "Cuba y las democracias latinoamericanas en los ochenta," *Documento de Trabajo PROSPEL*, no. 9 (Santiago de Chile: CERC/Academia de Humanismo Cristiano, 1987).

6. Ibid. pp. 8–9.

7. Former Argentinean president Raúl Alfonsín may have articulated this best in October 1986, when he asked Mr. Castro that "Cuba not transmit to the region, especially Central America, its conflicts or bilateral problems with the United States." *Somos* (Buenos Aires), 22 October 1986, pp. 9–12.

8. Enrique A. Baloyra, "The Madness of the Method: The United States and Cuba in the Seventies," in John D. Martz and Lars Schoultz, eds., *Latin America, the United States, and the Inter-American System* (Boulder, Colo.: Westview, 1980), pp. 115–44; Rafael Hernández, "Cuba and the United States: Political Values and Interests in a Changing International System," in Domínguez and Hernández, eds., *U.S.-Cuban Relations*, pp. 37–41; and Juan Valdés-Paz, "Notas sobre la formulación de la política exterior cubana," in

Roberto Russell, ed., *Política exterior y toma de decisiones en América Latina* (Buenos Aires: Grupo Editor Latinoamericano, 1990), pp. 113–17.

9. Enrique Baloyra-Herp, "Internationalism and the Limits of Autonomy: Cuba's Foreign Relations," in Heraldo Muñoz and Joseph S. Tulchin, eds., *Latin American Nations in World Politics* (Boulder, Colo.: Westview, 1984), pp. 168–85; Jorge I. Domínguez, *To Make a World Safe for Revolution: Cuba's Foreign Policy* (Cambridge: Harvard University Press, 1989), chaps. 5, 6; Hernández, "Cuba and the United States," p. 38; and Valdés-Paz, "Cuba's Foreign Policy," p. 117.

10. Valdés-Paz, "Cuba's Foreign Policy," pp. 180–81. Also Valdés-Paz, "Notas," pp. 116–17.

11. Valdés-Paz, "Notas," pp. 124–27.

12. For a more detailed discussion of this interpretation, see Domínguez, "To Make a World Safe," pp. 5–7, 248–53.

13. Baloyra, "Internationalism," pp. 182–83; Domínguez, "To Make a World Safe," pp. 1–7; Hernández, "Cuba and the United States," pp. 37–41.

14. For reasons of space I shall only comment on relations with Nicaragua. For more on Cuba's relations with other Caribbean nations, see Barry Levine, *The New Cuban Presence in the Caribbean* (Boulder, Colo.: Westview, 1983). Also see Carlos Moore, *El Caribe y la política exterior de la revolución cubana, 1959–1973* (San Germán, Puerto Rico: Centro de Investigaciones del Caribe y América Latina, 1986).

15. Moore, *El Caribe*, p. 6.

16. *FBIS-LAT* (90-79), 24 April 1990, p. 2.

17. Including M-19 (Colombia), Macheteros (Puerto Rico), Alfaro Vive Carajo (Ecuador), and the Tupac Amaru Revolutionary Movement (MRTA) of Peru. At this time, relatively cordial relations are maintained with the traditional Communist parties of the hemisphere, and it does appear that there is much similarity between their foreign policy priorities and those of the PCC. For illustration, see the text of the final 7 August 1988 communiqué of the Third Meeting of Communist Parties of South America in Montevideo in *FBIS-LAT* (88–160), 18 August 1988, pp. 1–2.

18. Bilateral trade is regulated by a 1977 partial agreement, but total annual trade has hovered around $150 million. To offer Cuba some of the benefits of the ALADI framework, tariffs were lowered in 1988. In 1991 Cuba and Mexico signed agreements on nuclear cooperation, tourism, and satellite communications in addition to the usual protocols on fisheries, trade, scientific-technological collaboration, and cultural and educational exchanges.

19. According to a 29 October dispatch by NOTIMEX in *FBIS-LAT* (90-215), 6 November 1990, p. 6.

20. In June 1991 the Cuban Embassy had to disavow José Luis Rodas, described by Mexican media as an official of the PCC. Allegedly, Rodas had said that Cuauhtémoc Cárdenas would be the next president of Mexico provided

the PRI did not repeat what it did in the 1988 election. NOTIMEX dispatch of 17 June, from *FBIS-LAT* (91-117), 18 June 1991, p. 3.

21. Homero Campa, "Salinas recibió a dos líderes anticastristas y Fidel desairó a la embajada mexicana en Cuba," *Proceso*, 28 September 1992, p. 26.

22. Two-part interview with Nancy López in Radio Havana Cuba broadcast on 18 and 19 June. See *FBIS-LAT* (91-119), 20 June 1991, pp. 2–3.

23. Directorate of Intelligence, Central Intelligence Agency, *Cuba: Handbook of Trade Statistics (U)*, ALA 93-10010 (July 1993): table 5, pp. 10–11.

24. Havana's Radio Progreso broadcast of 12 October 1991, citing a dispatch of the Italian news agency, ANSA. In *FBIS-LAT* (91-201), 17 October 1991, p. 8.

25. The G-3 consists of Mexico, Colombia, and Venezuela. The meeting took place on 23 October 1991. Castro was accompanied by Vice President Carlos Rafael Rodríguez and Deputy Foreign Minister Ricardo Alarcón. See *El Nuevo Herald*, 23 October 1991, pp. 1A, 4A; 24 October 1991, pp. 1A, 4A; and 25 October 1991, pp. 1A, 4A.

26. Radio Rebelde editorial of 30 December 1990, from *FBIS-LAT* (90-01), 2 January 1990, p. 6.

27. Shortly after the expulsion order, Cuban sources did not see a break with Panama, since in thirty years Cuba had only broken relations with the Dominican Republic, Chile, and Israel. NOTIMEX dispatch of 23 March 1990, from *FBIS-LAT* (90-58), 26 March 1990, p. 5.

28. For example, 4 June 1990 Ricardo Alemán, president of the Chamber of Commerce, Industry, and Agriculture of Panama, said his organization should not thwart continued contact between Panamanian and Cuban business firms. George Richard, former president of the association of Panamanian industrialists, said his country had a right to trade with anyone. *FBIS-LAT* (90-111), 5 June 1990, p. 5. At that time, it was estimated that Cuba was buying about $100 million from Panamanian companies every year.

29. Castro met practically all the other heads of state of the hemisphere at the inaugurations of Rodrigo Borja in August 1988 in Quito, Carlos Salinas de Gortari in December 1988 in Mexico City, Carlos Andrés Perez in February 1989 in Caracas, and Fernando Collor de Mello in March 1990 in Brasília. He was invited but unable to attend the July 1989 inauguration of Carlos Saúl Menem in Buenos Aires due to the domestic turmoil stemming from the trial of Division Gen. Arnaldo Ochoa and several codefendants (Cuba was represented by foreign minister Isidoro Malmierca). He missed the inauguration of Alberto Fujimori in August 1990 but sent a high-level delegation led by National Assembly of Popular Power (ANPP) president Juan Escalona. Castro was not invited to the inaugurations of Bolivian Jaime Paz Zamora (August 1989), Chilean Patricio Aylwin (December 1989), Colombian César Gaviria (August 1990), and Uruguayan Luis Alberto Lacalle (March 1990). Cuban vice president José Ramón Fernández was the highest-ranking Cuban official in

attendance at most of these other inaugurations or the first one to call shortly thereafter.

30. For a sample of his speeches and public appearances, see 11 August 1988 press conference in Quito, in *FBIS-LAT* (88-159), 17 August 1988, pp. 1–12; 4 February 1989 press conference in Caracas, in *FBIS-LAT* (89-027), 10 February 1989, pp. 2–16; and 14, 15, and 16 March 1990 interviews with Brazilian television in *FBIS-LAT* (90-063), 2 April 1990, pp. 7–14.

31. *FBIS-LAT* (90-053), 19 March 1990, p. 5.

32. *FBIS-LAT* (90-061), 29 March 1990, p. 11.

33. Such as the Cuban Institute for Friendship with the Peoples (ICAP) chief, the late René Rodríguez.

34. Communications agreements were subscribed in January 1987, followed by four somewhat less significant agreements in March of that year, covering scientific cooperation, facilitating Cuban exports to Brazil, creating an ad hoc ministerial commission of cooperation, and establishing periodic meetings between the foreign ministries but short of the frequent consultations characteristic of close partners. A transportation agreement was announced in April. At the end of that year Brazilian exports to Cuba were slightly under $2 million and a credit line of $100 million was reportedly under discussion. In January 1988 Cuban foreign minister Malmierca could not get the Brazilians to agree to draft agreements on science, ecology, and urban transportation that had been initially negotiated by Cuban vice president Carlos Rafael Rodríguez. In February the two countries signed a protocol on biotechnology, basic sciences, and meteorology. In October 1989 Brazilian foreign minister Paulo Tarso Flecha de Lima and Cuban foreign trade minister Ricardo Cabrisas subscribed a general agreement on trade and a partial scope agreement on tariff reduction, reducing duties by more than 60 percent on two hundred items. Two agreements were signed in January 1990; one covering medical and pharmaceutical matters, and another, a more comprehensive one, dealing with cooperation in matters of social policy.

35. Other bilateral agreements with Argentina cover maritime transport (March 1986) and nuclear cooperation (November 1986).

36. For example, following the G-3 Cozumel meeting of October 1991, Gaviria took Castro at his word that he would allow greater competition in direct elections to Cuba's national legislature and would be willing to leave power if he lost them. See Mimi Whitefield, "Is Castro Ready for Fair Vote?" *Miami Herald*, 25 October 1991, pp. 1A, 6A.

37. Bogotá, "Twenty-Four Hours," FINRAVISION TV-1, 29 October 1993, in *FBIS-LAT* (93-208), 29 October 1993, pp. 32–33.

38. "Evening Information Review," Radio Havana Cuba, 29 October 1993, in *FBIS-LAT* (93-208), 29 October 1993, p. 4.

39. Traditionally, discrepancies between country-generated and these data are due to differences in exchange rates (different rates may apply to dif-

ferent transactions), timing criteria utilized (entering data by contract versus delivery dates), and the fact that the Direction of Trade Statistics utilizes constant rates to derive CIF from FOB values. Two additional sources of distortion are at work here: one, that DOTS data for Cuba exclude trade with CAME and the Soviet Union in table 2, resulting in very inflated proportions for Latin America, and two, that Cuba may consistently underreport this trade. Cuban officials continually remind us that due to the provisions of the U.S. embargo many of their economic agreements with private parties and governments must remain confidential. For example, as discussed above, Cuban companies conduct a large volume of business through Panama. Yet Panama does not appear among the countries importing from or exporting to Cuba at least $50 million during 1985 to 1990.

40. Much of the import value is relatively inelastic, particularly since it concerns hydrocarbons, cereals, and spare parts for railroad and automotive equipment, which Cuba cannot or does not now produce. But grain and bean imports (from Mexico and Canada) are a direct result of excess land dedicated to sugar cultivation in Cuba, and this could be alleviated in the future.

41. See Susan Kaufman Purcell, "Demystifying Contadora," and Bruce M. Bagley, "The Failure of Diplomacy," both in Bruce M. Bagley, ed., *Contadora and the Diplomacy of Peace in Central America*, vol. 1 (Boulder, Colo.: Westview, 1987), pp. 159–77, 181–211; Luis Herrera-Lasso M., "México frente a Centroamérica," Rodrigo Pardo, "Entre la alienación y el pragmatismo," and Rita Giacalone, "La política centroamericana de Venezuela," all in Cristina Eguizábal, ed., *América Latina y la crisis centroamericana* (Buenos Aires: Grupo Editor Latinoamericano, 1988), pp. 145–68, 169–89, 191–209; and Fernando Cepeda Ulloa and Rodrigo Pardo, *Contadora: desafío a la diplomacia tradicional* (Bogotá: CEI and Editorial Oveja Negra, 1985).

42. Cynthia Arnson, *Crossroads: Congress, the Reagan Administration and Central America* (New York: Pantheon, 1989), pp. 203–6.

43. Concerning criticism of Arias, see "Our America," editorials of 13 April and 7 May 1988, in *FBIS-LAT* (88-072), 14 April 1988, p. 1, and (88-090), 10 May 1988, p. 4, respectively; "Our America," editorial of 26 July 1989, in *FBIS-LAT* (89-144), 28 July 1988, p. 1; Maggie Marín's article in *Bohemia*, 20 January 1989; and the Radio Rebelde editorial of 26 October 1989 calling Arias a "lackey" for excluding Cuba from the presidential summit of San José, in *FBIS-LAT* (89-207), 26 October 1989, p. 7.

44. *FBIS-LAT* (89-023), 6 February 1989, p. 1.

45. In this press conference, Castro also admitted that there was "something almost like a competition" going on between Cuba and Costa Rica. See *FBIS-LAT* (89-027), 10 February 1989, p. 5.

46. Articulated more explicitly by Cuban vice president Carlos Rafael Rodríguez on 28 June 1991, the eve of the Guadalajara Summit, when he told Mexican media that Cuba is interested in integration being united into a sin-

gle common process. NOTIMEX dispatch of 28 June in *FBIS-LAT* (91-125), 28 June 1991, pp. 1–2.

47. See OAS Vigésimo Primer Período de Sesiones, "Compromiso de Santiago con la democracia y con la renovación del sistema interamericano," OEA/ser. P, AG/doc. 2734/91, 4 June 1991.

48. See OAS, Vigésimo Primer Periodo de Sesiones, "Democracia representativa," OAS/ser. P, AG/doc. 2739/rev. 1, 5 June 1991; "Apoyo a la Iniciativa de las Américas," OEA/ser. P, AG/doc. 2762/91, rev. 1, 8 June 1991; and "Fortalecimiento de la OEA en materia de derechos humanos," OEA/ser. P, AG/doc. 2789/91, rev. 1, 8 June 1991.

49. See Radio Havana Cuba broadcast of 9 June in *FBIS-LAT* (91-115), 14 June 1991, p. 4; and "Our America," editorial of 11 June in *FBIS-LAT* (91-116), 17 June 1991, pp. 3–4.

50. "Palabras pronunciadas por el Presidente Carlos Salinas de Gortari, durante la ceremonia en la que inauguró la Primera Cumbre Iberoamericana," mimeo., Guadalajara, Jalisco, 18 July 1991, p. 1, my translation.

51. "Versión estenográfica de las palabras del Excmo. Señor Carlos Andrés Pérez," mimeo., Guadalajara, Jalisco, 18 July 1991, p. 2, my translation.

52. "Versión estenográfica de la conferencia de prensa . . . Excmo. Señor Felipe González Márquez," mimeo., Guadalajara, Jalisco, 19 July 1991, pp. 3–4. Also see Pablo Alfonso, "Felipe González fustiga a países 'antagónicos,'" *El Nuevo Herald*, 20 July 1991, p. 8A, my translation.

53. "Versión estenográfica de las palabras del Comandante Fidel Castro Ruz," mimeo., Guadalajara, Jalisco, 18 July 1991, pp. 2–4. Also Pablo Alfonso, "Discurso de Cuba fue 'jarro de agua fría' para mandatarios," *El Nuevo Herald*, 19 July 1991, pp. 1A, 4A, my translation.

54. Estados Unidos Mexicanos, Presidencia de la República, Dirección General de Comunicación Social, "Declaración de Guadalajara," mimeo., Guadalajara, Jalisco, 19 July 1991, my translation.

55. As stated by President Alfonsín in his address opening the 23–27 August 1988 meeting of the Latin American Parliament in Buenos Aires.

56. For the substance of some of those denunciations, see Ricardo Bofill, ed., *Cuba 1988: la situación de los derechos humanos*, mimeo., Comité Cubano Pro Derechos Humanos, n.d., pp. 122–52.

57. *FBIS-LAT* (90-046), 8 March 1990, pp. 3–4, 13.

58. Many Western European and Latin American countries, including Mexico, Canada, Great Britain, and Argentina, had already gone on record protesting sections 4 and 6 of the act. Respectively, these established sanctions against countries "providing assistance" to Cuba and mandating subsidiaries of U.S. firms engaging in trade with Cuba to disregard host-country legislation and abide by the provisions of the bill.

Part Three

**Toward the Twenty-first Century
Challenges and Opportunities**

Riordan Roett

The Debt Crisis and
Economic Development

When the debt crisis erupted in the summer of 1982, the "lost decade" began in Latin America and the Caribbean. The crisis management approach of the 1982 to 1988 period worked—barely. While
Brazil did declare a formal moratorium in 1987, after the spectacular
failure of its heterodox Cruzado Plan, other countries were pressured and encouraged to avoid taking the same step. Coordination
between the private commercial banks, the U.S. Treasury, and the
international financial institutions accomplished that task.

The crisis management approach was, however, just that—a
stopgap measure, because the crisis did not abate. In 1988 two new
administrations took office: Carlos Salinas de Gortari in Mexico and
George Bush in the United States. Salinas, an active participant in
the economic recovery program instituted in 1982 by his predecessor, decided that a major renegotiation of the Mexican debt was urgent if further reform efforts were to be meaningful. The Bush administration, sensitive to the politics of U.S. relations with Mexico
and convinced that a new policy was required, devised the Brady
Plan, named for the new secretary of the treasury. As David Mulford,
Brady's undersecretary for international affairs, has described it:

the turning point came in the spring of 1989 when the U.S. government . . .
designed a plan to crack the problem. This strategy replaced the previous
"new-money approach" by setting out a comprehensive plan based on the realities of the market. Policy reform by the debtor countries was still emphasized as the key for their recovery, but this time policy reform was supported
by a comprehensive plan for restructuring and reducing debt with the support of official sources.[1]

By mid-1992, twelve of the sixteen major debtor nations had
achieved debt reduction by refinancing agreements with their com-

mercial banks, accounting for 92 percent, or some $240 billion, of their outstanding commercial bank debt. Once completed, these agreements were expected to produce more than $50 billion in effective debt reduction, while lifting much more of the remaining burden from the debtors' backs through market-based collateralization.[2]

In response to the debt reduction schemes of the Brady Plan approach, the fiscal adjustment and structural changes in the major Latin American economies have made Latin America, once again, an attractive investment alternative. One sign was the activity in the stock markets:

of the world's six top-performing stock markets last year, five were in Latin America. . . . they were in Argentina, Colombia, Brazil, Mexico and Chile. . . . Investors who for a decade were intimidated by Latin America's mountain of debt now are pouring more than $40 billion per year into the region, turning once sleepy stock markets there into money machines—and attracting back billions in flight capital.[3]

The Inter-American Development Bank (IADB) was able to comment in its annual report (1992) that "in 1991 the long-awaited economic revival of Latin America began."[4] Net capital inflows more than doubled in 1991 to $36 billion, and the inflows continued in 1992 and increased in 1993.

The lost decade has ended from an economic and financial viewpoint. What is now needed is a decade of investment in social measures to compensate for the severe drop in living standards, wages, and social services in the last ten years. Governments are beginning to understand the urgency, in this decade, of not repeating the mistakes of the past. Many are seeking to use the Brady Plan reforms to initiate sensible macroeconomic management and to address long-ignored social issues.

We will only know at the end of this decade if this approach was both economically feasible and politically possible. Government planners often find it more challenging to deal with broader economic adjustment processes than with the more micromanagement required to achieve successful social investment goals. But it is clear to most observers that the impressive economic turnaround will be consolidated only if the social sector receives as much attention. Failure to do so will inevitably result in political unrest with unforeseen consequences for the region.

This chapter summarizes the evolution of the debt crisis in the 1980s and evaluates the state of play in the 1990s, including the status of the Brady Plan, the momentum of economic liberalization in the region, and the implications for the future of the striking turnaround in the region's fortunes.

The Debt Crisis in Perspective

As Pedro-Pablo Kuczynski has cogently summarized,

> there is . . . no great mystery about the origins of the debt crisis in Latin America: first, and most important, an extremely high level of external debt, most of it at floating interest rates; second, the impact of a very large rise in international interest rates, mostly denominated in dollars at a time of a rising U.S. dollar, upon the service of this debt; third, an eventual, but not immediate, decline in export earnings due to a deep international recession; and, finally, as in most debt crises, a loss of confidence on the part of the lenders, who initially started to lend at shorter terms and eventually stopped altogether, precipitating the suspension of debt service.[5]

During the 1950s and 1960s, the economies of Latin America and the Caribbean expanded. Growth was uneven, but the quality of life for millions of citizens improved. Income distribution remained badly skewed against the poor, but an expanding middle class offered new opportunities for mobility and inclusion in the modern sectors of the economy in many countries. The pattern slowed in the 1970s due to the heavy burden of oil import bills after the first petroleum crisis in 1973. It was also caused by slower growth in the industrial countries during the decade that reduced the demand for commodities exported by the developing nations.

Confronted with a decision to continue growing or introduce substantial cutbacks in spending, the region's governments opted for continued growth. To do so meant to borrow; hence, the massive public sector deficits that burden the region today. While the private sector borrowed, it was overshadowed by governments and the state agencies that garnered the bulk of the new lending flows. Flush with petrodollars, the world's commercial bankers were willing and anxious to find new customers. Latin America and the Caribbean were a godsend for them. The assumption of the borrowers was that world economic conditions, while not good, would not further deteriorate, allowing them to service the new debt. Careless about details, the region's financial and political leaders did not understand the implications of borrowing from commercial banks at floating interest rates and relatively short maturities.[6] As Barbara Stallings has commented,

in the 1970s there was a peculiar combination of cooperation and competition among the banks. Cooperation arose because the large loans were syndicated. A lead manager brought together a group of banks, which could number in the hundreds, and each took a piece of the loan and shared the risk.

Competition entered as the largest banks vied for the "mandate" to organize syndicates and obtain the front-end fees that were more lucrative than interest payments. Thus the lone investment banker traveling to a Latin American city in the 1920s in hopes of selling a $50 million loan was replaced by "pin-striped salesmen" [who] crowded each other in Intercontinental hotel lobbies and the reception rooms of finance ministers in order to offer $500 million. Also unlike the 1920s, U.S. banks were joined in the competitive fray by European and Japanese institutions as the 1970s moved on.[7]

The shift to private commercial bank loans paralleled a drop in loans from industrial countries and from the international financial institutions. These loans generally had fixed interest rates and relatively long maturities. The 1970s also saw a drop in direct foreign investment in Latin America. The savings level dipped in the region, public deficits grew, and erratic exchange rate and interest rate policies affected growth levels.

In the 1990s, a decade that will see almost all of Latin America and the Caribbean governed by civilian, democratic regimes, it is crucial to remember that there were few such governments in the 1970s. On the continent, only Colombia and Venezuela were democratic in the 1970s. Military authoritarian regimes were still in their heyday. They eagerly turned to the international commercial banks to maintain the only credibility they possessed—the capacity to generate high levels of growth. The policy decision to borrow was made by a small group; without functioning parliaments, interest groups, and the free press to challenge their authority, it was easy to justify the new credits as necessary for growth and development. The situation was even worse if one considers whether or not the borrowed funds were invested or saved. The evidence strongly suggests that they were not saved but were spent on pharaonic megaprojects with limited utility for social development, were dispensed as pay-offs, evaporated amid old-fashioned corruption, or left the country as flight capital, never to be seen again.[8]

The ship began to founder in the late 1970s. International oil prices tripled in 1979. The inauguration of Ronald Reagan in 1981 and the policies of his administration heightened the international economic crisis of 1980 to 1982 that produced unprecedented interest rate levels.[9] Interest payments exploded for the Latin American countries. In the short run, they borrowed more to service the debt, but export earnings were dropping precipitously as demand dropped sharply in the developed world. The banks reacted poorly to the Malvinas/Falklands War in mid-1982; confidence was weakening that Latin America was sufficiently stable to continue to service its debt; and a state of war, unthinkable just months before, raised new fears of disruption in the region.

The Crisis Erupts

In response to the turbulence in the world economy, high interest rates, and diminished export earnings for the Third World, the commercial banks stopped lending in mid-1982. In August of that year, Mexico informed U.S. officials that it was almost out of foreign exchange reserves and could no longer service its debt. During the "Mexican weekend" of 13–15 August, the patchwork response that continues today was cobbled together by the U.S. government and international financial institutions.[10]

Some observers believed that Mexico was an isolated case and that a package of international loans would be sufficient to tide it over. This belief was strengthened by the political nature of the debt announcement in Mexico; the Mexican leadership heralded the nationalization of the banking system and the reimposition of exchange controls by President José López Portillo on 1 September. The international community was quickly disabused of this false impression in Toronto in September 1982. At the joint annual meeting of the IMF and the World Bank, it was suddenly clear that Brazil was the emperor without clothes. Within eight weeks of the Toronto meeting, where Brazil failed to negotiate significant new loans, it too sought a moratorium on the repayment of principal to its commercial bank creditors. Within weeks, the rest of Latin America, with the exception of Colombia, moved to reschedule its outstanding debt.

From the position of the industrial country governments, it was critical to avoid a breakdown of the international financial system. Key to any policy response was a continuation of interest payments by the debtors; otherwise the private commercial banking system would be in serious danger of collapse. Of particular concern to the U.S. Federal Reserve System and to the White House was the poor health of many of the major banking institutions in the United States. U.S. banks were saddled with bad loans in the housing, agricultural, and energy sectors. To be hit with a moratorium by Third World debtors would prove disastrous.[11] Everything had to be done to maintain interest payments.

Paul Volcker, the head of the U.S. Central Bank, led the charge for the industrial countries. He organized a series of restructuring committees of international commercial banks whose task was to "advise" each of the debtors. The actual purpose of the committees was to coordinate the politics of the renegotiations among the commercial banks and to police the Latin American and Caribbean debtors to be sure they were tempted neither by a declaration of unilateral default nor the urge to organize a debtors cartel.[12]

Stabilization and Adjustment

An immediate consequence of the 1982 to 1983 debt crisis was the necessity for programs of economic stabilization and adjustment. The IMF played a critical role in this process. As Werner Baer and Howard Handelman have written,

all stabilization and adjustment programs require considerable economic sacrifice from much of the population. Such programs usually try to contain the forces that have produced inflation and to correct distortions that have grown out of the inflationary process. Orthodox programs, favored by the International Monetary Fund (IMF) and by monetarist policymakers, involve some combination of currency devaluation, reduction of import controls, credit restrictions, reduction of government subsidies on basic consumer goods (including fuel and basic foods), higher prices for public utilities, freeing of prices, wage repression, reduction of public employment, and reduction of the fiscal deficit. These policies usually produce a slowdown of economic growth, or even a period of decline. Thus, stabilization confronts policymakers with the problem of how to allocate economic sacrifices. Should they be evenly shared by all socioeconomic groups, or should they be borne more heavily by specific sectors?[13]

The answer, of course, is clear. The heaviest burden has been carried by the poorest segments of Latin America.

Government after government undertook IMF-monitored programs of adjustment and stabilization. The quickest way to achieve IMF goals, necessary for multilateral and private commercial bank credits, was to cut the social services budget. This was feasible in some countries because military governments could do so without fear of rebuke. Fledgling democracies did it with trepidation or postponed the inevitable for a year or two until forced to take the steps required to maintain their creditworthiness.[14] From the perspective of the industrial world, the issue was whether or not the Latin American governments would "bite the bullet" and do as they were told— or react collectively.

Latin America Reacts

The latter concern was a real one, from the position of the commercial banks and the industrial countries. As the frightening dimensions of the combined international economic crisis and the adjustment measures that were being demanded by the combined creditors became apparent to Latin American leaders, they reacted. President Osvaldo Hurtado of Ecuador wrote to the executive secretaries of the Economic Commission for Latin America and the Caribbean (ECLAC) and the Latin American Economic System (SELA) on 11 February 1983. The Ecuadoran chief executive requested the two entities to "prepare as soon as possible a set of proposals designed to develop the response capacity of Latin America and to consolidate its systems of cooperation."[15]

The two organizations drafted a document entitled "The Bases for a Latin American Response to the International Economic Crisis" in May 1983. The document was discussed at a meeting in Quito that month and again in August when a decision was taken to convene a heads-of-government conference in January 1984 in Quito. In the interim, the Inter-American Economic and Social Council (CIES) of the OAS organized a Specialized Conference on External Financing in Latin America and the Caribbean in Caracas in September 1983. The ECLAC/SELA basic document served as a "reference" document for the Caracas conference. Regrettably, the moribund meeting in Venezuela would prove to be the only spark of interest on the part of the OAS to join the debate about the resolution of the debt crisis.

In January 1984 at the heads-of-government meeting, a "Declaration of Quito" and a "Plan of Action" were approved. The declaration called for an immediate response from the creditor countries to ameliorate the dramatic fall in living standards and the economic and financial crisis that afflicted the region. It was widely noted that a democratic trend had begun in the region. Newly elected civilian regimes were desperate to find a solution both to the impossible situation they had inherited from their predecessors and the further worsening of the economic situation in the mid-1980s.[16]

In May 1984 the presidents of Brazil, Colombia, Mexico, and Argentina issued a joint letter that dramatically called for help from the industrial countries. It was ignored. In June 1984 seven Latin American heads of state addressed an urgent letter to the Group of Seven, about to convene for their annual economic summit in London. The letter called for a "constructive dialogue among creditor and borrowing countries." The Latin Americans stated that it was impossible to imagine that their financial problems could be resolved only by "contacting banks or through the isolated participation of international financial organizations." Deflecting the Latin Americans' entreaty, the final communiqué of the London summit brusquely rejected the call for negotiations and offered "help" only if the Latin governments reduced their spending and worked to put their houses in order.

The growing frustration of the Latin American political leaders led to the organization of the Cartagena consensus group in June 1984. Speaking at the opening of the meeting, then president Belisario Betancur of Colombia stated: "Latin America's foreign debt service has become so burdensome that it threatens the very stability of the international monetary system and the survival of the democratic process in various countries."[17] The Cartagena conference strongly endorsed the Quito declaration and called for a response from the industrial countries. The Cartagena group's finance ministers and foreign ministers met subsequently in 1984 and 1985 but without any meaningful outcome. Another letter was addressed to the economic summit, meeting in June 1985 in Bonn, but with no success.

It was clear that the strategy of the industrial countries was one of buying time—of the containment of the crisis by dealing with one country at a time and avoiding any contamination of the rest while the worst case was dealt with. Thus, a series of emergency packages, bridge loans, and credits were implemented from 1982 through 1985. A drastic cutback in the living standards in the debtor countries was the other side of the coin, of course. Imports were severely cut by Latin America, and large trade surpluses were generated to pay the interest on the outstanding debt. Latin America by 1983 had become a capital exporter, an anomaly in the theoretical development literature. Latin American governments, desperate to retain access to the international financial community, particularly for critical revolving trade credits needed to support the export surplus program, accepted the creditors' scheme.

Why did Latin America's efforts to act collectively fail? There is no easy answer to this question. A number of reasons account for the politically ineffective strategy of the Latin American states. Many were new democracies and their leaders were uncertain of how far they could go in pressing their case with the industrial countries. Any effective strategy would require the active involvement of both Mexico and Brazil, and one or the other was usually following its own strategy during the 1980s. The tactics of divide and conquer by the industrial countries were brilliant—from their perspective. The United States was given the lead in responding to Latin America and it was able to apply Paul Volcker's quarantine scheme with great success. Latin America found that it had few allies in the industrial world, and the Third World was a sympathetic but ineffective ally in the debt struggle. As Richard Feinberg has written,

the Latin American nations—individually or collectively—never really had their own debt strategy. . . . whereas the creditors—public and private— overtly organized to coordinate strategies for managing old debts as well as for providing new loans under certain conditions, the debtors remained independent from each other. Individual debtors, too, failed to devise or articulate very clear strategies beyond seeking to remain current on interest payments, regain credit worthiness, and minimize the costs of refinancing.[18]

Democracy also provided a surprising escape valve for the tensions in the Latin American countries. Contrary to many fears that the debt crisis would destroy fledgling democracies, they have survived the "Lost Decade" and have been able to convince their people of the need to work with, not against, the international financial community.[19]

The Baker Plan

By 1985, the industrial governments sensed a sharp increase in debt fatigue. At his inauguration in July 1985, President Alan García declared that Peru would allocate no more than 10 percent of its annual export earnings to service the debt. A "Declaration of Lima," signed by the Latin American leaders attending the Peruvian ceremony, called on the industrial countries to accept coresponsibility for the debt crisis and to recognize the linkage between interest payments and export earnings. At the same meeting, the Support Group was created to assist the Central American Contadora process in Central America. Fidel Castro convened a widely reported but ineffective series of debt meetings in Havana in the summer of 1985. And at the UN General Assembly meeting in September 1985, Presidents José Sarney of Brazil and Alan García of Peru, among others, were sharply critical of the lack of response to the plight of the debtor countries.

Important political changes had taken place in Washington in the ensuing years, one of which was James Baker's transfer from the White House to the U.S. Treasury. As treasury secretary, Baker was now the Reagan administration's coordinator for a response to the debt crisis. The second Reagan administration, while virulently ideological in its Central American policy, was more benign on broader hemispheric issues. At the joint meeting of the IMF and the World Bank in Seoul in October 1985, the Baker Plan was announced. It had three components. The first called for continued adjustment among the debtor countries; the second stipulated that the private commercial banks would lend an additional $20 billion over a three-year period; and third, the World Bank and the Inter-American Development Bank would provide new loans totaling $9 billion over three years.

The Baker Plan made good headlines but it did little to address the debt burden. The economic summit in Tokyo in June 1986 laconically endorsed the Baker Plan but did not indicate any change of policy on the part of the industrial countries. At the Venice economic summit in June 1987, Baker announced an "enhancement" of the Baker Plan that he termed a "Menu of Options." The menu was a wish list of possible financial mechanisms for reducing Latin America's debt, ranging from debt-equity conversion schemes, to exit bonds, to project lending, to on-lending. But the menu failed to reduce the debt. Many governments were wary of debt-equity schemes because they increased foreign ownership of vital resources and proved to be inflationary; capital markets were—and are—underdeveloped in most countries and the widespread use of equity swaps as a debt solution was not feasible. In addition, the secondary markets for debt-backed equities and securities are relatively thin in the region, and such instruments often fluctuate sharply in response to political statements or short-term economic developments in the debtor countries.

The announcement of the menu had been preceded by a dramatic decision at Citicorp, the lead bank in the restructuring process and one of the major creditors of all the Latin American states, that it would allocate $3 billion to its loan loss reserve fund precisely to protect itself from bad Third World loans. The U.S. Treasury and the Federal Reserve supported the decision; other commercial banks in the United States did not, since a comparable move by them would be highly costly in terms of earnings and investor returns.

The year 1987 saw a series of initiatives that indicated no one had any new answers to the debt crisis. In September the conservative *Financial Times* of London questioned whether or not a bits-and-pieces approach was sufficient:

the question is whether muddling through is still the best strategy or whether the governments of the developed countries should themselves provide resources to solve the problem. Muddling through is always easy, but is it enough? It is difficult to believe that the running sore of developing country debt will be healed without a willingness of major developed countries to contribute to the treatment.[20]

That theme was echoed by the newly organized Group of Eight Latin American states that met in Acapulco, Mexico, for their first summit meeting in 1987. In the final document, they declared that

the economic crisis undermines democracy in the region because it neutralises the legitimate efforts of our peoples to improve their living standards. It is contradictory that the same people who call for democracy also impose, in world economic relations, conditionality and adjustment schemes that compromise that very democracy, and which they themselves do not apply in correcting their own imbalances.[21]

Latin America Adjusts

Quietly, the democratic governments of Latin America had begun to realize in the middle of the Lost Decade that the old development models of the early post–World War II years were now inadequate. Some countries came to that realization sooner than others. Many viewed the dramatic reversal of Chile's economic fortunes in the mid-1980s with quiet admiration but often with the fear that it required an authoritarian regime to implement such drastic structural adjustment measures. The fact that the administration of Mexican president Miguel de la Madrid was beginning to do the same strengthened the apprehension. It was widely believed that the changes under way in Mexico were due to the pervasive influence of the Institutional Revolutionary Party (PRI) and its massive bureaucratic strength throughout the country.

The failure of the Cruzado Plan in Brazil in 1986 and the slow collapse of President Raúl Alfonsin's Austral Plan in Argentina further cautioned Latin America's leadership from embracing the siren call of deep adjustment.[22] But by the late 1980s, a number of countries had adopted far-reaching goals of internal change. The economies of the region were being opened to new investment; privatization schemes were under way to transfer to the private sector inefficient and bloated state companies; it became widely recognized that the internal debt was in most countries as serious, if not more so, than the external debt. Exchange rate policies had to be adjusted, exports diversified, and interest rates stabilized.

Latin America's leaders understood that they remained highly vulnerable to exogenous developments and trends. But by the last years of the decade, muddling through was all that was available. The international financial system had reached a steady state. Restructuring of the region's debt was an ongoing process, but always on a case-by-case basis. Volatile interest rates had steadied and dropped. Thanks to the absorptive capacity of the U.S. market, the region's export push succeeded in generating high trade surpluses for many countries.[23]

Did Latin America receive many benefits from its adjustment in the mid-1980s? Very few. Indeed, the situation tightened in 1987 to 1988 as regional banks in the United States began to write off Latin American debt. The Bank of Boston, for example, announced in December 1987 that it would write off $200 million. It was widely understood that the bank had given up hope of repayment of that portion of its loan portfolio to the debtor countries. Other regional banks followed throughout 1988. The decision of the regionals to opt out polarized the U.S. banking community. The so-called money center banks, primarily in New York and California, had comparatively thin reserves against their loans to the Third World but were under pressure within the Baker Plan to make new loans. The regional banks, with relatively small exposure, were healthier than the money center banks and able to reserve quickly against possible losses and to opt out of any forced new lending.

By 1988 to 1989, the decade's crisis had abated. The industrial countries were occupied with East-West questions. There was the general impression, with the exception of Chile, Bolivia, and Mexico, and a few of the smaller Central American and Caribbean states, that Latin American governments were irresolute, disorganized, well-meaning perhaps, but unwilling to understand the major trends in the globalization of the world economy. If they were unable to understand the need to restructure in order to compete, there was little the industrial countries could or would do to help them. Democracy had survived. Elites had not brought back the billions of dollars of flight capital that would provide a comfortable cushion for efforts at renewed growth in the region. And efforts such as those of the Group of Eight, and other regional groups, were ineffective and incapable of backing up their desperation with any action that would be seen as threatening to the industrial countries.

That perception changed sharply in the United States at the end of the Reagan administration. The new government of Mexican president Carlos Salinas de Gortari, who took office in December 1988, made it clear in 1989 that continued restructuring without debt relief was unacceptable. The Salinas government's willingness to challenge the conventional wisdom of the 1980s regarding the debt strategy was matched in the United States by a growing concern with the bilateral relationship. A period of Mexico bashing in the mid-1980s had yielded to a realization that American foreign policy and security interests were deeply affected by events in Mexico. If debt was a higher priority for Mexico, it would need to be for the United States as well.[24]

The Brady Plan

The year 1988 was a slide year in debt discussions. With the upcoming presidential election in the United States, it was clear that the Reagan administration would take no new action. Besides, Treasury Secretary Baker was deeply involved in running the campaign of then Vice President Bush. With the victory of the Bush-Quayle ticket in November 1989, the debt issue moved quickly. The president-elect met with Mexican president Salinas in Texas. It was "leaked" during the transition that the new American government would move beyond the Baker Plan and the Menu of Options soon after the inauguration in January 1989.

Secretary of the Treasury Nicholas Brady announced what has been termed the Brady Plan in March 1989. It stressed voluntary debt reduction by the banks—writing off loans in negotiation with the developing countries—as well as new lending to help them pay off old loans and develop the means to produce more foreign exchange and put their debt burden behind them. The plan relies heavily on the IMF and the World Bank to lend money to those countries and undertake structural reform to help them cut back on their outstanding obligations. A total of $28.5 billion was originally put forward in support of the new program, $24 billion from the IMF and the World Bank and $4.5 billion from the government of Japan. The goal was to reduce interest outflows by $7 billion a year for three years, but it was quickly pointed out that the U.S. target would require $40 to $50 billion of new funds.

At first, the private commercial banking community, highly vulnerable to reduction of its Third World debt exposure, resisted. Throughout 1989 they signaled their fatigue with Third World debt. In September 1989 Manufacturers Hanover announced that it would add $950 million of a Japanese infusion of $1.4 billion of fresh capital to its loan loss reserve fund. Chase Manhattan followed with a decision to increase its loan loss reserve by $1.9 billion. J. P. Morgan stated that it would add $2 billion to its reserve, a step that left it with 100 percent of its medium- and long-term exposure to Third World debt fully covered. The Morgan message was loud and clear. It indicated that it was turning its back on the new lending component of the Brady Plan. Now that it was fully covered, it had the flexibility to do with its loan portfolio what it wanted, without the pressure to grant new loans so that the old ones could continue to be serviced.

A second obstacle was the inability of the United States to provide more public funding for debt reduction. The debate between the U.S. private commercial banks and the Bush administration was clear—and bitter. The banks urged the Bush administration to make more resources available to encourage them to undertake greater debt reduction and to provide guarantees for new loans. The chairman of Morgan stated, when he announced the bank's loan-loss reserve decision, "we are very concerned about debtor countries' rising expectations of the magnitude of debt reduction possible under the Brady initiative, when sufficient resources to encourage sizable voluntary debt reduction programs have not been provided by industrial countries."[25]

By the end of 1989, a brief power struggle erupted. The players were the banks, the Third World countries, and the governments of the industrial countries. The issue was clear. Would the U.S. government and the other industrial countries provide sufficient enhancements for the private commercial banks to proceed with debt reduction? The banks were challenging a deficit-ridden U.S. administration to make a massive financial contribution to allow debt reduction to move ahead. To the degree that Latin America and the Caribbean are viewed by the industrial world as an area of special responsibility for the United States, they look to Washington to resolve the issue with minor contributions from the Japanese, who are seeking ways to buy friends with their trade surplus.

The issue was clear: "fundamental is the question about whether sufficient official funds will be available to provide significant debt relief for qualifying countries."[26] By 1990, few observers were willing to bet that the official funds would be made available. An alternative, of course, was for the industrial governments to apply more coercion against commercial banks to forgive debts, "a step that so far they have felt unable to take. Given a quasi-voluntary format, it is far less clear that there is enough."[27]

If a turning point can be identified that broke the logjam in 1990 to 1991, it was the Brady Plan negotiation between the banks and Mexico. The government of President Carlos Salinas de Gortari had inherited a difficult economic and political situation. While the initial reforms undertaken by his predecessor, Miguel de la Madrid, appeared promising, they had not yet restored confidence in the country's economy. The social fallout from the debt crisis in the 1980s had generated a strong, populist reaction to the Salinas candidacy. Only the indefatigable efforts of the ruling PRI, which has never lost a presidential election, guaranteed Salinas's hairline victory.

Salinas entered office with an excellent economic team, most of whom had worked with him in the 1980s in the de la Madrid government. Salinas was determined to continue the deepening of the reform process and to press immediately for international financial concessions to restore the creditworthiness of Mexico. That was essential, he reasoned, to begin to put the 1980s behind him and to begin to attract new direct foreign investment and capital flows. Ironically, what was viewed by Mexico as an important breakthrough when it was completed in February 1990 was interpreted otherwise internationally. One commentator stated that "the jury is now in on the 1989 debt restructuring agreement between Mexico and the international financial community. Unfortunately, the deal is a bad one for Mexico. The agreement, signed on Feb. 4, falls far short of the country's needs, has not and will not produce the desired effects, and leaves the nation in a woefully weak position for future negotiations."[28] Even the *Financial Times* laconically stated, "One hates to spoil a good party. But it is now clear that if Mexico eventually puts its debt problem behind it, the contribution from the new debt accord will have been modest indeed."[29]

Throughout 1990, additional voices were raised to express misgivings about the Brady Plan. The Institute of International Finance (IIF) in Washington, a think tank that speaks on behalf of the commercial banks, stated in May that the plan has encouraged an "alarming increase in country arrears to commercial bank creditors." The IIF report blames the Brady initiative for engendering "a loss of discipline in the [international financial] system and the build-up of payments arrears to commercial banks and official agencies."[30] The IIF concern reflects a related issue of growing concern in financial circles: the health of the private commercial banks. Third World debt is a critical element in the poor state of health of the commercial banks, but it is only one element. Bad loans in the real estate and energy sectors, the impact of the savings and loan fiasco, and a general sluggishness in the American economy have raised questions about the future of the private banking system as we now know it. The Latin American debt remains a problem for the private banks as much as it does the governments of the region.

It was in mid- or late 1990 that the terms of reference about the Latin American debt changed. The stark reality confronting Latin America in the 1990s was summarized by ECLAC in late 1989:

the economic crisis that has affected Latin America and the Caribbean during most of the 1980s persisted during the last year of the decade, as the average per capita product fell for the second year running, this time by 1%, while inflation averaged the unprecedented 1,000%.... the region's expanding trade surplus continued to be insufficient to cover the huge burden of debt service and only five Latin American and Caribbean countries managed to meet those commitments fully and timely in 1989.[31]

ECLAC continues to report that the net resource transfer abroad in 1989 reached nearly $25 billion—the equivalent of almost 18 percent of the value of the region's export of goods and services and of approximately 3 percent of its gross domestic product. If Mexico is excluded from these figures, the net resource transfer abroad in fact increased to nearly $23 billion, from less than $18 billion in 1988. The 1989 performance suggests that "most of the countries of the region seem now to be reaching the limits of their capacity for adjusting to external constraints, on the basis of their present structures of production."[32] But just as ECLAC was issuing its pessimistic assessment, the international financial markets rediscovered Latin America. That rediscovery has changed the nature of the debate regarding regional debt in the 1990s.

The Enterprise for the Americas Initiative

An additional factor in the debt debate emerged in June 1990 with the announcement at the White House of the EAI. It was heralded as a "new partnership for trade, investment, and growth" in the Americas. It called for free and fair trade within the hemisphere; domestic and foreign investment, new capital flows, a reduction in debt burdens, and an improvement of the environment; and additional support for debt and debt-service reduction.

As reported one year later, the initiative was "a triumph of timing which promised rewards for the sort of reforms the Latin Americans had already begun."[33] But the movement on specifics has been slow. Negotiations are under way on the North American Free Trade Agreement (NAFTA) with Mexico, Canada, and the United States seeking a new concept of North American trade. "Framework" agreements for freer trade have been signed with sixteen countries, as well as the southern common market of Argentina, Brazil, Paraguay, and Uruguay. Chile received the first enterprise debt reduction and investment package in 1991. Progress has been made in raising the $1.5 billion from the United States and other industrial countries for the creation of an investment fund proposed by President Bush. The fund is intended partly to support privatization efforts.

The problem has been the U.S. Congress, which has vocally endorsed the program but has been slow to pass legislation necessary for further action. Of all the trade, food, and foreign aid credits the president wants to make available for debt reduction, only forgiveness on some of the food debt has been authorized. Bills granting reduction on the rest moved slowly through both Houses.

The most dramatic result of the initiative has been the enthusiasm of the Latin American governments. President Bush visited South America in December 1990 and received a warm and enthusiastic endorsement for the initiative. All the Latin heads of states, during their visits to Washington, have supported the program. Combined with the economic restructuring that continues throughout the hemisphere, it has changed the tone and the nature of the debate about U.S.–Latin American ties for the first time in decades.

What remains to be done is substantial. But the successful conclusion of NAFTA will provide an important impetus for further trade action. Investment is returning to Latin America. But it is the stock of debt that remains the principal question mark to sustained, renewed growth in the hemisphere.

The New Realities of the 1990s

The successful conclusion of the Brady Plan for Mexico was followed with agreements for Costa Rica in May 1990, Uruguay in January 1991, and Venezuela in March 1990 (the formalities and legalities often took many additional months of discussion, but the fundamental agreement was the essential element in the negotiation). Chile and Colombia continued their successful policy of not seeking to renegotiate their foreign debt by prudent macroeconomic management combined, in the case of Chile, with an early commitment to liberalization, privatization, and an opening of its economy to foreign investment on very favorable and competitive terms. And to the surprise of many observers, Brazil successfully negotiated an agreement with the IMF in 1992 and concluded a Brady Plan debt rescheduling thereafter.

By 1992 the generalized commitment to reform in Latin America was recognized worldwide. Salinas in Mexico, Aylwin in Chile, Menem in Argentina, Peréz in Venezuela, and others were publicly and politically supportive of a rapid shift from the post-1945 economic development models. Only Brazil's president Fernando Collor de Mello, personally in favor of such reform, found himself blocked by a recalcitrant Congress, regional interests, and a new constitution approved in 1988 that tied the government's hands from moving rapidly to join the other countries in the hemisphere. The impeachment and removal from office of Collor at the end of 1992 probably signals a slower and more complicated adjustment process in the future for Brazil. While President Carlos Andrés Pérez has supported structural adjustment, he has had to contend with rising discontent with the impact of the reforms. Riots greeted the first announcement of the adjustment package in February 1989, and in February 1992 an attempted coup was partially justified in terms of the social costs of the macroeconomic changes then under way in Venezuela.

That commitment, and the successful completion of the Brady Plan negotiations, rekindled investor interest in the region—suddenly and dramatically. In August 1992 *The Economist* reported that "the reemerging markets of Latin America have become hot business. American securities firms are sterring private capital back there to profit from the economic reforms that are transforming the region. Inflows of new capital have jumped from around $8 billion a year in the 1980s to over $40 billion at an annual rate so far this year."[34] Shortly thereafter, ECLAC reported that

Latin America and the Caribbean debt burden has shown significant improvement over the last few years. For instance, in 1991, the region's coefficient of accrued interest payments/exports declined for the fifth consecutive year to 22%. This compares to 25% the previous year and represents the lowest level since the peak of 41% that was registered in 1982. The decline was due entirely to a US$3.5 billion fall in gross interest payments, a product of lower international interest rates, and the reduction of bank debt as well as the cancellation of some official obligations. Nevertheless a coefficient of 22% is still very high and reflects the serious debt problems that persist.[35]

One important indication of the growing financial interest in Latin America was the pattern of growth in the region's stock markets. In the early 1980s stock markets were viewed with suspicion. By the early 1990s, according to a survey by Salomon Brothers, "the return on investment in Argentina was 400 percent, and 100 percent in Mexico and Chile. Brazil's stock market opened to foreign investors only in mid-1991 but returned 150 percent to investors."[36] By the end of 1992 the Inter-American Development Bank reported that a sharp increase in capital flows in 1991 to the region caused problems for economic management in many countries. A more gradual and sustainable influx would have been preferable, commented the bank. Capital inflows to the region, estimated last year at $36 billion, had reached levels the IADB had assumed would not occur until the end of the century.

As the bank report explained, the inflows of capital were beneficial in principle as they relieved the decade-long constraint on investment and production caused by a lack of foreign exchange. However, in many countries the inflows meant governments had to either let real exchange rates appreciate and absorb the inflows through imports or maintain the exchange rate and allow foreign exchange reserves to rise. Expanding reserves threatened monetary stability and had to be offset by restrictive monetary and fiscal policies. If monetary policies were too stringent, however, the resulting high interest rates initiated a new round of capital inflows.[37] This was, of course, the sort of dilemma that few imagined possible a year or two ago. And from the operational perspective of finance ministers and central banks throughout the region, they would rather have the challenge of managing capital flows than worry if there would be any capital available at all for domestic investment needs.

Conclusion

As the Latin American debt crisis enters its second decade, it is no longer a crisis for many. The international financial community now views the region (at least its major countries) positively. The commitment to economic restructuring in the late 1980s by the democratic political leaders has succeeded in attracting the return of flight capital and new capital inflows. The successful Brady Plan negotiations were an essential prerequisite for new investment. Continued reform and liberalization, particularly the privatization of state corporations, has proven to be attractive to investors in search of new and profitable opportunities.

There are clearly dangers. The lack of an agreement in the Uruguay Round of GATT can impact negatively on Latin America's agricultural exports. The emergence of world trading blocs will have implications for the countries of the region. The continued sluggishness of the U.S. economy is of concern to the governments in the hemisphere. And the allure of Eastern Europe as an alternative to Latin America continues to concern the region. But the rapid negotiations on NAFTA between Mexico, the United States, and Canada; the South American Common Market (MERCOSUR) of Argentina, Brazil, Paraguay, and Uruguay; a possible common market among the countries of Central America and Mexico; and the bilateral free trade agreements being discussed (Chile and Mexico, Chile and the United States) offer new and important trade and investment opportunities in the hemisphere for the first time in its history.

The critical variables that are infrequently discussed are the costs of adjustment and the decrease of living standards during the 1980s. The challenge of the 1990s is to link the new flows of investment capital to social investment. Latin America's social agenda should be given a high priority between now and the end of the century. New capital investment should lead to higher levels of productivity. But that will require skilled, healthy workers, who are in short supply in the region given the lack of social investment in recent years. Continued political stability and social peace, at some point, will necessitate a shift in investment priorities on a sustained basis.

The task is not impossible. New resources are now available. The challenge to the successor governments—to follow those who undertook the hard decisions about economic liberalization and privatization—is to maintain the outward-looking economic model of recent years and address the human development challenge that confronts all the states in the region. The citizens of the region now await a repetition of the successful financial and economic engineering of recent years in improving the quality of life and addressing the human development imperative of Latin America and the Caribbean.

Notes

1. David C. Mulford, "Moving beyond the Latin Debt Crisis," *Wall Street Journal*, 21 August 1992, p. A7.

2. Ibid.

3. Lewis H. Diuguid, "Stock Markets Soaring across Latin America," *Washington Post*, 21 April 1992, p. 10.

4. "Virtue Rewarded," *The Economist*, 31 October 1992, p. 86.

5. Pedro-Pablo Kuczynski, *Latin American Debt* (Baltimore, Md.: Johns Hopkins University Press, 1988) p. 73.

6. For a comparative analysis of Latin America's phases of indebtedness, see Barbara Stallings, *Banker to the Third World* (Berkeley: University of California Press, 1987).

7. Ibid., pp. 97–98.

8. The capital flight issue is discussed in Donald L. Lessard and John Wil-

liamson, *Capital Flight and Third World Debt* (Washington DC: Institute for International Economics, 1987).

9. As I have written elsewhere, "by 1981 the warning signals were apparent to those who wanted to see them. While the ratio of debt service to export earnings in countries such as Indonesia, Korea, and Malaysia remained below the 'safe' level of 15 percent, the debt service ratios in Brazil and Chile rose above 30 percent and reached 35 percent in Mexico and Argentina. World Bank estimates indicate that a single percentage point change in short-term dollar interest rates has an impact each year of more than $1.2 billion on the combined net debt service of Mexico, Brazil and Argentina, Latin America's three largest borrowers. From 1979 to 1981 the debt servicing of these three key countries rose by $10 billion, or 170 percent." "The Debt Crisis: Economics and Politics," in John D. Martz, ed., *United States Policy in Latin America: A Quarter Century of Crisis and Challenge, 1961–1986* (Lincoln: University of Nebraska Press, 1988), pp. 242–43.

10. For the background to the Mexican debt crisis, see José Ayala and Clemente Ruíz Durán, "Development and Crisis in Mexico: A Structuralist Approach," in Jonathan Hartlyn and Samuel A. Morley, eds., *Latin American Political Economy: Financial Crisis and Political Change* (Boulder, Colo.: Westview, 1986), pp. 243–64.

11. The position of the private commercial banks is summarized in Terence C. Canavan, "The Threat to the International Banking System," in Robert A. Pastor, ed., *Latin America's Debt Crisis: Adjusting to the Past or Planning for the Future?* (Boulder, Colo.: Lynne Rienner, 1987), pp. 53–59.

12. On the strategy of the industrial countries, see Riordan Roett, "How the 'Haves' Manage the 'Have-Nots': Latin America and the Debt Crisis," in Barbara Stallings and Robert Kaufman, eds., *Debt and Democracy in Latin America* (Boulder, Colo.: Westview, 1989), pp. 59–73.

13. Howard Handelman and Werner Baer, "Introduction: The Economic and Political Costs of Austerity," in Howard Handelman and Werner Baer, eds., *Paying the Costs of Austerity in Latin America* (Boulder, Colo.: Westview, 1989), pp. 2–3.

14. See Eduardo Wiesner, "The State of the Debt Crisis: Benefits and Costs," in Pastor, ed., *Latin American's Debt Crisis*, pp. 25–31.

15. See Riordan Roett for a discussion of the 1983–84 response of Latin America in "Latin America's Debt: Problems and Prospects," *International Journal*, Canadian Institute of International Affairs, Vol. 43, no. 3 (summer 1988): 428–45.

16. For one of the earliest analyses of the relationship between debt and democracy, see Riordan Roett, "Democracy and Debt in South America: A Continent's Dilemma," *Foreign Affairs* 62, no. 3 (1984): 695–720.

17. See "Latin America's Response: Excerpts from Communiqués of the Cartagena Group," in Pastor, ed., *Latin America's Debt Crisis*, pp. 153–61.

18. Richard E. Feinberg and Ricardo Ffrench-Davis, *Development and External Basis for a New Debt in Latin America* (Notre Dame: University of Notre Dame Press, 1988), p. 60.

19. See Paul Drake, "Debt and Democracy in Latin America, 1920s–1980s," in Stallings and Kaufman, eds., *Debt and Democracy*, pp. 39–58, for a discussion of the survival of democratic regimes in spite of the debt overhand during the 1980s.

20. "Strategy for LDC Debt," *Financial Times*, 30 September 1987, p. 26.

21. "Acapulco Sparks a Sense of Unity," *Financial Times*, 1 December 1987.

22. For a discussion of the Austral and Cruzado Plans, see Robert R. Kaufman, *The Politics of Debt in Argentina, Brazil, and Mexico: Economic Stabilization in the 1980s* (Berkeley: University of California, Institute of International Studies, 1988).

23. David Mulford, a key architect of the Reagan administration's responses to the debt crisis and a major player in the Bush administration, summarizes his viewpoint in "The View of the Reagan Administration: Toward Stronger World Growth," in Pastor, ed., *Latin America's Debt Crisis*, pp. 81–86.

24. For background on the Mexican debt, see Thomas J. Trebat, "Mexican Foreign Debt: Old Lessons, New Possibilities," in Riordan Roett, ed., *Mexico and the United States: Managing the Relationship* (Boulder, Colo.: Westview, 1988), pp. 71–86.

25. Sarah Bartlett, "Third World Debt Woes," *New York Times*, 23 September 1989, p. 1.

26. Stephen Fidler, "One Step Closer to a Lighter Burden," *Financial Times*, 23 January 1990.

27. Ibid.

28. Jorge C. Castaneda, "Mexico's Dismal Debt Deal," *New York Times*, 25 February 1990.

29. "A Modest Deal for Mexico," *Financial Times*, 17 January 1990, p. 18.

30. Stephen Fidler, "Brady Debt Plan 'Encourages Arrears,'" *Financial Times*, 4 May 1990.

31. *CEPAL News* 9, no. 12 (December 1989): 1.

32. Ibid., p. 3.

33. "Bush Initiative Translates Slowly into Action," *Financial Times*, 18 July 1991.

34. See "Falling in Love Again," *The Economist*, 22 August 1992, p. 63.

35. "The External Debt of Latin America and the Caribbean in 1991," *CEPAL News* 12, no. 8, (August 1992), p. 2.

36 Diuguid, "Stock Markets Soaring."

37. Stephen Fidler, "Capital Flows to Latin America Trigger Problems," *Financial Times*, 20 October 1992, p. 16.

Christopher Mitchell

Policy toward Western Hemisphere Immigration and Human Rights

During the 1970s and 1980s, human rights and international migration gained importance as issues in U.S. policy toward Latin America and the Caribbean. The new weight of these concerns in U.S. foreign relations had a number of causes. Calculated policies of murder, torture, and imprisonment by some Latin American governments against their own citizens caused many Americans to question whether the United States should be extending aid to those regimes. Repression by states in Latin America and the Caribbean (and violence created by rebellions against some of those governments) forced many refugees into other countries, including the United States. Washington often could not avoid the policy dilemma of how to treat those newly arrived groups. In addition, at a time of periodic international shocks to the U.S. economy and slow economic growth, domestic groups, including trade unions and local governments, were worried by a large and perhaps increasing flow of unauthorized labor migration to the United States from Latin America and the Caribbean.

Matters of human rights and migration often presented themselves as separate issues in the making of U.S. hemispheric policy during the 1980s, but they shared an important characteristic: a focus on individuals in direct confrontation with state power. Quite often, as well, it appeared that U.S. government action might make a significant difference on both types of issues. By definition, the U.S. government deals directly with many arriving migrants, and in the case of human rights violations, if Washington could not dissuade the offending government at least it could disassociate itself from that state's abuses.

Issues such as these, which can readily be understood in terms of individuals' experiences, are likely to be presented with special vividness by the press, radio, and television. That circumstance may help account for a significant new pattern in policy making during the 1980s: the noteworthy influence of mobilized U.S. interest groups on Washington's actions toward both Latin American human rights and migration issues. Other factors, of course, also affected U.S. choices in these fields, especially ideology, economic interests, long-standing administrative practice, and the letter of immigration law. Policy makers in the executive branch retained the initiative in both fields during the decade from 1981 to 1991. However, they had to take new account of advocacy groups, which often sought alliances both in Congress and with broader currents of public opinion.

In dealing with Western Hemisphere immigration, the Reagan and Bush administrations accorded with a diffuse national majority that favored restrictionism. Both presidents opposed seaborne refugee migration from Cuba and Haiti and sought to reverse some large flows from Central American nations on the grounds that the migrants acted out of economic rather than political motives. Addressing labor migration from Mexico, the Reagan administration and congressional leaders succeeded in passing an Immigration Reform and Control Act (IRCA) in 1986 that for the first time forbade U.S. employers knowingly to hire unauthorized migrants. At the same time, special interests within the United States—economic, regional, ideological—were able to claim a share of influence. The Reagan administration, which had strong political alliances with conservative groups and Cuban Americans in South Florida, tended to offer a much warmer welcome to persons fleeing Nicaragua and Cuba than to those from El Salvador, Haiti, and Guatemala. Advocates for the latter groups, in turn, utilized legal appeals and congressional alliances in seeking to broaden or stabilize access to the United States for them. Only a complex compromise with U.S. agribusiness, to maintain certain labor flows from Mexico and Central America, made the passage of IRCA possible.

In the field of human rights, the Reagan administration sought a very marked break from President Jimmy Carter's policies, and the United States became far less exigent than before 1981 in urging Latin American governments to suppress political imprisonment, killings, and the use of torture. The ability of advocates for human rights to use publicity, however, rapidly convinced the new administration that it would need to maintain some human rights policy at (and somewhat beyond) the level of rhetoric. This decision ultimately contributed to the Reagan government's prodemocracy policy, with practical effects in a few Latin American nations.

Attentive segments of public opinion sometimes linked their views of U.S. policies toward migration and human rights in the Western Hemisphere, though policy makers seldom did so. Critics of the Reagan administration's policies in Central America, for example, viewed Washington as partly responsible for human rights abuses in nations like El Salvador. When, predictably, many Salvadorans sought political asylum in the United States, these critics were angered but not surprised by the official U.S. rejection of most petitions. U.S. foreign policy interests were seen as controlling the two policies. While many of the same denunciations were made of U.S. policy toward Haiti, at certain points in their dealings with that nation U.S. decision makers did try to restrain government abuse and thus reduce the level of forced migration.

This chapter first examines U.S. policies toward migration from Latin America and the Caribbean, covering population flows considered to be grounded in both economic and political motivations. I then explore the evolution of U.S. human rights policies toward the Western Hemisphere under Reagan and Bush, with attention to some of the links between the two issue areas. Finally, I consider whether the U.S. government or concerned interest groups were able to produce coherent policies toward human rights and inter-American migration capable of meeting the challenges of succeeding years.

Immigration Policies: Restrictionism, Foreign Policy, and Public Pressure

The 1980 crisis involving Cubans and Haitians marked a watershed for U.S. policy toward immigration from the Western Hemisphere. During the Carter administration's last year, over 125,000 Cubans and 25,000 Haitians came to the United States in small boats, seeking refuge from repression by the Castro and Duvalier regimes. This emergency, which made the Carter administration appear ineffectual in the midst of a U.S. presidential campaign, had the enduring effect of making immigration a more salient topic in U.S. political debates. Responding to an issue framed by the media and national public opinion as to "whether the United States can get control of its borders," the incoming Reagan administration was encouraged to adopt a generally restrictionist stance toward Western Hemisphere immigration. At the same time, the events of 1980 in South Florida raised two issues that were sometimes connected and that remained contentious for the following ten years. First, was the United States acting consistently and fairly toward migrant flows from different nations? If, for example, arriving Haitians were receiving systematically harsher treatment than Cubans, that raised questions both of basic even-handedness and of domestic ethnic and race relations. Second, what should be the relationship between U.S. immigration policy and general U.S. foreign policy toward Latin America? Should different migrant groups be handled differently because U.S. policies toward their home governments diverged?

The outgoing Carter administration stitched together a policy toward the Cubans and Haitians that reduced the crisis atmosphere by early 1981. The United States had traditionally welcomed refugees from Cuba, and most of the 1980 arrivees in the "boatlift" from the Cuban port of Mariel were rapidly released into U.S. society. However, since the size and makeup of the outflow from Mariel were being manipulated by the Cuban government, U.S. boats were forbidden to aid the migration, and in September 1980 the movement from Cuba ended. In the glare of national publicity surrounding the Cubans, Washington had to suspend for eight months its policy (in place since 1978) of opposition to Haitian migration to South Florida. A novel legal status was invented (Cuban-Haitian Entrant, Status Pending) under which migrants of both nationalities that had arrived during 1980 could remain in the United States.[1]

Toward the Caribbean, Central America, and Mexico, the new Reagan administration took restrictionism as its polestar in the migration field, though that policy proved far from uniform in application or effectiveness. Since the mid-1960s, public opinion in the United States had increasingly favored curbs on immigration, and that trend gained strength after 1980.[2] In relation to Cuba, the issue receded from view for several years, because Fidel Castro's government prevented emigration. As had frequently happened since 1959, Cuban policy was exerting a major influence over Washington's actions toward Cuban migration. To be sure, the U.S. government was faced with a nagging policy problem left over from the Mariel emergency: what to do with several thousand *marielitos* who were still imprisoned (because they were considered excludable from the

United States or because they had been convicted of crimes since arriving from Cuba). Washington wished to return these detainees to Cuba, but Havana would not take them without other foreign policy concessions from the United States.[3]

An instrument that would later be used to address this dilemma was pioneered by the United States in focusing on migration from Haiti. A diverse coalition of civil libertarians, black North American political leaders, and Haitians living in the United States was developing in opposition to the federal policy of detaining most Haitian asylum applicants in facilities that closely resemble concentration camps. Members of this coalition pursued an arduous but sometimes effective practice of mounting court challenges to federal treatment of Haitian asylum applicants. On the other side of the debate, strong pressure against further Haitian migration was being exerted by groups in the Miami area worried about unemployment and perhaps also motivated by racism; this pressure was transmitted to the national level through Congress. To respond to these demands, the executive branch needed a strategy that would prevent the very arrival of Haitian boat people, thus denying them or their advocates any standing in U.S. courts.

That strategy took shape as a formal agreement with the Haitian government, under which the Duvalier regime undertook to discourage emigration and permitted the U.S. Coast Guard to patrol the waters near Haiti. These cutters interdicted boats suspected of carrying unauthorized migrants and returned their passengers to Haiti following a shipboard hearing of any asylum claims. During the first ten years of these patrols, only twenty-eight migrants among the twenty-five thousand intercepted were judged potentially to qualify as refugees under U.S. law. Legal challenges to the policy were turned back by the U.S. courts.[4] Under Washington's intense persuasion (with the added inducement of continued U.S. economic aid), even the relatively feeble Haitian government proved able to reduce undocumented emigration considerably.

The migration agreement with Port-au-Prince did have one positive effect on political life in Haiti. The Mica Amendment (to U.S. foreign aid legislation) made U.S. assistance to Haiti conditional not just on Haitian aid in halting illegal emigration but on the improvement of the human rights situation in Haiti. The president was required to monitor Haitian official acts in both areas. As a result, the Haitian government's brutality came to be perceived as both less legitimate and less inevitable by Haitians, perhaps contributing to the Duvaliers' overthrow in February 1986.[5]

Along the nearly two-thousand-mile U.S.-Mexican border, it has never been practical to stop all migration physically. The majority of unauthorized migrants crossing that border has always come from Mexico, but at the start of the 1980s the flows from El Salvador, Nicaragua, and Guatemala increased notably. The civil strife in all three nations, partly rooted in radical uprisings that were tenaciously opposed by the Reagan administration, caused unprecedented migration within nations and within and beyond Central America. Appropriate government policy toward Central American migrants became one of the most contentious issues in U.S. domestic immigration debates, linking issues of immigration, foreign policy, and human rights.

By the middle of the 1980s, between seven hundred thousand and 1.2 million Central Americans were estimated to be living in the United States, including five to eight hundred thousand Salvadorans, one to two hundred thousand Guatemalans, and forty to eighty thousand Nicaraguans.[6] The Reagan administration pursued a consistently restrictionist policy toward granting both immigrant and refugee visas to migrants from all three nations.[7] However, the U.S. government clearly showed its foreign policy preferences in the handling of applications for political asylum from Central Americans who were arrested without documents in the United States. The executive branch was reluctant to depict politics in El Salvador and Guatemala as inspiring "a well-founded fear of persecution on account of race, religion, nationality, membership in a particular social group or political opinion," the legal criterion for the granting of political asylum. On the other hand, strong motives of ideology and foreign policy pushed the executive branch to portray the Sandinista regime in Nicaragua in just that light.

The Immigration and Naturalization Service (INS) nearly always followed the advice on asylum applications provided by the State Department's Bureau of Human Rights and Humanitarian Affairs (HA); the State Department country desks were also routinely consulted. This advice, frequently conveyed in form letters,[8] was that most Salvadorans and Guatemalans in the United States were "economic migrants" rather than "political refugees." In fiscal years 1983 through 1988, 3.4 percent of Salvadoran, 2.1 percent of Guatemalan, and 28 percent of Nicaraguan asylum applications were approved.

From 1984 through 1988, 37,143 Salvadorans and Guatemalans were deported or "required to depart" from the United States, while only 1,453 Nicaraguans faced those sanctions.[9] The district director of the INS in Miami was simply being unusually outspoken about this policy when he declared in 1986 that he would not send Nicaraguans back to Managua. His superiors in the Justice Department did not intervene.[10]

A remarkably widespread movement developed in the United States in opposition to these asylum policies and to the Reagan administration's policies in Central America, which were viewed as contributing to the refugee problem. For numerous church groups, social activists, and ordinary citizens, the pattern of Washington's policies toward Central America appeared simply outrageous. In this view, the Reagan administration bore major responsibility for generating refugees through its finance of the Salvadoran military and the Nicaraguan Contras. For the administration to claim that human rights conditions were improving in El Salvador and then to deport thousands of Salvadorans—while proceeding much more leniently with Nicaraguans—seemed the essence of hypocrisy and manipulation.

In 1981 and 1982, a sanctuary movement began to develop among churches in the southwestern United States and local governments in the San Francisco Bay Area. At the movement's height in 1985 and 1986, approximately three hundred churches, twenty cities, and the state of New Mexico committed themselves to protecting Salvadoran refugees (and sometimes aiding their travel to the United States), despite U.S. law and government policy to the contrary. As the best-known of these congregations wrote to Attorney General William French Smith in March 1982:

We are writing to inform you that Southside Presbyterian Church [in Tucson, Arizona] will publicly violate the Immigration and Nationality Act Section 274(a). We have declared our church as a "sanctuary" for undocumented refugees from Central America. . . . We believe that justice and mercy require that people of conscience actively assert our God-given right to aid anyone fleeing from persecution and murder. The current administration of U.S. law prohibits us from sheltering these refugees from Central America. Therefore we believe the administration of the law to be immoral as well as illegal.[11]

Assisting refugees had a special appeal to critics of U.S. refugee policy since it offered the chance—perhaps the obligation—to take practical action to aid some of the victims of Central American violence directly. For many of its participants, the sanctuary movement was also integrally linked to opposing the Reagan administration's foreign policy toward Central America. Reverend William Sloane Coffin Jr., of Riverside Church in New York City, observed in a 1985 debate with INS commissioner Alan C. Nelson:

Commissioner Nelson is quite right to say that this is not standard sanctuary. . . . The churches and synagogues provide food, shelter, clothing *and* a common platform on which both Central and North Americans can stand together to decry the deportation of innocent Salvadorans and Guatemalans. [We] urge the United States Government to stop funding the military in both Guatemala and El Salvador. Are we trying to embarrass the United States Government? No, we're trying to shame the government into changing its policies in Central America.[12]

Prosecution was virtually the only tool available to the government in dealing with the sanctuary movement, and even the Reagan administration showed no great eagerness to indict clergy, lay workers, and members of religious orders. When a small number of court cases were finally brought (primarily in Texas and Arizona), the political outcome was a draw. In the most publicized trial in Tucson in 1986, the Justice Department obtained six convictions for conspiracy to smuggle Salvadorans and Guatemalans into the United States, and these verdicts very likely discouraged some congregations and communities from joining the movement. However, the government's reputation suffered due to its reliance (for evidence) upon surreptitious recordings made at church meetings and Bible study sessions. The judge imposed only suspended sentences, and no further major cases were brought.[13]

The sanctuary movement lost momentum after the mid-1980s, but the year 1990 brought two major vindications of its efforts. The exertions of the movement's congressional allies finally bore fruit, as the Immigration Act of 1990 provided eighteen months of temporary protected status for most Salvadorans in the United States. On another front, a long-standing court challenge to government asylum practice was settled as the government promised to stop using foreign policy as a criterion in asylum cases and undertook to review the status of up to 500,000 Salvadorans and Guatemalans who had been denied asylum or had never sought it.

Central American refugee issues created occasional and significant political fireworks, but the biggest flow of undocumented migration was from Mexico. Demographer Michael S. Teitelbaum estimated that at the end of the 1970s between 3.5 and 6 million unauthorized immigrants were in the United States, augmented by annual new net arrivals of "at least several hundred thousand but considerably less than a million." Of these totals, he computed, Mexicans accounted for between 50 and 60 percent.[14] This large-scale process drew the Reagan administration and Congress into a search for new legislation to reduce the perception—and perhaps the reality—of hardly constrained population movement from abroad, especially from Mexico. This long and complex effort attracted extensive public attention in the United States. It may have altered government *actions* toward migration only to a limited degree, and (perhaps surprisingly) it did not greatly affect Washington's bilateral relations with Mexico. But it betokened a general effort by the U.S. government to mollify popular restrictionism by creating stronger controls over inter-American migration. These more routine procedures—whether in the form of legislation or international agreements—were intended to avoid the air of emergency improvisation that had made the Carter administration appear weak. Some limits to the success of this endeavor began to be demonstrated in dealings with Central America and the Caribbean during the Bush administration.

Between early 1981 and late 1986, the executive branch and Congress labored mightily over IRCA, often known as the Simpson/Rodino Act after its chief legislative sponsors, Senator Alan Simpson (R-WY) and Representative Peter Rodino (D-NJ). The social interests concerned with immigration issues proved to be diverse and vocal, including employers, labor unions both national and local, state and local governments, resident ethnic groups, and organizations dedicated to civil rights and civil liberties. The alignments of these groups often did not adhere to conventional Left-Right coalitions when it came to migration matters.[15] At the heart of IRCA was a pair of policies constituting a package deal that could win majority backing among legislators and interest groups. First, employers would, for the first time, be forbidden to employ undocumented migrants knowingly. Second, these employer sanctions would be balanced by a program of amnesty, permitting a good many resident undocumented migrants to attain legal status in the United States. Legalization garnered general support from ethnic and civil rights groups and from some labor unions with many immigrant members, while employer sanctions pleased national labor organizations, advocates of population control, and some local governments.

Business interests, especially those of large-scale agriculture, tended to be least pleased with these provisions, which seemed to portend higher wages and more government regulation. After many abortive efforts at legislative compromise to combine all these contending priorities, a provision was added that made passage possible in October 1986. A group of undocumented special agricultural workers (SAWs) would qualify for amnesty after as few as nine months in the United States, though other candidates for legalization had to have arrived prior to 1982. Moreover, additional replenishment agricultural workers (RAWs) might be legally admitted later if needed by the growers.[16]

Though northward migration had clearly become an important social process affecting both Mexico and the United States, it was not a very contentious theme in U.S.-Mexican diplomatic dealings in the 1980s. Neither government sought to politicize the subject, for differing reasons. For its part, Mexico saw little reason to make concessions on other matters (e.g., oil prices or supplies) to maintain a status quo on migration that it saw as acceptable and quite stable. Moreover, for Mexico to dicker with Congress over a new immigration law might be seen as intervention in U.S. politics. Members of Congress such as Senator Jesse Helms (R-NC) sometimes indulged in Mexico bashing on migration and other issues,[17] but for the most part the legislative bargaining on immigration reform was so intricate that discussion of international relations would have been an unwelcome complication.[18]

IRCA did not have much immediate impact on U.S. political relations with other nations in Latin America and the Caribbean. Immediately after the new law's passage, to be sure, the governments of such sending nations as the Dominican Republic, El Salvador, Guatemala, and Honduras expressed alarm that fewer of their citizens might be able to enter the United States and that indeed massive deportations might take place. The Reagan administration naturally did not change the letter of the law in response to these anxieties, but deportations did not rise and border arrests declined. Latin American governments soon stopped lobbying the United States on migration.[19]

One important effect of the Simpson/Rodino Act that may have implications for international dealings over the long term was that the new law led the U.S. public to expect that northward migration within the Western Hemisphere had been subjected to a control mechanism. This expectation, in relation to Mexico, had been thoroughly undermined by the early 1990s. The legalization program apparently reduced the flow of unauthorized migrants from Mexico in 1987 and 1988, but most of that effect was probably due to legalization rather than employer sanctions.[20] By 1989, forged documents had become inexpensive enough to undermine the identity checks performed by employers under IRCA, and in 1991 researcher Jorge Bustamante reported that illegal border crossing "has returned to business as usual."[21] Angry residents of the San Diego area, where half of all arrests along the U.S.-Mexican frontier took place, began holding monthly demonstrations to "Light up the Border" with their auto headlights.

In the Caribbean, the Reagan administration pursued a preventive policy against migration emergencies, even at some cost to its ideological preferences. Though Fidel Castro's government was anathema to the Republican Right,[22] a migration agreement was quietly negotiated with Havana in late 1984, under which 2,746 Cubans who arrived in 1980 were to be deported to Cuba from U.S. prisons as "excludable." In return, the United States would permit routine emigration from Cuba, which was viewed as a significant political safety valve for the Castro regime. As the State Department's coordinator for Cuban affairs stated, "this agreement provides that migration from Cuba to the United States will be 'normal'—the same in legal principle as migration from any other state to the United States."[23] The Mariel Agreement did not go into full effect until 1987, and news of it caused violent riots at two federal prisons among those slated to be deported. In the ensuing negotiations, advocates for the detained Cubans obtained more extensive judicial review of their cases, and the first expulsions did not take place until late 1988.[24]

In relation to Nicaragua and Haiti, the Bush administration had difficulty in handling migration emergencies, giving strong indications that no firm control had yet been established over U.S. borders. Would-be migrants retained considerable initiative; the INS and other agencies faced administrative obstacles and the legacy of old (occasionally contradictory) policies; advocates for migrant groups often skillfully used U.S. courts to challenge administration policies.

The crisis involving Nicaraguan migrants developed in South Texas, where the volume of asylum applicants from Nicaragua grew fivefold in six months, reaching over two thousand per week in December 1988.[25] Nicaragua's economy was in a disastrous decline compounded by natural disasters, and the political outlook remained uncertain despite Central American peace accords. The Reagan administration had, to a great degree, encouraged this population flow and increased its political visibility. In July 1987 Attorney General Meese had ordered that asylum standards be made more lenient for Nicaraguan applicants and also directed that they be issued work permits while their cases were under review. Under these rules, Nicaraguans usually sought asylum voluntarily upon entry through Texas, received work permits, and traveled on to Miami, where the INS was known to be lenient to them.

This process of de facto U.S. documentation for Nicaraguan migrants offered strong encouragement to emigration from that country. The Reagan policy also tended to make the flow through South Texas highly visible, and it included no safeguards against a greatly increased level of migration. Faced with protests from Texas border communities,[26] the incoming Bush administration reversed Meese's policy and sought blatantly to discourage Nicaraguans from coming to the United States. The INS began to conduct summary asylum adjudications as soon as migrants submitted their applications and detained thousands near Harlington, Texas, sometimes in makeshift prison camps and sometimes in the town's streets.

The emergency faded within a year, due to varied developments. Many incoming Nicaraguans simply traveled as unauthorized migrants to Florida, skirting the government's rough handling of asylum applicants; a total of 100,000 are estimated to have settled in Florida in 1988 and 1989. The Sandinista government's policies toward its opponents became more moderate as the 1990 elections approached in Managua. U.S. courts, as well, issued rulings questioning the legality of the INS's procedures in categorizing most Nicaraguans' asylum applications as frivolous. By January 1990 only 670 detainees remained in the Bayview, Texas, INS camp. As former acting INS commissioner Doris Meissner observed, "It is always the same story with detention plans: the I.N.S. launches them with great enthusiasm, but then it can't sustain them because of the costs, the vulnerability to litigation and the lack of public support."[27]

A similarly harsh U.S. policy, which also encountered political

criticism and legal challenge, was adopted toward a new Haitian influx in 1991–92. Haiti's first popularly elected president, Jean-
Bertrand Aristide, was overthrown by the army in September 1991,
and his supporters were widely persecuted in an atmosphere of un-
controlled official violence.[28] Soon increased numbers of rickety
boats full of Haitian migrants began embarking for the United States.
The Coast Guard followed its decade-old policy of interception but
did not at first return many of the migrants to Haiti. There were so
many (15,000 by early 1992) that a detention camp was built on the
U.S. naval base at Guantánamo Bay, Cuba, so that the Haitians
would not physically enter the jurisdiction of U.S. courts. Washington wished to return those picked up at sea on the traditional
grounds that they were economic refugees and had no standing in
U.S. courts anyway. The battle-weary legal advocates for Haitian
asylum seekers, especially the Lawyers' Committee for International Human Rights, did not prevail on appeal to the U.S. Supreme
Court. On 31 January the Coast Guard began shipping thousands of
Haitians back to Port-au-Prince each week.

The only real success for this policy was that it limited[29] the arrival of Haitians under emergency conditions in South Florida during a presidential election year. Otherwise, the policy for handling
the Haitians was improvised administratively and was politically
costly to the Bush administration. Even in Florida, overall public
opinion proved to favor granting temporary haven to those fleeing
from violence in Haiti, and the *Miami Herald* derisively dubbed
Bush's policy toward the influx "Operation Racist Shield."[30] Mayor
Xavier Suárez of Miami recalled his own arrival from Cuba as a refugee thirty-one years previously and distributed bumper stickers that
read "Interdict Drugs, Not Haitians."[31] Even conservative Republican senator Connie Mack of Florida introduced legislation calling
for temporary safe haven for the new wave of Haitians, and in the national media the administration was criticized for relaxing its economic sanctions against the Haitian junta so that the boat people
could be returned under more stable economic conditions.

Human Rights Policies: Rhetoric and "Quiet Diplomacy"

In the immigration field, there was considerable continuity between
the direction of U.S. policy development under Carter and that under Reagan. IRCA was a lineal descendant of a legislative proposal

submitted by the Carter administration in 1977, and the Caribbean interdiction policy was foreshadowed by U.S. handling of the Mariel exodus. In the area of human rights, the Reagan administration sought to reject Carter's policies decisively. During the election campaign, the Democratic administration's proclaimed stance toward human rights was sharply criticized by candidate Ronald Reagan, and cases from the Western Hemisphere such as Cuba, Chile, Argentina, and Brazil loomed large in Republican rhetoric. President Reagan's first ambassador to the United Nations, Jeane Kirkpatrick, tended to set the ideological pace in this field. A professor of political theory with a background in Latin American studies, Dr. Kirkpatrick took the Carter government to task for applying "double standards" that harassed right-wing "authoritarian" foreign governments (such as Chile) while indulging more rigid left-wing "totalitarian" regimes (such as Cuba). At his first news conference as secretary of state, Alexander Haig announced that "international terrorism will take the place of human rights in our concern because it is the ultimate of abuses of human rights."[32]

The new administration's first area of action in signaling a retreat from existing human rights policy was the State Department's Bureau of Human Rights and Humanitarian Affairs (HA), which had a legal mandate to advise within the State Department on human rights and to coordinate the department's human rights activities. This was a logical point of assault for the Reagan administration, since HA in the Carter years under the feisty leadership of Assistant Secretary Patricia Derian had been a key advocate for human rights activity within an often-less-than-enthusiastic foreign affairs bureaucracy. HA, frequently in alliance with members of Congress, their staffs, and human rights interest groups, had been a key force in bringing some of President Carter's rhetoric on human rights to practical implementation.[33] To succeed Derian, Reagan nominated Ernest W. Lefever, a clergyman and scholar who directed the Ethics and Public Policy Center in Washington. Though he had the credentials that might have been expected of a human rights activist, Lefever advocated a U.S. stance that few would describe as energetic. In his confirmation hearings before the Senate Foreign Relations Committee, Lefever outlined four ways in which "the United States can advance the cause of freedom and dignity beyond our borders": remain a good example of domestic human rights practices; "stand by our allies and our friends when their survival as independent states is jeopardized by external military pressure or political subversion"; utilize quiet diplomacy with states violating their citizens' human rights; and condemn "gross violations" that "at present . . . are perpetrated largely by adversary states, notably the Soviet Union."[34]

The Lefever nomination was strongly opposed by the domestic interest groups that had developed into the human rights community during the 1970s. There organizations believed that the new administration wished to do as little as possible to advance human rights, and the nomination hearings offered them a dramatic chance to focus their dissent on a clear up-or-down issue. Among those testifying against Lefever were leaders of Clergy and Laity Concerned, the Lawyers' Committee for International Human Rights, the NAACP, the National Council of Churches of Christ, and the United States Helsinki Watch Committee. A particularly vivid public impression was made by the attendance at the hearings of Jacobo Timerman, an Argentine editor and survivor of political imprisonment. Timerman's indictment of official torture and anti-Semitism in Argentina, *Prisoner without a Name, Cell without a Number*,[35] had just been published. The hearings became a major news story in the United States, and the committee reported adversely on the nomination by a vote of 13 to 4, with political moderates from the Republican committee majority joining all the Democratic committee members in opposition. Chairman Senator Charles Percy (R-IL) explained his negative vote:

On the basis of his long-held and firmly expressed views on human rights and foreign policy, Dr. Lefever's confirmation would be an unfortunate symbol and signal to the rest of the world. Whatever he may say, he is associated with a strident and vocal "hands-off" policy. His confirmation would be especially unfortunate if his intention, as the State Department's chief advocate for human rights, is to pursue quiet diplomacy as his general strategy, for he . . . fails to display the personal empathy and diplomatic qualities necessary to make such a strategy work.[36]

The Lefever nomination was withdrawn before a floor vote could be taken. The human rights community celebrated, and indeed they had shown the new administration (using a weapon—bad publicity—that Reagan's advisers were especially likely to take seriously) that a simple abandonment of Carter's human rights policies would not be feasible.[37] What lines of action *would* be pursued, however, came to depend on a combination of conservative ideology, political changes in Latin America, and (especially) policy entrepreneurship from within the Reagan camp.

The key policy entrepreneur in the human rights field during the Reagan years was Elliott Abrams, a young lawyer who began his government career as a staff aide to Senators Henry M. Jackson (D-WA) and Daniel P. Moynihan (D-NY). In late 1981 Abrams played an important role in devising a new human rights strategy for the administration. An "eyes only" memorandum for Secretary Haig that was at least inspired (and probably written) by Abrams stated: "Congressional belief that we have no consistent human rights policy threatens to disrupt important foreign-policy initiatives." The remedy should be to make clear that "human rights is at the core of our foreign policy" while adopting a definition of human rights as "political rights and civil liberties" and by implication placing less emphasis on protections of the person against torture, murder, and arbitrary imprisonment.[38] Under this new approach, the administration would be able to combine its strong emphasis on opposition to (nondemocratic) Communism with ostensible support for the cause of human rights. A week after the memorandum was sent, Abrams was nominated as assistant secretary at HA; he was confirmed easily.

Abrams developed a human rights policy toward Latin America that consisted of three main components. First, some stress was placed on reporting abuses of human rights by foreign governments, including those in Latin America. HA was already obliged by law to prepare annual *Country Reports on Human Rights Practices* in all foreign nations, and the Reagan administration at times displayed objectivity and energy in producing these reports. Human rights advocates were often of two minds about these documents. They gave credit to the administration for instances of clear reporting but also criticized what they saw as continued distortions in coverage of conservative regimes that enjoyed the backing of U.S. foreign policy.[39]

Second, the administration's rhetoric (even in some of the *Country Reports*) stressed political rights and the development of democratic practices such as elections. "Free elections are not simply a human rights goal," the new assistant secretary observed shortly after the 1982 election in El Salvador. "They are also the means which will guarantee that other human rights are also respected. . . . That is why free elections should be the very heart of the human rights movement."[40] This theme in human rights policy was compatible with the administration's idea for Project Democracy, launched with some fanfare by a presidential speech in 1982. This initiative aimed to diffuse democratic ideas and procedures through international education, student exchanges, and other means.

Third (and, some argued, most basically), few concrete policy steps were taken to challenge Latin American governments that abused the human rights of their citizens, except Cuba and Nicaragua. The administration frequently stated its devotion to quiet diplomacy as the best way to persuade errant governments to mend their ways. Yet one of the best kinds of evidence that such persuasion was being tried—the occasional eruption of public disputes such as had marked the Carter government's dealings with Argentina, Brazil, and other nations—was almost wholly lacking during the Reagan years. (One of the few documented instances of Reagan-era diplomatic pressure upon an ally on behalf of fundamental human rights was a visit by Vice President George Bush to El Salvador in 1983.)

Meanwhile, the United States moved to ease its policies toward a number of authoritarian governments with poor human rights records. Early in its tenure, the Reagan administration ceased opposing loans by international financial institutions to Argentina, Chile, Uruguay, and Paraguay;[41] military assistance in 1982 to Haiti's "Baby Doc" Duvalier was triple that provided by Carter the preceding year; limited military sales were resumed to Guatemala, and the administration fruitlessly sought congressional approval to reestablish military assistance to that repressive military regime.[42] Far from apologizing for this policy of selective action, Abrams argued strongly that human rights policy could not depart too far from what he saw as the broader goals of general foreign policy. Human rights, he stated, "are not a free-floating goal to be considered in isolation each morning. We do not betray the cause of human rights when we make prudential judgments about what can and can't be done in one place at one time."[43] Responding to critics of U.S. backing for the Salvadoran and Honduran governments in 1983, Abrams stated: "It is no part of a human rights policy to allow [these regimes] to be replaced by communist dictatorships. . . . our goal is not purity; we do not live in utopia. Our goal is effectiveness in a violent and bitterly divided area of the world."[44]

Human rights organizations viewed this three-part policy as too weak to be effective and as offering—in most instances—the mere pretense of opposing repression by Latin American governments.[45] In congressional testimony and in numerous publications, advocates for human rights adopted an approach of carefully distinguishing among the human rights policies followed by different segments of the executive branch toward different countries in the Western Hemisphere. At times, HA and Assistant Secretary Abrams were praised for specific decisions, while trenchant criticism was presented of other lines of action.[46] The public debate on U.S. policy toward hemispheric human rights sometimes became strident and polarized, a series of bitter polemics in which Abrams appeared to take some relish. Not surprisingly, the deepest division of views was over Central America, an area considered politically vital by the Reagan administration but one where Washington assigned a low priority to human rights. One administration critic wrote in 1983 that "in El Salvador and Guatemala the administration's acquiescence in practices of torture and mass murder by client governments comes perilously close to endorsement of offenses condemned at the Nuremberg War Crimes Tribunals," a charge Abrams dismissed as "slander" and "intellectual thuggery."[47]

Interest groups favorable to human rights were never able to force the Reagan administration to adopt an activist stance against official torture and murder in Latin America. Foreign policy administrators could frequently avoid the letter of legal requirements (with some limited exceptions in dealing with Central America), and the cumbersome legislative process was ill-suited to the job of enforcement.[48] In any case, the administration's emphasis on elections in Central America successfully drew attention away from human rights and produced such effective advocates for executive policies (in dealings with Capitol Hill) as President José Napoleón Duarte of El Salvador.[49] Administration planners did not fear losing the votes of human rights supporters, since they were assumed to be pro-democratic and "nothing will make them happy."[50] However, the human rights movement may have contributed to a major aspect of Reagan administration policy toward Central America: the absence of U.S. direct military intervention in Nicaragua or El Salvador, which seemed especially likely in late 1983 and early 1984. Human rights activists may have been a significant part of the chorus persuading the administration that it did not have public backing for a military adventure in Central America.

The United States continued to stress elections as a political recipe in Latin America after Abrams became assistant secretary for inter-American affairs in the second Reagan term, replaced by Richard Schifter, a quieter and less acerbic lawyer, at HA. This "pro-democracy" policy was very largely symbolic, but it did reap some political benefits for Washington in the late 1980s as most Latin American nations installed governments with at least nominal electoral backing. Most of these democratic or semidemocratic transitions were very much rooted in local political conditions and "mainly the result of internal dynamics."[51] U.S. policy did make a practical contribution to democratization in Chile, where administration planners after 1985 came to fear seriously that another Nicaragua might develop if deep polarization remained between the government headed by Gen. Augusto Pinochet and most civilian political groups. In a rare instance of coinciding views among the administration, nongovernmental organizations favoring human rights, and congressional human rights backers, U.S. policy worked actively for a fair plebiscite in 1988 in accord with Chile's constitution. Partly animated by U.S. Ambassador to Chile Harry Barnes, Washington helped to encourage and finance the Chilean opposition while warning Pinochet against closing off the consultative process prior to his October 1988 rejection by Chilean voters.[52]

The Haitian crisis that began in 1991 posed a very thorny challenge to U.S. human rights policy, as it did to the administration's handling of migration. Washington's ambassador, Alvin P. Adams Jr., had charted a farsighted course of support for the 1990 elections and for Aristide's fledgling government. After the Haitian president's escape to Venezuela following the coup, U.S. policy remained constructive in several key respects. The United States continued to recognize Aristide as Haiti's legitimate leader; Adams was withdrawn from Port-au-Prince in a sign of disapproval; and most important, through January 1992 the United States supported economic sanctions voted by the OAS intended to oblige the Haitian military and economic elites to restore Aristide to full authority.

Unfortunately, the Bush administration's urgent concern to stem the outflow of Haitian boat people severely undercut these positive steps. As soon as the U.S. courts gave permission, the great majority of the Haitians held at Guantánamo were forcibly repatriated to Haiti by the Coast Guard. At exactly the same time, U.S. backing for OAS sanctions was relaxed, with no political concessions forthcoming from the junta. This step was intended to improve the economic conditions that former refugees would find in Haiti and to avoid the clear self-contradiction that would be involved for the U.S. government in returning refugees to a nation while condemning its rulers as violators of human rights. The net result, however, was to render U.S. human rights policy (at least in Haiti) bankrupt for the time being. The United States had for ten years proclaimed that it backed democracy as the surest guarantee of effective human rights. In Haiti its policy had come down to supporting neither democracy nor human rights.[53]

By the beginning of the 1990s in most cases other than Haiti, El Salvador, and Guatemala, the key issues involving human rights in Latin America had changed from what they were ten years earlier. No longer was the central problem how to deal with murderers and torturers in full control of governments. Instead, the more usual question about Latin American nations had become, What is the quality of democratic practice, and what role will human rights play in improving prospects for democratic practice in the future? Human rights, though less often violated as a matter of national policy on the part of Latin American governments, continued to be politically important in two senses. In a number of nations civil-military relations were strained by the issue of how past human rights violations should be punished, if at all. In addition, some Latin American police forces continued to violate human rights routinely on the local level as part of long-established "anticriminal" campaigns.[54]

The Reagan and Bush policies toward human rights and Latin American democracy left the United States, for the most part, poorly prepared to deal effectively with these new questions. Having only a very limited record in condemning human rights abuses when they occurred, the U.S. government had little standing to aid hemispheric nations in retrospective searches for truth, justice, or both. Similarly, Washington's record of relative passivity when human rights victims included prominent elite leaders did not suggest that U.S. representatives would act effectively to oppose vigilante suppression largely aimed at the poorest classes.

Conclusion: Coherent and Coordinated Migration and Human Rights Policies?

Neither the executive branch nor mobilized interest groups and their occasional allies in Congress were able to produce fully coherent policies on Latin American migration or human rights during the 1980s. The Reagan and Bush administrations exercised the initiative in these fields, but each often pursued conflicting goals. Generally speaking, these chief executives sought to restrict unauthorized immigration. But concerns of ideology, broader foreign policy, and the varied costs of frontier enforcement kept qualifying this stance. Politically motivated migrants from Haiti, El Salvador, and Guatemala were to be deterred or deported, but most of those from Cuba and Nicaragua were made welcome. Undocumented migration from Mexico was to be reduced—except that U.S. agribusiness had to be mollified with SAWS, and it was well recognized that the U.S.-Mexican border could not be effectively sealed to exclude northbound workers. To confront migration emergencies on sea or land, the executive branch seemed to have prepared few administrative plans and virtually no blueprints for winning long-term domestic political support for restrictionist measures.

The two U.S. administrations of the 1980s tended to support Western Hemisphere human rights (usually defined as political rights) with rhetoric and better reporting but little action. The State Department and other U.S. agencies compiled their best human rights records in cases like Chile under Ambassador Barnes and Haiti under Ambassador Adams. In such instances, a committed diplomat on the scene could present—to Washington and to the local government—the defense of human rights and the pursuit of democracy as very closely intertwined. As state violations of human rights gradually diminished after the early 1980s, U.S. human rights policy was under less pressure to demonstrate activism. However, the seeming lack of basic conviction displayed by the Reagan human rights policies (most of which the Bush administration inherited) left them very vulnerable to renewed abuse of citizens by Latin American governments. In addition, as the Haitian case demonstrated in 1991–92, human rights considerations were likely to be subordinated to other policy priorities, including the exclusion of refugees from the United States.

Interest groups concerned with immigration policy and seeking to influence administration actions in that field tended to be much more diverse and divided than those focusing on Washington's human rights policies. Contending social interests on the matter of Mexican migration were so random that five years and parts of three congressional sessions were needed to produce IRCA. While spokespersons for specific migrant groups from Haiti and Central America used the courts and congressional lobbying with impressive skill, their movements faced stubborn administrative resistance and sometimes strong restrictionist pressure groups; many years were needed for them to produce measurable change in U.S. policy. The human rights movement, by contrast, became more consolidated and institutionalized during the 1980s but was able to produce only a modest practical response from HA and other U.S. agencies.

The Reagan and Bush administrations' policy disarray was most clearly visible in cases (such as El Salvador and Haiti) where crises of human rights and migration occurred simultaneously and abusive governments generated refugees. In these instances, domestic critics of administration policies in both issue areas tended to ally closely with each other, producing major political clashes with the Executive Branch in Congress and at the grass roots. At times, especially in its policies under the Mica Amendment and during President Aristide's government in Port-au-Prince in 1991, Washington sought a positive link between human rights and migration policies. For the most part, however, even in these critical cases the influence of ideology and broader foreign policy clearly outranked the U.S. government's nominal embrace of *both* human rights and even-handed policies toward migrants.

It appears likely that both migration and human rights—and the connections between them—will persist as significant concerns in inter-American relations in coming years. This is especially true in a period marked by continuing political conflict in Latin America, relatively easy population mobility among nations, and mass-media exposure able to dramatize the often-harsh encounter between individuals and the state. The policies followed by the United States during the 1980s toward these wrenching political and social processes offer only ambiguous guidance to assist with what may prove to be very difficult policy choices in the future.

Notes

1. Alex Stepick, "Unintended Consequences: Rejecting Haitian Boat People and Destabilizing Duvalier," in Christopher Mitchell, ed., *Western Hemisphere Immigration and United States Foreign Policy* (University Park, Pa.: Penn State Press, 1992), pp. 133–41; Wayne S. Smith, *The Closest of Enemies* (New York: Norton, 1987), chap. 8.

2. See Milton D. Morris, *Immigration: The Beleaguered Bureaucracy* (Washington DC: Brookings Institution, 1985), p. 25; Robert Pear, "New Restrictions on Immigration Gain Public Support, Poll Shows," *New York Times*, 1 July 1986, pp. A1, A21; and Edwin Harwood, "Alienation: American Attitudes toward Immigration," *Public Opinion* (June–July 1983): 50–51.

3. Jorge I. Domínguez, "Cooperating with the Enemy? U.S. Immigration Policies toward Cuba," in Mitchell, ed., *Western Hemisphere Immigration*, esp. pp. 47–50.

4. A federal appeals court ruled in 1985 that "because the statutory obligations [to permit applications for asylum] do not exist until an alien comes within the United States, plainly the Executive *can* avoid those obligations by interdicting the Haitians on the high seas. . . . Until a person has a right, there can be no denial of that right." *Haitian Refugee Center v. Gracey*, 809 F2d 794.

5. Stepick, "Unintended Consequences," pp. 147 ff.

6. Sergio Aguayo and Patricia Weiss Fagen, *Central Americans in the United States and Mexico* (Washington DC: Georgetown University Hemispheric Migration Project, 1987), p. 2A. The estimate of Salvadorans is for 1985, those for Nicaraguans and Guatemalans for 1986.

7. Lars Schoultz, "Central America and the Politicization of U.S. Immigration Policy," in Mitchell, ed., *Western Hemisphere Immigration*, esp. pp. 169–81. The Reagan administration consistently requested the allocation of a few refugee visas for Latin America and the Caribbean and planned to use most of those for Cubans. For 1986, for example, three thousand visas were requested for the Western Hemisphere, out of a worldwide total of 70,000. See "Proposed Refugee Admissions for FY 1986," U.S. Department of State, *Current Policy* 738, (September 1985): 1.

8. Patricia Weiss Fagen, "Applying for Political Asylum in New York: Law, Policy and Administrative Practice," New York University Center for Latin American and Caribbean Studies, Occasional Paper 41, 1984.

9. INS data, cited in Christopher Mitchell, "Changing the Rules: The Impact of the Simpson/Rodino Act on Inter-American Diplomacy," in Georges Vernez, ed., *Immigration and International Relations* (Washington DC: Urban Institute Press, 1990), tables 2, 3.

10. Robert Pear, "Key Federal Aide Refuses to Deport Any Nicaraguans," *New York Times*, 17 April 1986, pp. A1, A28.

11. Quoted in Robert Tomsho, *The American Sanctuary Movement* (Austin: Texas Monthly Press, 1987), p. 31.

12. "A Debate on Sanctuary," *Newsletter on Church and State Abroad* 7 (July 1985) (New York: Council on Religion and International Affairs), pp. 4–5.

13. "Six Convicted of Plot to Smuggle in Aliens for U.S. Sanctuary," *New*

York Times, 2 May 1986, pp. A1, A19. See also Tomsho, *American Sanctuary Movement*, chap. 9, 10.

14. Michael Teitelbaum, *Latin Migration North: The Problem for U.S. Foreign Policy* (New York: Council on Foreign Relations, 1985), pp. 24–25. See also Kenneth Hill, "Illegal Aliens: An Assessment," in Daniel B. Levine, Kenneth Hill, and Robert Warren, eds., *Immigration Statistics: A Story of Neglect* (Washington DC: National Academy Press, 1985), p. 243.

15. Michael Teitelbaum, "Right versus Right: Immigration and Refugee Policy in the United States," *Foreign Affairs* 59, no. 1 (fall 1980).

16. For the text of IRCA, see U.S. House of Representatives, 99th Cong. 2d sess., *Immigration Reform and Control Act of 1986* (report 99-1000).

17. Joel Brinkley, "U.S. Aides Harshly Assail Mexico on Drugs, Immigration and Graft," *New York Times* national edition, 14 May 1986, pp. 1, 4.

18. The most thorough examination of whether foreign policy issues affected the drafting of Simpson/Rodino is Carlos Rico, "Migration and U.S.-Mexican Relations," in Mitchell, ed., *Western Hemisphere Immigration*, esp. pp. 250–70.

19. Mitchell, "Changing the Rules," pp. 179–85.

20. Frank D. Bean, Barry Edmonston, and Jeffrey S. Passel, eds., *Undocumented Migration to the United States: IRCA and the Experience of the 1980s* (Washington DC: Urban Institute Press, 1990), esp. chap. 9.

21. Richard W. Stevenson, "U.S. Work Barrier to Illegal Aliens Doesn't Stop Them," *New York Times*, 9 October 1989, pp. A1, A13; Tim Golden, "Mexicans Head North despite Rules on Jobs," *New York Times*, 13 December 1991, pp. A1, A28.

22. Cf. *Reagan on Cuba*, a pamphlet published by the Cuban-American National Foundation (Washington DC: 1986).

23. Kenneth N. Skoug, "The U.S.-Cuba Migration Agreement: Resolving Mariel," U.S. Department of State, *Current Policy* 1050 (March 1988).

24. Colleen O'Connor with Ginny Carroll, "Men without a Country," *Newsweek*, 9 June 1986, p. 28; Ronald Smothers, "Court Orders Five Deported to Cuba," *New York Times*, 1 December 1988, p. A23.

25. Barry Bearak, "New Tide of Nicaraguans Swamps U.S. Border Cities," *Los Angeles Times*, 24 December 1988, pp. 1, 14.

26. Julie Morris, "Refugees 'Saturate' Texas County," *USA Today*, 5 December 1988, p. 6A. The Bush policy toward Nicaraguans well illustrates a broader pattern in U.S. government treatment of migrants from Latin American regimes perceived as politically hostile by Washington. Early waves of migrants from such nations, in which relatively affluent social and economic groups predominate, tend to be welcomed officially. Later waves containing larger numbers of the poor (and sometimes racial minorities) tend to face a harsher administrative response.

27. Quoted in Roberto Suro, "In Texas, the Door to Central Americans Opens a Crack," *New York Times*, 28 January 1990, p. 4.

28. Amnesty International reported that fifteen hundred persons had probably been killed following the coup. See Amnesty's report, *Haiti: The Human Rights Tragedy—Human Rights Violations since the Coup* (New York, 1992), p. 3.

29. Some Haitians (fourteen hundred by 10 February 1992) from the post-Aristide boatlift did reach Florida from Guatánamo Bay, as a result of INS asylum hearings held there that applied a more lenient standard than had been used at sea from 1981 to 1991.

30. 2 February 1992.

31. Larry Rohter, "Haven for Haitians Backed in Miami," *New York Times*, 5 February 1992, p. A8.

32. Quoted in Tamar Jacoby, "The Reagan Turnaround on Human Rights," *Foreign Affairs* 64, no. 5 (summer 1986): 1069.

33. Lars Schoultz, *Human Rights and United States Foreign Policy toward Latin America* (Princeton, N.J.: Princeton University Press, 1981), passim, esp. chaps. 3, 8. Some scholars contend that the Carter administration did more to implement its human rights policies in Latin America than in any other region; see David Carleton and Michael Stohl, "The Foreign Policy of Human Rights: Rhetoric and Reality from Jimmy Carter to Ronald Reagan," *Human Rights Quarterly* 7, no. 2 (May 1985): 205–29.

34. *Hearings on the Nomination of Ernest W. Lefever to be Assistant Secretary of State for Human Rights and Humanitarian Affairs*, Committee on Foreign Relations, U.S. Senate, 96th Cong. 1st sess., pp. 68–69.

35. New York: Alfred A. Knopf, 1981.

36. *Hearings on the Nomination of Ernest W. Lefever*, p. 506.

37. The Reagan administration was also becoming aware at this time that it would have to devise at least a minimal policy in the field of human rights in order to accord with legal mandates that called for reporting, certification, and other concrete administrative actions. A. Glenn Mower Jr., *Human Rights and American Foreign Policy: The Carter and Reagan Experiences* (Westport, Conn.: Greenwood, 1987), pp. 34–35.

38. Barbara Crossette, "Strong U.S. Human Rights Policy Urged in Memo Approved by Haig," *New York Times*, 5 November 1981, pp. A1, A11, and excerpts from the memo text, p. A10.

39. Human Rights Watch, together with the Lawyers' Committee for International Human Rights, publishes annual critical reviews of the *Country Reports*. See, for example, *Critique: Review of the Department of State's Country Reports of Human Rights Practices for 1987* (New York, 1988). That volume observes (p. 3) that "despite repeated criticism on this score, foreign policy considerations continue to taint the State Department's human rights

reporting." Cf. also Mower, *Human Rights and American Foreign Policy*, pp. 112–13.

40. Quoted in Charles Maechling Jr., "Human Rights Dehumanized," *Foreign Policy* 52 (fall 1983): 124.

41. Mower, *Human Rights and American Foreign Policy*, p. 109.

42. Thomas Carothers, *In the Name of Democracy: U.S. Policy toward Latin America in the Reagan Years* (Berkeley: University of California Press, 1991), pp. 60–63.

43. Quoted in Jacoby, "The Reagan Turnaround on Human Rights," p. 1078.

44. Abrams, "Human Rights Policy," in U.S. Department of State, Bureau of Public Affairs, "Human Rights and Foreign Policy," *Selected Documents* 22 (December 1983).

45. As Joseph Eldridge, director of the Washington Office on Latin America (WOLA), told a congressional committee in 1983, "The preponderance of the evidence suggests that the Reagan administration has simply not discharged its human rights obligations adequately. . . . The spirit of the human rights statutes is blithely ignored." *Review of U.S. Human Rights Policy*, Hearings before the Subcommittee on Human Rights and International Organizations of the Committee on Foreign Affairs, House of Representatives, 98th Cong. 1st sess., June 1983, pp. 117–18.

46. See the statements by Aryeh Neier, vice chairman of Americas Watch, and Jo Marie Griesgraber, deputy director of WOLA, in *Human Rights in Argentina, Chile, Paraguay and Uruguay*, Hearings before the Subcommittees on Human Rights and International Organizations on Western Hemisphere Affairs of the Committee on Foreign Affairs, House of Representatives, 98th Congress., 1st sess., October 1983, pp. 31–48, 97–116, respectively. Cf. also Cynthia Brown, ed., *With Friends Like These: The Americas Watch Report on Human Rights and U.S. Policy in Latin America* (New York: Pantheon, 1985), esp. chap. 1.

47. The critical quote is from Maechling, "Human Rights Dehumanized," p. 118; Abrams's response is in *Foreign Policy* 53 (winter 1983–84): 174. Cynthia Brown described Abrams's style as "argument-by-invective," *With Friends Like These*, p. 11.

48. Cf. David P. Forsythe, *Human Rights and U.S. Foreign Policy: Congress Reconsidered* (Gainesville: University of Florida Press, 1988), chap. 5.

49. Joseph Eldridge, "U.S. Human Rights Policy: Instruments and Directions," presented at Latin American Studies Association (LASA) 16th International Congress, Washington DC, 6 April 1991.

50. Presentation by Thomas Carothers at panel on Human Rights and U.S. Policy in Latin America, LASA 16th International Congress, Washington DC, 6 April 1991.

51. Francisco Orrego Vicuña, "Domestic Policies and External Influences

on the Human Rights Debate in Latin America," in R. J. Vincent, ed., *Foreign Policy and Human Rights: Issues and Responses* (Cambridge, England: Cambridge University Press, 1986), p. 112.

52. See Carothers, *In the Name of Democracy,* pp. 149–63; also Cynthia Brown and Katherine Rogers Hite, "U.S. Human Rights Policy toward Chile," presented at LASA 16th International Congress, Washington DC, 6 April 1991. The administration's human rights reporting on Chile for 1987 was lauded as "something of a model for how the State Department could be reporting on other countries." Human Rights Watch and Lawyers' Committee for Human Rights, *Critique,* p. 17.

53. On the intersection of human rights and migration issues in the 1991–92 Haitian events, see Doris Meissner, "The Crisis at Guantánamo Bay: Two Faces of U.S. Policy," *Foreign Service Journal* (March 1992); National Immigration, Refugee and Citizenship Forum, *Information Bulletin,* 6 March 1992, pp. 1–3; Amnesty International, *Haiti: The Human Rights Tragedy.*

54. Paulo Sérgio Pinheiro, "The Legacy of Authoritarianism in Democratic Brazil." Paper presented at the New York University Colloquium on Law and Society, New York, 17 February 1992.

William O. Walker III

Drug Control and U.S. Hegemony

This chapter analyzes the war on drugs in the Americas from 1960 to the present by asking a series of related questions: What were U.S. policy goals and options at any given time? What basic assumptions shaped the choices policy makers made? How did policy outcomes influence later efforts at drug control? To what extent did events external to drug control affect patterns of control? In other words, this chapter endeavors to find out what officials learned from earlier efforts to expand U.S.-style drug control throughout the Americas and how they incorporated what they did learn into subsequent policy. We begin with a brief assessment of the current situation.

During the 1980s the White House employed counternarcotics policy in a failed attempt to bolster U.S. hegemony throughout the region. That endeavor, as we shall see, had its roots in the 1960s, when traditional drug control policy and Washington's quest to define a common security agenda for the Americas initially coincided. The close association of drugs and security with the political economy of hegemony did not long endure and provided an ironic denouement to the war on drugs in the 1980s. That is, the more the United States managed to join drug control and security policies, the greater the autonomy Latin American leaders from Mexico to the Andean nations had to pursue antidrug policies of their own making.

By late December 1993 President Bill Clinton's drug control policy for the Western Hemisphere largely resembled that of his two Republican predecessors. The policy's twin pillars—control at the source and interdiction, with emphasis upon the former albeit through a reduced foreign assistance program—suggested the absence of historical memory and the paucity of imagination on the part of policy makers. These structural similarities, however, did not necessarily signify that Clinton's policy was serving the same function as had drug policy for Presidents Ronald Reagan and George Bush. Vestiges, though, of the drugs-cum-security policy link remained as the Clinton administration reportedly continued to rely on Haitian military officers as "intelligence assets" in the battle against drug trafficking in the Caribbean.[1]

The general outlines of inter-American drug policy at the end of 1993 are familiar to scholars, foreign policy analysts, and policy makers. That is, there exists a kind of grand strategy; the objective of the war on drugs has been to reduce the traffic in illegal opiates, cocaine, and marijuana. This supply-side approach to drugs has as its ultimate goal the maintenance of an antidrug regime, the contours of which have historically been set by the United States. Success in this endeavor means control at the source—specifically, a dramatic lessening of the production of raw drug materials. Despite the nearly total failure to reach this primary objective at any time in the course of the antidrug effort, no alternative strategy has been proffered to replace the supply-side approach. Such has been the practical effect of U.S. influence over the movement.

Along with control at the source, U.S. officials pursued the interdiction of drugs in transit as a primary strategy. Yet as early as the mid-1930s, the limits of interdiction were clear to U.S. drug control officials. In fact, rarely have they claimed more than a 10 or 15 percent rate of success for interdiction. Nevertheless, since at least 1969 the government has increasingly relied upon interdiction as a basic part of antidrug strategy. As a result, the high visibility of interdiction efforts, however successful, has been used to cast blame for the lack of control at the source upon producer nations. The premise underlying this development asserts that producer states lack the political will to control drugs. Recently, the United States has endeavored in a concerted fashion to reduce the laundering of drug money around the world. Revelations in 1991 about the drug-related activities of the Bank of Credit and Commerce International portrayed barely the tip of the laundering iceberg.[2]

The war against drugs in this century can be divided into five periods. The first two, 1909 to 1920 and 1921 to 1937, when the League of Nations Opium Advisory Committee led the antinarcotics movement, viewed drug control as a policy objective in its own right.

Then, with the outbreak in 1937 of the Sino-Japanese War, control and national security became one—a situation that lasted until Japan's defeat in August 1945. Next, U.S. drug policy was formulated in the shadow of Cold War security concerns. Even efforts to improve global instruments of control came within the context of larger policy concerns. Finally, Operation Intercept in 1969 enhanced public awareness of drug trafficking and usage, moving authorities in Washington to perceive drug control as a policy issue of the first priority. That they were prepared to do so reflects the joining of drug control with other objectives in U.S.–Latin American relations during the 1960s.

The aftermath of World War II witnessed an increase in drug consumption in the United States and the revival of an active, illicit drug trade from Mexico. Not satisfied with the responses of the Mexican government to diplomatic overtures, the United States chided Mexico in 1947 at the second meeting of the UN Commission on Narcotic Drugs (CND). This rebuke had the desired effect when officials in Mexico City promised to strengthen their domestic antidrug operations and soon took a far more active role in the work of the CND.

U.S. authorities also feared that postwar prosperity might stimulate an international trade in cocaine. Accordingly, they supported a UN mission sent to Bolivia and Peru to evaluate the role of coca in Andean society. The Commission of Inquiry on the Coca Leaf, evoking the traditional importance of coca, concluded that only improved socioeconomic conditions in producing regions or stronger government action could conceivably curb coca growing. Nevertheless, nothing in the commission's findings made U.S. officials doubt that Andean authorities were more or less favorably disposed toward the ultimate adoption of a U.S.-style program for coca control. That basic policy assumption withstood serious challenge until the 1960s.

Instances like those involving Mexico and Bolivia and Peru do not fully reveal the intersection of security policy and drug control activities in the early Cold War. Rather, it was in Asia that such a nexus became most discernible and where the stage was set for what later occurred in Latin America. Recent scholarship has clarified the place of opium in the making of modern Asia.[3] U.S. drug officials, in setting aside their own objectives in the larger search for security, lost a sense of proportion about drug control. The illicit traffic out of Asia constituted a serious foreign policy problem, not a dire threat to national security. Yet U.S. efforts to propagate a supply-side strategy rendered drug policy hostage to more important foreign and security policy interests. In this way the connection between drugs and security was cemented. To perpetuate the influence of the Federal Bureau of Narcotics (FBN), one of the Drug Enforcement Administration's DEA) predecessor agencies, drug control authorities had accepted a subordinate place at the policy-making table, one that all but guaranteed that the FBN and its successors would be included as appropriate in the making and implementation of national security policy.[4]

Turning drug control in the Americas into a security-related matter would not be accomplished as quickly. The effort actually had begun during the war as Peru supplied cocaine to the Allies for medical purposes under the Lend-Lease program. After 1945, however, with U.S. security policy primarily focused on Europe and Asia, the promotion of drug control in Latin America became the responsibility of the CND or was relegated to low-level U.S. diplomats serving in producer or transit states. The success of the Cuban Revolution in 1959 and the attendant rise of left-wing anti-Americanism in Latin America dramatically transformed the situation. The Western Hemisphere had become a major theater in the Cold War.

U.S. drug officials, led since 1930 by FBN chief Harry J. Anslinger, who possessed impeccable anti-Communist credentials, were predisposed to believe that revolutionaries would stop at nothing to achieve their goals. Anslinger had long charged the Chinese and other Asian Communists with trafficking in drugs. He therefore had no trouble in linking Fidel Castro's Cuba to the international drug trade, alleging that Cuba and China had formed an unholy alliance to undermine the West with drugs. Scholars have been critical of Anslinger on this issue, but he understood precisely what he was doing—as did Ambassador Lewis Tambs, who charged in the 1980s that narcoguerrillas were heavily involved in the South American cocaine trade. Anslinger was arrogating to the FBN a supporting role in the struggle against Communism.

Viewing the FBN as part of the national security state puts a far different analytical light than ever before on regional and global developments in drug control in the 1960s. The fashioning of a Single

Convention on Narcotic Drugs, finally accomplished in 1961, stands out not only as testimony to Anslinger's career-long advocacy of control at the source but also as evidence of how the United States propped up the existing international drug control regime and sustained dominance over it. In the process, security policy and antinarcotics activity became tightly enmeshed.

U.S. officials could only promote inter-American drug control as a foreign policy priority by defining cocaine production, for example, as a grave threat to the security of the United States, the producer nations, or both. Yet how, it must be asked, could cocaine undermine hemispheric security? Answering this question requires placing the political economy of the cocaine trade in a broader context. Understanding U.S. policy toward Latin America during the Cold War and also recognizing historic U.S. claims of hegemony in the hemisphere provide the appropriate framework.

Ideological ardor in the Cold War moved the United States to follow a two-pronged policy toward Latin America: opposition to the spread of Communism and support for the growth of a free market economy.[5] As needed, these pillars of U.S. policy also included the fashioning of economic development programs through private and public investment and reliance on counterinsurgency tactics (about which more later) to overcome perceived threats to political stability from anticapitalist, leftist revolutionaries. Political scientist D. Michael Shafer observes that U.S. policy thus emphasized the interdependence of development and security.[6] Without this explanatory framework, it is not easy to understand, for example, U.S. tolerance of the revolution in Bolivia in 1952, the unrealistic expectations that shaped Washington's response to selective democratic reforms in Colombia in the early 1960s, or U.S. concern about the revolutionary military regime in Peru in the late 1960s and the 1970s.

By 1969 U.S. policy makers concluded that controlling the illegal drug traffic would help maintain U.S. hegemony over Latin America because the trade threatened development and, hence, undermined security.[7] In the 1960s two important developments influenced U.S. drug policy. First, the signing and ratification of the 1961 Single Convention on Narcotic Drugs indicated that a global consensus had been reached favoring the supply-side approach to control. Thereafter, narcotics control almost imperceptibly yet inexorably became a matter of international as well as national security.

Also the response in Washington to the Single Convention was to emphasize bilateral relations. Doing so made frustration the order of the day as drugs from Southeast Asia continued to flow into the West and Latin America became a greater source than ever for cocaine, marijuana, and heroin. Demand for these drugs by recreational and heavy consumers seemed to rise exponentially. Yet organizational changes failed to curb demand; the FBN, mired in scandal, became in 1968 the Bureau of Narcotics and Dangerous Drugs (BNDD). But the BNDD had no one of Anslinger's stature to dominate the policy-making process, an organizational debility that may have ironically accelerated the association between security and drugs throughout the federal bureaucracy.

Chaos did not necessarily reign supreme, however. The 1960s opened with an urgent appeal from Mexico City to the Eisenhower administration for antidrug cooperation and assistance. The tone of the appeal and U.S. responses throughout the decade served the political needs of those who defined drug control as a security matter. By 1964 the Agency for International Development (AID) in the Department of State had devised a program that anticipated future U.S. antidrug assistance programs. Included in the aid package were funds for both crop eradication and the purchase of weapons to stanch the illicit trafficking out of Mexico. Under President Lyndon B. Johnson, officials tried to formalize all transborder antidrug operations with Mexico but failed because of the largely unilateral nature of the plans. Such was one of the grave drawbacks of U.S. assertions of hegemony.[8] Put another way, U.S. plans for inter-American narcotics control tended, at that time and later, to compromise the sovereignty of producer and transit states—or so charged critics of U.S. policy.

In the Andes, an Inter-American Consultative Group on Coca Leaf Problems met at Lima in 1964, achieving only meager results as it sought ways to restrict the production, distribution, and consumption of coca and its chief by-product, cocaine. Bolivia would not even sign the Single Convention until 1975; and Peru, although a signatory power, declared that reduction of the coca crop could not even be considered for perhaps twenty-five years. Complicating the already sensitive relations between Washington and Lima was the establishment of a national coca monopoly in 1969, the Empresa Nacional de la Coca.[9] As was the case with the state-run opium and opiate monopolies in an earlier era in Asia, a coca monopoly in the

Andes directly threatened U.S. objectives in the antidrug effort there.

Both the Mexican and Peruvian cases reveal how important the issue of political will had become to Washington's quest for more effective drug control. After the early 1960s, U.S. authorities no longer assumed that Latin American states were predisposed to adopt U.S.-style controls. Indeed, the state-as-actor approach, a corollary of the supply-side philosophy that had long informed regional drug policy, gradually became the recalcitrant state-as-actor perspective. Thus arose the atmosphere of suspicion that has pervaded drug control in the Americas ever since.

Proposals for narcotics control would thereafter emphasize law enforcement as part of an overall foreign aid package. U.S. policy makers in the 1960s worried that the "revolution of rising expectations" in the Third World, which encompassed virtually all drug-producing countries, could not easily be controlled. They nevertheless sought to do so by tying together development and security assistance as provided to local law enforcement programs by AID, part of which was to be used for narcotics control. The existing data do not reveal whether the drug control performance of producer states improved, but that is doubtful given the level of funding that Washington made available in the 1970s and after. Almost imperceptibly, drug control had vanished by the late 1960s as an autonomous foreign policy issue. In its stead, the linkage between drugs and security had become tighter than before, a bond that Operation Intercept would reaffirm.[10]

Intercept enabled the Nixon White House to seize political control of the drug issue, which was commanding the attention of the public because of rising heroin addiction among U.S. soldiers returning from Indochina, and simultaneously to assert hegemonic authority in the hemisphere. Intercept subjected all traffic at the border to lengthy delays in order to impede the flow of drugs north from Mexico; in so doing the Nixon administration had two objectives. First, it made interdiction as important as control at the source. Second, and more significant, it served notice that the production of illegal drugs threatened U.S. security and demonstrated a lack of political will by the country of origin in the struggle against drugs.[11] In due course, U.S. policy makers would employ the political and economic instability of the 1980s in the Andes, for example, to their advantage, even though the extensive, illegal cultivation of coca and the traffic in cocaine were only symptoms of that instability. They accomplished this feat programmatically by joining drug control assistance with the established practice of providing aid for military, police, and counterinsurgency forces.

On this latter point some further explanation is in order. The Kennedy administration had raised counterinsurgency policy to the level of doctrine. In doing so, the vigorous men of the New Frontier were merely building upon a tradition that reached back to pre-Revolutionary days, found systematic expression in the Indian wars of the nineteenth century, and then manifested itself abroad for the first time in the Philippines at the turn of the century. Working on the basic assumption that the revolution of rising expectations could not fully be met, U.S. policy makers in the Cold War shouldered the imperial burden of forcing demands for development and modernization into acceptable channels. In operational terms, this effort entailed creation of the Office of Public Safety (OPS) in AID; extension of military assistance abroad to contain the spread of Communism; and establishment of the International Military and Education Training program (IMET) in an attempt to reshape the overly negative attitudes of Third World military officials toward development.

The Andean nations of Bolivia, Colombia, and Peru received a sizable amount of Washington's development-cum-security funding. The Public Safety Program of OPS, which became the most notorious of these assistance programs, dispensed funds liberally for the purpose of enhancing local law enforcement capabilities. This objective closely resembled the goal of U.S.-style institution building that would characterize Operation Snowcap in the Andes twenty-five years later. The United States also sent military assistance to the three countries under a variety of programs and trained under IMET several thousands of their military personnel in the first thirty years of the Cold War.

Providing such assistance set the stage, as Michael T. Klare has shown, for the extensive paramilitary aid that has dominated U.S. drug-control funding in Latin America since the early 1970s. Indeed, when the U.S. Congress denounced and abolished the Public Safety Program as of 1 July 1975, the International Narcotics Control (INC) program had already been in place for nearly four years. The Nixon administration designed INC as a way of going to the source of illicit narcotics production. Mexico initially benefited the most from the program, while Bolivia, Colombia, Peru, and Ecuador were no less vital to its ultimate success.

Following Operation Intercept, both the United States and Mexico endeavored to put the best possible face on a contentious situation by devising what they termed "Operation Cooperation." By the mid-1970s, authorities in Mexico City initiated La Campaña Permanente, in which Mexican resources together with assistance from the DEA were employed in a modestly successful endeavor to curtail opium poppy growth and heroin production.[12] So far as the available data reveal, the Mexican drug-control record during the late 1970s was a relatively good one.

Even as the United States and Mexico were defining drugs as a mutual security problem, political developments in Washington were making that task more difficult. First, as early as 1971, the House Foreign Affairs Committee expressed concern about the abuse of Southeast Asian heroin by U.S. troops who served in Indochina. One committee report held, in line with traditional U.S. policy, that "the problem must be attacked at the source."[13] What differed was the manner of attack that Congress had under consideration, namely, a preemptive buy of the Southeast Asian heroin supply. Officials in the executive branch had rejected this proposal at least twice by mid-decade. Despite the high unknown costs that annual preemptive buys would have entailed, the White House strenuously opposed the idea because it meant reviving drug control as a matter to be handled sui generis, which would have undermined the recently established drug-security relationship. Also, the House Select Committee on Narcotics Abuse and Control (HSC) came into existence in 1976. Headed by representatives who were dedicated to crop eradication and who hoped to strengthen the antidrug fight, the HSC looked beyond promise and began to assess performance in Latin American drug control programs.

As before, Mexico caught the eye of the proponents of strict drug control in the United States. President José López Portillo doubtless had in his government officials who were profiting from drug production and trafficking. What López Portillo knew about that situation remains unclear; in any event, by the time Reagan took office in 1981, members of Congress and some administration officials, although few then in DEA headquarters, were doubting Mexico's good faith regarding drug control. Ironically, Mexicans had their own doubts about the U.S. antidrug commitment because of strict legal prohibitions against the spraying of paraquat on domestically grown marijuana. But the stark realities of power in U.S.-Mexican relations made that concern largely irrelevant in the bilateral relationship during the Reagan era.

The INC programs failed to achieve desired results in South America in the late 1970s and early 1980s despite, for that time, extensive funding. Amounts appropriated for Colombia's antidrug program compared favorably with the funding for Mexico. But as the trade in marijuana and cocaine gradually turned into a multibillion-dollar business, corruption within drug police and the military and indecisiveness in Bogotá limited the effectiveness of U.S. aid. Similar problems also compromised U.S. programs in Bolivia, Ecuador, and Peru, where the smuggling of coca paste and cocaine became highly organized. The presence in the Andes of DEA agents in a training capacity had little discernible impact on the illegal trade. Incipient local efforts to restrict coca growing were largely ineffective because coca remained the most lucrative and, in some areas, the only cash crop. Then, when the global inflation of the late 1970s rendered both fiscal planning and reliance on monetary policy inadequate tools for maintaining economic stability, dependence on cocaine trafficking for foreign exchange coincided nicely with the expanding appetites for drugs among North Americans.

The patience of the United States for the evident inability of Latin American nations to control either drug production or trafficking was disappearing by 1980. As that happened, the politics of pressure dominated drug control in the Americas as never before. Colombia focused attention on itself both when it considered legalizing and taxing the marijuana trade and as the boom in cocaine production became public knowledge. Further, Peru and Bolivia were widely criticized in Washington for failure to implement controls on coca cultivation as mandated by the 1961 Single Convention. Bolivia especially fell out of favor with the United States during and after the seizure of power in July 1980 by Gen. Luis García Meza in what has accurately been termed a "cocaine coup." To U.S. authorities, Bolivia seemed little more than a nation in thrall to the coca leaf and, hence, to the trade in cocaine. Throughout the Andes, it appeared as though the so-called kings of cocaine, with their headquarters in Medellín and Cali, Colombia, were constructing powerful, albeit decentralized, empires.[14]

Viewed from the perspective of official Washington, it is not surprising that pressure increasingly characterized U.S. drug policy. Both Congress and the Reagan administration sought in various, occasionally competing ways to transform drug-control policies and operations in Latin America. More than any other congressional committee, the HSC, under the powerful leadership of Representative Charles Rangel (D-NY), held to account Latin Americans in Mexico and South America for the integrity of their respective antidrug activities. The HSC also arrogated to itself the role of watchdog over U.S. policy. With no particular mandate, save the presumed interests and fears of an ill-defined constituency, Rangel's committee held hearings, conducted study missions, and released reports about the deteriorating status of drug control in the hemisphere.

Officials in Washington, realizing that available resources were not sufficient for controlling coca and cocaine, were forced to reconsider their policy options. García Meza's cocaine coup had rendered that decision all the more necessary. INC programs, military assistance, and several AID projects directly related to coca control were placed on hold or sharply curtailed throughout the Andes. The Bureau of International Narcotics Matters (INM) in the Department of State, DEA, and other U.S. agencies, such as Customs and the Coast Guard, participating in antidrug activities nevertheless decided not to revise their traditional response to the drug problem. Turning once again to control at the source, as if it were some modern Holy Grail, the United States resumed assistance to Bolivia and Peru. By late 1983 both countries had established mobile narcotics enforcement units, known as Unidad Móvil de Patrullaje Rural (UMOPAR). The Bolivian government of Hernán Siles Zuazo signed in August 1983 a series of coca-control agreements with the Department of State, and Peru accepted U.S. financing for a coca eradication project known as Control y Reducción de Cultivos de Coca en el Alto Huallaga (CORAH).

The DEA participated in these Andean coca-control programs by providing advisers to train the U.S.-equipped strike forces. Politicians in host countries may have reacted adversely to the presence of DEA agents but generally accepted it as the price for continued development aid from the United States. The mission of the agents included monitoring crop eradication. When it became apparent that Bolivia was failing to meet agreed-upon goals, the White House ordered military and economic assistance suspended. Nowhere was the DEA presence more controversial than in Mexico, where in 1985 Agent Enrique Camarena Salazar and his Mexican pilot were abducted, tortured, and killed. The case remained unsettled to the satisfaction of the DEA for some years despite the arrest and successful prosecution of many persons allegedly responsible for the crime.[15] Demonstrating how negatively the Camarena case affected U.S.-Mexican relations was the publication in *Proceso* in April 1990 of the names of DEA agents operating in Mexico.

DEA agents in the field insisted that the Camarena issue be resolved even if it impaired U.S-Mexican relations, whereas DEA headquarters could not afford to be so uncompromising. Were the agency to withdraw its agents from foreign operations, one raison d'être of the DEA, the existence of the agency might be placed in jeopardy. Thus, high officials at DEA did not make settlement of the Camarena dispute a sine qua non for cordial relations with Mexico.

There existed before President George Bush visited Mexico in November 1990, however, something of a carrot-and-stick approach. The U.S. Customs Agency, at least until Commissioner William von Raab resigned in July 1989, would not be outdone in its vehement denunciation of Mexico. So flamboyant and strident was von Raab that he publicly voiced his antipathy toward Mexico whenever the spirit so moved him. Likewise, Senator Jesse Helms (R-NC) of the Senate Foreign Relations Committee denounced the administration of Mexican president Miguel de la Madrid Hurtado as though it were sponsoring drug smuggling into the United States as a matter of policy. If Helms possessed no special expertise concerning the drug issue, he did have an eye for an attractive political issue and frequently made the most of it.

Helms, Representative Larry Smith (D-FL) of the Foreign Affairs Committee, and like-minded members of Congress doubtless seemed like something of a rogue elephant to State Department officials in charge of drug-control policy. Indeed, the requirement that the president of the United States certify the antidrug record of sovereign states in Latin America placed the department on the defensive in the bureaucratic battle to define the contours of U.S. policy. Nevertheless, the printed record in the 1980s of testimony before Congress by the several assistant secretaries of state for international narcotics matters does not show a bureau that found the politics of pressure disagreeable. As such, the national interest certification given Mexico in 1988 may have been purposefully intended by the White House to elicit demands from Congress to place additional pressure on Mexico about drug control.

Not only in the 1980s did the HSC rally support throughout Congress for a foreign policy promoting extensive eradication of crops in the Andes and in Mexico, it also called for a dramatic improvement in the rate of drug interdiction, thereby directly criticizing the antidrug efforts of the Reagan administration. In that regard, committee leaders encouraged a militarization of the drug war over the opposition of Secretary Caspar Weinberger's Department of Defense (DOD). Likewise, the House Foreign Affairs Committee, under Smith's leadership, called for a more active war on drugs.

Although certain officials in INM were receptive to the idea of an intensified drug war, as seen in the earlier development of INM's air wing and its other assistance programs, DOD certainly viewed the matter in an altogether different light. Fighting the drug war was not seen as part of DOD's mission, primarily because the war could not be won under any acceptable definition of the term. Further, the renascent Cold War with the Soviet Union and its putative allies in Central America and the Caribbean still commanded the nation's defense priorities. President Reagan was quick to attack drugs with strong rhetoric but was reluctant to make the drug war a policy priority of the first order.[16] His reluctance would change in 1986, however. For policy analysts, the transformation affords an opportunity for examining what, if anything, U.S. officials learned from earlier experiences.

Reagan issued National Security Decision Directive No. 221 on 8 April 1986, proclaiming that drug production and trafficking threatened U.S. security. As a result, all nations under attack from drugs, especially in the Andes, should defend themselves—individually or in concert. In practice, Reagan's announcement meant a greater emphasis on control at the source and even more vigorous efforts in source countries to interdict illegal drugs. The United States would provide advice, training, and equipment, and the war against drugs would be waged on the ground in Latin America as well as in international waters.

Reagan apparently brought the CIA into the war on drugs at that time. The agency initiated operations to infiltrate trafficking organizations by employing informers, a tactic of uncertain value essayed by Anslinger years earlier. If success depended upon the incarceration of numerous cocaine cartel leaders, then the CIA endeavor badly failed—at least on an operational basis. Organizationally, though, the agency would prosper as the Cold War ended with the creation of its Counternarcotics Center.

Reagan's 1986 strategy studiously ignored competing security objectives that partially compromised U.S. antidrug goals, thus confusing policy ends and means. Gen. Manuel Antonio Noriega of Panama, for example, was arguably the Reagan administration's most vital security asset in Central America, notwithstanding a well-deserved reputation for double-dealing. Noriega was deemed indispensable to the United States and, hence, remained in power as long as William Casey headed the CIA.[17] Furthermore, the administration chose to overlook the involvement of an unknown number of Honduran military officials in the drug trade because Honduras was serving as a sanctuary for the Nicaraguan Contras. Such contradictions in security priorities were not lost on those nations, notably Colombia, that were being asked to serve on the front lines of the drug war.[18]

The United States virtually insisted that the battle against drugs be taken to the source countries. To be sure, aid for some military operations came after being requested by Latin American governments. Yet it seems reasonable to ask how much of a choice Bolivia had in March 1986, when Operation Blast Furnace was being proposed.[19] It is unlikely, too, that Colombia had many options other than a war with the Medellín cartel after the assassination of presidential candidate Luis Carlos Galán in August 1989. The Bush White House partially viewed the response to the killing as a test of the political will of the government of Virgilio Barco Vargas. Accordingly, when Barco's successor, César Gaviria Trujillo, sought to devise a Colombian response to the violence of the Medellín cartel, Bob Martinez, then director of the Office of National Drug Control Policy (ONDCP), declared that Colombia was on trial before the world.

South American unwillingness to strike directly at illicit production and trafficking would have jeopardized U.S. economic and military aid programs. Armed with this implicit threat, the United States—in 1987, well before Galán's murder—had fashioned an extensive antidrug strategy for the Andes, Operation Snowcap. But Snowcap, slow in getting under way, soon ran into difficulty, especially in Peru, where the Maoist Sendero Luminoso, or Shining Path, controlled coca-growing areas in the Upper Huallaga Valley. Proposals late in the decade to dispatch U.S. Special Forces into the Andes were too controversial to accept openly, although by mid-1991 President Alberto K. Fujimori did agree to their limited use, a tactic that further involved the United States in the drug war on the ground in South America.[20]

Developing a more aggressive antidrug strategy inevitably created greater expectations regarding Latin American performance in Congress and the Executive Branch. The control of drugs moved into the highest rank of foreign policy priorities for the United States, at least rhetorically. Yet crop eradication programs and drug interdiction campaigns, together with the incarceration or death of a number of drug kingpins (despite several spectacular, singular achievements), did not noticeably impede the global flow of drugs, as annual reports from the State Department attested.[21]

One expected result of neutralizing major traffickers was a decline in money laundering. Hence, the toppling of Noriega and subsequent arrest of the executive officers of several Panamanian banks held out the promise of greater success, a hope that was leavened by the realization that the laundering of money remained in 1993 a vexing problem for Panama, a country whose government after 1989 owed its very existence to the United States. Whether in Panama or elsewhere in the Americas, the remarkable ability of money launderers to operate with virtual impunity posed a serious threat to U.S. policy and definitely had further the potential to corrupt any nation in thrall to the drug business.

The Bush administration had gone beyond its predecessors in trying to prevail in the drug war. Galán's killing provided the pretext for implementing Washington's Andean Drug Strategy, which was intended to elicit broad support for an intensified campaign against drug production and trafficking. The short-term costs of this quixotic endeavor were especially high in Bolivia, Colombia, and Peru. In attempting to replicate the century-long effort to control drugs at their source and in transit, President Bush and his colleagues nearly shook governments across the Andean ridge to their very foundations.

Regime stability hung in the balance from Bogotá to Lima to La Paz as Washington dangled the carrot of multibillion-dollar antidrug aid in front of politicians, police, and the military. Autonomous sectors in each state remained under the sway of coca and cocaine, giving rise to the preconditions for prolonged civil strife if not actual civil war. Indicative of this situation was the pervasive role of Sendero Luminoso in the Peruvian drug trade and the existence in Colombia of ad hoc alliances of convenience between rebels and cartels in order to maximize profits from the cocaine business and an emerging commerce in heroin. Meanwhile, the doctrine followed by the Bush administration to wage war on drugs, calling for "low-intensity conflict," evoked an unexpected reaction. Andean leaders insisted upon a multilateral approach to the war on drugs, a development that would have met with much favor in the United States in the 1960s. Yet by the late 1980s, multilateralism threatened to undermine the linkages between drug policy and U.S. hegemony.

By interpreting hegemony as a negotiated phenomenon, it is arguable that the Andean nations held certain advantages over the United States when the four heads of state gathered at Cartagena, Colombia, in February 1990. Barco reminded Bush and Secretary of State James W. Baker III that Colombia remained the major theater in the drug war, a fact emphasized by the assault on the judicial system in the form of bribery and murder of judges by the cocaine cartels. Peru's Alan García Pérez even brought a coca farmer to Cartagena in order to put a human face on his request for greater assistance for economic development, the need for which seemed abundantly clear to Bolivia's Jaime Paz Zamora.

U.S. responses to the call for multilateralism demonstrated the resilience of hegemony and a lack of learning by authorities in Washington. To be sure, Bush and Baker did acknowledge the importance of addressing the demand for drugs at home and gave vague promises of development assistance and balance-of-payments support. At the same time, a "Marshall Plan" for the Andes—an idea advocated by several prominent Latin Americans—was beyond the realm of possibility. Further, as the drug war intensified in the two years after Cartagena, Congress increasingly tied aid to performance. At length the logic of the Andean Drug Strategy led to a diminution of respect for human rights throughout the Andes as military resources intended for the war on drugs were employed to control all manner of domestic dissent.[22]

By the end of the Bush presidency, Congress was criticizing how the war against drugs was being fought. Nevertheless, this critique generally failed to question the basic premises behind U.S. drug policy. Rather, Congress was asking the White House to achieve historic goals of control at the source and interdiction with significantly fewer resources. As for economic development, the assistance cupboard—through AID—remained off-limits to the three Andean nations. As a result, following a second antidrug summit, convened at San Antonio, Texas, in February 1992, Mexico—a participant at the gathering—and Colombia took the lead in fashioning a Latin American approach to drug control. Although the effort portended little more than frequent consultation about drugs, its very existence underlined the bankruptcy of the Andean Drug Strategy and the limits of traditional U.S. drug policy. At most, Washington had achieved a "stalemate, not victory," in the war on drugs.[23]

Equating drugs with national security did have some positive consequences for inter-American relations. Bush had achieved a semblance of order in U.S. policy by defusing drug control as the volatile political issue that it had been since 1969. More than at any other time since the inception of the international drug control movement over eighty years earlier, the United States had sought to integrate producer and transit nations into an overall counternarcotics strategy. From Mexico to Colombia, Bolivia, and Peru, and elsewhere in the Americas, the administration promoted drug control in one important way that transcended past practice: the drug problem was one of demand as well as supply.

Accepting the drug threat as a common societal malaise did not indicate that the century-long war on drugs had ended. What Bruce M. Bagley terms the "new hundred years' war" found a home, albeit a modest one, in the early Clinton administration.[24] The oversight agency for drug policy, the ONDCP, saw its operating staff trimmed to less than 20 percent of its size under Bush. As if to cushion the bureaucratic shock, Clinton added the head of ONDCP to his cabinet. Although many critics of drug policy and numerous observers on Capitol Hill were calling for an extensive program of education, treatment, and rehabilitation along with tough law enforcement at home, Clinton's drug policy for the mid-1990s—announced by new ONDCP chief Lee Brown—differed far more in degree than in kind from that of the previous twelve years.

Conditions giving rise to a hemispheric drug war since 1980 had scarcely changed as Clinton took office. The Department of State's annual International Narcotics Control Strategy Report, issued in April 1993, documented a steady rise in the amount of opium under cultivation regionally and reported that the hectarage of coca being grown in the Andes remained stable, but it could not estimate how much cocaine was available for public consumption. At the same time, drug-trafficking organizations were employing sophisticated techniques over a complex network of routes that made interdiction of readily transportable drugs like cocaine and heroin extremely difficult. Moreover, multilateral operations to disrupt money-laundering operations were meeting with only scant success.[25] Thus, the war on drugs—in its 1980s incarnation—was continuing, with considerably less fanfare but without noticeably better results.

Clinton's transition team had paid precious little attention to drug control, and the State Department decided not to prepare a position paper on drug policy for the new president. Moreover, one of the final duties of Stephen M. Duncan, assistant secretary of defense for drug enforcement policy and support, was to cut $211 million from the 1993 fiscal year budget for the Pentagon's role in the drug war—a move reducing the allocation of the DOD to about $1 billion in a $12.7 billion budget. Moreover, at the outset of the Clinton presidency, the policy role of the State Department's Bureau of International Narcotics Matters, the main operational agency in the drug war, remained unclear. The White House did finally decide to merge INM into a comprehensive unit responsible for terrorism, crime, and drugs, but the House of Representatives temporarily blocked the move, fearing a rise in terrorism at home.[26] Another plan to restructure the drug policy apparatus would have incorporated the DEA into the Federal Bureau of Investigation, but DEA backers in Congress killed the change. At the least, wrangling on Capitol Hill about the organizational status of the antidrug bureaucracy demonstrated that drug policy had become as much a product of interagency disputes as a matter of intergovernmental relations.[27]

Even so, the grand strategy U.S. policy makers historically have employed in their campaign to control drugs in the Americas remained unchanged at middecade. Control at the source on the cheap defined the contours of inter-American drug policy for the Clinton administration. Thus, a cut in funding for the drug war in the Andes of more than 30 percent, down to $90 million, did not lead to a reconsideration of basic U.S. assumptions. To do so "would be to doom a number of these countries to even greater attack by narco-traffickers," opined Timothy E. Wirth, the State Department's adviser to the White House on drug policy.[28]

This pursuit of traditional objectives meant unaccustomed flexibility—the legacy of Bush's Andean Drug Strategy—for Latin American leaders in defining a response to drug problems in their own nations. Yet so long as U.S. aid for sustainable development was not forthcoming, the responses were unlikely to be more than half-hearted ones. If it was true that U.S. officials refused to learn the lessons contained in a history of drug policy failure, it was also true that Latin Americans could not respond to drugs as a national security matter. In that regard, it did not matter that the United States had created the issue in the 1960s, when it first associated drugs with hemispheric security. The inability to address the profound threat of drugs to political and economic stability left the sovereignty of producer and transit states in question. Furthermore, it invited future U.S. interventions and assertions of hegemony.

In an important book about the tasks confronting the Latin American Left in the wake of the Cold War, prominent Mexican intellectual Jorge Castañeda writes of the need to complete the job of nation building in order to remove the justifications for intervention. Controlling drugs is fundamental to that process, he argues, if the shadow of U.S. domination is ever to recede.[29] Democratization might therefore revitalize sovereignty and bring a real measure of equality to inter-American relations. In doing so, it might successfully challenge the strategy and tactics that have characterized drug control in the Americas for over three decades.

Notes

1. *Washington Post*, 24 October 1993, pp. A27, A28.

2. "The Dirtiest Bank of All," *Time*, 29 July 1991, pp. 42–47.

3. Alfred W. McCoy, *The Politics of Heroin: CIA Complicity in the Global Drug Trade* (Brooklyn: Lawrence Hill Brooks, 1991); William O. Walker III, *Opium and Foreign Policy: The Anglo-American Search for Order in Asia, 1912–1954* (Chapel Hill: University of North Carolina Press, 1991).

4. Walker, *Opium and Foreign Policy*, chaps. 8, 9; and Douglas Clark Kinder, "Bureaucratic Cold Warrior: Harry J. Anslinger and Illicit Narcotics Traffic," *Pacific Historical Review* 50 (May 1981): 169–91.

5. David Green, *The Containment of Latin America: A History of the Myths and Realities of the Good Neighbor Policy* (Chicago: Quadrangle Books, 1971), pp. 255–90; and Roger Trask, "The Impact of the Cold War on United States–Latin American Relations, 1945–1949," *Diplomatic History* 1 (summer 1977): 271–84. See also Stephen G. Rabe, *Eisenhower and Latin*

America: The Foreign Policy of Anticommunism (Chapel Hill: University of North Carolina Press, 1988), pp. 16–25, 63–68, 77–83, 126; and Jerome Levinson and Juan de Onís, *The Alliance That Lost Its Way: A Critical Report on the Alliance for Progress* (Chicago: Quadrangle, 1970).

6. D. Michael Shafer, *Deadly Paradigms: The Failure of U.S. Counterinsurgency Policy* (Princeton, N.J.: Princeton University Press, 1988), p. 79.

7. Guy Poitras, *The Ordeal of Hegemony: The United States and Latin America* (Boulder, Colo.: Westview, 1990).

8. See Mexico, Country File, National Security File, Lyndon Baines Johnson Library, University of Texas, Austin, Tex.

9. William O. Walker III, *Drug Control in the Americas*, rev. ed. (Albuquerque: University of New Mexico Press, 1989), p. 197.

10. Michael T. Klare, *Supplying Repression: U.S. Support for Authoritarian Regimes Abroad* (Washington DC: Institute for Policy Studies, 1977), pp. 7–25.

11. Richard B. Craig, "Operación Intercepción: Una política de presión internacional," *Foro Internacional* 22 (October–December 1981): 203–30.

12. Richard B. Craig, "*La Campaña Permanente:* Mexico's Antidrug Campaign," *Journal of Interamerican Studies and World Affairs* 20 (May 1978): 107–31.

13. U.S. Congress, House of Representatives, *Report of Special Study Mission,* "The World Heroin Problem," 92d Cong., 1st sess., 27 May 1971 (Washington DC: U.S. Government Printing Office, 1971), p. 1.

14. Rensselaer W. Lee III, *White Labyrinth: Cocaine and Political Power* (New Brunswick, N.J.: Transaction Publishers, 1989); Guy Gugliotta and Jeff Leen, *Kings of Cocaine: Inside the Medellín Cartel—An Astonishing True Story of Murder, Money, and International Corruption* (New York: Simon and Schuster, 1989).

15. Elaine Shannon, *Desperados: Latin Drug Lords, U.S. Lawmen, and the War America Can't Win* (New York: Viking, 1988).

16. For an assessment of INM's air wing in Mexico, see U.S. General Accounting Office, *Drug Control: U.S.-Mexico Opium and Marijuana Aerial Eradication Program,* GAO-NSIAD-88-73 (Washington DC: U.S. Government Printing Office, 1988).

17. John Dinges, *Our Man in Panama: How General Noriega Used the U.S.—And Made Millions in Drugs and Arms* (New York: Random House, 1990).

18. Bruce Michael Bagley, "Dateline Drug Wars: Colombia: The Wrong Strategy," *Foreign Policy* 77 (winter 1989–90): 154–71.

19. Michael H. Abbott, "The Army and the Drug War: Politics or National Security," *Parameters* 18 (December 1988): 95–112; and Lt. Col. Sewall H. Menzel, U.S. Army, Ret., "Operation Blast Furnace," *Army* 39 (November 1989): 24–32.

20. U.S. Congress, House of Representatives, *Thirteenth Report by the Committee on Government Operations,* "Stopping the Flood of Cocaine with Operation Snowcap: Is It Working?," 101st Cong., 2d sess., 14 August 1990 (Washington DC: U.S. Government Printing Office, 1990).

21. See the U.S. Department of State's *International Narcotics Control Strategy Report,* issued annually with midyear updates.

22. See, for example, Americas Watch, *Peru under Fire: Human Rights since the Return to Democracy* (New Haven, Conn.: Yale University Press, 1992), and *Political Murder and Reform in Colombia: The Violence Continues* (New York: Americas Watch, 1992).

23. Robert A. Pastor, *Whirlpool: U.S. Foreign Policy toward Latin America and the Caribbean* (Princeton, N.J.: Princeton University Press, 1992), p. 101.

24. Bruce Michael Bagley, "The New Hundred Years War? U.S. National Security and the War on Drugs in Latin America," *Journal of Interamerican Studies and World Affairs* 30 (spring, 1988): 161–82.

25. U.S. Department of State, Bureau of International Narcotics Matters, *International Narcotics Control Strategy Report,* April 1993.

26. *Washington Post,* 22 July 1993, p. A29.

27. A further manifestation of this phenomenon became public in November 1993, when the *New York Times* reported that the CIA had authorized the shipment of nearly a ton of pure cocaine into the United States from Venezuela in 1990. What this revelation meant for further operations of the agency's Counternarcotics Center was unclear at the time. *New York Times,* 20 November 1993, pp. 1, 5.

28. *New York Times,* 21 November 1993, p. 10.

29. Jorge G. Castañeda, *Utopia Unarmed: The Latin American Left after the Cold War* (New York: Alfred A. Knopf, 1993), pp. 298–302.

Joseph S. Tulchin

The United States and
Latin America in the World

In the euphoria that followed the dramatic razing of the Berlin Wall in November 1989, President George Bush triumphantly declared the end of the Cold War and summoned the beginning of a New World Order. The phrase was catchy and seemed to match the momentous quality of the events that had preceded the celebration in Berlin. At the time, no one was quite sure what the president's term meant, although it was plain that he intended to convey optimism, a sense that an era of instability and threat was behind us and that all the nations of the globe could look forward to a period of relative peace and goodwill.

Not long after the president had put his rhetorical stamp on the end of the Cold War, the deputy director of the State Department policy-planning staff and an analyst of international affairs at the Rand Corporation, Francis Fukuyama, explained that the end of the Cold War was in effect the end of history. A follower of Hegel, Fukuyama saw in the collapse of the Soviet Union and in the triumph of one of the contending parties the sudden end of a terrible dialectical struggle for the domination of the organization of the world. With that triumph, total and unconditional, the United States and the way of life it represented—democratic capitalism—would sweep all before it.[1] Fukuyama's essay was but one statement in a debate that continues to this day about how best to characterize the post–Cold War world. Events have made a mockery of President Bush's phrase. Indeed, within a year, it had become common to dismiss his bon mot by referring to the New World *Dis*order. The dominant theme was that confusion characterized official thinking about foreign policy in the Bush and Clinton administrations.[2] The peace, the goodwill, the sense of an inertial, almost inevitable drive toward a world community that moved constructively forward, implicit in the president's remarks, were hard to find or even imagine. Everywhere one turned there was conflict, disaster, and a threat of worse to come.

But if there was no consensus about the future, there was no disagreement that the Cold War had ended. Indeed, in the aftermath of the dismantling of the Berlin Wall, nothing was more amazing than the implosion of the Soviet Union. Almost overnight, one of the world's superpowers was reduced to a congerie of independent states, many of which were warring with one another over ethnic identity, territory, economic issues, or a combination of all of these. Even Russia, the largest and most powerful of these states, appeared on the verge of economic collapse and political chaos. Whatever was to follow the Cold War would almost certainly not be characterized by a bipolar struggle for hegemony between rival empires that represented conflicting ideological systems. The precise implications of this change would have to be worked out gradually, on a case-by-case basis, in which each crisis would be used by the parties to evaluate their stake, their commitments, their willingness to act, and their ability to influence other parties involved to act in a particular manner. Speaking to the Trilateral Commission in 1992, Henry Kissinger remarked on the speed of the current world transformations, saying, "If we look at history, there have been many periods when there have been changes in the nature of the components that constituted the international order and in the way they interacted with each other. . . . What has not occurred before is the rapidity of change, the global scope of the change, the ability of various regions to communicate instantly with all other regions of the world, and the interconnection—economically and therefore politically—of all the regions."[3]

How would these dramatic changes influence relations between the United States and Latin America? How would the various nations of Latin America, experiencing a wide variety of economic conditions but, for the first time in the history of the region, all (except for Cuba) governed by civilian, democratic regimes, react to the changes that had impressed Henry Kissinger?

The debate in the United States over the New World Order said very little about Latin America. It was assumed by most authors who studied the international system that the United States would maintain its paramountcy within the Western Hemisphere. Several conservative writers worried that the end of the Cold War meant that the United States would pay even less attention to Latin America than it had in the recent past, although some noted casually that such disinterest was only right and natural, since Latin America was not likely to present a threat to U.S. interests.[4] Liberals tended to see an opportunity to achieve the partnership between the United States and Latin America that had been frustrated by the myopic policies of the Cold War. They argued (or hoped) that the United States would now pay more attention to Latin America.[5] During this discussion, the Bush administration concentrated a great deal of energy on NAFTA, first agreed with Canada and then with Mexico. In fact, the United States and several of the nations in the region seemed to be making economic activity central to their new international relationship. The only policy dealing with Latin America that Bush's administration announced with great fanfare was the Enterprise for the Americas Initiative, which seemed to signal the primacy of economic relations, especially free trade, throughout the hemisphere.[6] Some authors, however, took this as an oversold safety precaution against the possibility that Europe and Japan might consolidate economic blocs that would exclude the United States, or at least make it more difficult for the United States to gain access to the markets represented by those blocs.[7]

One policy option that appears to have been shunted aside was neo-isolationism. The United States was not ready to withdraw from the international arena. The vast military and economic power accumulated since World War II, together with nearly fifty years' experience of throwing around the nation's geopolitical weight, made it hard for the United States to bury its head in the sand. Weakness or geopolitical timidity on the part of other powers, especially Germany and Japan, the United States's major economic rivals, only served to make the last more disposed to strut on the international stage. Moreover, there was an idealistic strain in U.S. policy, a desire to do the right thing and to perform humanitarian deeds in the name of democracy. Yugoslavia, the former Soviet Union, Somalia, South Africa, China, the Middle East, Haiti—all were crisis areas that, either because of the human misery they produced or because they threatened to spill over their borders, cried out for some sort of external mediation.[8]

By the middle of the Clinton administration, a pattern was emerging in the international affairs of the United States that would affect its relations with Latin America. First, an emphatic Europocentrism had developed in the nation's foreign policy concerns. Second, Congress and the public seemed to pay attention to Latin America as a region only in terms of trade or economic relations—what one observer called the NAFTA-ization of inter-American relations.[9] There appeared to be exceptions to this (the attention accorded the crises in dealing with the military dictatorship in Haiti, for example, or the pressure brought to bear by the Cuban-American Foundation to tighten sanctions on Fidel Castro), but these were more issues of domestic politics than debates over foreign policy. Third, there was a reemergence in U.S. policy of a Wilsonian urge to drive the nation to do good works on behalf of democratic capitalism and to teach other nations how to behave and how to enjoy the benefits of the American way of life. Fourth, working against the Wilsonian urge was the Vietnam syndrome, which continued to exert a powerful influence on U.S. thinking in order to ensure that—no matter how worthwhile—the nation did "not get bogged down" in international adventures.

The sum of these tendencies suggests that United States policy toward Latin America sought to avoid "getting involved" except where the former's domestic politics made avoidance impossible. It was a policy that focused on trade and economic issues, because Latin America could be understood within the global framework of U.S. economic relations. Aside from these issues, the U.S. government seemed to act with extreme caution in handling other items on the inter-American agenda, such as the protection of democracy, the elimination of poverty, the curtailment of the drug traffic, environmental protection, the treatment of refugees and illegal immigration, the proliferation of weapons of mass destruction, and corruption. Because the United States did not want to get involved and because neither the government nor the public focused its attention on Latin America, there appeared to be an incipient tendency on the part of the United States to go it alone, acting unilaterally in hemispheric affairs while dealing with the nations of the hemisphere in a bilateral fashion, despite the fact that the Clinton administration began with all sorts of encouragement for multilateral peacekeeping.

Historically, the United States has considered Latin America as something of a nuisance or potential source of trouble. When at the end of the nineteenth century export markets became increasingly important to the United States, Latin America was taken more seriously, but the former remained concerned about the latter's instability, which was seen as an excuse for foreign intervention as well as a threat to the northern nation's economic interests in its southern neighbors. Today, foreign intervention is no longer considered a threat, but instability is still looked on by the United States as a problem. Underdevelopment, too, is worrisome because it makes Latin America less valuable as a trading partner and a recipient of U.S. investment. At the same time, underdevelopment is seen not only as a cause of instability but also as a perpetuator of the human misery that is a constant reproach to the international capitalist system.

§

How are the nations of Latin America to deal with current changes in the international system? How are they to define their role in world affairs? And, inevitably, how will they deal with the United States? First, like the United States, they must come to terms with the very transformations mentioned by Henry Kissinger, especially the liberalization of world trade and the increasing globalization of capital, information, and technology. In the same way that Latin American countries differ markedly in size, economic capacity, natural resource endowment, and so forth, so too will global changes affect these countries in different ways and degrees. Nevertheless, it is true for all of them that their ability to deal with the changes will determine how they take advantage of the space available to them for autonomous action in the international system.

Crucial to the way in which the nations of Latin America deal with the transition to the post–Cold War world will be their ability to estimate the power of the United States. A significant feature of the debate over U.S. standing centers on the rise of Japan and its satellites among the East Asian "tigers" and a unified Europe in the global economy. Some experts are convinced that the world will soon be divided quite sharply into three economic blocs: the Western Hemisphere, led by the United States; Asia, led by Japan; and Europe, led by an institutionalized European community. This argument is based as much on such factors as efficiency, competitiveness, and growth—where the United States was considered to be lagging badly—as on actual size or a broader definition of power.[10]

Others argue that while the United States remains—and will remain—the largest economy in the world, its relative weight in the international system will decline as Japan and the European community grow at a faster rate and as the world evolves toward interdependence. This prospect suggests a tendency toward multilateral peaceful settlement of disputes. Such a trend, it is argued, will favor Europe economically, enhance collective security organizations, and accelerate the decline of the United States as a dominant power, since economic power or capacity will gradually replace geopolitical power in determining international influence.[11] Finally, there is the *real politik* position that holds firmly to the view that the United States is the only world power, because it is the only nation with the capacity and the will to project its influence beyond its borders, by military means if and when necessary. The war in the Persian Gulf lent credence to this position.[12] Most commentators at the end of the 1980s and into 1990 focused on the Big Bang, the date in 1992 when Europe would become a single, unified market. That was to be, symbolically, the date when the United States would no longer be able to extend its influence around the globe. In such a world, the argument runs, Latin America should rethink its dependence on the United States and scramble to line up friends, allies, and patrons in the new trading blocs, especially in Europe.

But very shortly after those optimistic essays were written, the Big Bang, while not quite a whimper, was reduced radically. To begin with, the cost of absorbing East Germany was to take far more resources and to absorb more political energy than had been anticipated. At the same time, unemployment in the east and other factors led to a resurgence of crude neo-Nazi movements, which alarmed all political groups in Germany as well as most people in the rest of Europe. The Germans by 1992 were much more preoccupied with domestic issues than they were before 1990 and were much less confident about their role in world affairs.[13] The civil war in Yugoslavia became increasingly brutal, and the carnage in Bosnia, driven by Serbian desires for ethnic cleansing, seemed to undermine the civilized behavior and sense of community that lay at the core of the new Europe and that proponents of the European community assumed would lead to their ascendancy over the United States. Europe, however, seemed impotent in the face of events in Yugoslavia; it also appeared to be reduced to a catatonic passivity in the face of ethnic conflict and growing economic malaise in the former Soviet Union, the well-publicized starvation in Somalia, and even the gathering criticism of the Maastricht treaty of unification. At the end of 1992, it was difficult to anticipate how soon Europe would resume its drive toward unification, but it seemed fairly clear that sooner or later there would be a single European market that would make Europe more protectionist than it had been at any time since World War II.

At the end of 1992, the world community could act in Somalia only on the coattails of the United States, which agreed to send troops to protect the humanitarian groups delivering food to a starving population preyed upon by rival armed clans. In announcing his decision to send troops to eastern Africa, President Bush said he was doing so because the United States simply could not stand by and not act. The event held enormous potential significance, and where this now put the new "red line" limiting the use of U.S. power was not clear.[14] In commenting on U.S. intervention in Somalia, Reverend William Sloane Coffin, one of the historic figures of the pacifist movement in the United States, said, "Moral isolation is simply not a defensible position for those opposed to war. There is great anguish and confusion. We are groping for some kind of legitimate police action on an international scale."[15] A year later, the intervention in Somalia had all but self-destructed. U.S. troops were withdrawn in haste, with officials in Washington talking about the need to have "exit scenarios" before intervening anywhere else. The UN Command was at odds with governments that sent troops to participate in the peacekeeping, and the warlords looked as if they were back in control by 1994.

Latin America, meanwhile, had to deal with the harsh fact that as a region its trade had declined in the world economy from 12 percent in 1960 to 6 percent in 1980 and 3 percent in 1990. During the same period, the region suffered a similar decline as a factor in the U.S. economy, dropping from 25 percent in 1960 to 13 percent in 1985. Latin America as a total of U.S. overseas investment fell in these same years from 40 to 13 percent. In addition, while the crisis may have passed, the nations of the region were still digging out from under the burden of a debt that exceeded $500 billion. Repaying that debt, for some of the smaller economies, threatened to stall or stunt economic recovery in the 1990s and complicated the process of economic reform for even the largest of the nations in the region.

The globalization of the world economy, especially finance, was something with which the leaders of Latin America would have to deal. The world's stock markets were evolving toward operation as one seamless web. Traders in New York got up early to monitor the Nekkei index on the Tokyo stock exchange. Major brokerage houses in New York had international desks that worked twenty-four hours a day. At the height of the Japanese boom, it looked as if Japanese investors would buy half of California and all the golf courses in the hemisphere. When the Japanese stock market collapsed in 1992, the expectations for Japanese capital were reduced, but the Japanese economy was still considered to be something akin to a juggernaut, ready at any moment to resume its unstoppable expansion around the world. As trade became increasingly free, under the influence of the GATT negotiations, and as communications and computer technology together made the flow of information and capital easier, the movement toward a truly global economy, especially in financial and capital markets, seemed close at hand, although the final negotiations to sign the GATT agreement at the end of 1993 brought to the surface some ugly protectionist feelings, especially on the part of the French. While the globalization of the economy suggested greater flexibility and autonomy for Latin America, it also implied the triumph of a capitalist model that many Latin American economists had long believed discriminated against Latin America. It implied, too, that the nations of Latin America would have to throw themselves into an increasingly competitive international economy and that their historic comparative advantage in the export of primary products was no longer of much value. In this "new" global economy, it appeared that the nations of the region would have to find niches for themselves—whether in primary products, manufacturing, or services—in which they could compete with producers in the industrialized societies of Europe and North America, as well as with the aggressive exporters of the East Asian "tigers."

One of the peculiar effects of globalization that complicated Latin American relations with the United States was the increasing importance of technology and the diffusion of its use. The United States insisted on making access to technology and the protection of intellectual property rights one of the central issues of international trade negotiations. Traditionally, Latin America had never given much attention to the matter and, along with some of the countries in the Pacific Basin, was notorious for its failure to crack down on violations of copyright. Further, Latin America never had been highly successful in the creation of technology. The key to growth in the 1990s and beyond appeared to be the ability to attract technology, to attract qualified people, and to attract capital. The technologies that mattered most were transportation and information.[16] These were not areas in which Latin America ever had enjoyed a comparative advantage. If the world economy of the future were to be driven by ever more rapid rounds of technological innovation, the old import substitution model of growth would have to be abandoned along with the older model of primary product exports based on comparative advantage, and all the countries of the region would have to throw themselves into the new international market, modernizing their economies as quickly as they could.

Another major trend in the international system to which the nations of the region were forced to adapt was the growing significance in the international agenda of what had come to be called global issues. In his remarks to the Trilateral Commission in 1992, Henry Kissinger stated that there were "issues now in the world that go beyond anything previous leaders have had to deal with—environment, population, nuclear issues, problems that genuinely concern all of humanity and that can only be solved on a global basis."[17] Latin Americans did not create these issues, but they cannot be avoided and they can be dealt with effectively only on a multilateral basis. This may prove more frustrating for the United States, accustomed as it is to protecting its own national security by maximizing its autonomy, but such issues affect the nations of Latin America as well. Sometimes they are protagonists, as in the case of Brazil and the protection of the rain forest; sometimes they are victims, as in the depletion of the ozone shield and the frightening effects on animals and humans in the south of Chile and Argentina; but one way or the other, Latin American nations must participate in dealing with global issues. At the very least, in order to trade with the United States, all the region's nations will have to devote considerable resources to environmental regulations. That seems to be the minimum requirement for access to the U.S. market.

Some of the emerging global issues represent real threats to the national security of nations in Latin America and create tension in their international relations. The traffic in drugs, for example, has undermined the national sovereignty of Colombia and strains the capacity of both Peru and Bolivia to control their national territory. More complicated is the question of how to limit the international traffic in drugs. Members of the Reagan and Bush administrations claimed they could solve the drug problem in the United States by preventing the illegal importation of the offending materials—a policy known as interdiction. In the face of mounting evidence of the failure of interdiction, some members of the U.S. government suggested that the United States, in defense of its national interests, should send troops to one or more of the Latin American producers of drugs in order to cut off the production of the substances at their source. The effort to use military force to limit or end production or to reduce the traffic complicated U.S. bilateral relations with a number of countries in the region and created considerable tension in the relations among the nations of the Amazon basin. The kidnapping of a Mexican national on Mexican soil by the U.S. Drug Enforcement Agency embarrassed the Salinas government, which went to great efforts not to let the issue escalate in domestic politics, and made it more difficult for the Mexican president to push his free market policies and NAFTA, a result unanticipated and certainly not desired by the Bush administration. The Clinton administration decided that its predecessor's policies had failed but had difficulty coming up with a new policy. Several countries proposed using multilateral approaches, but by 1994 multilateral solutions were less popular in Washington than they had been a year earlier.

Other global issues that threaten to create tensions between the United States and Latin America are the defense of human rights, the protection of democracy, the proliferation and export of arms of mass destruction, emigration, and population control. Central to the discussion of these issues is what forums can be used to discuss them and what institutional mechanisms should be used to adjudicate disputes between parties. How much sovereignty will each nation be willing to cede in order to allow multilateral agencies to deal with these issues? Are these issues in which the various, often conflicting traditions of international law can help by creating the bases for consensus, or will the several national traditions divide the hemispheric community?

Aside from these general trends in world affairs, the directions of which are hard to predict and the implications of which for Latin American policy are often obscure, the one obvious change that the conclusion of the Cold War will bring to U.S.–Latin American relations is an end to a tightly focused definition of national security in terms of bipolar competition. This inevitably will lead to a redefinition of the terms of conflict resolution in the hemisphere.[18] How are the nations of Latin America to take advantage of this redefinition in order to maximize their international autonomy?

As a counterpart to the notion that the end of the Cold War would create a major role for the UN, many in Latin America hoped that the elimination of the Soviet Union as a factor in hemispheric affairs would be an excellent opportunity for the OAS. Indeed, several of the countries in the hemisphere, led by Argentina and Chile, tried to make the OAS both an instrument of protection for democracy and human rights and an effective forum for the discussion of the new global issues, especially the environment.[19] Although significant progress was made in strengthening the OAS and major steps toward reforming its charter were taken, it was clear that in the short term the OAS would not enjoy any more success than the UN as a major factor in the New World Order. Three elements appear to undermine efforts to make the OAS a significant medium for the resolution of hemispheric conflicts. First and foremost of these is the powerful tendency of U.S. administrations to act independently, to avoid feeling constrained by other states or multilateral organizations. Second is the reluctance on the part of many nations in Latin America, especially Mexico, to cede any iota of their national sovereignty to an international organization in which the United States plays a prominent role, although this may change with the signing of NAFTA. Finally, there was some evidence in the 1990s that the sudden end of the rigid zero-sum, bipolar framework for national security debates would stimulate neonationalist postures in Latin America, just as it had in Europe and the former Soviet Union.[20]

The challenge for Latin America in the 1990s is to devise new modes of conflict resolution that will not simply recapitulate earlier chapters in inter-American history, with the hegemony of the United States, while dealing with the dramatic salience of the new global issues that are shaping the new security agenda. Of particular concern to Latin Americans will be the following questions: Will the world economy move toward freer trade or will it slip into rigid, exclusionary trading blocs? Will this new economy become a complex, shifting hybrid, requiring extreme flexibility and the heightened capacity to adapt? How will the New World Order be governed? As far as the nations of Latin America are concerned, the key to these questions lies in how the United States defines its role in the world.

§

In moving to define its role in world affairs, the United States seemed pulled in two different directions. By the time Bill Clinton took office as president in 1993, the view that the New World Order would be an era of peace governed by the UN was held by very few, and their predictions receded further and further into the future. The opinion that the United States was the only nation capable of projecting its power beyond its borders seemed to hold sway in discussions about the appropriate posture for the United States in the still uncertain emerging international order, but the notion was countered or questioned internally by a powerful reluctance to pay for international adventures and by a growing insistence that the nation's energies should be devoted to solving problems at home. Clinton's electoral campaign had revolved around this point and, while avoiding direct criticism of anything George Bush had done in foreign policy, insisted that it was time to focus on domestic questions.

The decision to send troops to the horn of Africa seemed to be the defining case. It was a good cause; no one opposed feeding the starving of Somalia. The objectives were well defined, and the time frame within which the operation would be conducted appeared short. Finally, the cost was considered small and would be paid for through the UN. Most important, the American people did not see a quagmire or a military struggle that might escalate and leave the country bogged down in a local dispute incapable of settlement. When President Bush was asked why the United States was intervening in a country so far from home, he responded, "It was the right thing to do." Would the United States become the world's policeman and a nation of good works? Probably not, because nowhere would the definition of "doing the right thing" prove so simple, stimulate so little controversy at home or among the international community, and cost so little. None of the other issues on the international front burner at the time—Yugoslavia, the former Soviet Union, Liberia, the Kurds, Iraq's nuclear program, Haiti, the Middle East—was amenable to so straightforward a solution. As if to emphasize the points, U.S. officials, much to the irritation of Secretary General Boutros Boutros-Ghali, persistently denied that the troops would disarm the warlords. And when several U.S. troops were killed and the body of one dragged through the streets of Mogadishu, public reaction in the United States was fierce. The Clinton administration decided it would not act alone in any of the world's hot spots, even in Haiti, within the Caribbean Basin.

As far as Latin America is concerned, the end of the Cold War certainly marked the end of the tight definition of national security in terms of the former bipolar competition with the Soviet Union. Such an obsessive focus had distorted U.S. policy in the hemisphere, reaching the point during the first Reagan administration when debates over all facets of policy toward Latin America (military aid, development assistance, defense of democracy and human rights, trade) were decided by the perception of exogenous factors, that is, the Cold War, rather than endogenous factors, such as social malaise, state terrorism, and the like.[21] Such a change in the focus of U.S. policy almost immediately led to a shift in how the United States approached conflict resolution in the region.

Nations that had been the subject of intense scrutiny by the United States, welcome or not (Nicaragua is one example), suddenly found themselves off the front pages of U.S. newspapers and out of the minds of U.S. policy makers. Nicaragua became so insignificant to the Bush administration that Senator Jesse Helms, with little more than a whimper out of the administration, was able to hold up aid to the government of Violeta de Chamorro for more than a year and scuttle the appointment of a professional diplomat as ambassador to Managua. Elsewhere in the region, as nations explored the possibilities of multilateral organizations and joint or collaborative ventures, such as MERCOSUR, the Group of Three, the Group of Rio, the negotiations between Chile and Argentina, the ongoing series of talks among the presidents of the Central American nations, and the efforts to breathe more life into the Caribbean associations, the U.S. government made approving noises without ever quite expressing enthusiasm for these efforts.[22] Decision makers in Washington were unwilling to champion any collective or multilateral initiative by Latin American nations that smacked of limiting U.S. freedom of action, a traditional posture.[23] Some of this effort by Latin Americans was a response to Bush's Enterprise for the Americas Initiative, but a good deal of it was in the nature of probing the limits of the autonomy of action that might be available to the nations of the region once the Cold War framework had been removed and was part of several nations' efforts to redefine their own security.[24]

One of the greatest beneficiaries of the new sense of freedom to explore new modes of action and their possibilities was the OAS. The United States did not want to arbitrate all interstate disputes in the hemisphere or have its hand forced in any conflict, so for a while, at the beginning of the Bush administration, it looked as if the OAS would become its chosen instrument. Luigi Einaudi, a strong personality and a respected Latin Americanist, was appointed U.S. ambassador to the OAS. In conjunction with a group of "Young Turks" from Latin America led by Heraldo Muñoz of Chile and Juan Pablo Lohlé of Argentina, and later Hernan Patiño Mayer of Argentina, Einaudi provided energetic leadership for the OAS. He was a powerful proponent within the State Department of using the OAS as the principal vehicle of U.S. policy in the region.[25]

The alliance among the strongest advocates of democracy in the hemisphere was attractive and congenial to U.S. policy, and the seeming willingness on the part of the OAS to take on tough cases, like the transition to peace in El Salvador, the military coup in Haiti, and a definition of a hemispheric agenda for the environment, meant that the United States could assume a low profile in the hemisphere until and unless it had reason to do otherwise. Unfortunately, this quickly proved an illusion. The very first test for the "new" OAS, that of dealing with the military coup in Haiti, proved too complex and involved too many commitments from too many members of the organization. Several prominent members remained unalterably opposed to an interventionist role for the organization, which had the effect of blunting the force of any collective statement about the crisis. Furthermore, Haiti proved too difficult to handle even within the OAS, although it is hard to imagine that the Haitian case would be less difficult than dealing with the protection of democracy in Venezuela or Peru. President Jean Bertrand Aristide was an uncooperative, uncompromising ally, and no nation in the region would step forward to provide the resources—financial or military—to carry out a solution determined by the majority. Worse, from the U.S. point of view, the OAS was unable to help on the Haitian refugee issue, which soon became a bitter dispute in U.S. domestic politics. The more sensitive the issue became, the less patience the U.S. government had with the OAS. When the OAS could not agree on a policy, the United States found itself in the unacceptable position of having to go it alone with regard to the growing numbers of Haitians who risked their lives in tiny boats to cross the water to Florida. When the United States tried to get its allies in the OAS to defuse the refugee question by agreeing to take quotas of the Haitians so that the United States would not have to take them all (a measure that would prove unacceptable to the Congress), there was a babble of explanations as to why this country or that other country would not be able to take two thousand or ten thousand refugees. At that point, at the beginning of the Clinton administration, the U.S. government left negotiations with the Haitians to the UN while the administration devoted itself to dealing with the domestic fallout of the refugee problem. The UN imposed sanctions on Haiti, and the United States joined with France, Venezuela, and Argentina to form the ad hoc Friends of Haiti in an effort to broker a solution to the problem.

Other items on the agenda of hemispheric conflict resolution—democracy, governance, emigration, civil-military relations, the environment, drug traffic, poverty, and misery—were even more complex issues and prompted lower levels of consensus among the membership. Here the United States was content to allow the OAS to discuss endlessly, since it was unlikely that anything would result that might embarrass the United States.

The failure by either the Bush or Clinton administration to adopt with enthusiasm a leadership role for the United States in the OAS was due in part to a long-standing reluctance to allow the organization to compromise U.S. independence of action and in part to a widespread disdain within the policy-making bureaucracy for the institutional capacity of the OAS. At the same time, the failure was also the result of a genuine confusion within the government as to the direction of foreign policy. In the first place, there was confusion on strategic issues and uncertainty over what constitutes a threat. The Department of Defense convened a working group at the end of 1991 to discuss the military's mission in the Western Hemisphere. Through a series of sessions that included commissioned papers from a fairly wide spectrum of civilian analysts, the military and the intelligence community sought some guidance as to what it should be doing in the years ahead. The National Defense University did the same in 1993, and SOUTHCOM held a conference on the same subject in 1994.[26] The military, particularly leary of becoming the policemen of the hemisphere, did not want to be drawn casually into seemingly minor confrontations that ought to be dealt with by police forces in the affected countries, especially if there were any hint of domestic disagreement over the use of U.S. forces. Such a prospect was the setting for a quagmire, an unwinnable war, a no-win situation. The public and the Congress shared a reluctance to get sucked into foreign adventures. What has been called the Vietnam syndrome was still powerful in U.S. public opinion in all sections of the country and in all segments of the political spectrum.[27]

The U.S. military took the side of the governments of Latin American nations in opposing the use of U.S. troops in the effort to restrict the production and shipment of drugs from Latin America to the United States. Hemispheric discussions of drug trafficking rarely got very far. The United States took the position that the problem was on the supply side, while the Latin Americans maintained—with varying degrees of insistence—that the problem was at least half on the demand side and that solutions that focused exclusively on elimination of supply or interdiction of trade in drugs were doomed to failure. At one point, the Bush administration offered to send aircraft carriers to the coast of Colombia to prevent planes from leaving Colombian soil en route to clandestine airstrips in the United States. The public outcry in Colombia ended the adventure even before it began. More complex was the effort to get Peruvian president Alberto Fujimori, whose campaign platform had included strong attacks on the drug trade, to accept some form of military support in his efforts to eradicate or reduce the manufacture of cocaine paste on Peruvian soil and its shipment to sites in Colombia or directly to the United States. The Peruvians were anxious to keep U.S. military involvement quiet and as small as possible. That proved to be ineffective, as the drug lords had private armies that outmanned the joint forces of the Peruvian government and the U.S. Drug Enforcement Agency. The U.S. military resisted becoming directly involved, although the air force did provide surveillance craft for patrols over the area. Even that was ended when the Peruvian air force fired on one of the patrol planes in what was described as a breakdown in communications.[28] Not surprisingly, nationalists of the Left and the Right opposed giving the U.S. military an important role in fighting the drug lords. Conservatives in the U.S. Congress were frustrated by what they considered the reluctance on the part of Latin American governments to cooperate with the United States in combatting the traffic in drugs. Drug policy in the hemisphere was subjected to a formal review that lasted through most of 1993 without remarkable results.[29]

The United States did not want to become the policeman of the hemisphere because it did not consider it a worthwhile activity. Whatever the theoretical implications of U.S. hegemony, the U.S. government did not want to become responsible for settling conflicts in the region. Latin America seemed to have lost whatever geo-political or strategic significance it had had before and during the Cold War. The initial historical premise for the United States's polic-ing of the Western Hemisphere was to avoid intervention by outside powers whose presence might endanger the United States. Who was going to intervene in Latin America in the 1990s? Yugoslavia, the former Soviet Union, the Middle East—these were areas in which conflicts, if allowed to get out of hand, would threaten the stability of the world and endanger U.S. national interests. No one in official Washington during the Bush or Clinton administration believed that political instability in Brazil, an economic meltdown in Argen-tina, or a "white coup" in Peru could threaten U.S. interests. In the cases of Peru and Venezuela, the United States protested its support for democracy, but the measures taken to back up those declarations were meek and mild compared to what the United States indicated it might do in trouble spots elsewhere in the world. The U.S. public was more concerned with crises in Europe and the Middle East than in Latin America. The only exceptions were Haiti and Cuba, because both represented the leverage of local Florida groups over national politics and because the plight of the Haitian refugees stirred the hu-man rights community and portions of the black community.

The old joke told during the Nixon years that the administration would do anything for Latin America but pay attention to it seemed to fit the Bush administration. The Clinton administration could claim that it paid attention to Latin America, but it could not decide what to do about the region. Haiti, drug traffic, the debt crisis—so far each of these issues has been handled by the government in such a way as to keep them circumscribed, to reduce U.S. commitment of resources, and to make sure that they did not impinge on broader areas of the nation's concern. Protestations of Latin America's im-portance to the United States were based on projections of future economic interest. Some argued that a revived Latin America would be a major market for the United States and a perfect field for U.S. in-vestments, especially if the European common market proved to be less open than the GATT negotiations promised, but until the revival took place, the fact remained that Europe and Asia were both far more important to the U.S. economy. Other arguments in support of Latin America's significance to the United States, such as a shared historical experience, shared democratic aspirations, cultural affini-ties, and feelings of brotherhood, always seemed to lose out in the setting of priorities to more pragmatic, immediate considerations in which strategic concerns seemed more clearly defined.

Further complicating U.S. policy in the hemisphere during the Bush and Clinton administrations was a curious resurgence of Wilsonianism, that urge—born of a certitude that the U.S. system is the best and the best for everyone, everywhere—to teach the benefits of liberal democracy to anyone, even with the use of force. Emerging from the final years of the Cold War and from the bitter internal debate over intervention in El Salvador and Nicaragua, new domestic and international alliances had formed that were ferociously activist on matters of human rights and the defence of democracy. The National Endowment for Democracy (NED) interpreted its successful intervention in Chile in favor of democracy in the plebiscite organized by the military dictator Augusto Pinochet as a demonstration that it was possible to intervene on the side of democracy without stirring a nationalist backlash and without upsetting the bipartisan coalition in Congress, which provided their funding. The NED began to look around for other fields to conquer and increased the pressure on Cuba while it mounted technical assistance missions to nations in the former Soviet bloc to teach them how to organize judiciaries, write legal codes, and establish political parties and the other institutions of democracy. The Democracy Project in AID quickly became the U.S. government's largest single foreign aid program and the core of AID's policy of sustainable democracy.[30]

The defense of democracy was a policy around which Democrats and Republicans could build coalitions; the virtues of democracy brought liberals and conservatives together. Both seemed to be convinced of the universality of democratic values as well as of the efficacy of collective action in preserving, protecting, or even creating the institutional mechanisms of democracy. Some who had been staunchly opposed to intervention in the 1980s began to assume the postures of Wilsonian interventionism.[31] The Cuban American community used the democracy issue to insinuate itself into the mainstream debate on foreign policy and to win allies among human rights groups and others who for years had shunned the Miami Cubans as selfish reactionaries. It was no accident that candidate Clinton indicated his support for the Toricelli Bill, which banned trade with Cuba by foreign subsidiaries until Fidel Castro made clear steps to restore democracy, and that insiders spoke of the Cuban American "litmus test" for the new administration's appointees who would have anything to do with Latin America. For nearly a month after the inauguration, the Cuban American lobby seemed to control the formulation of Latin American policy.[32] The conservative supporters of democracy and the more progressive advocates of U.S. intervention against dictators had trouble agreeing over how the United States should play its role as protector of democracy in the hemisphere.

In the aftermath of the Cold War, and with the transition to democracy well advanced in Latin America, the human rights community consciously set out to reinvent itself and to define its new mission now that the United States apparently was not going to engage in clandestine interventions in the hemisphere or in operations supportive of dictatorships or other regimes that blatantly violated the human rights of their citizens. Organizations such as the Washington Office on Latin America (WOLA), Americas Watch, and the various church-related human rights groups sought ways to remain effective in helping the forces of democracy in the hemisphere consolidate their strength and extend to more and more people. The transnational nongovernmental organizations (NGOs) had come to play a critical role in defining Latin American interests as well as in influencing U.S. policy. Theirs, too, was a posture of universalism and activism. It was a position that staked out the moral high ground for the United States and justified intervention for just cause, as in Somalia. The problem, however, was that the NGOs had served also to confuse the line between domestic and international issues. They were anxious to get the UN involved but sensitive to the need to define carefully the parameters for multilateral action, and they were conscious of the ambiguity toward the UN within the U.S. foreign policy establishment.[33]

In attempting to maintain its credentials as a supporter of democracy while not getting sucked into one intervention after another in countries that were alleged to violate the human rights of their citizens, the Bush administration had been caught in this ground swell of Wilsonian interventionism. While there really was no dissent over the importance of human rights, the question was how to intervene to accomplish special purposes without getting trapped in a quagmire. Intervention was not so simple.

But if the Bush administration was ambivalent over how to export democracy in the hemisphere, it had no doubts about how to solve Latin America's economic problems. The free trade treaty with Canada seemed to be going well. The U.S. position in the GATT negotiations clearly favored freer trade. Mexico was about to join Canada and the United States in forming a North American Free Trade Area. Why not extend the benefits of NAFTA to the entire hemisphere? This seemed to fit in with the efforts of multilateral lending agencies to push the governments of Latin America to get their economic houses in order, to restructure their economies and modernize their policies, and to make their nations more competitive. It was in this context that on 27 June 1990 President Bush announced the Enterprise for the Americas Initiative.

The administration emphasized that the president's new policy was part of a worldwide phenomenon, part of a broad swing toward market economies and democratic polities. The policy itself, according to Roger B. Porter, a presidential adviser on economic matters, was part of a "vision for Latin America that is built on a foundation of partnership: partnership between Latin America and the Caribbean on the one hand and the United States on the other; partnership among the governments in the Hemisphere and their private sector; and partnership among the private sectors of the countries in the region."[34] This official explanation of the EAI recognized that there were scant government resources involved. That was the point—the EAI was about markets, eliminating barriers to trade and to entrepreneurship and reducing statism. "The challenge to Latin governments under the Bush initiative," Porter said in a speech to the Americas Society in the fall of 1990, "is to remove obstacles to efficiently functioning markets and to create a climate for entrepreneurship." States should not be involved in production but should "implement regulations which safeguard foreign investments and facilitate the entry and exit of capital."[35]

President Bush, by nature an optimist, saw a global trend toward market economics and democratic politics. He was particularly encouraged by the movement toward freer international trade. He believed profoundly in the efficacy of untrammeled international exchange. This was the government's recognition of the consensus with respect to the transformation of the international market. Reflecting a view long advocated by international lending agencies and the IMF and now legitimized by a broad consensus among academic economists, the so-called Washington Consensus stressed the virtues of the free market and the need to restructure the command economies of the former Socialist bloc and the protectionist economies of the Third World along lines congenial to the policies of the industrialized nations of the developed West.[36] According to this view, with the end of the Cold War there was a growing trend toward openness in the international economy based on increasingly free trade and growing ease of movement of capital, labor, and information across national boundaries. Such restructuring by the developing nations would permit their reinsertion into the increasingly competitive world economy, where efficiency and comparative advantage appeared to be the keys to success.

The end of the Cold War freed the nations of Eastern Europe to join in a movement already well advanced in the Western Hemisphere, where, with the exception of Cuba, each nation was ruled by civilian, elected governments, an alignment unique in the region's history. Moreover, many of the governments had set out on economic reforms of profound significance, turning away from the import substitution models of development that had dominated policy making virtually since the Great Depression and that had been an article of faith since the 1950s to open their economies to the international market. The Washington Consensus seemed global in its reach. It was the economists' version of Fukuyama's end of history.

Despite these trends, Bush had been upset by the lament of the presidents of the Andean nations with whom he had met early in 1990 to discuss the vexing issue of drug traffic. President Bush had gone to the meeting in Cartagena expecting enthusiastic cooperation from his Latin American colleagues. Instead, the leaders of Bolivia, Peru, and Colombia had reported to him that their countries and the other countries of the region were caught in an economic tailspin. They reported that the 1980s had been a lost decade for Latin America. The region had gone backward in economic terms, pinned down by the heavy burden of the enormous unpaid international debt that had brought the flow of private capital to a standstill and dragged most of the hemisphere into a recession that was undermining the new and fragile democracies. In the face of severe recession, the civilian governments were unable to raise the revenue to satisfy the legitimate needs of their population.

To compound the problem, the restructuring programs that were imposed on Latin America by the international banks as a condition for renewed loans, and sometimes by the U.S. Treasury as a condition for credits by the Export-Import Bank or other federal agencies, were sapping the strength of the state. This came precisely at a time when a strong state was needed to consolidate a fledgling democracy and to respond to legitimate social needs such as staggering unemployment and to threats such as drug trafficking, environmental degradation, and terrorism—all of which were at the top of the U.S. agenda for the hemisphere. But President Bush was not attracted to a program of official aid. Such a program went against his own philosophy, and he knew that even if he were to adopt one he would have a tough time selling it to the Congress and to the American people, who were leery of the lingering recession and of the costs of the savings and loan scandal that hung over their heads. Historically, with the exception of the Alliance for Progress, the United States had responded to Latin American requests for economic help by urging them to open their markets and allow U.S. capital to solve their problems. "Trade not aid" was the response of U.S. officials after World War II to Latin American colleagues who asked for a hemispheric equivalent of the Marshall Plan. Bush was not the first U.S. president to believe in the magical healing powers of the international market.

These general concerns were focused for the president and his immediate advisers on the specific instance of Mexico, whose young Harvard-educated president, Carlos Salinas de Gortari, had embarked on a bold reform program designed to open the Mexican economy, jump-starting it with massive infusions of foreign capital and privatizations. For many years Mexico, to the United States, had been a special case. Aside from the obvious ties created by intertwined histories, a two-thousand-mile common border, and a high level of economic interdependence, the two countries were forced to confront together the most significant emigration—legal and illegal—in the hemisphere. As Texans, President Bush and Secretary of State James Baker had a greater awareness of Mexico than most Americans, and they also had an acute sense that they should do something about and for Mexico. As Texans, too, they tended to confuse the rest of Latin America with Mexico. What was good for Mexico undoubtedly would be good for the rest of the region.

Gathered on the president's ranch in southern Texas, Bush and Baker took into account their recent decision to begin talks with Mexico for a free trade zone, which, when added to Canada, would constitute a North American Free Trade Area. They also thought about the president's forthcoming trip to South America in September.[37] What emerged—the result of policy planning within the

Treasury Department by a small group called together by Secretary Nicholas Brady—seemed the perfect package. The subsequent plan —aimed at Mexico but to include the rest of the hemisphere—was designed to deal with the major preoccupations of Latin America: debt, trade, and economic well-being. Consistent with administration policy in the Uruguay Round of the GATT negotiations, the initiative strengthened the commitment of the Latin American nations to the multilateral trade reform central to those discussions. Finally, by its insistence on partnership and hemispheric togetherness, the plan aimed at allaying the deep-seated anxieties of Latin Americans about the residual urges of the United States toward hegemonic behavior in the hemisphere.

In and of itself, the Enterprise for the Americas Initiative accomplished little. A more serious problem was that it was oversold in Latin America.[38] Even if all barriers to trade with the United States were eliminated, nontariff barriers included, Latin American exports to the United States would increase by only 8 percent. That amount would not be enough either to solve Latin America's economic woes or to fuel the engines of growth for very long. The indirect gains, however, have been significant. At the very least, in a worst case scenario, the possibility of a free trade area in the hemisphere would protect the Latin American nations from a resurgence of U.S. protectionism, although nontariff barriers have become so complex and the asymmetry between the U.S. economy and the economies of the Latin American nations so vast that true free trade would, under the best of circumstances, be decades away and under more difficult circumstances hopelessly delayed. Still, the EAI has provided important indirect benefits even if we take a cynical view of its short-term accomplishments. There has been a palpable increase in investor confidence in Latin America, as shown by the impressive demand for securities on a growing number of exchanges in the region, and there has been a significant flow of private capital into a few of the countries, mainly Chile and Mexico. If the EAI has provided a buttress for free trade policies that are historically anomalous, politically vulnerable, and subject to domestic attack, then by making the economies of the Latin American nations more competitive in the international marketplace, the plan may prove to be a self-fulfilling prophecy of the most positive sort.

Perhaps most important, in rushing to join the hemispheric free trade area the EAI gave the nations of Latin America a powerful stimulus to intraregional integration efforts, pushing them further toward realization than at any previous time. Should such projects as MERCOSUR and the Andean Pact be brought to fruition they will strengthen the economies of Latin America at a critical time and prove to be a powerful support for the self-esteem of the peoples of the hemisphere. Ironically, by pushing the Latin American nations to restructure their economies, then leading them to expect great things from an EAI given a splashy inauguration, then suggesting that a NAFTA for the hemisphere was the solution to their problems, and finally frustrating them by bureaucratic inadequacy and partisan wrangling, the United States may end up strengthening Latin American regionalism.[39]

Historically, the United States has preferred to deal with Latin American nations on an individual basis and has gone to great lengths to discourage multilateral efforts. Today, in the aftermath of the Cold War, the United States needs Latin America to join with it in the settlement of hemispheric disputes, just as the United States needs European and other allies to deal effectively with crises in Yugoslavia, Cambodia, Iraq, or elsewhere, whether through the UN or other forms of collective effort. In the Western Hemisphere, the United States needs allies to deal with crises in Haiti and Peru, drug trafficking, terrorism, and threats to the environment. This need for partners may produce some unanticipated changes in U.S. policy that run counter to the United States's historic need for a free hand in hemispheric action. The Bush administration gave every indication that it preferred to act alone. Historically, the Democrats have been more inclined toward multilateral cooperation with Latin America. The Bush administration was willing to have multilateral organizations operate as long as they did not threaten U.S. national interests or force U.S. intervention and as long as they followed the emerging code of good behavior that protected human rights and democracy. The Clinton administration began by trumpeting its support for multilateralism, but such enthusiasm dissipated quickly in the face of public reaction to unanticipated complications in Haiti, Somalia, and Bosnia.

The end of the Cold War brought a remarkable reemergence in the United States of some traditional approaches to dealing with Latin America, approaches that seemed to be drawn from the distant past and to rely upon deeply felt and widely shared assumptions about U.S. relations with the rest of the hemisphere. Briefly, these attitudes—they cannot be called a coherent or conscious policy so much as a set of concurrent attitudes—include an aversion to interference by outsiders, a compulsion to prevent any instability that threatens the United States, and a desire to preserve U.S. autonomy of action so that its global interests are not compromised. Taken together, these attitudes, if formulated deliberately as policy, would indicate a hemispheric hegemon whose major preoccupations were elsewhere, one that preferred not to get involved, if at all possible, and one that would like to reserve the region as a kind of preserve, a safety area that might be redefined as an economic bloc should that prove necessary. In dealing with Latin America, such a traditional posture would emphasize what the Founding Fathers called propinquity. The United States would be primarily concerned with the countries and issues closest to its territory and most likely to threaten its well-being. Thus, Mexico gets greater attention than Brazil and the broad, intense discussion of and support for NAFTA.

Of course, new technologies and new global issues have altered our sense of distance, but the same rules appear to apply today as they have over the past two hundred years. Emigration is currently a source of deep concern, and countries that send large number of immigrants to our shores are considered close in every sense. The importance of environmental issues in U.S. politics is influenced by the public perception of how close or immediate the threat is. The destruction of the Amazon rain forest seems more immediate than the problem of acid rain in Canada, more threatening than the destruction of the rain forest in Puerto Rico or Costa Rica, and (now that the Soviet Union is not seen as a party to the conflict) much more threatening than civil disorder in Nicaragua. The debate over Cuba seemed to have less to do with foreign policy and international affairs than it did with the extraordinary leverage over the U.S. political discussion exercised by the Cuban American Foundation, which suggests that countries in Latin America are close as they become part of the domestic political debate.

The implications of this concept of distance seemed to be that the farther from the United States, the more removed from the nation's attention, the greater the autonomy of action available to the countries of Latin America. Actions by one country may be seen as unobjectionable, while the same actions by another country may be considered dangerous. By the same token, similar actions by the same country at two different moments might well elicit different responses from the United States. In calculating foreign policy responses to Latin America, so much depends on how the situation is perceived in the United States and how deeply inmeshed the issue becomes in U.S. domestic politics. In less than two years, Nicaragua went from an issue central to the foreign policy debate in the United States to one of a nation pleading for attention from the U.S. government.[40]

§

How is Latin America to deal with the New World Order after the Cold War? What are the options available to the nations of the region? In one sense, Latin America found the end of the Cold War liberating, for it would no longer be necessary for Latin American nations to define their own national security and to have their policies evaluated and defined in terms of U.S. perceptions of their impact on the bipolar struggle. On the other hand, while it was maddening and, in the last analysis, demeaning to define one's national security in terms of the perception of another nation, the bipolar competition did allow for a certain amount of playing off of one great power against the other. Such gambits had their cost (the United States never took kindly to Latin American flirtations with the Soviet Union), but they brought some benefits as well, at least in the short term. Trade with the Soviet Union, as Argentina carried out when no one else would buy its grain, was less objectionable than establishing links that carried political or military implications. Cuba, of course, was the most extreme example.[41] Once the Soviet Union began to pull back from its Cuban commitments, the United States responded with vindictiveness. Instead of welcoming Cuba back into the hemispheric fold, the United States tightened its embargo with the Toricelli Bill and threatened subsidiaries of U.S. corporations that traded with Cuba. The signals to Latin America were mixed and difficult to interpret.[42]

But there was as much, if not more, confusion in Latin America as in the United States over what might be an appropriate foreign policy in the post–Cold War world. Several important efforts were made to define national security policy in an autonomous fashion.[43] In many countries a great deal of attention was paid to what was known as the reinsertion into the international market. For the most part, the discussion was driven by economic issues and, again, the framework seemed to be determined from outside the region in the so-called Washington Consensus. As had been the case through most of the Cold War, the nations of Latin America were anxious about their development model. A Chilean general commented that "underdevelopment was the principal security threat to Latin America."[44] In such a case, Latin Americans did not seem to have much choice. How were they to be competitive in the global marketplace? Modernization was the key, and the modalities of modernization were taken for granted. The Latin American dilemma seemed all the more acute as the nations of Eastern Europe and the former Soviet Union rushed to create the trappings of democracy and free market capitalism. How frustrating for Latin American leaders to do everything possible to hurry the restructuring of their economies, at cruel social cost, only to see potential investors rush to Eastern Europe and hesitate to venture south. Meanwhile, these leaders waited and waited for their own investors to bring home the billions of dollars stashed abroad that were needed to stimulate and revive the economies of their own countries.[45] Some people in Latin America, worried about the social cost of restructuring or unconvinced of the virtues of the Washington Consensus, began to explore alternative models and look for other "possible capitalisms."[46]

The requirements for successful reinsertion into the global market and a key to Latin America's future success in the international system appeared by the beginning of the 1990s to be set by what we might call an international code of good behavior. Rarely explicit, its elements were obvious in the reactions of the United States and other major economic powers to dealings with the developing nations. First and foremost, it was necessary to have a democratic government. Second, it was essential to guarantee the sanctity of property and to welcome capital in its various forms—the code for this was to have an "open" economy. Every nation in the hemisphere, even Cuba, tried to be more open than it had been, although the pace and comprehensiveness of the openness varied widely from country to country. Finally, and most difficult, it was necessary to be "transparent" in the conduct of international affairs and in the protection of human and property rights. This was a touchy subject, because it ran into a combination of long-standing protection of certain local production (the computer industry in Brazil, pharmaceuticals in Argentina) and corruption. It became clear that traditional forms of influence peddling in Latin America could become a limiting factor in the creation of new markets and, more important, in a nation's capacity to attract new investment.[47]

To maximize their autonomy in the world marketplace, the nations of Latin America had to be competitive. That meant they had to produce products at attractive prices. It also meant that they had to prepare their labor force to produce new products in an efficient and competitive fashion. Otherwise, they would be condemned to the perpetual exportation of primary products, prices for which were at best unstable and more often soft, or else held to serve as cheap labor *maquiladoras*. The escape from the cheap labor trap would be through the creation of a labor force capable of handling increasingly sophisticated manufactured products. This, however, raised the thorny questions of technology transfer and education reform. Would the nations of Latin America be able to gain access to the technology necessary to produce the manufacturers they might want? Would Latin Americans be able to restructure their education systems to adapt to new global demands?[48]

Even if Latin Americans followed all the prescriptions of the international lending agencies and opened their economies, even if these nations were transparent in their international dealings and remained steadfast in their political democracy, their capacity to exert influence in the international system—the space they would enjoy within the system—would be determined in part also by their ability to deal with their own increasing poverty. The debt crisis and the restructuring programs together had forced severe restrictions in government welfare programs and, in some cases, recession. These contributed to massive increases in the incidence of poverty and, in some countries, to more marked inequities in the distribution of income.[49]

In some cases, the perception of inequity together with corruption was a volatile mix. It produced two attempted coups against the regime of Carlos Andrés Pérez in Venezuela and social disturbances throughout the hemisphere.[50] A democratic government's capacity for action in the international system was seriously restricted by the spread of poverty among its people and by its own inability to deal with that poverty. Moreover, the threat to democracy that growing social inequity represented could so focus the attention of a government on domestic issues that it might become weaker in its international dealings. Its international space would be reduced. Similarly, its ability to speak with authority in an international forum would be influenced by such things as social inequity, corruption, and the perceived propriety of its democratic government. Costa Rica is the most extreme example of a country that has based its international role on the consolidation of its democracy. The government of Carlos Menem in Argentina tried to use a single-minded defense of democracy as an instrument of foreign policy to increase the influence of Argentina in international organizations such as the OAS.

No matter what their economic strategy, no matter what their view of how the post–Cold War world will be organized, the nations of Latin America will have to deal with the fact that the United States will continue to be the unrivaled hegemonic power in the hemisphere. Whatever their view of the debate over the decline of the United States, there is no challenger to the United States in the Western Hemisphere. Even in cases where Europe or Japan have a larger share of a nation's trade than the United States or where one or another of the rival economic blocs is making significant investments in the economy of a Latin American nation, neither Japan nor any of the nations of Europe is interested in or capable of exercising influence within the hemisphere that comes remotely close to hegemony. The Latin Americans will have to deal with the United States or come up with an independent posture that takes the United States into account. For good or for ill, Japan and Europe are preoccupied with what is happening in Eastern Europe and the former Soviet Union. They accord even less attention and priority to Latin America than does the United States. Disturbances in the Eurasian land mass, especially in the former Soviet Union, elicit a reaction markedly different from disorder in Brazil or Kenya. This disparity is likely to hold at least for the next decade.

Relative inattention is damaging to the national ego but represents a historically unique opportunity to create a role in international affairs. U.S. preoccupation with Europe means that Latin America can exercise considerable autonomy in the definition of its own role in world affairs. As long as they are democratic, and as long as they do not glaringly violate the emerging Wilsonian code of international behavior, the nations of Latin America will have considerable autonomy to help define the nature of the new national security agenda. The United States will be more than happy to cede leadership to a democratic Latin America in an equitable solution to such problems as Haiti, Cuba, drug trafficking, and the entire gamut of global issues. The U.S. military has indicated that it is willing to collaborate with Latin American partners in its expanding "non-traditional" mission in the hemisphere.[51] Confusion in the United States over what its role in world affairs should be and a lack of consensus on the value of multilateral organizations to enforce the international code of behavior and to resolve conflicts makes that autonomy greater still.

The dilemma for Latin America is that it never before has been in a position to assume real autonomy or real responsibility and it is seriously inhibited. There is little awareness that in order to exercise responsibility in world affairs a nation must be prepared to sacrifice some measure of sovereignty. This is difficult for Latin American countries, which have exerted most of their international effort since independence to protect their sovereignty, particularly in this century from the United States, and will not easily give any of it up, even though this may be the only way a nation can carve out a role of increasing influence and responsibility in the international system. The Declaration of Santiago, in which the nations of the region pledged to act against a military coup in any country, appears to be just the right sort of mechanism through which the Latin American nations can take their destiny in their own hands. The question is how it will be used, if at all.[52] It was applied successfully by an ad hoc multilateral group in Guatemala in 1993 but could not be invoked with effect in dealing with Haiti.

The OAS is both a key to and a reflection of what is happening in Latin America and in the hemisphere as a whole. Indeed, it is fair to say that the OAS today is also a reflection of what is happening in the global system. Whatever else it might be or become, the OAS is currently a critical forum in which the nations of Latin America define their concept of their own security. For nearly a hundred years the nations of Latin America have been searching simultaneously for a way of living together and a way to curb the tendency of the United States to act unilaterally within the hemisphere in defense of its own national interests, often at the expense of the national interests and even the sovereignty of one or more of the other nations in the hemisphere. The central question has become, Will the nations of Latin America define their security in strictly national terms or in terms that take advantage or require some measure of regional cooperation or integration?[53] Whatever the answer, it appears fairly certain that in the foreseeable future the ability to control or inhibit the individual action of the United States will depend upon the ability of the Latin American nations to cooperate with one another in either regional or subregional groups. In the short term, it may prove easier for them to operate in ad hoc groups in which a common interest is clear (the Esquipulas group, the Group of Rio, the Group of Three, for example), rather than in the OAS itself, which is hampered by its comprehensive membership, its historical baggage, and its institutional clumsiness.

Will Latin Americans succeed in defining their own positions with regard to the emerging global agenda so that they can accommodate or combine their respective positions with that of the United States? Or will they remain reactive, responding to the U.S. definition of how the hemisphere should deal with these issues while considering U.S. national interests? Some Latin American analysts suggest that such definitions may prove divisive and not cohesive.[54] In this context it is clear that the OAS can do no more than the member states have the will to do and that smaller, more flexible groups may have greater leverage.

These possibilities present Latin America with a fearsome challenge and represent a historic opportunity. Never before have the nations of Latin America had a similar chance to define their roles in the world community and to contribute in a meaningful, substantial fashion to the shaping of the hemispheric community. They must act—and soon—or the opportunity may pass and a new framework be imposed on them that could reduce their autonomy to less than it is today or what it was in the past. The United States will not willingly or deliberately remain in the state of confusion in which it found itself at the beginning of the 1990s. More than at any time since their independence, the nations of Latin America have their destiny in their own hands.

Notes

1. F. Fukuyama, "The End of History?" *National Interest* 16 (summer 1989); the piece, with the comments and rejoinder to the comments, was converted into a book, *The End of History and the Last Man* (New York: Free Press, 1992).

2. For example, Kim R. Holmes, "The New World Disorder," in *The Heritage Lectures,* and the Staff of the Heritage Foundation, *Making the World Safe for America: A U.S. Foreign Policy Blueprint* (Washington DC: Heritage

Foundation, 1992). For another view of the same subject, see Stanley Hoffman, "Delusions of World Order," *New York Review of Books*, 9 April 1992.

3. Kissinger, "Unsolved Problems," in *Lisbon 1992* (Trilateral Commission, 1992).

4. Mark Falcoff, article in the *Washington Post*; and Holmes, "The New World Disorder."

5. Robert Pastor, *Whirlpool: U.S. Foreign Policy toward Latin America and the Caribbean* (Princeton, N.J.: Princeton University Press, 1992); Abraham Lowenthal, "Latin America and the New Winds," *Miami Herald*, 25 March 1990; *The United States and Latin America in the 1990s: Changing U.S. Interests and Policies in a New World* (Washington DC: Inter-American Dialogue, 1991); "The United States and Latin America in a New World," *North-South* (June–July 1992). See also Peter Hakim, "The United States and Latin America: Good Neighbors Again?" *Current History* 91, no. 562 (February 1992); and Richard Feinberg, "Latin America: Back on the Screen," *International Economic Insights* (July–August 1992). Looking beyond the Bush administration, Inter-American Dialogue indicated that "opportunities for sustained cooperation [never] had been greater." *Convergence and Community: The Americas in 1993: A Report of the Inter-American Dialogue* (Washington DC: Aspen Institute, 1992).

6. Roger B. Porter, "The Enterprise for the Americas Initiative: A New Approach to Economic Growth," *Journal of Interamerican Studies* 32, no. 4 (winter 1990): 2; Peter Hakim, "The Enterprise for the Americas Initiative," *Washington Quarterly* 15, no. 2 (spring 1992). Also see his "The Enterprise for the Americas Initiative: What Washington Wants," *Brookings Review* (fall 1992).

7. Tulchin, "The Enterprise for the Americas Initiative," in Roy Green, ed., *United States Trade Relations* (Boulder, Colo.: Praeger, 1993).

8. One survey of post–Cold War approaches to foreign policy gives greater importance to the neonationalist position. See Alan Tonelson, "Beyond Left and Right," *National Interest* (winter 1993–94). It is my view that the internationalists still dominate the academic debate as well as the policy community.

9. Interview with Moisés Naim, Carnegie Endowment, 18 January 1993.

10. Paul Kennedy, *Imperial Overreach* (New Haven, Conn.: Yale University Press, 1990); David Calleo, *Declining Hegemon* (Baltimore, Md.: Johns Hopkins University Press, 1991); Samuel P. Huntington, "The U.S.—Decline or Renewal?" *Foreign Affairs* 67, no. 2 (winter 1988–89).

11. Robert O. Keohane and Joseph S. Nye Jr., *Power and Interdependence*, 2d ed. (New York: Scott, Foresman, 1989); and Nye, "Arms Control after the Cold War," *Foreign Affairs* 68, no. 5 (winter 1989–90); a few European authors in 1990 anticipated Europe's arrival on the scene as a major force, although they differed among themselves as to the consequences this might have for

the polarity of power in the international system. On the role of the UN and collective security, see Thomas G. Weiss and Meryl A. Kessler, eds., *Third World Security in the Post–Cold War Era* (Boulder, Colo.: Lynne Rienner, 1991); and Thomas G. Weiss, ed., *Collective Security in a Changing World* (Boulder, Colo.: Lynne Rienner, 1993).

12. John Lewis Gaddis, "Toward the Post–Cold War World," *Foreign Affairs* 70, no. 1 (winter 1990–91); and Charles Krautheimer, "The Unipolar Moment," *Foreign Affairs* 70, no. 2 (spring 1991); Robert W. Tucker and David C. Hendrickson, *The Imperial Temptation: The New World Order and America's Purpose* (New York: Council on Foreign Relations, 1992); and Susan Strange, "The Persistent Myth of Lost Hegemony," *International Organization* 41, no. 3 (autumn 1987). For an interesting collection of views with some historical perspective, see Michael J. Hogan, ed., *The End of the Cold War* (New York: Cambridge University Press, 1992).

13. For example, see the pamphlet by W. R. Smyser, *Germany's Domestic Situation and U.S. Relations,* Institute for Defense Analyses, 12 August 1992.

14. *New York Times,* 5 December 1992, p. 1.

15. *New York Times,* 21 December 1992, p. 1.

16. John Kasarda, "Jobs, Migration, and Emerging Urban Mismatches," in Michael G. H. McGeary and L. E. Lynn Jr., eds., *Urban Change and Poverty* (Washington DC: National Academy, 1988); and Kasarda, "Structural Factors Affecting the Location and Timing of Urban Underclass Growth," *Urban Geography* 11, no. 3 (1990).

17. Kissinger, "Unsolved Problems."

18. Augusto Varas, "Global Transformations and Peace: Arms Control, Disarmament and the Resolution of Conflict in the Western Hemisphere in the Post–Cold War Period: A Framework for Analysis." Ms. prepared for a workshop at the Woodrow Wilson Center, 16 November 1992.

19. José Baena Soares, "The Future of the Organization of American States," Woodrow Wilson Center, 15 April 1991; Heraldo Muñoz, *Environment and Diplomacy in the Americas* (Boulder, Colo.: Lynne Rienner, 1992); speech by Ambassador Hernan Patiño Mayer at Tufts University, 6 February 1992.

20. A. Varas, "Los nuevos parametros estratégicos en el cono sur." Paper presented at the North-South Conference, Miami, 7 December 1992.

21. Lars Schoultz, *National Security Policy in U.S.–Latin American Relations* (Princeton, N.J.: Princeton University Press, 1986), and *Human Rights and United States Policy toward Latin America* (Princeton, N.J.: Princeton University Press, 1981); Luis Maira, ed., *Estados Unidos: una visión latinoamericana* (Mexico City: CIDE, 1984); Walter LaFeber, *Inevitable Revolutions* (New York: Norton, 1983); and Thomas Carothers, *In the Name of Democracy* (Berkeley: University of California Press, 1991).

22. Anthony Bryan, "A Wider Caribbean . . . at Last?" *North-South* 1, no. 5 (February–March 1992); Jorge I. Dominguez, Robert A. Pastor, and R. DeLisle Worrell, *The Caribbean Prepares for the* 21st Century (Boston: World Peace Foundation, 1986); also in Robert A. Pastor and Richard Fletcher, "The Caribbean in the 21st Century," *Foreign Affairs* 70, no. 3 (summer 1991); Andrés Serbin, "The Caribbean: Myths and Realities for the 1990s," *Journal of Interamerican Studies* 32, no. 2 (summer 1990); Andrés Serbin, "The Caricom States and the Group of Three: A New Partnership between Latin America and the Non-Hispanic Caribbean?" *Journal of Interamerican Studies* 33, no. 2 (summer 1991); and speech by Jamaican ambassador to the United States Richard Bernal, reprinted in *Enterprise for the Americas Initiative*, Report No. 8 (Woodrow Wilson Center, September 1992), and Statement before the House Committee on Small Business, "Impact of NAFTA on the Economic Development of the Caribbean and U.S./Caribbean Trade," 16 December 1992; Roberto Bouzas, "A U.S.-MERCOSUR Free Trade Area," in Sylvia Saborio, ed., *The Premise and the Promise: Free Trade in the Americas* (Washington DC: ODC, 1992); "The Southern Cone Countries in the International Political Economy," (Buenos Aires: FLACSO, 1992); Felix Peña, "Competividad, democracia e integración en las Americas." Paper presented at a seminar organized by the Fundação G. Vargas, 21 August 1992.

23. Tulchin, "Enterprise for the Americas Initiatives."

24. Paul C. Psaila, "Redefining National Security in Latin America: A Workshop Report," Wilson Center Latin American Program, Working Paper No. 24 (1993).

25. See, the remarks by Luigi Einaudi and Heraldo Muñoz in Baena Soares, "The Future of the Organization of American States."

26. L. Erik Kjonnerod, ed., *Evolving U.S. Strategy for Latin America and the Caribbean* (Washington DC: National Defense University Press, 1992); and the series of publications by the National Defense University; for example, Samuel J. Watson, ed., "Proceedings of the Latin American Strategy Development Workshop Series" (May 1992).

27. Tulchin, "Estados Unidos y la crisis en Centroamérica: una perspectiva histórica," in Juan del Aguila et al., *Realidades y posibilidades de las relaciones entre España y América en los ochenta* (Madrid: ICI, 1986).

28. *New York Times*, 23 October 1992. For a comprehensive treatment of the drug issues, see the special issue "Drug Trafficking Research Update," *Journal of Interamerican Studies* 34, no. 3 (fall 1992); and Peter H. Smith, ed., *Drug Policy in the Americas* (Boulder, Colo.: Westview, 1992); and "United States Drug Policy toward Latin America," Woodrow Wilson Center Working Paper No. 194 (1991). For a Latin American view of the issue, see Diego Cardona y Juan Gabriel Tokatlian, "El sistema mundial en los noventa," *Colombia Internacional* 13 (January–March 1991); Adrian Bonilla, "Teoria de las relaciones internacionales como discurso político: el caso de la guerra de las

drogas," *Colombia Internacional* 15 (July–September 1991). More sensational treatments are Clare Hargreaves, *Snowfields: The War on Cocaine in the Andes* (New York: N.p.., 1992); and Michael Smith, ed., *Sharecropping for the Drug Lords: Narcotics and Development in the Third World* (New York: N.p., 1992); and Rensslaaer W. Lee III, *The White Labyrinth: Cocaine and Political Power* (Rutgers: Transaction, 1989).

29. Remarks by Congressman Benjamin Gilman, House Committee on Foreign Affairs, 3 February 1993. On the policy review, see the *Washington Post*, 6 November 1993, p. 1.

30. Carothers, *In the Name of Democracy;* on the activities of the NED, see its annual reports for the years 1988 to 1992. On the role of the NED in Chile during the plebiscite, see Joseph Tulchin and Augusto Varas, eds., *From Dictatorship to Democracy* (Boulder, Colo.: Lynne Rienner, 1991); and Thomas E. Skidmore, *The Media and Politics in Latin America* (Baltimore, Md.: Johns Hopkins University Press, 1993).

31. See, for example, *Convergence and Community*.

32. See Hearings of the House Foreign Affairs Committee, 3 February 1993. Freedom House, a human rights NGO that had been active in Eastern Europe, was represented in Washington by Frank Calzon, who identified himself as Cuban, not Cuban American.

33. Interview with Alexander Wilde, Washington Office on Latin America, 21 February 1992; also Douglas W. Payne, "Latin America and the Politics of Corruption," *Freedom Review* (January–February 1993).

34. Porter, "The Enterprise for the Americas Initiative."

35. Ibid., p. 6.

36. John Williamson, "What Washington Means by Policy Reform," in John Williamson, ed., *Latin American Adjustment: How Much Has Happened?* (Washington DC: Institute for International Economics, 1990).

37. The trip subsequently was postponed until December 1990.

38. Hakim, "The Enterprise for the Americas Initiative."

39. See the articles by S. Weintraub, Felix Peña, and Roberto Bouzas cited previously. For a summary of U.S. and Latin American views of the Enterprise, see Francisco Rojas, ed., *América Latina y la Iniciativa para las Américas* (Santiago: FLACSO, 1993); and Roy E. Green, ed., *The Enterprise for the Americas Initiative: Issues and Prospects for a Free Trade Agreement in the Western Hemisphere* (Westport, Conn.: Praeger, 1993).

40. For a detailed discussion of this concept with reference to the Caribbean, see Tulchin, "The Formation of United States Policy in the Caribbean," *Annals* (spring 1994).

41. Trade always has been considered more natural to U.S. leaders than entangling alliances. See Felix Gilbert, *To the Farewell Address* (Princeton, N.J.: Princeton University Press, 1961).

42. On the confusion in U.S. foreign policy formulation, see the Stanley

Foundation, *Global Changes and Institutional Transformation: Restructuring the Foreign Policymaking Process* (Muscatine, Iowa: Stanley Foundation, 1992).

43. See especially the work of several scholars at FLACSO, Chile; for example, Varas, "Global Transformations," and the joint project by FLACSO and the Woodrow Wilson Center that conducted national and regional seminars on the subject to encourage public debate. Another effort in Argentina is represented by Roberto Russell, ed., *La política exterior Argentina en el Nuevo Orden Mundial* (Buenos Aires: GEL, 1992).

44. Remarks by Gen. Fernando Arancibia during the seminar Los Dividendos de la Paz, conducted by RIAL, Santiago, Chile, 25 October 1990.

45. For a Bolivian lament by the minister of finance, see Jorge Quiroga et al., "Reviewing Bolivia's Economic Transformation," Woodrow Wilson Center, Latin American Program, Working Paper No. 201 (1992). On the restructuring programs, see Richard E. Feinberg and Valeriana Kallab, eds., *Adjustment Crisis in the Third World* (Washington DC: ODC, 1984); Howard Handelman and Werner Baer, eds., *Paying the Costs of Austerity in Latin America* (Boulder, Colo.: Westview, 1989); and Nora Lustig, *Mexico: the Remaking of an Economy* (Washington DC: Brookings Institution, 1992).

46. Simon Teitel, ed., *Towards a New Development Strategy* (Baltimore, Md.: Johns Hopkins University Press, 1992); and Enrique Iglesias, *Reflections on the Development Process* (Baltimore, Md.: Johns Hopkins University Press, 1992)

47. See, for example, the public discussion of a complaint by Terrence Todman, the U.S. ambassador to Argentina, of corruption affecting a U.S. firm attempting to do business in Argentina, *Clarin*, 23 March 1992; *Pagina 12*, 24 March 1992; and the scathing exposé published by Heracio Verbitsky, *Robo para la corona* (Buenos Aires: Planeta, 1992).

48. Simon Schwartzman, "Technology Transfer and the New Model of Economic Development," ms. in the possession of the author; Gustav Ranis, "International Migration and Foreign Assistance: Concepts and Application to the Philippines," ms. in possession of the author.

49. Advocates of the reforms insisted equity would come eventually through the "equity of the market": A. Alsogaray, "Va a ser resistencias," *La Nación*, 9 December 1992; and, more generally, Felipe Larrain and Marcelo Selowsky, eds., *The Public Sector and the Latin American Crisis* (San Francisco: ICS, 1991).

50. On the Venezuelan case, see Joseph S. Tulchin and Gary Bland, *Venezuela: The Lessons of Democracy* (Boulder, Colo.: Lynne Rienner, 1993). On the links between poverty and social tension, see John Walton, "Global and National Sources of Political Protest: Third World Responses to the Debt Crisis," *American Sociological Review* 55 (December 1990); and John Wal-

ton, "Debt Protest and the State in Latin America," in Susan Eckstein, ed., *Power and Popular Protest* (Berkeley: University of California Press, 1989).

51. Remarks "not for attribution" by a senior Defense Department official, at the conference Warriors in Peacetime: The Military and Democracy in Latin America, New Directions for U.S. Policy, 11–12 December 1992. It is worth noting that this official indicated he considered the traditional concept of sovereignty to be "impractical" and that it was being replaced by a concept of "national integrity" in the definition of the conditions for "humanitarian intervention." For a Latin American view of shared security, see Francisco Rojas, "Toward a Hemispheric Regime of Shared Security," in Bruce Bagley et al., eds., *The United States and Mexico: Economic Growth and Security in a Changing World Order* (Miami, Fla.: University of Miami Press, 1993).

52. Nathaniel C. Nash in *New York Times*, 9 June 1991, pp. iv, 2.

53. See V. P. Vaky and Heraldo Muñoz, *The Future of the Organization of American States* (New York: Twentieth Century Fund, 1993).

54. Monica Hirst and Carlos Rico, *Regional Security Perceptions in Latin America*, FLACSO, Serie de Documentos e Informes de Investigación (Buenos Aires, May 1992).

John D. Martz

The Championing of Democracy Abroad: Lessons from Latin America

North Americans may still remain resistant as a people to soccer—
to *fútbol*, in the Latin American vernacular. Yet they need make no
concessions to their fellow Americans to the south in regard to their
mania for sports. Throughout all the Americas, competition is important, nowhere more so than in politics. Outcomes are critical. For
better or worse, competition is omnipresent, and North Americans
display a cultural fixation on winning. All too often the inclination
is to accept nothing short of complete success. Returning to sports
analogy, baseball aficionados recall the unforgettable Durocher Dic-
tum, in which the legendary "Leo the Lip" assured the citizens of
Flatbush and the nation that "nice guys finish last." And in politics
as well as sports, victory is required. Where foreign policy is concerned, the notion of victory is buttressed by a traditional North
American belief that its own ideas, philosophies, and policies
should be those of other nations as well.

Alliterative references to sports, then, should underline the relevance of cultural and national attitudes concerning U.S. policy toward Latin America. There is a deeply rooted conviction, in some
ways idealistic and well intentioned, that the presumed uniqueness
of our democratic system must, indeed should, be transported to foreign shores. Geography suggests that this is especially true of Latin
America. From such attitudes spring forth a national vision with
messianic overtones. There is a sense of responsibility that embraces the championing of democracy abroad. Presumably, if U.S.
values, attitudes, and political institutions do not win ultimate acceptance across the hemisphere, the game will have been lost. While
advocacy of democracy *a la norteamericana* has long since become
globalized, there is a special relevance for the Western Hemisphere,

where paternalism has so often been associated with interventionism.

To probe North American definitions of democracy, especially as manifested toward Latin America, remains an ongoing task for scholars and decision makers alike. At this historical moment, given the extraordinary events of recent times, the need for reassessment is undeniable. As the United States attempts to champion democracy abroad, the lessons of the recent past cannot be ignored. Yet the context has changed dramatically, even while the North Americans reassert the conviction that they are engaged in a kind of crusade wherein policy somehow is either "won" or "lost."

Politics, Perceptions, and Preaching the Faith

As the United States entered the final decade of the twentieth century, its international policies clearly required a determined accommodation and adjustment to changing international and regional realities. In a penetrating essay that confronts the necessity of a far-reaching reorientation of policies, G. Pope Atkins has questioned whether the United States is "intellectually, politically, or materially equipped to seize the moment and engage Latin America on a partnership basis, given the doctrinal baggage carried over from the past, enormous domestic problems that reduce its international capabilities, and the high-priority international challenges elsewhere."[1] While Atkins's own expectations were not unduly discouraging, there was no denying the fact that with the international system entering the post–Cold War era, there were few guidelines for policy makers, while perceptions were difficult to change. George Bush was not alone in an absence of vision or imagination that might give substance and meaning to empty rhetoric promising a so-called New World Order. Thus, given our particular concern with U.S. policy toward democracy in the Americas, deeply entrenched attitudes are not readily discarded.

While North American perceptions of democracy have varied from one administration to another, they have often been at odds with Latin American views as well. To some degree this responds to contrasting cultural and intellectual patterns, to the Iberian and Thomistic tradition as distinct from the Enlightenment preachments of Locke, Montesquieu, Mills, and others. In addition, Latin America's experience with U.S. interventionism, often an alleged manifestation of a commitment to the diffusion of democratic attitudes and institutions, has produced a somewhat jaded reaction. This was eloquently expressed in the mordant statement of Kalman H. Silvert, a preeminent advocate of true democracy, in distinguishing between the developed and the developing nations. He argued that while the former might themselves be at least partially democratic, "for the poorer parts of the world they are only the extra actors of surplus value, the imposers of colonialism, the buyers of local elites, the prompters of worldwide dislocation, as they move about in the ceaseless search for economic advantage and military security."[2]

Perceptual difficulties also result from the common sin of overgeneralizing about Latin American polities. For instance, the nations of Central America and the Caribbean have been the predominant targets of direct U.S. intervention. History reminds us that classic Yankee involvement early in the twentieth century included a direct presence in Cuba, Haiti, the Dominican Republic, Panama, Honduras, Guatemala, and Mexico. For those who prefer more recent experience, where has the United States been most directly and obviously involved? Cuba, Grenada, Panama, Nicaragua, and El Salvador in particular come to mind. For these nations, as Silvert would have it, images of democracy will inevitably be blurred; "democracy" is not a meaningless concept but, as symbolized by their observation of the North Americans, embraces ingredients of hypocrisy and disingenuousness. In a number of these relatively less developed polities, moreover, their own domestic experience with democracy is limited. As Brazil's Fernando Henrique Cardoso saw it, in such countries elections were not sacrosanct and constitutional guarantees are subject to multiple interpretations.[3] The point is readily reinforced by the diverse opinions expressed by competing power contenders in El Salvador, Guatemala, Panama, and Nicaragua during the early 1990s. Other nations, however, politically more developed and geographically more distant from Washington, hold more internationalized definitions of democracy and less painful experience with blatant interventionism from the north. With the political maturation of Latin American nations far more advanced in some countries than in others, then, both institutional and intellectual perspectives are diverse.

A final addition to the preceding array of problems emanates from the irrepressible North American proclivity toward preaching the faith. This faith, of course, is couched in the tradition of the U.S.

democratic experience and in the unwavering sense of mission toward the world at large. This has meant a historical process whereby the United States has passed through "alternating cycles of trying to make the world safe *for its type of democracy* [my emphasis] and of endeavoring to make its type of democracy safe from the world."[4] Few presidents in this century have resisted the impulse. Theodore Roosevelt guaranteed Panamanian secession from Colombia while characteristically expounding his responsibility to police the Caribbean states until they became competent to do so themselves. Woodrow Wilson, an ardent exponent of the democratic ethos to the roots of his Princetonian philosophy, repeatedly intervened self-righteously in Mexico to shape its government to his own liking. Franklin D. Roosevelt, even at the zenith of his prewar advocacy of the Good Neighbor Policy, had no qualms in warmly greeting such visiting chiefs of state as Anastasio Somoza. Dwight D. Eisenhower believed his policies were for the ultimate benefit of liberty and freedom in the Americas, while John F. Kennedy sent warships to the Dominican Republic as a threat to elements Washington saw as politically unacceptable. More recently, Henry Kissinger was willing to justify unilateral actions designed to alter Chilean voters' freely expressed choice in the 1970 elections. Even more current was Washington's patent unwillingness to accept as legitimate the results of Nicaraguan elections until—wonder of wonders—its preferred candidate, Violeta de Chamorro, led anti-Sandinista forces to victory.

The paternalistic impulse toward preaching the faith—not totally different from the Spanish *conquistadores* nearly five centuries earlier—cannot be dismissed without acknowledgment of racist elements. In our first volume on U.S.–Latin American relations I referred to the sense of mission that had been demonstrated in the Philippines early in the century—another formerly Spanish colony where the subsequent U.S. presence was pronounced. This provided a basis for political discrimination that is best described as "Little Brown Brotherism." Let us cite once more the trenchant sarcasm of Mark Twain in his sardonic criticism of efforts to convert the politically pagan Filipinos, as the North Americans saw them. The language is richly exemplary.

Extending the Blessings of Civilization to our Brother who Sits in Darkness has been a good trade and has paid well, on the whole; and there is money in it yet if carefully worked—but not enough, in my judgment, to make any considerable risk advisable. The People that Sit in Darkness are getting to be too scarce.[5]

Although writing of imperialism at the turn of the century, Twain could well have been reiterating similar sentiments for the world of the late twentieth century.

While elements of racism have not vanished from U.S. foreign policy and attitudes, reference to Little Brown Brotherism represents a figurative expression of paternalism toward the presumably less enlightened and politically immature Latin Americans. The arrogance of ethnocentrism, while sometimes submerged, nonetheless provides a basis on which political leaders, foreign policy decision makers, and independent commentators conduct their affairs. Preaching the faith comes all too naturally when the subject is democracy. Yet this very concept itself defies easy definition. A selective examination of its many facets should therefore precede further analysis of democracy and inter-American relations.

Dimensions of Democracy: The State and the Citizen

There is a broad definitional consensus supporting the concept of democracy as requiring that society be ruled through the consent of its members. At a minimum, the state is responsible for the designing of political structures and the elaboration of mechanisms capable of assuring self-determination. Constitutions, laws, parties, and elections become central to this notion of democracy. To go a step further, however, is to argue that individual rights must also be enshrined, incorporating the observance of civic freedoms and a respect for basic liberties. Even more sweeping is the view that democracy embraces economic and social as well as political dimensions. Without repeating my discussions in other works (including the predecessor of this volume),[6] it is worth recalling that in the original Greek, *demokratia* referred to a government requiring participation by all the citizenry, including the lowest social strata. In a perfect world, it could be practicable for democracy to guarantee access to socioeconomic justice and well-being as well as enjoyment of a wide range of political rights. To deal with the real world of imperfection, in contrast, demands an explicit understanding of the dimensions that must be confronted not only by academics but by policy makers.

A central point of contention revolves around the role of the state in its responsibility toward the citizen. For some, it is impractical to go beyond a narrow and orthodox interpretation. Alexander Wilde, writing of Colombia's formalistic democracy as spawned by its so-called Frente Nacional, reflected this view in emphasizing institutionalization. Thus, democracy might be defined by restricted procedural rules "that allow (though they do not necessarily bring about) genuine competition for authoritative political roles. . . . Such rules would include freedom of speech, press, and assembly, and the provision of regular institutional mechanisms for obtaining consent and permitting change of political personnel (normally, elections)."[7] In short, the political dimension was the focus of Wilde's analysis—scarcely inappropriate for studies of Colombian politics at that time.[8] A less restrictive treatment, while still focused on the political dimension, is presented in John Booth's more recent study of democracy in Central America. Sensitive to criticisms of the classic pluralist-elitist model, he stresses direct popular participation in the governance of the state. Public choice also requires conditions favorable to the unfettered exercise of civic rights. Basic democracy, for Booth, includes "the right to speak freely and to publish political opinion, the right to oppose incumbents in office and to remain safe and free, the right to associate and assemble freely for political ends, the right to petition the government, and the right to seek and win redress from abuses of authority by incumbents in power."[9]

At least by implication, this suggests a distinction between those political rights that might be labeled respectively as procedural and civic. This is the conceptualization articulated recently by a non–Latin Americanist, eminent sociologist Alex Inkeles. Writing as editor for a special issue of *Studies in Comparative International Development* in which contributors analyzed the problems in the measurement of democracy, Inkeles drew a line separating political rights and structures from civic rights or civil liberties. He sees political rights as mechanisms through which the people may express their preferences and promote their implementation. These are meaningless, however, without a concomitant defense of basic civil rights. For Inkeles, "political structures are important in their own right, but without significant opportunity to exercise such structures there can be no effective exercise of the political rights generally placed at the core of any definition of democracy."[10] Speaking of what he terms civic rights and liberties, Inkeles cast forth a reminder that for the individual citizen, human rights constitutes a primordial dimension of democracy. He effectively argues not only that human rights are important to definitional considerations of democracy but that there must be sensitivity toward the variegated character of human rights.

This is not the place for extended discussion. From the perspective of U.S. policy concerning immigration and human rights, the chapter by Christopher Mitchell provides a penetrating analysis. In addition, the contribution by William Walker demonstrates that the links between narcotics and the protection of individual well-being cut very close to the bone. Indeed, it may well be that human rights have their own definitional dynamics. Without engaging here in dissection of works by authors such as Farer, Pastor, and others, suffice it to say that the North American championing of democracy in Latin America has sometimes given substantial weight to human rights as a fundamental dimension. In theoretical terms, Cole Blasier has provided an especially thoughtful categorization of democratic characteristics. He first writes of personal security, which includes freedom from arbitrary treatment by the state—arrest, torture, imprisonment, exile, execution, and the like. Second come those basic economic needs such as food, shelter, clothing, and health care. His final category embraces political rights such as freedom of speech, press, and religion. It is this last that lies closest to traditional concepts of democracy and human rights as conceived in the United States.[11]

Taking all the preceding into consideration, it is redundant to elaborate further on the self-evident diversity of democracy. However, the range and variability assure that policy makers will encounter both theoretical and practical difficulties. Moreover, the potential for perceptual conflict between Latin and North Americans also takes on large proportions. In the first place, definition may focus not only on political rights but, more narrowly, on institutional and procedural manifestations of democracy. This may or may not be seen as carrying over to participatory activities. Be that as it may, there are also important considerations regarding the four freedoms: speech, press, assembly, and religion. Also, there is an empirical question whether or not personal security, defined as protection against arbitrary state action, is to be included. Beyond such manifestations of political rights and freedoms lie concerns over economic rights. Classic theory has tended not to reach this far in philosophic terms, but for Latin America and for U.S. policy makers any such assumption is arguable. For any Third World society—and increasingly for the First World as well—there are both ethical and political questions that revolve around the economic status and health of large sectors of the population.

Few examples could be more compelling than the claims of Cuban revolutionaries in the early 1960s. They argued that the failure to honor Fidel Castro's repeated promises of free elections was meaningless, for his wide popularity was unquestioned. What mattered was the development of policies assuring economic and social democracy. *Fidelista* loyalists insisted that this was the most fundamental element of true democracy. Thus, if the Cuban Revolution could assure the economic well-being of the ordinary citizen without recourse to the electoral process, then the significance of democracy would have been proudly and productively served. In due course, the revolution had to confront the cold realities of political and economic life, notwithstanding ideological preachments. At the same time, comparisons can be found in ideologically different circumstances where the setting is anything but revolutionary. The Chile of Augusto Pinochet scarcely took a back seat to other regimes in its conscious violation of human rights and degradation of individual freedoms over the better part of two decades. The dictatorship made a mockery of electoral and procedural democracy as well. Yet its economic policies, despite severe shortcomings and internal contradictions, served the nation less poorly than those adopted by several of its less authoritarian neighbors.

Such are the multilayered dimensions of democracy, then, that it is no small matter to dissect them, identify policy priorities, and formulate rational and productive alternatives. This is further complicated by the conflicting perspectives mirroring the thinking of Latin Americans and their counterparts from the north. There are ample reasons for Latin American cynicism over U.S. policy initiatives that are justified on the grounds of exporting democracy. In practice, most North American administrations have encouraged procedural forms and systemic institutionalization; the Carter government was the one major exception over the past half-century. Washington is consequently seen as supporting a status quo that is nonthreatening to its own interests. An apt guideline would be Leonardo Molina's interpretation in a recent volume on newly emergent democracies: "Democracy is a regime in which the government cannot abuse its public powers because of the constraining effect of autonomous intermediary institutions; a set of institutions and rules that allows competition and participation for all citizens considered as equals."[12] Once again, it is the political dimension and its procedural forms that are emphasized.

Nonetheless, it is difficult to exclude the direct personal participation of the citizen from operational democracy. The use and abuse of arbitrary authority on the part of the state can scarcely be overlooked, even by policy-making elites who would prefer to be unfettered by the presumed chains of public opinion. The record from Washington is mixed and demands at least a summary of the experience in recent years. What emerges is an erratic course of policy and action, one that more often than not has favored the state as the pre-eminent preoccupation for the United States in its avowed advocacy of democracy abroad.

Retrospective Realities: Of Naïveté and Innocence

There are substantive reasons to regard Woodrow Wilson as a genuine champion of democracy, individual freedom, and self-determination. It is also true that his perceptions of the world, including the nation that bordered the United States to the south, led to policies that were an admixture of naïveté and innocence, as shaped by a woeful ignorance of the Americas. Wilson dispatched troops to northern Mexico under the command of Gen. John J. Pershing and sent marines to Haiti, the Dominican Republic, and Nicaragua. He also intervened with unconscionable self-confidence in the revolutionary turbulence in Mexico, never doubting either the practical or the moral propriety of such actions.[13] This combination of narrowly defined national interest, Christian moralizing, and personal sanctimony has periodically returned in less blatant form. All too often a lack of basic knowledge or empathy has also heightened the innocence of policy emanating from Washington.

By way of illustration, consider briefly the attitudes and assumptions of four North American administrations: those of the Eisenhower, Kennedy, Carter, and Reagan governments. They provide two natural analytic pairings. In the case of Eisenhower and Kennedy, competing world visions led to contrasting policies toward democracy in Latin America. The former shared with his secretary of state,

John Foster Dulles, the conviction that international Communism was the principal threat to the United States.[14] They reasoned that the best insurance against Communist subversion was a strengthening of the Latin American military. They consequently pursued cordial relations with such dictatorships as Marcos Pérez Jiménez in Venezuela, Fulgencio Batista in Cuba, Anastasio Somoza in Nicaragua, Rafael Leónidas Trujillo in the Dominican Republic, and others. Questions of true democracy received minimal attention. In the absence of better-informed opinion at the higher levels of government, it was erroneously believed that the dictators were staunch bulwarks against international Communism. Washington's ideological bias blinded policy makers to the opportunism of tacit coexistence between military regimes and Communist parties in such places as Cuba and Venezuela, to mention but two.

The conscious policy of strengthening presumably sympathetic military leaders was shaped through provisions of the Mutual Security Act of 1951, adopted after the outbreak of the Korean War, which produced numerous military agreements with Latin American nations. U.S. attitudes were further dramatized by the 1954 intervention in Guatemala, which was also highly damaging to the self-assumed championing of democracy in Latin America. Only the innocent and the naive believed for a moment that the action was designed to further the cause of democracy. Washington pledged to help Guatemala become a showcase for democracy, while Secretary Dulles promised "to support the just aspirations of the Guatemalan people." More to the point, however, was his interest in alleviating conditions "which might afford Communism an opportunity to spread its tentacles throughout the Hemisphere."[15] Latin Americans were far from persuaded and anticipated the emergence of the U.S.-backed regime of Col. Carlos Castillo Armas as yet another military dictatorship. Washington's subsequent decision to decorate Castillo with the Legion of Merit during a state visit was especially damning, as was a similar honoring of Venezuela's Pérez Jiménez later by the Eisenhower administration.

The president and his advisers held a narrowly simplistic belief that revolutionary change was axiomatically perilous, that Communist subversion bore all the responsibility for unrest, and that a championing of democracy was of secondary importance. Only toward the close of the 1950s did Washington undergo a policy reexamination that accepted the importance of economic assistance. This led to the joining with Latin America in the 1960 creation of the Inter-American Development Bank. As Frederico G. Gil wrote in the earlier companion volume, this indicated a shift from the policy that "maintained that private investment should carry the greater burden of Latin American development and that international governmental aid should be limited."[16] As he further noted, however, policy toward Latin America amply corroborated Hannah Arendt's contention that "fear of revolution has been the *leitmotif* of postwar American foreign policy in its desperate attempts at stabilization of the *status quo*, with the result that American power and prestige were used to support obsolete political regimes that long since had become objects of contempt among their citizens."[17] This fear was by no means dissipated by John F. Kennedy's arrival at the White House in 1961, although the prevailing apprehension over Communist expansion also was accompanied by the realization that an absence of operative democracy simply encouraged the spread of injustice, inequality, and a violation of individual rights.

As the incoming president and his New Frontiersmen looked to the south, they were no more modest than their predecessors in the conviction that they knew what was best for Latin America. If the paternalism remained, however, the policy orientation changed. Political democracy in an institutional sense became an important priority, while Kennedy himself was sympathetic to the importance of promoting democracy and popular government.[18] He also believed that U.S. interests were best served by extensive socioeconomic reforms and thus labored to bring forth the Alliance for Progress, as adopted in August 1961 at Punta del Este. It is well to recall that the preamble to the charter advocated "accelerated economic progress and broader social justice within the framework of personal dignity and political liberty." Furthermore, the twelve basic objectives of the alliance were framed to achieve "maximum levels of well-being, with equal opportunities for all, in democratic societies adapted to their own needs and desires."[19] In short, the Kennedy administration—notwithstanding such disasters as the Bay of Pigs adventure—reflected a concern with democracy at the levels of both the state and the citizen. This was no mean achievement, although there was an innocence that accompanied the idealism embodied in the alliance itself. There was also naïveté in official expectations concerning the efficacy of diplomatic pressures on behalf of civilian governments besieged by restless or disenchanted military establishments.

In such instances as the Peruvian *golpe de estado* in 1962, U.S. pressure up to and including the recalling of the ambassador from Lima merely strengthened that regime while Peruvian nationalism was bestirred against the United States. Roughly similar responses were produced by attempted pressures in the Dominican Republic and Honduras, among others. The reformist, prodemocratic zeal of the Kennedy administration was therefore on the wane prior to the president's assassination in 1963, and its shortcomings in championing democracy in the Americas mirrored an innocent belief that goodwill and sympathetic intentions were sufficient to carry the day. The president himself, his appreciation of Latin American political realities honed by the fires of direct experience, learned to be more probing and less ideological in his judgments. Indeed, as his speechwriter and longtime confidant Theodore C. Sorensen later wrote, Kennedy had concluded that in some instances, military usurpers "were neither unpopular nor reactionary; and those able and willing to guide their countries to progress he wanted to encourage. Unfortunately, he had learned, many of the more progressive civilian governments in Latin America (as elsewhere) were less willing or less able to impose the necessary curbs on extravagant projects, runaway inflation and political disorder."[20]

Moving the clock forward from Eisenhower and Kennedy, our retrospective tour of attitudes and policies leads to a second pairing: the administrations of Jimmy Carter and Ronald Reagan. The former judged the time conducive for a recrudescence of democracy and constitutionality. The promotion of human rights in Latin America drew unparalleled attention. For Carter, the advocacy of democratic reform was founded on the fashioning of an activist human rights policy. The administration left little question that, as Kryzanek put it, "the United States was firmly behind those governments that protected individual freedom and opposed to those regimes that engaged in harsh, repressive practices in order to limit dissent."[21] Even before reaching the White House, Carter had declared, "We can live with diversity in governmental systems, but we cannot look away when a government tortures people or jails them for their beliefs."[22] Once in office, he applied a variety of mechanisms to attack human rights abuses.[23]

Individual governments perceived as violators of personal security and freedom were penalized by a reduction or elimination of military assistance. Authoritarian regimes in Argentina, Brazil, Chile, Guatemala, Paraguay, and Uruguay were all subjected to these sanctions at one time or another. The Carter administration also adopted such measures as quadrupling the budget and staff of the Inter-American Commission on Human Rights and promoting the American Convention on Human Rights, previously signed at San José, Costa Rica, in 1969. The president's commitment was further underlined by the creation of a new assistant secretary for human rights within the Department of State, the responsibilities of which included annual publication of a report on the status of human rights in every nation. In the final analysis, the Carter policy will ultimately be judged by history for two fundamental efforts: renegotiation of the canal treaties with Panama, and the active promotion of human rights.

Jimmy Carter himself never doubted the importance of the latter; neither did he question a broad definition of democracy, one embracing an explicit commitment to a broad panoply of individual freedoms and liberties. Nearly a decade after leaving office he described the relationship of democracy and human rights in the following language: "The global movement to defend human rights has made possible the spread of democracy in the western hemisphere, and democratic governments have proven the best means of defending human rights."[24] Carter also made clear his own priorities, having concluded when he ascended to the presidency in 1977 that protection of one's personal integrity from abuse and arbitrary violence was paramount. Carter felt compelled "to give highest priority to the victims of arbitrary arrest, torture, and murder by death squads associated with military governments."[25] Perhaps it might have been different had the Latin America of the late 1970s not been the locale for human rights abuses by a number of notably vicious authoritarian regimes. Given the horrific character of repression, however, Carter's sense of compassion was so offended as to guarantee the emphasis of his Latin American policy.

Whatever the verdict of history on the totality of the Carter experience, our present concern is focused on questions of democracy; there are valid grounds to view his emphasis on human rights as both realistic and appropriate. For critics, to be sure, he had embarked on an idealistic voyage across waters made tempestuous by the winds of international Communism. At the same time, one should note that in the early 1990s, there remains in Latin America itself a deep reservoir of approval for the basic Carter policy. Questions about the realism of his approach to hemispheric affairs are more likely to center on misjudgments or misperceptions that influenced U.S. actions in such contentious arenas as Nicaragua, El Salvador, and Cuba. On balance, however, I would argue that the championing of Latin American democracy by the Carter administration was by no means alien to the political conditions of the times.

With the advent of the Reagan administration, a preoccupation with human rights was superseded by a focus on leftist terrorism, with the menace of Communist expansion provoking Washington to concentrate on Central America and the Caribbean. Such key officials as Secretary of State Alexander Haig insisted that security interests demanded the courting of even the most arbitrary dictatorships. UN Ambassador Jeane Kirkpatrick held similar views. While Secretary Haig proposed that the United States go to the source by pressuring Cuba, Dr. Kirkpatrick was paying cordial visits to Santiago and Buenos Aires, where she pointedly rejected any contact whatever with human rights activists. There was symbolic meaning in the fact that the first Latin American leader to visit President Reagan was Gen. Roberto Viola, strongman of the ruthless Argentine military government.

While the administration concentrated on Central America, a striking transformation was taking place elsewhere in Latin America. As Pastor reminds us in his chapter, there were competitive elections in Brazil, Grenada, Guatemala, and Uruguay, while new civilian governments took power in Bolivia and Peru. The twenty-year rule of Forbes Burnham in Guyana was terminated by his death in 1985, and in February 1986 three decades of family dictatorship in Haiti were ended by the flight to France of Jean-Claude Duvalier. With the growing shift from military authoritarianism to civilian, electorally based government, the Reagan White House responded by a grudging effort to proclaim its own advocacy of democracy in Latin America. Powerfully influenced by the remarkable mobilization of "People's Power" in the Philippines, which toppled the Marcos dictatorship (despite Reagan's profound reluctance to accept the ouster of his longtime friend), the administration gradually recognized that democracy abroad could have political benefits.[26]

The first Reagan term, according to a sympathetic account by Margaret Daly Hayes, selected three major themes for particular attention; human rights was not among them.[27] During the second term, however, President Reagan responded to the process of systemic democratization that was spreading across Latin America, seeking to claim the lion's share of credit. In point of fact, administration actions to stimulate democratization were modest and certainly far from decisive. Washington's understanding of democracy was relatively narrow, translated into a policy emphasis on formalist and constitutional elements. There was little to dissipate the image of an administration that itself viewed Latin America through the distorting optics of Cold Warriorism. In 1984 the report by the government's own widely heralded Kissinger Commission on Central America presented a multifaceted panorama that the White House received with predetermined selectivity. It simply ignored such findings as the commission's view that indigenous factors were crucial to the crisis gripping the region.[28] Meanwhile, the record showed that in supporting numerous right-wing regimes, Washington was failing the forces of democracy in Latin America. Its ideologically simplistic generalizations were the hallmark of a less than benign approach to the region.

Realities of the Day: Democracy in the Naughty Nineties

If we are indeed confronting a contemporary demarcation of dramatic proportions between two historical eras in world affairs, does it also follow that U.S. advocacy of a global democratic ideal may itself undergo far-reaching changes? Moving from the previous retrospective interpretation, it is critical to recognize that hemispheric relations are being couched within a new global context. The decade of the nineties may lead to fundamental shifts in attitude and policy. However, the nineties may well tantalize us with visions that proved either ephemeral or, at the least, misleading. What little evidence now exists to help in elucidating future patterns of behavior and action requires an examination of events transpiring during the 1989 to 1993 Bush administration.

Several of our contributors have addressed President Bush's record at some length. In this instance, of course, our theme is democracy. Rather than repeating material from other chapters, then, let us select a few cases where Latin American democracy, including the protection of human rights, has been most seriously challenged: from the Caribbean, Cuba and Haiti; and from the South American continent, Peru and Venezuela. Outcomes are still uncertain at this writing, but these instances provide a range of national settings, from Marxist authoritarianism to nepotistic dictatorship, and from a fledgling democracy to one that had been the most active and relatively most participatory in the region.

In many ways there is little to be said about once-revolutionary Cuba that does not appear in the chapter by Enrique A. Baloyra. As the Castro regime proceeds along the lines he has so vividly etched, however, it is useful to recall contemporary attitudes and policies emanating from Washington. They are inextricably intertwined with electoral considerations. The attitudes of Cuban Americans in Dade County and environs have been less monolithic than fervently anti-Castro organizations and lobbyists would concede. At the same time, they cannot be ignored by office-seekers, especially given Florida's electoral clout. For the desperately embattled campaign of George Bush in the fall of 1992, each visit required a host of carefully scripted messages, unfailingly presented at appropriate public gatherings. It was simple enough for the administration to leave in place the long-standing blockade of the island. When candidate Bush expressed the hope of being the first U.S. president to visit a democratic Cuba, he received the plaudits of partisan crowds. Yet he could remain passive as a decision maker; the costs were minimal. Moreover, he could largely ignore the ongoing debater over the fate of Radio Martí.

The point is not to contest the wisdom of U.S. policies toward Cuba nor to pursue analysis of partisan electoral calculations during a heated presidential campaign. Rather, one must ask if the United States were championing democracy and to what effect. The relative inactivity of the Bush administration, given Cuba's internal conditions, was less than startling. Even so, it is difficult to champion a cause by doing nothing. In light of continuing human rights violations in Cuba, it is legitimate at least to ask whether or not patience and inactivity are sufficient. This also raises questions about the character and persona of a post-Castro government. It would be disheartening to learn that Washington is merely engaged in a rhetorical game of blind man's bluff with Havana. State, Defense, and the CIA all presumably have their own expectations about who and what may follow Fidel. But there is no way to claim that U.S. policy in the early nineties constitutes meaningful advocacy of democracy for Cuba. Neither can it be said that abuses of human rights have received priority attention.

If the latter is true of Cuba, it is even more evident with Haiti, where conflict has weakened fragile institutions and facilitated ongoing abuse of individual rights. The earlier involvement of the Reagan administration is relevant to the contemporary situation. When the twenty-nine-year dictatorship of the Duvalier regime was drawing to a close, Washington cut off aid. Jean-Claude Duvalier fled Haiti on 7 February 1986, but according to President Reagan himself, the United States had never urged his departure.[29] When subsequent efforts to organize free elections disintegrated in the face of bloody attacks by the Haitian military in November 1987, thereby shutting down the electoral process, the Reagan administration issued a strong protest and terminated all remaining aid to the ruling junta. This was later restored, accompanied by demands for electoral democratization. Events proceeded haltingly toward installation of a constituted government through a sweeping victory at the polls by Father Jean-Bertrand Aristide. On 29 September 1991 Aristide was ousted by the military, leaving the Bush administration to face a series of complicated policy issues, including a restoration of constitutional government, while issues of human rights became especially vexing. The Haitian *golpistas*, viciously abusive of civil liberties, engaged in the indiscriminate persecution of suspected opponents as well as countless innocent bystanders, provoking a massive flight of Haitians from the island. Thousands sought refuge, and the United States could not duck the ensuing problems.

Efforts to reverse military intervention continued. Secretary of State James Baker promised that "this coup must not and will not succeed."[30] However, sanctions visited greater deprivation on Haiti's poor while the traditional oligarchy and its military spokesmen were immune. In February 1992 the Bush administration unilaterally softened the economic trade embargo, while the program of forced repatriation of Haitian refugees continued. The OAS and Latin American foreign ministers wrestled with the problems of constitutional restoration, whether or not Aristide himself returned to the island. Institutional redemocratization staggered along while the plight of the refugees worsened. By May the *New York Times* was reporting an increasing exodus, with an estimated 29,000 Haitians having tried to reach the United States by boat since the ouster of President Aristide.[31] Toward the end of the month Washington issued an executive order that the boat people would be returned to Haiti directly, without any semblance of administrative review. Political asylum was to be denied, and the U.S. Coast Guard was directed to transfer them to Haitian officials. President Bush expressed the hope that lives might be saved by discouraging the dangerous sea passage from Haiti to southern Florida. His announcement of a new policy also reversed a 1981 directive by Ronald Reagan, wherein immigration officials were responsible for determining immediately whether or not fleeing Haitians were truly political refugees.

As a practical matter, the Bush policy bore profoundly negative implications for Haitians. It constituted a virtual invitation to human rights violations on the part of the military in Port-au-Prince. Presumably, boat people would be required to stand in line for hours, even days, outside the U.S. Embassy, awaiting a questioning of their concerns and interests by overworked consular personnel. This automatically labeled them as opponents of the regime and openly encouraged the punitive actions that characterized Haitian authorities. More than 34,000 Haitians had taken to the seas by late June, but the executive order from Washington included severe implications for official abuses of human rights. The *Miami Herald*, for years an ardent monitor of Latin American affairs, was scathing in its assessment of the Bush policy. In its lead editorial of 27 May entitled "A Human Rights Outrage," the *Herald* assailed the president for having "hung the bunting of shame upon this nation's history as haven for the persecuted and the oppressed." While granting that the executive order reflected in part the overcrowded status of the refugee camp at Guantánamo Bay, the newspaper critically dissected the administration's efforts at self-justification. Citing the UN Convention Relating to the Status of Refugees, the editorial urged congressional action. "Let Congress act swiftly to reverse Mr. Bush's human-rights outrage and guarantee that any alien has the right at least to argue his case for political asylum."[32]

Given the complexity of the situation, it may be unfair to charge the Bush administration with callousness toward democracy and human rights. At the very least, however, Washington could not argue convincingly that it was acting in defense of these principles. The growing concentration of attention to Haitian refugees and to immigration policy led the United States to veto or to ignore efforts by the OAS to ameliorate the suffering of refugees while negotiating a modicum of constitutionality and legitimacy with officials in Port-au-Prince. Repeated OAS initiatives were met with unenthusiastic rhetoric from Washington. By September 1972, a full year after Aristide's removal, the former president resisted direct communication with Marc Bazin, the handpicked spokesman of the military government. The proposed return of Aristide to the island was unacceptable to Port-au-Prince. Neither side was inclined to compromise, and Washington's influence was largely irrelevant. Human rights abuses continued while the stalemate endured, and George Bush was charged with racism in his forced repatriation of refugees. His administration continued to grant political asylum to virtually all Cubans reaching Miami, even as it asked the courts for a ruling that the thousands of Haitians were economic rather than political refugees and therefore subject to forced repatriation by the Coast Guard.

The difficulty in applying U.S. pressure in favor of democratization was underlined by the experience of the Clinton administration. After having sharply criticized George Bush during his presidential campaign, Bill Clinton found himself confronted by the intransigence of the Haitian military, the inflexibility of Aristide, and the same domestic pressures in Florida that had influenced his predecessor. On 27 June 1993 talks began in New York between Aristide and Haitian military representatives, culminating in an agreement that included Aristide's return on 30 October as president of Haiti. Lt. Gen. Raoul Cedras subsequently reneged on the agreement, and by the beginning of 1994 he remained in power while Aristide enjoyed exile in the United States. An attempted landing of U.S. troops on behalf of the multinational UN mission to restore democracy had been withdrawn in the face of armed opposition by military-sponsored thugs in Haiti. Thus, whatever the substantive and procedural problems with both the Bush and Clinton administrations, the United States was unable to bring about even a formalized restoration of democracy in a weak and impoverished Caribbean state.

While the military intervention in Haiti against civilian rule was scarcely surprising, events in Peru and Venezuela emerged from very different circumstances. In both instances, Washington's capacity to alter conditions and strengthen democracy has been minimal. The *autogolpe* of Peruvian president Alberto Fujimori in 1992 came by way of an arbitrary closing of congressional doors and a suspension of constitutional rights. Despite a range of justifications, it was clear that Fujimori had unilaterally usurped power unto himself. The self-proclaimed civilian dictatorship was received with dismay and dis-approval across the Americas. Fujimori was denounced and Peru was marginalized by regional Andean organizations as well as hemi-spheric meetings of foreign ministers. Washington joined in the chorus of criticism but also feared that its antidrug campaign would suffer. In due course Fujimori manipulated a new constituent assem-bly into the drafting of a charter that would allow for his reelection. This in turn was approved by referendum late in 1993. Whatever the evolution of Peruvian politics from this point forward, it is clear that the United States exerted precious little influence on basic decisions concerning democracy. Both President Fujimori and his opponents were sensitive to Washington's responses but fundamentally pro-ceeded within the context of domestic Peruvian considerations. The North American banner of democracy was not a decisive force.

Lastly, we came to Venezuela, where, for a third of a century, the beacon of democracy had provided inspiration to all the Americas. Without digressing into the details of the political situation,[33] suf-fice it to say that knowledgeable observers had been well aware of systemic deterioration and a hardening of the arteries.[34] Yet two mil-itary uprisings (although representing minority elements within the armed forces) bespoke of resentment against the entire political leadership in general, as well as President Carlos Andrés Pérez in particular. Reverberations resonated across the hemisphere, and declarations of support for President Pérez included explicit state-ments from Washington. This at least stood in contrast to the histor-ical record, for the United States had readily accepted coups in Car-acas in 1945, 1948, 1952, and 1958. When Pérez was brought down by domestic opponents in mid-1993, the United States forcefully re-stated its support for constitutional procedures, which Venezuela was already honoring through selection of an interim president.

In December 1993, when national elections took place as sched-uled to choose a new president and Congress, Washington made clear its commitment to democracy. Two major Latin Americanist policy makers from the Clinton administration visited Caracas to deliver pointed if undiplomatic messages about the sanctity of elec-tions. President Clinton subsequently sent his congratulations to the victor, Rafael Caldera; messages of approval also went to the interim government and, quietly, to the Venezuelan military. Granted the goodwill and positive intentions from Washington, it was also true that statements by Clinton's representatives were not appreciated in Venezuela and, furthermore, that the nation's adherence to constitutional procedures was a reflection of national attitudes and a deep democratic vocation. If the United States stood on the side of the angels, its influence was negligible. There is little reason to believe that preelection "warnings" to ranking Venezuelan military leaders swayed their decision to support electoral procedures.

Analysis of North American advocacy of democracy abroad cuts both ways. On the one hand, it defies common sense to argue that the United States had the means to alter significantly the course of events unfolding in Venezuela. It was for the Venezuelans themselves to resolve their problems. This very fact underlines a fundamental theme in this chapter; namely, that there are very real limits to Washington's influence, especially where political and institutional crises are at hand. At the same time, official declarations and ceremonial rhetoric are not without their value. It is ironic that President Pérez, amid his own problems of sheer political survival, remained an eloquent defender of Jean-Bertrand Aristide while sharply denouncing Alberto Fujimori's violation of constitutionality in Lima. There would have been little to lose if George Bush had issued a ringing denunciation of military adventurism and *golpismo*. Official statements from Washington, instead, were diplomatically proper while lacking the fire of conviction that is particularly relevant in Latin America. There was no Klaxon call alerting antidemocratic forces throughout the hemisphere to a powerful and profound antipathy in Washington. Neither were there persuasive indications that the United States would act unsympathetically toward future military interventionism. Whatever messages may have been sent in private, they lack the impact that can only be exerted by firm and unqualified public presidential declarations.

The decade of the 1990s is not yet far advanced, and challenges to democracy can be expected to increase. Some will emerge in forms unimaginable in earlier years. The drug war, for example, had not been anticipated. Now it constitutes a socioeconomic and political problem of international proportions and is of direct relevance for democracy in the Andean states, the Caribbean, and the United States itself. Environmental questions have rapidly gained in significance. There will soon be other matters that will further crowd the policy-making agenda. Consequently, reference to the "Naughty Nineties" is more than an empty alliterative phrase. The multiplication of problems and challenges, of civic concerns and socioeconomic problems, staggers the imagination. Perhaps it is only with the omnipresence of the Computer Age that citizens and policy makers alike can sort out, absorb, process, and respond to the realities of contemporary times. In this sense there is truly an element of naughtiness, of teasing provocation that complicates these final years of a tumultuous century. Among other things, the Naughty Nineties should not only remind us of prevailing political realities but also of ever-more-complex challenges to the Democratic ethos.

The Foibles and Follies of External Democratizing

Diverse political and cultural traditions underlie the images of democracy observable in the Americas of the late twentieth century. The resultant diversity and contradictions complicate greatly the task for North Americans dedicated to the championing of democracy abroad. Basic definitions and concepts are heterogeneous, and cultural pluralism is evident. Thus the often ethnocentric paternalism of Washington, deeply rooted in old attitudes and habits, constitutes a sharp limitation on the actions of the government. A longstanding inclination to exaggerate political trends in Latin America and to overgeneralize through simplistic views of a democracy-dictatorship dichotomy has further complicated the process of decision making. It should also be recognized that misunderstandings and misinterpretations born of ethnocentric bias are far from one-sided. The certainty with which Latin American critics judge democracy in the United States is itself a by-product of inadequate information and distorted half-truths. Neither Latin nor North Americans have a monopoly on self-satisfied analyses that do little justice to political realities.

Consider briefly two controversial situations that have recently produced oversimplified assumptions and perceptions on both sides. First is the suspension of $116 million of U.S. aid to Nicaragua in mid-1992 on the grounds that President Violeta de Chamorro was tacitly selling out democracy by including Sandinistas at high levels of her government. From her perspective, an eventual unification of the Nicaraguan family required broad collaboration and coexistence. It could also be noted that the Sandinistas had polled some 40 percent of the vote while being defeated and thus should not be denied any role whatever in the government. The U.S. aid suspension, powerfully supported by rightist congressmen, came just as a horrendous seaquake and tidal wave hit Nicaragua on 1 September, taking a toll of over one hundred dead and five hundred injured. The president could only protest vainly that she refused to sell her country in order to gain access to desperately need frozen funds. However, she was forced to retreat, yielding to external pressures that were atavistic attacks by a minority in Washington with little concern for democracy and for its institutional fragility in Nicaragua. With George Bush caught up in his final desperate efforts to cling to power, policy makers in Washington could scarcely claim to have encouraged democracy in a tiny country whose politics had responded to the demands of the northern colossus throughout the entire century.

A second illustration comes from Colombian preoccupations with the possibility of direct U.S. military intervention to kidnap prominent *narcotraficantes* for prosecution in the United States. When the Supreme Court issued a ruling in support of the earlier seizure of an accused Mexican torturer of U.S. drug agents on Mexican territory, it was seized upon as confirming a North American policy of direct intervention in other nations. From one perspective, the extreme Colombian nervousness demonstrated a misunderstanding of North American traditions of constitutional separation of powers. It also showed a relative ignorance over earlier declarations and actions of the Bush administration that had been a matter of public record. When the president spoke to the press following the Court's decision, he emphasized the independence of the Supreme Court from the Executive Branch. The ruling, he declared, "does not mean that there will be a wave of kidnappings." For most Colombians, however, there was a virtual certainty that the legal decision constituted a declaration of new U.S. policy. Thinking about democracy, then, was not beneficial to an understanding of the process. Historic and cultural chasms were not bridged.[35]

Cultural blinders and diverse ethnocentric assumptions and attitudes, to repeat, place a formidable barrier in the path of would-be champions of international democratization. In addition, a second array of problems has emerged as a consequence of the collapse of

Communism. The United States has scarcely begun to comprehend, let alone respond to, the disappearance of the singular external threat that so dominated thinking about both domestic and foreign policy for half a century. It is scarcely surprising that policy toward Latin America has floundered and that a long-range vision has been absent. Until the close of the 1980s, two basic and uncomplicated perceptions had been at war with one another. Kryzanek put it well in counterposing the reformist and realist schools of thought. As he saw it, "the dilemma over steadfast support of democratic principles versus toleration of authoritarianism as a means of containing Marxist revolution became an issue that divided presidential administrations, congressional leaders, professional foreign policy bureaucrats, and the U.S. populace."[36] Now the basic premise guiding both schools of thought has disappeared with stunning rapidity. The hands of the clock cannot be turned back. While the conflict with international Communism has lost relevance, the struggle for democracy, in any and all of its manifest forms, has never been more acute.

The international maturation of Latin America had become evident even prior to the dissolution of the Soviet empire. Regional and subregional activism has moved forward often without U.S. participation: from the Contadora Group to the Andean Pact; from the Group of Rio and environmentalism to MERCOSUR; from a renewal of ties with Spain to more far-reaching links to the European community. All these efforts and more are examples of forward-looking Latin American initiatives. Yet at the same time, the magnitude of socioeconomic problems requires external involvement—in terms of human resources as well as financial assistance. Perhaps nowhere is this more important than in the process of organizing and servicing human needs. If a true definition of democracy extends beyond the state, beyond the political system that intelligent politicians will always manage to control, divert, or shape for their own purposes, then the dimension of the individual becomes paramount. Whether one prefers to speak about freedom of self-expression, public liberties, and political participation or rather concerns of social justice and economic well-being, in the final analysis the individual relies upon or at least is directly affected by the state.

The record demonstrates that U.S. policy makers are limited in their capacity to influence Latin America. The fate of democracy itself, however defined and conceptualized, can be influenced but by no means dictated from Washington. If history in any meaningful sense is our guide, this might entitle us to a deep sigh of relief. At the same time, prospects for the inherent and immutable rights of the human being in the Americas of the nineties are intimidating. The fate of constitutional democracy rests on shaky foundations. Furthermore, individuals may scarcely fare better in their daily lives with a democratic than with an authoritarian regime. This very statement logically brings us to the heart of a philosophical and pragmatic debate that cannot be probed at length in this chapter. For the moment, it is important to remember that many powerful forces work against the efforts of even the most enlightened policy makers in Washington. The differences of cultural outlook and contrasting historical traditions are also influential in every nation, not solely in the United States. There is no Yankee monopoly on these problems.

In looking ahead, it is important also to recognize yet another basic political reality: for better or for worse, Latin America is not a high-priority policy area for the United States. Those with expertise in the region tend not to be in government service or, alternatively, are serving loyally in locales that their nonregional colleagues tend to view as Siberias that assure slow professional advancement. To lament this reality does not alter it, nor does it change the fact that the limits of U.S. power in the region are influential, sometimes even decisive. Such considerations cannot be ignored, even though they do not justify any relaxation of efforts to encourage democratization. There are those who would call upon the United States first to address more effectively its own failings at extending the benefits of democratization to its people at home. Fair enough. But this still spares neither North nor Latin Americans from their fundamental responsibilities. The relative diminution of traditional U.S. domination is healthy; at the same time, it also demands greater Latin American efforts on behalf of democracy, at the level of the individual citizen as well as the state writ large.

Underlying all the preceding is a passionate belief in the profound significance of Democracy, as defined in broad terms and deserving of a capital *D*. In the long and inexorable unfolding of history, the democratic ethos must ultimately prevail. For the short term, however, it can be taxing to maintain the faith. Five years ago, conditions were sufficiently discouraging that my closing remarks were guarded at best:

it is incumbent upon the U.S. political leadership to understand and respond to the realities of hemispheric affairs. To do otherwise is to suggest that, even with the best of intentions, the United States will ill serve the cause of democracy in Latin America. If history is to be our guide, the prospects are much more a cause for lamentation than for optimism.[37]

Today, an examination of events and conditions makes it difficult to deny a deterioration over the intervening half-decade. Rodgers and Hammerstein's "cockeyed optimist" would not have found it a congenial time. Neither have the millions of Latin Americans for whom the myriad conceptualizations of democracy so often are nothing more than hollow rhetoric that fails to touch their lives.[38]

Notes

1. G. Pope Atkins, ed., *The United States and Latin America: Redefining U.S. Purposes in the Post–Cold War Era* (Austin: University of Texas Press, 1992), p. 1.

2. Kalman H. Silvert, *Essays in Understanding Latin America* (Philadelphia: Institute for the Study of Human Issues, 1977), p. 58.

3. Fernando Henrique Cardoso, "On the Characterization of Authoritarian Regimes in Latin America," in David Collier, ed., *The New Authoritarianism in Latin America* (Princeton, N.J.: Princeton University Press, 1979), pp. 33–60.

4. Frederick B. Pike, *The United States and the Andean Republics: Peru, Bolivia and Ecuador* (Cambridge: Harvard University Press, 1977), p. 303.

5. As noted in my earlier essay, the quotation was taken from David Haward Bain, *Sitting in Darkness: Americans in the Philippines* (Boston: Houghton Mifflin, 1984).

6. See John D. Martz, "Images, Intervention, and the Cause of Democracy," in Martz, ed., *United States Policy in Latin America: A Quarter Century of Crisis and Challenge, 1961–1986* (Lincoln: University of Nebraska Press, 1988), pp. 307–30; also see Martz, "Democracy and the Imposition of Values: Definitions and Diplomacy," in Martz and Lars Schoultz, eds., *Latin America, the United States, and the Inter-American System* (Boulder, Colo.: Westview, 1980), pp. 145–73; also Martz, "Latin America and the Caribbean," in Robert Wesson, ed., *Democracy: A Worldwide Survey* (New York: Praeger, 1987).

7. Alexander W. Wilde, "Conversations among Gentlemen: Oligarchical Democracy in Colombia," in Juan J. Linz and Alfred Stepan, eds., *The Breakdown of Democratic Regimes: Latin America* (Baltimore, Md.: Johns Hopkins University Press, 1987), p. 29.

8. There are numerous works treating the Frente Nacional from a variety

of perspectives. Several are reviewed in John D. Martz, "Democratization and National Development in Colombia," *Latin American Research Review* 27, no. 3 (1992): 216–27. Also of special note is Jonathan Hartlyn, *The Politics of Coalition Rule in Colombia* (Cambridge, England: Cambridge University Press, 1988).

9. John A. Booth, "Elections and Democracy in Central America: A Framework for Analysis," in Booth and Mitchell A. Seligson, eds., *Elections and Democracy in Central America* (Chapel Hill: University of North Carolina Press, 1989), p. 14.

10. Alex Inkeles, "Introduction: On Measuring Democracy," *Studies in Comparative International Development* 25, no. 1 (spring 1990): 4.

11. Cole Blasier, "The United States and Democracy in Latin America," in James A. Malloy and Mitchell A. Seligson, eds., *Authoritarians and Democrats: Regime Transition in Latin America* (Pittsburgh, Pa.: University of Pittsburgh Press, 1987), p. 227.

12. Leonardo Molina in Enrique A. Baloyra, ed., *Comparing New Democracies: Transition and Consolidation in Mediterranean Europe and the Southern Cone* (Boulder, Colo.: Westview, 1987), p. 303.

13. See Martz in Martz and Schoultz, eds., *Latin America*, p. 148.

14. Federico G. Gil, *Latin American–United States Relations* (New York: Harcourt Brace Jovanovich, 1971), pp. 214–15.

15. *New York Times*, 1 July 1954, pp. 1, 8.

16. Gil, "The Kennedy-Johnson Years," in Martz, ed., *United States Policy*, p. 7.

17. Hannah Arendt, *On Revolution* (New York: Viking Press, 1963), p. 47.

18. Arthur M. Schlesinger Jr., "The Alliance for Progress: A Retrospective," in Ronald G. Hellman and H. Jon Rosenbaum, eds., *Latin America: The Search for a New International Role* (New York: John Wiley and Sons, Sage Publications, 1975), pp. 58–59.

19. The text is found in a brief commentary by one of the architects of the alliance. See Lincoln Gordon, *A New Deal for Latin America: The Alliance for Progress* (Cambridge: Harvard University Press, 1963).

20. Theodore C. Sorensen, *Kennedy* (New York: Harper and Row, 1965), pp. 535–36.

21. Michael J. Kryzanek, *U.S.–Latin American Relations*, 2d ed. (Washington DC: Praeger, 1990), p. 75.

22. From a speech reprinted in Jimmy Carter, *A Government as Good as Its People* (New York: Simon and Schuster, 1977), pp. 166–71.

23. Among other useful overviews, see Abraham Lowenthal, "Jimmy Carter and Latin America: A New Era or Small Change," in Kenneth Oye, Donald Rothchild, and Robert Leiken, eds., *Eagle Entangled: U.S. Foreign Policy in a Complex World* (New York: Longman, 1979), pp. 290–303.

24. Jimmy Carter, "Human Rights and Democracy," in Robert A. Pastor,

ed., *Democracy in the Americas: Stopping the Pendulum* (New York: Holmes and Meier, 1989), p. xv.

25. Ibid., p. xvi.

26. Among the better sources, see Raymond Bonner, *Waltzing with a Dictator: The Marcoses and the Making of American Policy* (New York: Times Books, 1987); Stanley Karnow, *In Our Image: America's Empire in the Philippines* (New York: Random House, 1989); and David Wurfel, *Filipino Politics: Development and Decay* (Ithaca, N.Y.: Cornell University Press, 1988).

27. Margaret Daly Hayes, "Not What I Say, but What I Do: Latin American Policy in the Reagan Administration," in Martz, ed., *United States Policy.*

28. For the full text, see *The Report of the President's National Bipartisan Commission on Central America* (New York: Macmillan, 1984).

29. See the report of the relevant Reagan press conference in the *New York Times,* 12 February 1986, p. 10.

30. "Haiti: 'We Could Turn Our Back,'" *Newsweek,* 24 February 1992, p. 16.

31. *New York Times,* 18 May 1992, p. 1.

32. *Miami Herald,* 29 May 1992, p. A12.

33. For a current analysis, see John D. Martz, "Political Parties and the Democratic Crisis in Venezuela," October 1992 paper to be published in the forthcoming volume edited by Joseph S. Tulchin and Moises Njaim, to be published by Lynne Rienner.

34. Among other works, see John D. Martz, "Peligros de la petrificación: el sistema de partidos venezolanos y la década de los ochenta," in Enrique A. Baloyra and Rafael López Pintor, eds., *Iberoamérica en los años 80: perspectivas de cambio social y político* (Madrid: Centro de Investigaciones Sociológicas, Instituto de Cooperación Iberoamericana, 1982), pp. 149–87; Martz, "Political Parties and Foreign Policy in Venezuela," in Heraldo Muñoz and Joseph S. Tulchin, eds., *Latin America in World Politics: Comparative Perspectives* (Boulder, Colo.: Westview, 1984), pp. 133–50; and Martz, "The Malaise of Venezuelan Political Parties: Is Democracy Endangered?" in Donald L. Herman, ed., *Democracy in Latin America: Colombia and Venezuela* (New York: Praeger, 1988), pp. 155–75.

35. My own extensive lecturing in Colombia during the summer of 1992 at both undergraduate and graduate levels as well as discussions with faculty in Bogotá and in the interior provide strong and dramatic confirmation of the complicated and often contradictory perceptions mentioned briefly with regard to extradition, kidnapping, drug criminality, and the like.

36. Kryzanek, *U.S.–Latin American Relations,* p. 168.

37. Martz, "Images, Intervention, and Democracy," in Martz, ed., *United States Policy,* p. 327.

38. For further discussion of the themes examined here, significant works

are Abraham F. Lowenthal, ed., *Exporting Democracy: The United States and Latin America: Themes and Issues* (Baltimore, Md.: Johns Hopkins University Press, 1991); Thomas Carothers, *In the Name of Democracy: U.S. Policy toward Latin America in the Reagan Years* (Berkeley: University of California Press, 1991); and Robert A. Pastor, *Whirlpool: U.S. Foreign Policy toward Latin America and the Caribbean* (Princeton, N.J.: Princeton University Press, 1992).

The Contributors

Enrique A. Baloyra is professor of political science in the Graduate School of International Studies at the University of Miami. His publications include numerous works on Cuba and El Salvador, in addition to theoretical investigations of regime transitions. An early example of the latter is his *Comparing New Democracies* (Chapel Hill, 1987).

John A. Booth is Regents Professor of Political Science at the University of North Texas. A specialist on Central America, his recent works include coeditorship of *Elections and Democracy in Central America* (Chapel Hill, 1989) and two editions of *Understanding Central America* (Boulder, 1989 and 1993).

George W. Grayson is Class of 1938 Professor of Government at the College of William & Mary. His books include *The North American Free Trade Agreement* (Foreign Policy Association, 1993), *The Church in Contemporary Mexico* (Center for Strategic and International Studies, 1992), and *Oil and Mexican Foreign Policy* (University of Pittsburgh Press, 1988).

Michael J. Kryzanek is professor of political science at Bridgewater State College. He has written extensively on the politics of the Dominican Republic and on U.S. policy in the Caribbean. Recent publications include *United States–Latin American Relations* (Praeger, 1985 and 1990) and *Leaders, Leadership, and U.S. Policy in Latin America* (Westview, 1992).

John D. Martz is distinguished professor of political science at Pennsylvania State University. He has been editor of *Studies in Comparative International Development* since 1989. He is currently completing research for his eighteenth book, a comparative study of the three Grancolombian nations.

Christopher Mitchell is professor of politics and director of the Center for Latin American and Caribbean Studies at New York University. With baccalaureate and doctoral degrees from Harvard University, he is the author of *The Legacy of Populism in Bolivia* (Praeger, 1977) and editor of *Changing Perspectives in Latin American Studies* (Stanford University Press, 1988) and *Western Hemisphere Immigration and United States Foreign Policy* (Penn State Press, 1992).

Eul-Soo Pang is professor of international development and policy studies and director of the International Institute at the Colorado School of Mines. The holder of a Ph.D. in history from the University of California at Berkeley, he is currently completing a book comparing state-owned enterprises and their role in the development of Argentina, Brazil, and Chile under military rule.

Robert A. Pastor has been professor of political science at Emory University and director of the Latin American and Caribbean Program at Emory's Carter Center since 1986. Director of Latin American and Caribbean Affairs on the National Security Council from 1977 to 1981, Dr. Pastor is the author of eight books, including *Whirlpool: U.S. Foreign Policy Toward Latin America and the Caribbean* (Princeton University Press, 1992). His 1994 nomination as ambassador to Panama was later blocked by Sen. Jesse Helms.

Riordan Roett is the Sarita and Don Johnston Professor and director of Latin American Studies at the Paul H. Nitze School of Advanced International Studies at the Johns Hopkins University. The author of *Brazil: Politics in a Patrimonial Society* (Praeger), which is now in its fourth edition, his many publications include his edited *Political and Economic Liberalization in Mexico* (Lynne Rienner, 1993) and *Mexico's External Relations in the 1990's* (Lynne Rienner, 1991), which also appeared in Spanish translation.

Steve C. Ropp is professor of Political Science and director of International Studies at the University of Wyoming. He is the author of *Panamanian Politics: From Guarded Nation to National Guard* (Praeger, 1982) and coeditor with James A. Morris of *Central America: Crisis and Adaptation* (New Mexico, 1984). Recent analysis of

Panamanian politics can be found in "Explaining the Long-Term Maintenance of a Military Regime: Panama before the U.S. Invasion," *World Politics* (January 1992).

Joseph S. Tulchin is director of the Latin American Program at the Woodrow Wilson International Center for Scholars in Washington DC. His publications include *Argentina and the United States* (Twayne, 1990) and edited volumes, including *Problems in Modern Latin American History* (SR Books, 1994), and he has written at length about U.S.–Latin American relations.

William O. Walker III is professor of history at Ohio Wesleyan University. He is the author of *Drug Control in the Americas*, rev. ed. (New Mexico, 1989) and *Opium and Foreign Policy: The Anglo-American Search for Order in Asia, 1912–1954* (North Carolina, 1991), and numerous articles on U.S. drug policy.

Howard J. Wiarda is professor of political science at the University of Massachusetts–Amherst and professor of national security studies (on leave) at the National War College of the National Defense University in Washington DC. He is the author, most recently, of *Latin American Politics: A New World of Possibility* (Wadsworth) and *Latin American Politics and Development* (4th ed., Westview).

Index